ECONOMIC PHILOSOPHY OF B.R. AMBEDKAR

ECONOMIC PHILOSOPHY OF B.R. AMBEDKAR

Dr. Chandrakant Singh

CENTRUM PRESS
NEW DELHI-110002 (INDIA)

CENTRUM PRESS
H.O.: 4360/4, Ansari Road, Daryaganj,
New Delhi-110002 (India)
Tel: 23278000, 23261597, 23255577, 23286875
B.O.: No. 1015, Ist Main Road, BSK IIIrd Stage,
IIIrd Phase, IIIrd Block, Bangalore-560085 (INDIA)
Tel: 080-41723429
Email: centrumpress@gmail.com
Visit us at: www.centrumpress.com

Economic Philosophy of B.R. Ambedkar

First Edition, 2011

ISBN 978-93-80836-44-7

PRINTED IN INDIA

Printed at Mehra Offset Press, Delhi

Contents

Preface

Dr. Ambedkar was an economist by his basic training. His career was characterised by two distinct phases : the first one up to 1921 as a professional economist contributing scholarly books and the second one as a political leader thereafter until his demise in 1956, during which he made pathbreaking contributions as a champion of human rights for the untouchables.

Dr. Ambedkar wrote three scholarly books on economics:

(i) Administration and Finance of the East India Company,

(ii) The Evolution of Provincial Finance in British India, and

(iii) The Problem of the Rupee: Its Origin and Its Solution.

The first two represent his contribution to the field of public finance: the first one evaluating finances of the East India Company during the period, 1792 through 1858 and the second one analysing the evolution of the Centre- State financial relations in British India during the period, 1833 through 1921.

The third book, his *magnum opus* in economics, represents a seminal contribution to the field of monetary economics. In this book Dr. Ambedkar examined the evolution of the Indian currency as a medium of exchange covering the period, 1800 to 1893 and discussed the problem of the choice of an appropriate currency system for India in the early 1920s. On his return to India, Dr. Ambedkar did not write any book on economics *per se*, though several of his other contributions during that period carry a distinctive imprint of the economist in him.

A distinctive feature of Dr. Ambedkar's scholarly contribution is his perceptive analysis of economic dimension of social maladies, such as, the caste system and untouchability.

While Mahatma Gandhi had defended the caste system on the basis of division of labour, Ambedkar came out with a hard-hitting critique in his book '*Annihilation of Castes*' (1936), pointing out that what was implicit in the caste system was *not* merely division of labour but *also* a division of labourers. Dr. Ambedkar's attack on the caste system was not merely aimed at challenging the hegemony of the upper castes but had broader connotation of economic growth and development. He argued that the caste system had reduced the mobility of labour and capital which in turn, impeded economic growth and development in India.

The book, which provides a rare opportunity to debate and discuss the contribution of Dr. Ambedkar in nation-building, will be great interest to all sections of people.

—*Dr. Chandrakant Singh*

1

The Evolution of Provincial Finance in British India

For a long time to come students will be saved the conventional humiliation of making an apology for presenting a study of Indian Finance or Economics. But it will, on the other hand, be necessary, I fear, for an equally long period, for them to tender an apology for the shortcomings of their respective investigations. Even when the treatment of a subject is analytical, a good analytical study often requires an historical setting. Unfortunately no spadework has been done in the field of Indian Finance. Consequently the difficulties which beset a pioneer in that field are immense.

There is occasionally the difficulty owing to the antecedents of some point not having been quite completely elucidated. Often there is the apprehension of some error having crept in, and, when there is hardly anyone to save the student from it, there is nothing but to smart under a sense of irritating affliction. Not very seldom does it happen that a pioneer student is jubilant over his find of material bearing on his subject, but it is not without a long and wearisome search that he is able to sift the grain from the chaff. Again, sources sometimes prove false guides, so that a perusal of them only ends in a considerable waste of time and energy.

Precisely these have been the difficulties besetting the present task. There are no books to prepare the student for his work and hardly any savant to lighten his labour or set him on the proper track. Not withstanding such odds, an attempt is made to make this study thorough without being too detailed. This has rendered the undertaking quite a laborious one. But I do not wish to speak of the labour that is involved, nor do I wish to astonish the reader with what might appear to be a formidable list of books and documents consulted in the preparation of this monograph. What I am anxious to speak of are its shortcomings. There are indeed many of them which a well-versed critic may spot out. It is my hope that they are not of such a character as seriously to impair the value which this monograph may otherwise be said to possess. My regrets are with regard to only a few of them.

I have specified a date as to when Local Decentralisation of Finance commenced in India; but I feel that date may not be the earliest and that there may be a date earlier than that one given by me. I wish I had settled that point finally. But that would have been a task analogous to that of searching for a needle in a haystack, and it is doubtful whether the value of that result would have been commensurate with that labour. Besides, although I am not confident of my date, my feeling is that later researches may after all confirm my statement. Another matter which I have not dealt with, but which I would have liked to have dealt with, was the inter-relation of Provincial and Local Finance. This I had originally planned to do, but left pursuing it because I found that the chief subject I was dealing with, namely, the Provincial Decentralisation of Imperial Finance, began to be overlaid by facts and arguments not germane to that topic.

These shortcomings will, however, be removed by a supplementary monograph on Local Finance in British India, which is well under way and which I hope to publish before long. Occasional repetitions may also be pointed out as a defect of this monograph. That they should be avoided is all very well. But where economy in the words of explanation are likely to obscure, repetitions such as are I unavoidable must be justified, for the interests of clarification should always outweigh the tedium they involve.

I cannot conclude this preface without thanking Mr. Robinson, the Financial Secretary at the India Office, for many valuable suggestions and for the loan of many important documents bearing on the subject. I am also thankful to Prof. Cannan, of the University of London, who has read the rough draft of a small part of the manuscript. My debt to Prof. Seligman, my teacher at Columbia University, is of course immense : for from him I learned my first lessons in the theory of Public Finance. I am obliged to my friend Mr. C. S. Deole for assistance afforded in the dreary task of reading the proofs.

Foreword

The problem discussed by Mr. Ambedkar in his excellent dissertation is one that is arousing a growing interest in all parts of the world. From the very beginning we find fiscal burdens imposed by both central and local governments. As soon as there was a political organisation, the conduct of war on the one hand and the provision of local protection and convenience on the other called for expenditures on the part of both state and local authorities. It was only at a later period that there was interpolated between the local and the central political organisations the intermediate form which Mr. Ambedkar calls the provincial government. The names applied to these various classes of expenditure differ with the authorities themselves.

In India, we speak of local, provincial, and imperial expenditure; in Germany, of local, state, and imperial expenditure; in the United States and Switzerland, of local, state, and federal expenditure; in Australia, of local, state, and commonwealth expenditure; in South Africa and Canada, of local, provincial, and federal expenditure; and in France, of local, departmental, and general expenditure. In some cases, as in the British Empire, there is being developed a still more comprehensive class of expenditures, borne by the empire at large.

The character and importance of these various classes of expenditure and the relations between them are undergoing a continual change, due to an alteration in the functions of government. This is itself largely due to a change in the general economic conditions, resulting in a gradual modification either of political structure or of administrative activity. In some countries, as in Canada, Argentine and Brazil, the provinces are really a creation of the central government; in other countries, as in the United States, Germany, and Switzerland, the federal government is the creation of the originally sovereign states. In some countries the intermediate (provincial or state) government is suffering a loss of importance as compared with the local or central governments; in other countries, the reverse is true.

With the increasing pressure of taxation and the development under modern democracies of augmented governmental functions, the problem of the equitable distribution of burden among these various forms of government is becoming more or less acute. What Mr. Ambedkar calls assignments, assigned revenue, and share revenue, is symptomatic of the choice of methods in all countries. One of three fundamental plans must be pursued. Either the central or the provincial government may be maintained by the other, according to the relative degree of strength : in former times, in the United States, and in Germany the states were supposed to support the central government, either wholly or in large measure; in modern times, in Canada and Australia, the reverse is true. Or, secondly, distinct revenues may be allocated to the separate governments : until recently the federal government in the United States, Germany, and Switzerland was supported primarily by indirect taxes; the state governments by direct taxes. Or, thirdly, the revenues may be collected by one government and a portion of the proceeds allotted to the other : there are many instances of a state or provincial tax being shared with the federal government, and still more examples of a federal or central tax being shared with the state or provincial government. In the United States at present the proper disposition of the inheritance tax as between state and federal government is fast becoming a burning question; in Germany the fiscal relations of state and federal government are in the forefront of political discussion.

The value of Mr. Ambedkar's contribution to this discussion lies in the objective recitation of the facts and the impartial analysis of the interesting development that has taken place in his native country. The lessons are applicable to other countries as well; nowhere, to my knowledge, has such a detailed study of the underlying principles been made.

It is true that only half of the picture is presented. For the situation has everywhere been complicated by the entrance of the local authorities into the field; and by their claims to fiscal consideration as compared with both state (provincial) and general (federal) demands. In the United States, for instance, the now widely debated problem of financing the schools is largely dependent for its solution on the proper answer to be given to the question of fiscal interrelations. To this question Mr. Ambedkar proposes to devote himself in a subsequent study. If he succeeds in illumining that situation as successfully as he here deals with the initial problem, he will lay us all under still deeper obligations.

Introduction

Definition and Outline of the Subject

A student of Indian Finance has two chief sources of information and guidance open to him. One is the Annual Budget Statement, and the other is the annual volume of Finance and Revenue Accounts. Though separately issued, the two are really companion volumes inasmuch as the financial Statement forms, so to speak, an exhaustive explanatory memorandum of the annual financial transactions, the details of which are recorded in the volume of Finance and Revenue Accounts.

Helpful as these sources are, they are not without their puzzles. A reference to the latest volume of Finance and Revenue Accounts will show that the accounts therein are classified under four different categories:—(1) Imperial, (2) Provincial, (3) Incorporated Local, and (4) Excluded Local. But this is by no means uniformly so. For instance, a volume of the same series before 1870 will not be found to contain the accounts called "Provincial," nor will the accounts styled "Local "be found in any volume prior to 1863. Similarly, any volume of the Financial Statements before 1870 will be found to divide the financial transactions covered therein into—Imperial and Local only. But a volume of the same series after 1908 curiously enough groups the accounts not under Imperial and Local but under (1) Imperial, and (2) Provincial, while the financial Statements after 1921 cover only the Imperial Transactions. Nothing is more confusing to a beginner than the entrance of the new, and the exit of the old, categories of accounts.

The natural question that he will ask is, how did these different categories evolve, and how are they related to one another ?

In the present study an endeavour is made to explain the rise and growth of one of them, namely, the "Provincial." But in order that there may be no difficulty in following the argument it is deemed advisable to preface this study with an outline defining its subject-matter and indicating the interrelations of the parts into which it is divided. To facilitate a thorough understanding of the subject the study is divided into four parts, *each* one dealing with the Origin, Development and Organisation of Provincial Finance and the final form in which it was cast by the constitutional changes of 1919. In Part I a somewhat thorny and yet necessary ground has been covered in order to give a complete idea of the origin of Provincial Finance.

While due homage is paid to the adage which requires students of the present to study the past, nothing more than the past of the present has been dealt with. In Chapter I, Part I, an attempt is made to present a picture of the system of Finance as it existed before the inauguration of the Provincial Finance and to state the causes that called for a change in its organisation. In Chapter II a rival system of Finance proposed during the period of reconstruction is brought to light and shown why it failed of general acceptance. Chapter III is devoted to the discussion of a plan which was a compromise between the existing system and its rival, and the circumstances which forced its reception.

Having explained the Origin in Part I, the Development of Provincial Finance is made the subject of Part II. How far the arrangement followed in Part I is helpful must in the absence of anything to compare with it be left to the opinion of the reader. In regard to Part II, however, it is to be noted that the arrangement is different from what is adopted in the only fragmentary sketch published on the subject of Provincial Finance in 1887 by the late Justice Ranade. As will be seen from a perusal of Part II, that one of the features of Provincial Finance was that the revenues and charges incorporated into the Provincial Budgets were revised every fifth year.

Justice Ranade in his pamphlet, which simply covers the ground traversed in Part II of this study, and that too up to 1882 only, has taken this feature as a norm by which to mark off the different stages in the growth of Provincial Finance from one to another.

Consequently, each quinquennial period to him becomes a stage, and in his hands the history of Provincial Finance falls into as many stages as the quinquenniums into which it can be divided. It may, however, be submitted that if every revision had changed the fundamentals of Provincial Finance, such an arrangement would not have been illogical. But as a matter of fact, Provincial Finance did not change its hue at every revision. What the revisions did was to temper the wind to the shorn lamb.

If the history of the development of Provincial Finance is to be divided into stages according to the changes in the fundamental basis thereof, then emphasis has to be laid on features altogether different in character. Writers on the theory of Public Finance seem to conceive the subject as though it were primarily a matter of equity in taxation and economy in expenditure.

But to a Chancellor of the Exchequer finance is eminently practical with a problem to solve, namely, how to bring about an equilibrium in the Budget. If we scan the history of Provincial Finance in British India with a view to discover the method of meeting the problem of equilibrium in Provincial Budgets and the changes introduced in it from time to time, we shall find that Provincial Finance has evolved through three distinct stages, each with its own mode of supply, namely, Assignments, Assigned Revenues and Shared Revenues. Consequently, instead of following the mechanical plan of Justice Ranade, it is believed to be more logical and instructive to divide the stages in the growth of Provincial finance according to the method of supply to the Provincial Governments adopted by the Government of India. Consequently, Part II, which deals with the Development of Provincial Finance, is divided into three Chapters: (1) Budget by Assignment, (2) Budget by Assigned Revenues, and (3) Budget by Shared Revenues.

This discussion of the Origin and Development of Provincial Finance is followed in Part III by an examination of its Organisation. Chapter VII in Part lit is devoted to the analysis of the hitherto neglected rules of limitations on the financial powers of Provincial Governments primarily to bring out the fact that Provincial Finance was not independent in its organisation.

The analysis of the true position of Provincial Finance is, however, reserved for Chapter VIII, in which the conclusion is fortified by a reference to the character of these limitations, that, notwithstanding the high-sounding appellation of Provincial Finance, there were neither provincial revenues nor provincial services as separate from Imperial revenues and Imperial services, so that instead of being federal in its organisation the system remained essentially Imperial. Chapter IX discusses how far it was possible to enlarge the scope of Provincial Finance without jeopardy to the constitutional responsibilities of the Government of India under the old law.

Part IV is a discussion of the changes introduced into the mechanism of Provincial Finance by the Reforms Act of 1919. Chapter X of this Part is devoted to the analysis of the causes which led to these changes. In Chapter XI a full description of the changes effected by the new law is given, while Chapter XII forms a critique of the new regime.

In view of the fact that students of Indian Finance ordinarily content themselves with the phrase "Decentralisation of finance," to indicate Provincial Finance, a word of explanation in justification of what may rather be called the too cumbersome title of this study. No student of Indian Finance, who is sufficiently acquainted with the branching off of the system in different directions, will fail to mark the inadequacy of the phrase Decentralisation of Finance to mean Provincial Finance.

If there were in the Indian system only the Provincial Decentralisation there would have been no necessity to labour for a new title. As a matter of fact, the starting points of decentralisation are by no means the same, and the systems evolved through it are quite different in character. For instance, the centre of decentralisation and the systems evolved by the policy of decentralisation brought into operation in 1855 were different from the centre and the systems evolved there from by the policy of decentralisation initiated in 1870. Again, the centre which is gradually being decentralised since 1892, be it noted, is different from those affected by the decentralisation of 1855 or 1870. To put it more clearly, the decentralisation of 1855 was the decentralisation of *Indian* Finance resulting in—

(I) the separation of Local from Imperial Finance.

The decentralisation of 1870 was the decentralisation of Imperial Finance resulting in—

(II) the separation of Provincial from Imperial Finance.

And the decentralisation commencing from 1882 is the decentralisation of *Provincial* Finance resulting in—

(III) the separation of Local from Provincial Finance.

Obviously then, "Decentralisation of finance "far from being indicative of Provincial Finance, is a general name for this variegated and multifarious process of decentralisation described above, and it cannot but be confusing to use as a title to the study of one line of decentralisation a phrase which can be generically applied to all the three lines of decentralisation distinguished above.

In order, therefore, that this study may not be taken to pertain to a line of decentralisation other than the one it purports to investigate, it has been thought proper to designate it "The Evolution of Provincial Finance in British India "with a sub-title, "A Study in the Provincial Decentralisation of Imperial Finance," where the words Provincial and Imperial must be read with the emphasis due to them. How careless the phraseology often is may be instanced by the fact that Justice Ranade's pamphlet referred to above is styled "Decentralisation of Provincial Finance." Although it deals with the development of Provincial Finance, it is likely to be passed over by the student, for its title implies that its subject-matter must be the growth of Local Finance. If Justice Ranade had been conscious of the varieties of decentralisation, he would have probably realised that the title of his pamphlet was false to its contents.

Provincial Finance : Its Origin

The Imperial System

Its Growth and its Breakdown: The Imperial system of Government in India dates from the year 1833. Of the two chief motives which led Parliament to establish it, one was to replace the existing multiplicity in the systems of justice and police by a uniform system of the same, common as far as possible to the whole of India with its varieties classified and systematised. Under the existing system then prevailing such multiplicity was inevitable, for not only the civil and military government and the ordering and management of the revenues of each of the three Presidencies, Bengal, Madras and Bombay, were vested in their respective Governors in Council, but each Governor in Council was also empowered to make and issue such rules, ordinances and regulations for the good order and civil government of the territories he individually commanded, provided that they were just and reasonable and not repugnant to the laws of the British realm.

To the codes of law promulgated by these authorities must be added the whole body of English Statute law introduced in India so far as it was applicable, by the charter of George I in 1726 and such other English Acts subsequent to that date as were expressly extended to particular parts of the country.

The work of administering such a diverse body of laws proved so embarrassing that it was the view of the supreme Court of Calcutta that "no one person can pronounce an opinion or form a judgement... upon any disputed right of persons, respecting which doubt and confusion may not be raised by those who may choose to call it in question; for very few of the public or persons in office at home, not even the Law Officers, can be expected to have so comprehensive and clear a view of the Indian system of law, as to know readily and familiarly the bearings of each part of it on the rest."

The other motive was to create a strong central government to deal effectively with the European settlers in the country. It is to be noted that if the native population suffered under the uncertainties of law, the British population lived under the most galling restrictions.

The revelations of oppressions by Englishmen practised, in the early days of British Rule, contained in the report of the Secret Committee of the House of Commons appointed in 1771 to inquire into the affairs of the East India Company, were followed by very stringent laws governing the entry and residence of private British subjects in India. No British subject of European birth was allowed to reside in India beyond 10 miles from any one of the principal settlements without having previously obtained a special license from the Company or the Governor-General of India or the Governor of the principal settlement in question.

The Court of Directors of the Company, subject to revision of the Board of Control were empowered to refuse such licenses and the Governments in India were strictly enjoined not to sanction the residence of British subjects on their own authorities except under special circumstances and were authorised, in cases they deemed proper, to declare licenses otherwise valid as void.

Counterfeiting licenses and unlicensed residence were made crimes punishable with fine or imprisonment; and persons who were dismissed from, and who had resigned service, were declared guilty of illicit trade if they lingered beyond the 10-mile limit after their time had expired. Unlicensed British subjects were made liable to be deported and such as were licensed were required to register themselves in the court of the district in which they resided.

Subjected as they were to the regulations of the Local Government they were made amenable to justice in India as well as in Great Britain for all illegal acts done in British India, or in Native States. To render them impotent to cause complications, they were not allowed to lend money to or be concerned in raising any for native princes or foreign companies or foreign European merchants. Similarly to protect the natives from their oppression they were forbidden to lend money to the latter at a rate of interest exceeding 12 percent per annum on penalty of forfeiting for every offence treble the value and they were placed under the jurisdiction of the Justices of the Peace in all cases involving assault or trespass on, and small debts due to, the natives of India.

Moreover, every British subject of European birth was required to register in the office of his district the name, etc., of his native stewards, agents, and partners, on penalty of being disentitled to recover or receive any sum or sums of money by reason of the joint concern or to compel an account thereof by any suit in law or equity in any court within the provinces.

The ruling race had long chafed at these restrictions, under which it was placed, without much avail. They were evidently aimed at keeping out an element dangerous to the stability of the Indian Empire, but, as time went on, and as the Indian Empire was consolidated by successive victories over the native princes, there was raised against these restrictions such a storm of indignant criticism that even those who had acquiesced in their virtue were forced to admit that they had outlived their purpose.

While the British Parliament could not help abiding by the sentiments of the time, it refused to disregard the consequences which it thought would inevitably attend upon the free ingress of British subjects of European birth under the then existing system of government.

It realised that a harmonious treatment of the immigrants and an effective control over them was absolutely essential. Parliament was afraid that the different governments armed as they were with co-equal and independent powers of legislation and administration by exercising these powers with regard to the immigrants entering their respective territories, with different views and according to inconsistent principles might integrate the whole mass of them into a disaffected body difficult to be dealt with. Besides the necessity of a harmonious treatment based on uniform principles, the fears of Parliament that the ingress of British immigrants would result in the revival of oppression on the natives were not completely allayed. As its recrudescence was felt to be a likely event, Parliament desired to subject them to a strong and uniform central control, so that the offender in one jurisdiction might not be able to find an asylum in another.

Thus, whether considered from the standpoint of bringing about uniformity of laws or securing stringency of control over elements subversive of order, the then existing system of government with its divided jurisdiction was ill-suited for the purpose held in view. An all-powerful Central Government legislating for and controlling the affairs of India as a whole was deemed to be the only solution for the emergency.

Accordingly there came to be enacted in 1833 that "the Governor-General in Council (at Fort William in Bengal) shall have power to make laws and regulations for repealing, amending, or altering any laws or regulations, whatever, now in force or hereafter to be in force in the said territories or any part thereof, and to make laws and regulations for all persons, whether British or native, foreigners or others, and for all Courts of Justice, whether established by His Majesty's Charters or otherwise and the jurisdictions thereof, and for all places and every part of the said territory, and for all servants of the said Company within the dominions of princes and states in alliance with the said Company. . . . ;

A Central government was thus created by vesting the legislative power exclusively in the Governor-General of India in council. But it could not have been all-powerful had the two Presidencies of Madras and Bombay remained as heretofore invested, by law, with the civil and military government of their respective territories.

On the other hand, if Parliament had stopped short of divesting them, there would have ensued the possibility of a conflict between these governing authorities and the sole legislative authority newly created. Being responsible for peace, order and good government, the former could have refused to govern according to laws made by the latter, and all the gain expected to arise from the institution of a central and strong government would have been lost. To eliminate this element of weakness in the Indian politics newly established, Parliament proceeded to divest the presidencies of Bombay and Madras of the high status which they hitherto occupied as *responsible* governments, so that according to the new Constitution

"......the Executive Government of each of the several Presidencies ...... (was to be) *administered by* (not vested in as heretofore) a Governor and three Councillors.

While "......the Superintendence, Direction, and Control of the whole civil and military government of all the...... territories and Revenues in India (was) vested in a Governor General and councillors styled the Governor-General of India in Council."

Thus came to be established in India the Imperial system of government. It is true that long before its establishment the Government of Bengal had the supreme power, not only of superintending and controlling the government and management of the Presidencies of Madras and Bombay in the matter of commencing hostilities, or declaring or making war against any Indian prince or power, or for negotiating or concluding any treaty of peace or other treaty with them, except in case of emergency, but it also possessed by a later enactment the power of superintendence in all such points as related to the collection or application of revenues, or to the forces employed, or to the civil or military government of the said presidencies.

But it must not be supposed, as is often done, that before 1833 the two Presidencies were in any real sense subordinate to Bengal in their domestic affairs. The fact that Madras and Bombay were required constantly and diligently to transmit to the Government of Bengal true and exact copies of all orders and resolutions and their acts in Council, and were enjoined to pay due obedience to the orders of the Government of Bengal, must not be construed to mean any subordination in their internal affairs.

For, barring the extra territorial authority vested in the Government of Bengal, it must be borne in mind that, equally with Bengal the Governments of Madras and Bombay were *vested each* with the civil and military government and also with the ordering and management of all territorial acquisitions arid their revenues. Along with the Government of Bengal they possessed as stated before co-equal and independent powers of legislation within their respective jurisdictions. A truer view therefore seems to be that they forwarded the copies of their proceedings to the Government of Bengal for information rather than for orders.

At any rate, such seems to have been the view taken by the Government of Bengal itself, for, though it had the power to issue orders and compel obedience to them it had in practice confined its supervision and control "to pointing out an irregularity and requesting that it be not repeated." More than this was thought inadvisable and it is doubtful whether it would have been constitutional.

The Imperial system of Government was necessarily accompanied by the Imperial system of Finance. Before the inauguration of the Imperial system of Administration the several Presidencies were like separate clocks each with its own mainspring in itself. Each possessed the powers of sovereignty, such as the legislative, the penal, and the taxing powers. They were independent in their finance. Each was responsible for the maintenance of services essential for peace, order and good government within its jurisdiction and was free to find money by altering or levying taxation or borrowing on credit to meet its obligations.

For their ways and means they often drew upon the resources of one another, not, however, because their exchequers were not distinct, but because they were parts of a common exchequer belonging to the East India Company All this was changed by the Act of 1833, which vested the revenues and the government of the different territories in the Governor-general of India in council.

The revenues and the services became by law the revenues and the services of the Government of India. The provinces became the collecting and the spending agencies of the Government of India. They ceased to levy any new taxes or to collect the old ones in their own name. In like manner the services they administered became a charge of the Government of India, which distributed among the various provinces sums from the consolidated fund for the maintenance of the services. It was by law provided that without the previous sanction of the Government of India the provinces were not to spend the fund allowed to them in creating any new office or granting any salary, gratuity, or allowance. The public debt was no longer a charge upon the revenues of any particular Presidency alone, nor did there remain any question of primary or secondary liability as between the revenues of the other Presidencies. Ail the provincial debts became the debts of the Government of India and were charged to the revenues of India as a whole In short, the financial system which was roughly analogous to the system of separation of sources and contributions from the yield was changed into a system of aggregation of sources and distribution of the yield; for, as observed in a Government Resolution by virtue of the Act of 1833,

"British India, though for the sake of convenience subdivided into Presidencies under separate locally controlled governments, (became) in reality one sole grand Power in dependence on Great Britain, having undivided interests, a single exchequer, and controlled in all essential and general principles by one Government—the Governor- General in Council....... The entire resources of India (were) applicable to one purpose only, the discharge of its engagements and those connected with its management in England, and to whatever section of British India funds (were) wanting, funds (were) supplied, as a matter of course, without any reference to the particular source from which they were derived. So comprehensive did the system of Imperial Finance become in time that when in 1858 the Crown took over from the Company the government of India it was found that

"no province had any separate power of legislation, any separate financial resources, or practically any power of creating or modifying any appointments in the public service; and the references to the Government of India which this last restriction involved gave that Government the opportunity of interference with all the details of provincial administration."

Whatever may have been the merits of the Imperial system of Government from the military, political, legislative, or administrative points of view, it is a melancholy fact that as a system of finance it proved unequal to the strain imposed upon it. From its very start it suffered from the fatal disease of financial inadequacy, and it was only occasionally that the efforts of the Finance Ministers were successful in restoring an equilibrium and slaving off the hour of crisis. How chronic the deficits were may be seen from the following 'figures:—

Year	Surplus	Deficit	Year	Surplus	Deficit
1834-35		194477	184647		971,322
1835-36	1,441,513		47_48		1,911,986
1836-37	1,248,224		48_49		1,473,225
1837-38	780,318		49_50	354,187	
1838-39		381,787	50_51	415,443	
1839-40		2,138,713	51_52	531,265	
1840-41		1,754,852	52_53	424,257	
1841-42		1,771,603	53_54		2,044,117
1842-43		1,346,011	54_55		1,707,364
1843-44		1,440,259	55_56		972,791
1844-45		743,893	56_57		143,597
1845-46		1,496,865	57_58		7,864,222

Anyone who ponders upon this pitiable story of Indian Finance as revealed by these deficits can hardly fail to wonder with Disraeli who remarked in the House of Commons that—

"able as has ever been the administration of India, considerable and distinguished as have been the men whom that administration had produced, and numerous as have been the great Captains, the clever diplomatists, and able administrators of large districts with whom the Government has abounded, the state of the finances of India has always been involved in perplexity, and India that has produced so many great men, seems never to have produced a Chancellor of the Exchequer."

The causes of this collapse, however, are not far to seek. The inadequacy of Indian Finances is mainly to be ascribed to an unsound fiscal policy. The policy was unsound for various reasons. In matters of state economy it is usual to argue that the expenditure to be incurred should determine the magnitude of revenue to be raised.

But experience has shown that this stock maxim has proved ruinous wherever its limitations have failed to receive their due weight. It cannot be too often said that the growing expenditure of the State can only be sustained from the growing wealth of the society. Nor can it be too strongly emphasised that the test of sound finance does not merely consist in being capable of raising the requisite amount of revenue.

It must be remembered that the *mode* of raising the revenue is an aspect of the question which is fraught with tremendous consequences for the stability and productivity of the nation. It is too obvious to be denied that a tax system by its unequal incidence may cause social upheavals, just as by its unwise incidence on trade and industry it may impoverish society by setting out of gear its economic mechanism and technique and eventually beggar the State by impairing the productive powers of society.

Wisdom therefore requires that those who are entrusted with the financial management of the State should look beyond the more immediate object of raising and spending of money, for the "hows" of finance are very important, and can be seldom neglected in practice with impunity.

The wealth of society is the only patrimony on which the State can draw, and the State that damages it cannot but end in damning itself History abounds with instances of States wrecked by the unwise neglect of these evident truths, but if an illustration be wanted in further proof thereof, the system of Imperial Finance established in India is matchless for the purpose.

The land tax was the heaviest impost of the Imperial revenue system in operation. The underlying doctrine of the tax in India has been that it is of the nature of rent paid by the cultivator to the State in virtue of the theory that the land in India has from immemorial times been regarded as the property owned by the State. The cultivator is not the proprietor, but is the occupier of the land. The land is let to him and the State is therefore justified in claiming the whole of the economic rent arising from the land. On this assumption the land tax has been imposed irrespective of the question of necessity or justice.

Besides this legal fiction of State landlordism there was also another economic principle, which was, taken to be the justification for the enhancement of the land revenue. There is reason to believe that the Physiocratic doctrine of *produit* net had its influence in the management and fixing of the land tax in India.

We find high officials in .India arguing in the early stages of the revenue management that "whether or not the principle of the French Economists of laying all the taxes on the land be...... erroneous or otherwise, it is certainly conformable to the prevalent system in India; nor is that theory supported by the French alone, but by respectable authorities in England, who contend that all taxes fall ultimately on the products of the soil, and that in advancing a different doctrine the eminent author of *The Wealth of Nations* is at variance with himself, inasmuch as his previous data lead to that conclusion." (this footnote is given below) Whatever may have been the reasons for augmenting the land tax, few can deny that a heavy consolidated impost on the first exertions of any species of industry absorbing the whole or nearly the whole of its profits in ruinous and impolitic.

It becomes an effectual bar to the creation of that produce on which the future exertions might be profitably employed and through the medium of which individual wealth and public revenue may be increased to an almost inconceivable extent. A land tax of this nature was sure to blast the very production of that wealth which industry would have otherwise brought into being the land tax was so heavy that the system of tax prevailing in India might well have been called a near approach to the single lax system.

The ratio of the land revenue to the total revenues of India was as given below :—

Year	Ratio
1792-93 to 1796-97	50.33
1797-98 to 1801-02	42.02
1802-03 to 1806-07	31.99
1807-08 to 1811 –12	31.68
1812-13 to 1816-17	53.33
1817-18 to 1821-22	66.17
1822-23 to 1826-27	61.83
1827-28 to 1831-32	60.90
1832-33 to 1836-37	57.00
1837-38 to 1841-42	59.05
1842-43 to 1846-47	55.85
1847-48 to 1851-52	56.06
1852-53 to 1855-56	55.40
Average for 64 years	54.07

While the land tax prevented the prosperity of the agricultural industry the customs taxes hampered the manufactures of the country. There were internal customs and external customs, and both were equally injurious to trade and industry. The internal customs were made up of transit and town duties.

For the purposes of transit duties the country was artificially divided into a number of small customs areas. Goods may be manufactured and consumed *ad libitum* within each customs area, but the moment they left their own division they became liable to duty. The injurious effects of this regulation, though concealed, were none the less real. The transit duties held up trade, which in its turn reacted adversely on the manufacturers of the country. Adam Smith has told us how the growth of industry depends upon the extent of the market. Here for the purposes of the transit duties the whole country was cut up into small bits after the manner of squares on a chess board. What wonder is there if trade, and its handmaid, industry, both languished to a serious extent.

The adverse effect on the transit duties was also felt in another way. In every country somewhat industrially advanced there is not only a social division of labour, but there is also a territorial division of labour, otherwise called localisation of industry. Evidence is not wanting to show that the localisation of industry formed a prominent feature of Indian economy. Under it each locality in India specialised in a particular art or industry; for instance, cotton was grown in one locality, woven in another, and bleached in a third place.

But it often happened that these localities were situated in different customs areas, and a raw good might have had to pay the transit duty many a time before it reached its finished stage. To avoid this each locality was obliged to waste its energies along unprofitable lines in order to escape the transit duties.

The town duties, which formed a part of the internal customs, also worked in their effects towards de-urbanisation. Commercial entrepots are admittedly vast instruments of the trade of a country.

The opportunity of ready purchase and sale of almost every kind of commodity in any quantity, accumulated capital, extended credit, general information all meet here as in a centre. They support, encourage and give lift to commerce and to the trade of a country. But the direct effect of the town duty was to distract and drive away trade, for under the system every article which was subject to it had, after the payment of transit duty, to pay on entry, in the town, the town duty and, if it underwent any change of form by manufacture within the town of entry, it could not have been furnished to any neighbouring place without a second impost being paid upon it under the transit duty system, enhanced in proportion to the increase of value it might have acquired from the labour and the skill bestowed upon it, The consequence was that towns dwindled both in trade and industry owing to the reason that merchants ceased to frequent them and that no manufactures of articles subject to the transit duty were capable of being established in them except for their own supply.

It was in this depressed condition that the Indian industries were called upon to meet foreign competitors. But the external customs cannot be said to have protected, much less fostered them. As a rule commercial tariffs are based upon what is called commodity competition.

The import tariffs are designed to check by means of higher duties the importation of such foreign commodities as are likely to interfere in the successful manufacture of the same commodities at home and the export tariffs are framed principally with a view to give bounties to such of the home commodities as have a chance of securing a foothold in foreign markets.

But the theory of external customs in India had no connection with the theory of commodity competition In comparison with the policy actually adopted even a protectionist would have preferred to see trade left perfectly free, for the tariff was based on political rather than economic considerations. The Indian Import Tariff varied not with the nature of the imports but with the origin of the imports and the bottom on which they were shipped.

Being political in character it was preferential in design and in its framework. It is to be regretted all the more that the preference involved an unmitigated loss to the people and to the government.

It was excusable to have admitted into India goods of English origin and shipped on English bottoms at a rate half of what goods of foreign origin and shipped on foreign bottoms were charged with. But nothing can extenuate the sacrifice imposed upon the Indian industries by letting in British goods at lower rates than what the Indian goods had to pay under the internal customs; and this was done when, be it remembered, England was prohibiting by high tariff the entry of India-made goods and India-built ships!

But while the import tariff made it easy for the foreigners to compete successfully with Indian manufactures burdened as they heavily were by the weight of the internal customs, Indian goods found it considerably difficult to compete in foreign markets under the incubus of export duties which formed one of the most lamentable features of the Indian tariff and which endured long into the nineteenth century. Thus the customs laws internal and external blockaded trade and smothered industry. The comparatively paltry revenues derived from them is the best proof of their ruinous effects.

The following table gives the ratio of the Customs Revenue to the total revenue :—

Year	Ratio
1792-93 to 1796-97	2.38
1797-98 to 1801-02	3.10
1802-03 to 1806-07	4.16
1807-08 to 1811 –12	5.04
1812-13 to 1816-17	6.68
1817-18 to 1821-22	8.32
1822-23 to 1826-27	7.58
1827-28 to 1831-32	8.12
1832-33 to 1836-37	7.19
1837-38 to 1841-42	6.76
1842-43 to 1846-47	6.02
1847-48 to 1851-52	5.40
1852-53 to 1855-56	5.52
Average for 64 years	6.22

When these resources failed the Government resorted to some very questionable means of raising revenue.

On an impartial survey of the revenue system as prevailed under the Imperial regime one is constrained to say that justice in taxation was conspicuous by its absence. It was a cruel satire, or at best an idle maxim, for the lancet was directed not where the blood was thickest but to that part of the body politic which on account of its weakness and poverty most meekly bore the pang.

The landlords who passed their lives in conspicuous consumption and vicarious leisure on the earnings of the poor tenants, or the many European civil servants who fattened themselves on pay and pickings, were supremely exempted from any contribution towards the maintenance of the Government whose main activities were directed towards the maintenance of pomp and privilege. On the other hand, the salt tax# and the Moturpha, and other oppressive taxes continued to harass the industrious poor.

#The percentage ratio of the salt revenue to the total revenue at different times was as follows:—

Year	Ratio
1792-93 to 1796-97	14.13
1797-98 to 1801-02	12.10
1802-03 to 1806-07	11.09
1807-08 to 1811 –12	11.14
1812-13 to 1816-17	10.92
1817-18 to 1821-22	11.25
1822-23 to 1826-27	11.87
1827-28 to 1831-32	12.03
1832-33 to 1836-37	9.72
1837-38 to 1841-42	12.37
1842-43 to 18 46-47	11.65
1847-48 to 1851-52	9.14
1852-53 to 1855-56	9.17
Average for 64 years	11.07

Hendricks, *op. cit.*

It is indeed true that many petty and vexatious taxes prevalent under the native rule were abolished; there is, however, enough evidence to show that the revenue thus lost was made up by enhancing those that were continued to be levied, particularly the land tax. The latter charge has always been officially denied, but none the less it remains true that the land tax has been consolidated and increased concurrently with, if not consequently upon, the abolition of such other taxes as being raised from the poor cost the Government more than their yield.

Under the injurious revenue system described above, the taxing capacity of the people decayed so that notwithstanding its numerous resources# from which it derived its revenues the Imperial Government was unable to make both ends meet.

#The following is a conspectus of the taxes levied :—

Source of Revenue	Amount of Revenue raised in Millions	Period		Locality and Date of Commencement
		No. of Years	Dates	
Land Revenue	662.308	64	1792-93 to 1855-56	Throughout the period in Bengal, Bombay and Madras since 1834-5 in N.W.P. and 1849-50 in the Punjab.
Sekyer & Abkary	9.729	20	1836-37 to 1855-56	Throughout the period in Bengal, N.W.P., Madras and Bombay, and since 1849-50 in Punjab.
Excise	4.987	"	"	Bengal accounts exclusively.
Moturpha	6.455	"	"	Madras accounts exclusively.
Salt	135.532	64	1792-93 to 1855-56	Bengal since 1792, Madras 1822, Bombay 1822, N.W.P. 1839.
Opium	106.707	"	"	Bengal since 1792, Bombay since 1820.
Post Office	8.888	"	"	Bengal and Madras since 1792, Bombay since 1813, Punjab 1849, N.W.P. 1835.
Stamps	16.697	59	1797-98 to 1855-56	Bengal from 1797, Madras from 1813, Bombay from 1819, N.W.P. from 1834, Punjab from 1849.

Customs Duties				
Internal 1. Transit 2.Town External 1. Import 2. Export	76.179	64	1792-3 to 1855-56	Bengal, Madras and Bombay from 1792-3, N.W.P. from 1834-5, Punjab since 1849-50.
Mint	3.221	"	"	Bengal from 1792, Madras and Bombay from 1813.
Revenue Tobacco	1.437	18	1836-37 to 1853-54	Madras 1836 on.
Miscella-neous	194.777	64	1792-93 to 1855-56	Same as under land revenue.

It ought to serve as an object lesson to all financiers to show that when their revenue laws are harmful to the resources of the people they must blame none but themselves for their empty treasury.

Was the money raised by such injurious taxes without reference to their effect on the productive powers of the country spent on such public utilities as were calculated to enrich and elevate the economic life of the tax-paying population ? A glance at the following table giving the distribution of the expenditure by decades on the different services will show how the money was spent:—

Distribution of the Expenditure

Percentage Ratio of Total Expenditure			**in the Year**			
on	1809-10	1819-20	1829-30	1839-40	1849-50	1857
Military	58.877	64.290	53.754	57.721	51.662	45.55
Interest on debt	18.010	12.805	12.124	9.756	10.512	7.19
Civil and Political	7.221	8.900	9.575	12.296	8.902	9.62
Judicial	7.525	6.800	7.107	9.565	7.180	}

Provincial Police	1.991	2.093	1.535	2.062	2.062	} 9.38
Buildings, Fortifications, etc.	1.639	1.756	2.810	1.428	1.661	

Prominent among this array of figures are those on the military expenditure and though they have dwindled in years they have invariably consumed more than one half of the total revenues of the country. But the stupendous figures opposite military do not represent the true burden of that expenditure. To them must be added the figures for the interest charge on debt, for the debt incurred was entirely a war debt. India was all throughout this period a battle-ground between the Country Powers and the East India Company.

The two Mahratta Wars, the three Mysore Wars, the two Burmese Wars, the two Afghan Wars, and the Carnatic Wars, not to speak of the numerous other minor engagements, were fought in the interests of adding India to the dominions of the Company and of the Crown. While Parliament claimed that the dominions of the East India Company were the dominions of the Crown it must be borne in mind that it refused to pay a farthing of the purchase money. On the other hand, the entire cost of these wars was borne by India as so much dead weight on her scanty resources.

The charges shown separately under buildings and fortifications must also be included in the military expenditure, to which category they really belonged. On making these needful additions we find the unparalleled fact of a country wasting between 52 to 80 percent of its precious little money on war services. It may, perhaps be argued on the other hand that much of the military expenditure, large though it was, went back into the coffers of the Indians themselves as they formed the bulk of the forces employed in the country. The Indians of course, formed a very large portion of the military# and if the scales of salaries fixed for the European and native forces were equal the result would have been favourable to the natives of the country, though it cannot be said to have excused that huge military expenditure.

Strength of the Indian Army before the Mutiny

	European	Native	Total
Artillery	6,419	9,138	15,577
Sappers	110	3,043	3,153
Cavalry	3,456	30,533	32,989
Infantry	29,760	188,660	218,420
Total ...	38,745	231,374	270,119

Report of Major-General Hancock on the Reorganisation of the Indian Army, Parliamentary paper of the year 1859.

But the scales of salaries for the Europeans and natives were so grossly unequal# that one European drew on an average more than the salaries of four natives put together.

#This is indicated by the following table :—

Cost of an Infantry Regiment Per Month

European

	Details			Total		
Officers	Rs.	As.	Ps.	Rs.	As.	Ps.
37 Officers	14,734	14	3	21,779	2	7
Staff and Establishment	4,515	12	4			
Command and other allowances	2,528	8	0			
Men				25,999	8	0
117N.C.O.S.	2,289	4	5			
950 Privates	11,203	8	4			
Rations, clothing and other charges Total	12,506	11	3			
				47,778	10	7

So this expenditure, whether from the standpoint of public utility or private employment, did not benefit the population which contributed to the revenues of the State.

The civil and political charges which absorbed nearly 10 percent of the revenue can hardly be said to be recuperative in their effect. This part of the expenditure again was not shared by the native population which bore its burden. As a result of conquest the natives naturally came to occupy a secondary position; but the conquest had done more than merely degrade their status.

It had engendered a certain sense of distrust for the natives in the minds of Englishmen. Conquered and distrusted the natives since the commencement of British rule had come to be excluded from the higher administrative posts of the country#.

#Before 1833 the very meagre scale on which they were employed is disclosed by the following figures :*—

Native Civil Servants of the 1st Class attached to the Secretariat of the 3 Precidencies Receiving per Month Salaries of Rs.	Bengal		Madras		Bombay		Total	
	No.	Total Salary Drawn	No.	Total Salary Drawn	No.	Total Salary Drawn	No.	Total Salary Drawn
500 and upwards	5	2,700			5	2,500		
400 and upwards	2	800			1	400		
350 and upwards	4	1,400	1	350	1	350		
300 and upwards	3	900			2	600		
250 and upwards	5	1,250			1	250	89	20,690
From Rs. 250 to 200	17	3,460	5	1,155	1	200		
From Rs, 200 to 150	10	1,590	4	682 1/2				
From Rs. 100 to 150	5	550	5	525	5	330		
Below Rs. 100	6	470	1	871/2	2	140		
Total	57	13,120	16	2,800	16	4,770		

NATIVE						
	Details			Total		
Officers	Rs.	As.	Ps.	Rs.	As.	Ps.
26 Europeans	9,861	2	1			
20 Natives	940	0	0	13,527	8	7
Staff and	1,209	1	4			
EstablishmentCommand	1,517	5	2			
and other allowances						
	1,780	0	0			
Men	7,000	0	0	9,606	14	0
140 N.C.O.s.	826	14	0			
1,000 Sepoys						
Charges						
Total				23,134	6	7

It was to remove this injustice that Parliament in the Act of 1833 provided "that no native of the said territories, nor any natural-born subject of His Majesty resident therein, shall, by reason only of his religion, place of birth, descent, colour or any of them be disabled from holding any place, office, or employment under the said Company".

It is evident from this table that if we deduct the salary of 26 European officers and command and other allowances shown under the heading "Native" which amounts to Rs. 11,378 7. 3. we shall find that 1,104 Europeans drew Rs. 47,778 10. 7. while 1,160 natives drew only Rs. 11,755 15. 4.

But, as a matter of fact, till after the Mutiny not one of the natives was appointed to any office except such as they were eligible for before this Statute was passed, because the Court of Directors in interpreting it advised the Government of India at the very start that by this enactment "practically...... no very marked difference of results will be occasioned.

The Judicial and police charges, which together absorbed something like 10 percent of the total revenue raised, can only be regarded as protective in their distinction between the situations allotted to the covenanted service and all other situations of any official or public nature will remain generally as at present." Thus the bulk of the money raised by injurious taxes was spent in unproductive ways.

The agencies of war were cultivated in the name of peace, and they adsorbed so much of the total funds that nothing practically was left for the agencies of progress. Education formed no part of the expenditure incurred and useful public works were lamentably few. Railways, canals for navigation or irrigation and other aids to the development of commerce and industry for a long time found no corner in the Imperial budget. For a total area of 837,000 square miles there were constructed a few miles of railways, 2,157 miles of land ways, 580 miles of waterways and 80 miles of telegraph. Or speaking in terms of money spent, we find that for the entire period of fifteen years from 1837-8 to 1851-2 the average expenditure of a productive character amounted only to £ 299,732 a year.

There is a principle well known to farmers that constant cropping without manuring ends in the exhaustion of the soil. It is, however, capable of wider application, and had it been observed in the State economy of India the taxing capacity of the country would have grown to the benefit of the treasury and the people. Unfortunately it was lost upon the financiers of India to the detriment of both.

But if the chance of augmenting the resources by judicious taxes and productive expenditure to cover the chronic deficits was forfeited, there was at least the way open for economy in expenditure. As might be supposed, a strong Central Government of the kind established in 1833 was capable of effecting economy wherever possible. As a matter of fact, the centralisation was of the weakest kind. *De jure* there was an Imperial system of administration, but the *de facto* administration was conducted as though the primary units of executive government were the Provinces and that the Government of India was only a co-ordinating authority. This was obvious from a variety of circumstances. Legislation was, it is true, centred in the Government of India; none the less the laws that were passed by the Government of India were passed *for* the different provinces as though the initiative in legislation still lay in the Provinces and that the Government of India was only a sanctioning authority. Each Province had its own customs, internal as well as external, a survival of their sovereign status.

Each Province continued to have its own Army. Notwithstanding centralisation, the account system still remained provincial, sustaining the sense of their financial independence. The work of administration and collection of revenue being still conducted by them, the provinces behaved as though they were the lawful authorities charged with the responsibilities of Government.

This spirit of independence bred insubordination, and some of the Provinces, particularly Bombay and Madras, endeavoured to resist the attempts of the Government of India to tax the people under their jurisdiction when the cost of the mutiny compelled it to levy fresh burdens. The point to be borne in mind is that the Act of 1833 made an unfortunate divorce between the legal and administrative responsibility. The Imperial Government were responsible in law but did not administer the country.

The Provincial Governments administered the country but had no responsibility in law. This divorce had a fatal effect on the economy in the finances of the country. As was inevitable extravagance in expenditure had become the rule in practice and it was inherent in the Imperial system itself. Economy is begotten of responsibility, and responsibility is obtained where a government has to *find* the resources to meet the charges it desires to incur. Prior to the inauguration of the Imperial system the Provincial Government had the obligation to raise money for the charges included in their budgets. Consequently they had to be economical.

But under the Imperial system, while the budgets for the various services were prepared by the provincial authorities, the responsibility for finding the ways and means rested on the Government of India. Formerly "They knew the limits of the purse they had to draw upon, but under the Imperial system they

"had no means of knowing the measure by which their annual demands upon the Government of India ought to be regulated. They had a purse to draw upon of unlimited because of unknown depth. They saw on every side the necessity for improvements, and their constant and justifiable desire was to obtain for their own provinces as large a share as they could persuade the Government of India to give them out of the general revenues of the Empire. They found by experience that the less economy they practised and the more importunate their demands, the more likely they were to persuade the" Government of India of their requirements. In representing these requirements, they felt that they did what was right, and they left to the Government of India, which had taken upon itself, the responsibility of refusing to provide the necessary means".

To these extravagant demands the Government of India had often to yield; for, till very late, it did not possess the machinery to appraise the demands and to control the expenditure on them. It is not usual to expect much efficiency from any Imperial system of administration, much less when it covers not a department, not a province, but a country as big as a continent. Merely from being huge it is slow to move. Much slower would it necessarily be if it were a system as unorganised and unconsolidated as the Indian system was. First of all, the Imperial system in India was without its executive machinery of control. The Act which created it must be said to have grievously erred in uniting into one the Government of Bengal and the Government of India. As a result of this fusion the machinery was over stained. Its duties as the Government of Bengal left it very little time to attend to its duties as the Government of India. There was not only a common executive, but there was also a common Secretariat charged with the work of the two Governments. Overworked as the Secretariat was, its efficiency was considerably lowered by the absence of any officer specially charged with the duty of handling the finance of the country till 1843.

It was in that year that Lord Ellenborough, the then Viceroy of India, separated the Secretariat of Bengal from that of India and attached to the latter a distinct office called the Financial Secretary to the Government of India unencumbered with the details of any other Department of State except that of finance. But while the want of a scrutinising officer was thus made good by this appointment of a distinct Secretary of Finance, it was not possible for him to enforce economy in expenditure in the absence of a centralised system of audit and account and of an appropriation budget. Notwithstanding the establishment of the Imperial system of finance, the officers of audit and account remained attached to the Secretariats of the various Provincial Governments. They were not accountable to the supreme Government on whom the responsibility for the ordering and the management of the revenues of India had by law devolved. Being attached to the provincial Secretariat the Government of India could issue orders with regard to the accounts and the audits not directly but only through, and with the interpretation of, the Local Government concerned. Secondly, the budget system, though good enough for the purposes of mercantile accounts, that is, record, was useless for the first and elementary purpose of all good State accounts, namely, check. There were indeed three estimates (sketch, regular, and budget) prepared for the purposes of the financial administration of the country showing the amount of money required for the carrying on of each of the different services. But this distribution of public money on the different services was not held to mean appropriation. It was only treated as cash requirements. Owing to this fact the grants were never carefully prepared nor was the limit set on them observed in practice. As there was no budget of specific votes or sanctions for each of the services the audit and account was simply concerned with noting whether record was kept of all the money that was received and paid through the public treasury.

It is evident that in the absence of an appropriation budget the primary object of all State accounts and audit, namely check on the spending authority to abide by the sanction, was never achieved. The Provincial Governments, extravagant in their demands, were also careless in the matter of expenditure. So long as the Government of India remained without an appropriation budget and a centralised system of audit and account, it continued to be only a titular authority in the matter of financial control, and the provinces, though by law the weakest of authorities in financial matters, were really the masters of the situation.

To its inability to curb the extravagant habits of the provincial authorities generated by a financial irresponsibility on the part of the Provincial Governments and inefficiency on the part of the Central Government must be added the general spirit of apathy which marked the Executive Council of the Government of India in matters of finance. While it was true that nothing could be spent from the revenues of India without the specific vote of the Executive Council, it does not appear that the Council from its way of working could have taken any keen interest in promoting economy in expenditure. The Council acted collectively, and there was no distribution of executive work among the different members which composed it. With the exception of the Department of War and Legislation the whole work of the Government was brought before the Governor-General and his Councillors. As a result of its collective working

> "every case actually passed through the hands of each member of the Council, circulating at a snail's pace in little mahogany boxes from one Councillor's house to another."

Under such a system nobody was a Chancellor of the Exchequer to urge economy, because everybody was supposed to be one. The result was that finance in being everybody's business suffered from being nobody's business, so that funds were distributed not according to the genuine needs of the services, but according to the relative claims and persistency of the clamour made for them.

Sufficient evidence has been given to show that the collapse of the Imperial system was due to a faulty fiscal system marked by injurious taxes and unproductive and extravagant expenditure. It must not, however, be supposed that this faulty fiscal policy commenced with the inauguration of the Imperial system. On the other hand, it was a heritage which descended to the Imperial system from the past. None the less it is obvious that a timely revision of the fiscal policy and the strengthening of central control would have solidified the foundation of the Imperial system. But a much too long continuance thereof undermined its financial foundations, and as it could get no more money to meet its rising expenditure from a people whom it had beggared, the Imperial system succumbed to the shock of the Mutiny, never to rise again in its original garb.

2

Imperialism V. Federalism

As the result of the cost of the Mutiny of 1857 the already precarious condition of the Imperial Finance became so grave that no problem during the succeeding decade can be said to have engrossed the attention of responsible authorities as the one relating to the rehabilitation of that tottering system. Although the controversy as to the proper line of reconstruction to be adopted was long drawn out, the causes of the collapse were so patent that all those who had anything to do with Indian Finance unmistakably laid their finger on one supreme defect in the system whose breakdown they had witnessed, namely, the irresponsible extravagance it engendered in the Provincial Governments. To obviate this evil it was sought on the one hand by some responsible authorities "to make the Local Governments partners in the great joint stock of Indian Finances, and, so to enlist their interest and animated co-operation with the Government of India, instead of keeping them on the footing of agents and servants, who, having no motive for economy and using the means of their masters, think only of enhancing their own demands by comparisons more or less well founded, with the indulgence conceded to others."

This view gradually led to the formation of a considerable body of well-trained opinion for changing united India into the United States of India, by making the provinces into separate and sovereign States. The aim was to substitute a Federal system for the Imperial system and to assimilate the financial position of the Central authority in India to that of the Central authority in the United States. For the consummation of the Federal plan it was urged that the revenues of India should not be dealt with as one income, collected into the Imperial Treasury and thence distributed among the different Provincial Governments. According to the plan each province was to be allowed to keep its revenues and meet its charges from them. The Central Government was to have its own separate resources and, if need be, supplemented by contributions from the provinces as their share of the expenditure of the Central Government based on some equitable standard. Thus under the Federal plan the consolidated Imperial Budget with its formal division between Imperial and Provincial was sought to be replaced by the creation of distinctly separate budgets, Central and Provincial, based on a genuine division of services and allocation of revenues.

Many advantages were claimed in favour of the Federal plan. First it was believed that the separation of the revenues and services would lead the ways and means of the Central as well as of the Provincial Governments to be clearly defined, so that each one of them would be responsible for administering its affairs within the funds allotted to it. Heretofore the Provincial Governments sent up their estimates of revenue and expenditure as returns unconnected with each other, and the task of balancing them was left to be done by the Supreme Government upon the aggregate of the different provincial estimates submitted to it. Under the Federal plan the provincial estimates would have to be balanced accounts of receipts and charges made over to them. Though primary it was not the only advantage which the Federalists claimed for their plan, for it was advanced not only as a measure to set bounds to the extravagant expenditure of the Local Governments by limiting the funds on which they were to draw, but also as a measure for setting bounds to the growing expenditure of the Central Government as well. The Federalists did not conceal the fact that the Central Government, being in a position to draw upon the total resources of India as a whole, was inclined to be extravagant in its own expenditure. They therefore thought that the Federal plan, involving as it did the allocation of revenues and services, would result in enforcing economy on the Central as well as on the Provincial Government. The Federal plan was not only proposed by its advocates in the interests of economy and responsibility, but also in the interests of plenty. The Federalists denied that India offered few sources of revenue for the growing expenditure of the State. Though the Indian Finance ferry was water-logged, it was their view that there were many sources of taxation with the outpourings of which it could be set afloat. But they argued that these available sources were left untapped, as the Imperial Government, which could tap them, would not do so because of their restricted *locale',* and Provincial Government, which would like to tap them, because of their restricted *locale* could not do so under the existing constitutional law. But if the Provincial Governments were vested or rather re-vested with the powers of taxation as they would be under the Federal plan, such sources of taxation as were given up for being too regional-in character by the Imperial Government would be used by the Provincial Government to the great relief of Indian Finance as a whole.

Not only was Federalism advocated in the interests of economy and plenty, but also in the interests of equity. It was contended that the existing system resulted in an iniquitous treatment of the different provinces. If we take public works of provincial utility and the expenditure incurred upon them in the different provinces as the criterion, the criticism of the Federalists cannot be said to have been unfounded. On the other hand, the following figures go to substantiate a very large part of their arguments :—

Outlay on Public Works

Average for the Years 1937-8 to 1845-6

Province	*Population in thousands*	*Area in sq. miles*	*Revenues in hundreds of Rs.*	*Revenues in Public works in hundreds of Rs.*
Bengal	40,000,000	1,65,443	10,239,500	1,79,812
N.W. P.	23,200,000	71,985	5,699,200	1,41,450
Madras	22,000,000	1,45,000	5,069,500	30,300

Complied from *Calcutta Review,* 1851, Vol. XVI, p. 466.

Thus the outlay on public works was in Bengal 1 3/4 percent.; in North-Western Provinces, 2 1/2 percent.; and in Madras a little over 1/2 percent/of their respective revenues. This favoured treatment of some provinces as against the others was justified by the Imperial Government, which distributed the funds, on the ground that the favoured provinces showed surpluses in their accounts.

But the Federalists pointed out these deficits and surpluses ascribed to the different provinces were grossly fictitious. They were the result of a bad system of accounts. The system was bad for the reason that it continued to show the accounts of the financial transactions of the country not according to Heads of Account but according to the provinces in which they occurred as used to be the case before 1833 when there was no common system of finance. With the passing of the Act of 1833 this system of accounts had become quite out of keeping with the spirit and letter of that Act.

This would not have mattered very much if the All-India items were separated from the purely provincial items in the General Heads of Account.

In the absence of this the evils of the system were aggravated by entering exclusively into the accounts of a province the charges for what was really an All-India Service, so that it continued to show deficits, while others which escaped continued to show surpluses and claim in consequence the favoured treatment given to them. The Presidency of Bombay offered to the Federalists a case in point. The demands of the Presidency were invariably received with scant courtesy by the Government of India, for in its history Bombay seldom showed any surplus in her accounts.

But, if it had been realised that the deficits were caused by the barbarous system of accounts which kept on charging the Presidency with the cost of the Indian Navy, it undoubtedly would have fared better. Such vicious ways of appointment were not the only evil features of the system of accounts. Under it it was quite common to charge one Presidency with the cost of a service and to credit another with the receipts thereof. How the deficits found in the Madras accounts were inflicted upon it by the erroneous system of accounts may be seen from the following :—

Cost of the Army of Occupation		*Revenues derived from the Occupied territory*	
Debited to	***Amount Rs.***	***Credited to***	***Amount Rs.***
Madras	79,83,000	Bombay	20,00,000
		Bengal	1,04,22,870

Taking into consideration the iniquities involved in such a system of accounts, it is beyond dispute that the advantage claimed by the Federalists for their plan was neither fictitious nor petty. A division of functions between the Federal and Provincial Governments would have in itself been an advantage by comparison with the existing chaos. And, if it did not result in equity, it had at least the merit of opening a way for it.

When however the Federal plan was put before the authorities in the form of a practical proposal, it gave rise to a determined opposition. The challenge was at once taken up by the supporters of the Imperial system who, be it noted, were mostly military men in civil employ. They opened their attack on the Federal plan from two sides, that of practicability and expediency.

Is it possible, asked the Imperialists, to localise the revenues and charges of India as belonging distinctively to one particular province? They insisted that,

"from the commencement of (the British) power (in India)...... the interests and affairs of (the) presidencies and the provinces have been interwoven and interlaced—one often overlapping the other, and vice versa—in a manner from which extrication or disentanglement is now impossible, without making changes which would entail inconveniences greater than any entailed by the existing system...... The army of Bengal Presidency is quartered not in the rich districts of the Lower Ganges, but mainly in the poorer districts of the Punjab. Thus placed, that army defends virtually the whole Presidency. The Madras army is not kept within that Presidency, but holds, besides the Madras country, the Deccan, the Central Provinces, and British Burma.

Similarly the Bombay army holds, besides its own Presidency, the State of Rajputana and of Malwa. The Lower Provinces or Bengal proper are in themselves rich; but besides their own revenues they receive large customs receipts, which belong partly to them, but largely also to the other Divisions of the Bengal Presidency. Even Bengal opium does not entirely belong to Bengal, a large portion being raised in the North-Western provinces. In Bombay the opium revenue does not, strictly speaking, belong to that Presidency at all, being raised beyond its limits, in the territories which, if included in any Presidency at all, would pertain to that of Bengal. Some of the Salt Duties, both of Madras and of Bombay, are raised on salt destined for consumption in Central India, and, in strictness, should be credited to the Government of India. Instances might be multiplied; but it becomes instantly evident that, if an adjustment of these matters with a view to complete localisation of finance were to be attempted, many difficulties, perhaps even disputes, would arise......

Arguing in the same strain, Lord Lawrence, the then Viceroy of India, wrote:

"Experience has shown that it is convenient that the resources of British India should be considered in the aggregate and not with reference to the particular province in which it is raised. If the rule were otherwise, we must enter into the question—what are the revenues which each province may fairly claim? What are the items of expenditure which may justly be charged to each? Is the Punjab, for instance, to be charged for all the British troops located in the hills for sanitary considerations ? Is the whole of the force ranged against the Northwestern border to be similarly debited ? Are the troops quartered in Rajputana to be charged to the Bombay Presidency to which they belong, or in what manner is their cost to be arranged for ? On the other hand, we may be asked, why should not Bengal in particular—which, having no foreign neighbours, and a docile and timid population, requires only a minimum garrison—have the benefit of her surplus revenues ? Why on the opposite view of the question should not Bengal bear her share of the cost of the troops located in the North-Western Provinces, the Punjab and Central India, which guard her from such invasions as those of the Rohillas, the Mahrattas and the Pindarics of former times? These are all questions which would require solution if each were to have a financial system of its own" and in his opinion the question was impossible of solution.

But the Imperialists went further than this and argued that, even if it were possible to distinguish and localise the charges and the revenues into provincial and central, it was inexpedient to do so. Under the existing system of finance, they held that

"the Imperial Government, disposing of financial resources of the whole of India, can carry those resources at once where they are most needed. There are objects which have a truly national importance, though they may appear chiefly beneficial to a particular district. There may be evils, necessities and dangers in particular districts, which it is the duty of the supreme Government to correct and remedy at the charge of the whole. The creation or improvement of a part may have a national importance, though the expenditure on it may seem unfairly beneficial to a particular locality. A road, a canal, a railway from a cotton district or a coffee district, or a tea district, may have a vital significance to the whole people and commerce of India ; and yet the expenditure on such a work be out of all proportion to the present revenue of the district which it is destined to develop...... or the supreme Government may find it necessary to lay out, for moral and social purposes, larger sums on recently conquered, savage, or dissatisfied provinces than the revenues of those provinces seemed to warrant, in order to remove causes of disturbances or dangers, and to force those provinces into some degree of harmony with the long settled, pacified, reclaimed portions of the Empire....... The old provinces of the Empire conquer the new provinces. The old are bound in duty to civilise what they conquer. We have no right to annex a country and then throw it on its own resources. Conquest has its own duties as well as its rights."

"I venture to demur," wrote Lord Napier of Merchiston, President of the Council of Madras, "to the policy of those who would restrict the benefits of the supreme Government to its receipts, and who would measure out in a parochial spirit to every province appropriations proportional to its specific returns. On the contrary, it ought to be a satisfaction to the rich to help the poor; to the old to protect the young; to the good to improve the bad; for thus all can co-operate in building up the glorious fabric of a—United India. Such ends can only be attained by a Central Government disposing of the financial resources of a whole Empire.

It is evident that arguments or sermons such as the above by themselves could never have supported the cause of the Imperialists. Notwithstanding the emphasis laid upon the difficulty of separating the revenues and charges into Imperial and Provincial, it must be conceded that the task was by no means so insuperable as the Imperialists made it out to be. The difficulty of apportioning the military charges could have been easily obviated by centralising the military and making it a charge of the Central Government. On the same basis all those services charged to a particular Presidency or Province, but which from their nature benefited the whole Empire, could have been easily incorporated into the budget of the Central Government. Similarly it was possible in practice to allocate the existing sources of revenue between the Central and the Local Governments. The Central Government could have been allowed to retain for its use such sources of revenue the *locale* of which extended beyond the limits of a Presidency or the maximum yield of which depended upon a uniform administration of the same throughout the country. While on the other hand the Provincial Government could have been allowed to appropriate such sources which were restricted in their *locale* or the yield of which depended upon local vigilance. For instance, the customs duties could have been easily made a central resource, not only because their incidence was wider, but because they required a common and uniform policy of legislation and administration. The opium revenue could have been treated as a central source of revenue, and the same treatment could have been granted to the salt revenue. Of course it would have been difficult to effect a separation of the sources of revenue in such a way as would have granted to each of the several Governments concerned resources adequate to meet the charges devolving upon them. A certain adjustment of funds by contributions from the provinces to the Central Government or from the Central Government to the provinces would have been inevitable; neither could it have been possible to obviate the adoption of principles more or less arbitrary in the matter of apportionment of revenues or of charges. But admitting the difficulties and arbitrariness involved in the problem of separating the Imperial Budget into a Central and several Provincial Budgets, it must still be said that it was quite capable of satisfactory solution. Colonel Chesney in response to the challenge thrown out by the Imperialists had made a notable attempt to distinguish the existing heads of charges into Imperial and Provincial. In his Indian Polity he says :

"The items of Imperial expenditure for which contributions would be required consist apparently of—(1) the Home Establishment and charges disbursed by the Secretary of State ; (2) interest on Indian debt; (3) Establishments of the Government of India ; (4) Diplomatic establishment ; (5) Army ; (6) Imperial Services—Post Office and Telegraph Department ; (7) interest guaranteed on railway capital ; to which must be added (8) grants in aid to some of the poorer provinces (which do not at present pay their expenses)."

This and other efforts convinced the Imperialists that their argument from practicability was bound to fail. Consequently they shifted their emphasis from the argument from practicability to that from expediency. Expediency furnished a better ground for attacking the Federal plan. Can a Federal Government be as efficient as the Imperial Government? Can its credit be as high? Can its prestige be as great as that of the existing Imperial system? It must be premised that it was fresh in the minds of the people that it was the Imperial system with a strong power of control that had saved the country to the British from the hands of the mutineers of 1857. The survival value of the Imperial system had been proved in the struggle. By a clever maneuver the Imperialists turned to the authorities and asked them to consider what had sustained the Imperial system throughout the struggle. They did not fail to emphasise the point that it was because the Imperial system of finance had given into the hands of the Imperial Government the control over the management of the revenues and disbursements of the Empire that the latter, in an emergency like the Mutiny, could stimulate every source of income, close every avenue of outlet, and concentrate all its expenditure on the capital object at stake— the energetic prosecution of hostilities.

They showed that, without the Imperial system of finance, the Imperial Government would have had to deal with lukewarm, reluctant, hesitating or even hostile partners, perhaps not directly concerned in the struggle or convinced of its necessity, and solicitous for exoneration or delay. Further they made out that the Imperial management of finance was vital not only in heightening the efficiency of government, but also in maintaining the high state of credit. Credit, it was argued, depended upon the magnitude of the revenue, and to disintegrate the revenues was tantamount to lowering the credit.

The Federal plan was also accused of abrogating the European tradition which has given prestige a very high place in its code for Asian government. It was inconceivable to the Imperialists that the Central Government could maintain its prestige without centralisation in finance, for it was the system of Imperial Finance which, having collected the leading strings in political and administrative matters into the hands of the Imperial Government, enabled that Government to dictate a policy and have it executed to its own satisfaction. But who could uphold the prestige of the Central Government, if it became a pensioner of the Local Governments subordinate to it?

Looked at from the vantage ground of detachment from the time of the controversy one may wonder what strength there was in the argument from expediency which gave the Imperialists such an easy victory over the Federalists. Federal Governments such as those existing in America, Germany or elsewhere do not lend support to the view that in their working there is bound to be a loss of efficiency, credit, or prestige. Their history has belied all these gloomy foreboding. But it should be remembered that at the time the controversy raged in India, much of the history of Federalism was a blank page, for Federalism was itself in its infancy. People, however, sided with the Imperialists, not because they could not draw upon the history of Federalism for arguments in its favour, but because the events of the time had inclined them to support the Imperial system.

The Imperial system had saved India from the hands of the Mutiny of 1857, and when their fears of its repetition were not yet allayed it was too soon to expect them to consent to disrupt a machine that had just then proved its worth in the great contest. Conscious though they were of its defects, people recoiled from any attempt to tamper with it. So strong was the partiality of the people for the Imperial system that, notwithstanding the many defects which to their knowledge detracted from the efficiency of the system, they could give a sympathetic hearing to the Hon'ble Major-General Sir H. M. Durand, who wrote:

"I assert confidently that at present there is absolutely no ground whatever for the allegation that the financial control of the Government of India goes to undue lengths in what it attempts, and miscarries miserably. On the contrary, any partial miscarriage of control is no proof whatever that the rules are faulty, but that their relaxation is highly inexpedient, and that more rigid subordination of them should be enforced both by the Government of India and the Home Government. To subvert the financial control of the Central Government because one out of nine administrations has proved rather refractory, is about as sensible a procedure, to my mind, as to annul the articles of War and the powers of the Commander-in-Chief because a regiment should somewhat happen to misbehave. I venture to doubt the statesmanship of ruling either India or armies in this way."

Notwithstanding the victory of the Imperialists, it must be said the Federalists lost a cause which was bound to succeed. For the sentiment of the time, however favourable to the retention of the Imperial system, was powerless to resist the force of events. The Imperial Government had to be extricated from the state of chronic penury in which it had fallen, and if statesmanship did not favour the system of Federal Finance as a means, financiers soon learnt that the system of Imperial Finance was doubtful as an end.

The Compromise

Imperial Finance without Imperial Management

If the Federalists failed to carry the day, they at least led their opponents to improve the system by removing some of the most radical defects from which it suffered. Attention was mainly directed towards revising the revenue laws and improving the machinery of control so that more revenues be obtained and less wastefully spent. With the primary object of making the Imperial system strong and prosperous, serious attempts were made about the close of the rule of the East India Company to do away with the oppressive taxes which had so long retarded the prosperity of the people and consequently of the Government. The internal custom duties were done away with, and the country was not only freed from all restrictions which hampered the growth of trade and industry, but positive encouragement was given to them by introducing the element of protection in the import tariff and trade was facilitated by equalising the duties on English and foreign shipping. Articles of export were also relieved from the handicap of export duties and efforts were made to improve the cultivation and pressing of cotton, tea and other staples which commanded a great market in Europe and elsewhere.

The administrative machinery was next subjected to revision. Advantage was taken of the Indian Councils Act of 1861 authorising the Viceroy "to make from time to time rules and orders for the more convenient transaction of business in his Council," to bring legally to an end the system under which the whole Council was supposed to take part collectively in the disposal of all the business of the Government by assigning to each member of the Council the charge of a separate department of administration: the Council was thus virtually converted into a Cabinet of which the Governor-General became the head. In this manner a place for a Chancellor of the Exchequer was created to which was appointed the well-Known financier, Mr. James Wilson. The attention of Mr. Wilson was directed first of all to the improvements in the machinery of fiscal administration. The credit of establishing in India a uniform system of accounts, centralisation of civil and military audit, and the introduction of an appropriation budget, rightly belongs to him. With the improvement in the revenue laws and the check on waste through improved and efficient administration was combined the policy of retrenchment in expenditure, and the budget and audit rules were "so framed as to leave to the head of each Local Government or of each branch of administration a much larger *(sic)* discretionary power than......here to fore...... allowed in rearranging the details of expenditure" if that led to retrenchment. So drastic was the economy practised that, soon after the inauguration of the policy of spreading education throughout the country initiated by the dispatch of the Secretary of State in 1854, a stop was put to any increase of expenditure on education.

But notwithstanding all these efforts at betterment howsoever diligently sustained, they did not improve the finances of India materially; at any rate. Mr. Wilson in his Financial Statement for 1860-1, by way of summing up the financial situation, said: "we have a deficit in the last three years of £ 30,547,488; we have a prospective deficit in the next year of £ 6,500,000; we have already added to our debt £ 38,410,755." To meet this huge deficit Mr. Wilson was obliged to augment the stamp duties, double the external customs, and impose an income tax, hitherto unknown to the people. Even the yield of these "three tremendous taxes" did not help Mr. Samuel Laing, the successor of Mr. Wilson, to a prosperous condition, for he too in his Financial Statement for 1861-2 wanted £ 500,000 fairly to weather his deficit and get into smooth waters with a small surplus. A few years of financial prosperity intervened. But Mr. Massey, who relieved Mr. Laing in 1866, "upon a review of the financial condition of the Empire and the increasing demands made upon its resources...... deemed it expedient to make provision for a permanent addition of a million sterling at the least to the existing revenue"

Why the efforts of these successive Finance Ministers were not crowned with success is to be explained chiefly by the fact that the administrative and public needs of the country had grown beyond measure. After the Mutiny "thousands of Englishmen, not only soldiers, but Englishmen of almost every class, poured into India. Ten thousand things were demanded which India had not got, but which it was felt must be provided. The country (had to be) covered with railways and telegraphs, roads and bridges. Canals (had to be) made to preserve the people from starvation. Barracks (had to be) built for a great European army, and every sort of sanitary arrangement which would benefit the troops (had to be) carried out. This was not only true in regard to matters of Imperial concern. Demands for improvements similar to those which fell upon the Central Government cropped up in every town and in every district controlled by the Local Government. The demands for improved administration also made themselves effective. The police was in a shameful condition throughout India and the inadequacy of the pay given to native judges and other subordinate officers employed in the posts of importance in the courts was declared by Lord Lawrence when he was Viceroy to be a public scandal. Among more than four thousand of these officers in the Bengal Presidency, the highest paid of all, and these were very few, received £180 a year. The great majority received from £12 to £24 a year sums less than those earned in many parts of India by common bricklayers and carpenters. All these had to be put on a completely new footing.

While the needs for expenditure were thus growing, economy in expenditure became difficult of achievement. Comparatively easy at first, each successive measure of economy became directly, as well as relatively, more arduous than its predecessor. The growing needs of improvements, hitherto neglected, and the contracting scope for economy, combined to demand an ever-increasing scale of taxation. The dangers of increased taxation by an alien Government of a people not interested in obtaining the amenities of life, much less at the cost of a tax, were uppermost in the minds of the three great financiers who were sent out from England in succession to rehabilitate the finances of India on a sound and stable basis. They realised that unless bounds were set to these demands for improved administration and improved material and moral conditions, the immediate benefits of which were enjoyed more by the European than the native population, taxation howsoever high would be inadequate for financial solvency, besides being dangerous to the political stability of the Empire. Under the existing system of barren uniformity and pedantic centralisation their object was thought to be impossible of achievement; for the Local Governments, on which alone the Central Government could depend for economy, rendered at best to that Government not only a cold and languid support in financial vigilance and reform, but too often exhibited a passive resistance, and even countenanced evasions of regulations intended to be conducive to economy.

The only way to make Local Governments economical in their ways was to give them the power and responsibility of managing their own affairs. As a matter of administrative experience the financiers had found that while some of the branches of revenue and expenditure were truly imperial, there was a wide field of both of them which was properly local in character, and ought to have been entrusted to Local Governments.

They were convinced that there could be no standard of economy until the requirements of the Local Government were made absolutely dependent upon known means, and nothing they thought would serve to make known to the Local Governments the means available for their outlay than to carve out from the Imperial purse a separate purse of definite magnitude for the use of Local Governments and to throw on them the responsibility of meeting their demands and maintaining an equilibrium in their finance. Thus they were led to the same conclusion as the Federalists.

However, to make the plan acceptable to the Imperialists, they made certain concessions without seriously compromising the working of the plan. The Federal plan required a change in the constitution of the system of government in India. It necessitated a *legal* partition of the revenues and charges of India between the Central and the several Provincial Governments. While all, including the Imperialists, recognised in the Federal plan a powerful measure for enforcing financial responsibility and economy, the chief objection to it arose from the fact that it sought *legally and permanently to* divest the

Central Government of the resources of India. The financiers as practical politicians soon found out a way to obviate this defect in the Federal plan.

By virtue of their experiences of the working of the British Parliament they found that there was no necessity to resort to a constitutional change. Convention was deemed to be as good as law and, once established, can seldom be altered without disturbance. Separation of charges and revenues between the Central and Provincial Governments was therefore proposed to be made a matter of convention which could be upheld so long as it was profitable for the parties concerned to do so.

This gave all the advantages of the Federal plan without legally divesting the Central Government of its control over the resources of India. In its nature it was a compromise between constitutional Imperialism and constitutional Federalism.

It meant Imperial finance without Imperial management. Under the compromise the revenues and charges remained Imperial in their status, but their management was to be provincialised, so that each of the Provincial Governments was given to administer a part of the Imperial charges incurred in its territory within the limits of a part of the Imperial revenues collected within its territory. This was the essence of the new plan. It differed from the Federal plan in retaining to the Imperial Government the supreme controlling, counselling and regulating authority in all matters pertaining to Indian Finance, without its being actually engaged in the details of the administration of a *part* thereof.

In the essence of the plan as described above all the three finance ministers who were called upon to undertake the task of reconstruction had agreed. They differed, however, in the scale on which it was to be carried out. Whether Mr. Wilson had ever elaborated his own skeleton of the plan is doubtful; but that the idea of it had occurred to him seems pretty certain. The Income Tax Act XXXII of 1860, imposed by him

"was meant to consist of two parts—first, a variable tax, originally fixed at 3 percent on incomes, which percentage it was intended should be raised or lowered as the general exigencies of the Empire required, and which might if the state of the finance should ever permit, be entirely remitted; and secondly, a permanent tax of 1 percent., which was to be at the disposal of the local administration, and to be expended on roads, canals, and other reproductive public works, within the area which paid the tax (*vide* sections 190-4 of the Act). This portion of the tax was never intended to be remitted. It was always to be kept up, not only to meet the charges to which it was applicable, but in order to maintain the machinery of the tax so that at any moment of exigency, after a temporary remission the other portion of the tax, applicable in aid of the general finances, might be re-imposed without agitation, discussion, or trouble."

But, as Mr. Wilson did not live long enough to elaborate his ideas into a scheme, it is difficult to say to what extent he intended to work them out in practice.

Mr. Laing, the successor of Mr. Wilson, put it in a much more definite shape. His budget for 1861-2 was for a deficit caused chiefly by the pressing demands of the Local Governments for useful public works, and his sense of financial safety compelled him "to curtail roads, canals and other useful works of this description, to the allotment on which they (had) been carried on or rather...... starved, since the Mutiny."

But his anxiety to promote the useful public works, the urgency of which he fully recognised, led him to propose to the Provincial Governments a method of supplementing the scanty Imperial grants made to them. He said to them: "Take what we are able to give you, and for the residue take certain powers of taxation and raise it yourself.. ....for there are certain subjects which can be dealt with far better by local than by Imperial taxation..."

His object was to enact local budgets "not merely to meet a temporary difficulty but to inaugurate a permanent improvement," to the relief of the Imperial treasury and the benefit of the Provincial Governments. This scheme involving the management of the public works charges by the Local Government with an allotment from the Imperial revenues supplemented by the power to tax had secured a general approval. But at the time when the scheme was put forward the Local Government was without the requisite machinery for carrying into execution the powers of legislation necessary to impose the taxes proposed to be given to them. The execution of the scheme had therefore to be postponed pending the enactment of local legislative councils then undertaken by Parliament. But, the ensuing years having been years of financial prosperity, the interest in the scheme relaxed and it was consequently dropped *sine die.*

This spell of prosperity, however, proved to be only a passing phase and the stress of returning adversity which beset Mr. Massey compelled him to revive the scheme in a much more enlarged form. He proposed that: "In considering the ways and means by which the additional amount (of one million sterling) should be raised ...... the most convenient mode of proceeding would be by a partial transfer of charges of a local character from Imperial to local account."

As the annual produce of local funds applicable to local purposes in India did not much exceed two million sterling, it was proposed to make the moderate addition to this amount of £1,200,000 in round numbers to be raised in rateable proportions in the several Presidencies and Local Governments, and applied in relief of a corresponding amount of charge for local services then borne by the Imperial revenues. The above-mentioned sum of £1,200,000 was arrived at by an assessment of 4 percent on the estimated revenues of the several Local Governments (except Burma) for the current year, after excluding customs duties and the income tax. The heads of charges to which the proceeds of the new funds were applicable were (1) education, (2) police, (3) district jails, (4) public works, (5) repairs and maintenance of roads.

The list of taxes suggested to provide ways and means included (1) a license tax on trades and professions, (2) a house tax, (3) an octroi duty in towns, and (4) a succession duty on lands which did not pay revenue. The Local Governments were to be left free, subject to the approval of the Government of India in Council, to select the particular tax most suited for being levied in their respective territories so as to yield the full amount required, after deducting the cost of collection, and spend the proceeds on the services mentioned above, on all or any of them, according to their discretion.

The replies of the Local Governments and administrations addressed in connection with this scheme, indicated a general agreement as to the practicability of such a transfer of charges being made and being met by new local taxation, though there was also a general disposition to object to the transfer of charges without a simultaneous transfer of revenue with which to meet the expenditure on them. Under the circumstances the Government of India agreed to reduce the expenditure to be transferred to the Local Governments to £ 800,000 and to transfer to them the proceeds of the license tax as a means for making adequate provision for the same.

The favourable reception accorded to the scheme and the sympathetic criticism to which it was subjected led Mr. Massey to extend and modify it. In his exposition of the new and enlarged scheme Mr. Massey wrote: "my first object has been to select, for the first series of charges to be transferred to local authorities, those items of expenditure which being least susceptible of control by the Government of India, give as a whole, an amount of such dimensions as will not be difficult to manage, and yet will be of sufficient importance to indicate that the measure is intended to be a reality, and a step towards the more complete transfer of the financial administration to the local government.

Taking the civil estimates...... it seems to me, plainly, the most convenient method of proceeding to transfer a few entire grants or section of grants, in preference to selecting special items from several grants...... By adopting the plan...... no change whatever in the system of accounts will be called for; and the only alteration will be, that certain sections of the grants for various purposes, will be provided in a special manner. The only exception to this rule... is in dealing with a head' Miscellaneous 'which...... is rather an incongruous collection of charges.

Among these will be retained, for transfer to local management, all those items which would reasonably be termed local.... and the residue.... could easily be classed under some of the other main heads of charge. The most important of the charges which I should propose to transfer is that for 'Jails' subordinate to ' Law and Justice,' which may... be taken in lump. The charges for ' Registration ' and ' Tulubana ' also under ' Law and Justice ' follow. These are met from special fees credited under the head of ' Law and Justice'. To set off against these charges, a transfer of the revenue under ' Law and Justice ' is also proposed... Under ' Education' the ' Miscellaneous ' charges are proposed to be transferred to the corresponding transfer of the revenue credited under' Education'. Next follows the whole of the charges under ' Medical Services ' except the fixed ' Medical Establishments and Chemical Examiners'.

The entire charge under ' Stationery and Printing ' is also taken. Under ' Police ' the charges met by contributions from local sources are transferred, including the Railway Police. Against this is set off the receipts under ' Police'. ' Besides the above it is proposed to transfer a portion of the charges, for the collection of the Land Revenue and of the Income Tax and License Tax, which... I have assumed as likely to be levied in future. It has been necessary to assign a sum sufficient to cover the general charges which would be transferred and the propriety of transferring a corresponding portion of the cost of collection seems apparent. Under the designation of charges of collection of the Land Revenue were not included the cost of the Revenue Survey or Settlement as they were exceptional and variable, though the charges under ' Allowances to Village Officers ' were included.

"The first and principal transfer of revenue will be a portion of the Land Revenue, which I propose to fix at 1/16th or one anna in the rupee. The same rate will govern the proportion of the charges for collection transferred......

"The next item of revenue which I assume at one-fourth of the Income Tax and License Tax, which I shall suppose to be raised.

"It is next proposed to transfer the whole of the receipts under the following heads : (1) Law and Justice, (2) Police, (3) Education, (4) Miscellaneous, except items of a financial nature, and also (5) all income under Police Works excepting that derived from Irrigation.

The items of expenditure under Public Works proposed to be transferred are (1) Roads, (2) Repairs of Civil Buildings, (3) Miscellaneous works both new and repairs, and (4) Tools and Plant."

The scheme thus enlarged was discussed at length from various points of view. But though it won the approval of cautious critics the scheme was too large for the Imperialists. And as the two greatest of them, Lord Lawrence, the Viceroy of India, and Lord Napier of Merchistoun, Governor of Madras, disapproved of it, it failed to materialise in consequence of their opposition.

But unfortunately for the Imperialists, throughout this decade during which they were stubbornly objecting to any surgical operation on their patient—the Imperial system of Finance—it did not show any sign of convalescence.

On the other hand, the delay in the operation aggravated its ills. Notwithstanding the constant enhancement in taxation and the reduction in expenditure, the three Chancellors of the Indian Exchequer sent from England could point to only three years of surplus during the decade between 1860 to 1870.

On the other hand, to the embarrassments due to constant deficits was added the bewildering breakdown of the budget system created to bring about order and economy in the public finances of the country. Not to speak of its efficiency as an instrument of economy, the budget system under the strain due to excessive centralisation proved useless even as an instrument of order. The finances fell into a chaos. Notwithstanding the elaborate circulars and orders issued with regard to the accuracy in the framing of the budget estimates, it was an extraordinary phenomenon which confronted the Finance Ministers when the budgets, which were begun with large estimated surpluses, strangely enough closed with large actual deficits.

To what extent the actuals erred from the estimates may be seen from the following table:

Year	Estimate Deficitsurplus	Actual Deficitsurplus
1866-67	-66,700	-2,307,700
1867-68 ...	1,628,522	-923,720
1868-69 ...	1,893,508	2,542,861
1869-70 ...	48,263	1,650,000 (est)

From the above table it is clear that the estimates for 1868-9 and for 1869-70, which were based on the revised estimates of 1868-69, were expected to end with an estimated surplus of £1,893,508 and £48,263 respectively. But when the actuals of the year 1868-69 showed that instead of a surplus there was to be a large deficit, Lord Mayo, who was in the meantime appointed to the Viceroyalty of India, became convinced that if his budget was recast on the basis of these results, it would close with an actual deficit instead of the estimated surplus. This financial surprise threw his budget into confusion, and to restore order he was obliged to adopt the unusual procedure of addition to taxation and the reduction of expenditure in the midst of the fiscal year.

So grave was the crisis that with all these measures he could do nothing more than close his budget with an estimated deficit of £1,650,000 which would have been inevitable had it not been for certain windfalls such as the recovery of the value of supplies in the Abyssinian War and the adjustment of other large outstanding accounts which enabled him to convert his large deficit into a small surplus. Happy as he was over the immediate results of his efforts, Lord Mayo was convinced that there was something rotten in the system of Imperial Finance and, while anxious not to end it, he courageously set forth to mend it by inaugurating the scheme of Provincial Finance represented by the compromise the growth of which will be the subject-matter of Part II of this study.

3

Provincial Finance : Its Development

Budget by Assignments

1871-72 TO 1876-77

The origins which led to the formulation of the scheme of Provincial Budget having been presented in the foregoing part of this study, we may now proceed to examine the constitution of the scheme as it was introduced and the changes which it underwent from time to time.

With his sureness of instinct Lord Mayo traced the financial deficits and surprises to the inefficiency of the Imperial and the irresponsibility of the Provincial Governments, and was led to the conclusion that the inauguration of Provincial Budgets was the only remedy equal to the malady.

But it must be recalled that the situation was yet dominated by Imperialistic considerations, and while every one in charge of the affairs was desirous, even anxious, to ease the situation by some means or other, few were willing to do so at the cost of Imperial control. Even Lord Mayo was not without his Imperialistic leanings.

But the force of the baffling circumstances compelled him to break through the hitherto prevailing spirit of hesitation and indecision, although the steps he took in determining the constitution of the Provincial Budget were slow and cautious.

The scheme which actually came to be introduced from the financial year 1871-2 was first adumbrated in a confidential circular of the Home Department of the Government of India, dated February 21, 1870. Enlarging upon the policy of retrenchment by which the road grant for 1869-70 fixed in the beginning at £ 1,236,000 came to be reduced at the close of the year to £1,021,178 and that estimated for 1870-1 at £ 1,000,000 came to be finally settled at £ 784,839 supplemented by £29,110 for Miscellaneous Public Improvements, the circular gave the Provincial Governments

"to understand that the diminution that has been made in the Imperial grant for communications and roads is not a temporary diminution caused by present financial pressure. It is the result of a settled policy, deliberately adopted, independently of temporary considerations, and it is far more probable that in future years the special grant for these purposes will be reduced than that it will be increased.

It therefore becomes a matter of very urgent necessity that no time should be lost in providing from local sources the funds necessary for the maintenance of the existing provincial and district roads, and for the construction of the new lines of communications which become every day more necessary."

That local wants should be met by local resources had been the ideal of Indian financiers during the entire period of its reconstruction.

But that the view had by that time passed beyond the stage of academic discussion is obvious, for the Circular stated that "the Governor-General in Council had fully resolved that he will insist on full effect being given to this principle "in future. Many of the Local Governments took the sentiments of the Government of India conveyed in the Circular in all the seriousness in which they were meant to be taken and had begun to develop their local resources.

In the Bombay Presidency a cess of 6 1/4 percent. On the Land Revenue was levied and two-thirds of it was set aside for roads and works of public utility. The Madras Government under an old Act of 1866 levied a cess of one-half of an anna on every rupee of annual rental equal to 3 1/8 percent. On the Land Revenue for purposes of district roads. The Bengal Government had declared its intention to follow the Madras Presidency. Encouraged by the steps taken by these Local Governments the Circular urged upon other Local Governments and Administrations in Northern India, namely, North-Western Provinces, Punjab, Oudh and Central Provinces, to consider the expediency of increasing their road cesses on the land revenue to 5 percent. The object of the move evidently was to relieve the Imperial treasury of the road grant, once the Provincial Governments were in possession of adequate local revenues.

In this way the Circular contemplated a very meagre scheme of Provincial Budget, incorporating only the charges on local public improvements and the revenues derived from local resources to meet them. But before it could be set into operation the financial difficulties of the Government of India called for a larger measure of relief. Bad as the position already was, there was little confidence to be placed in the stability of the opium revenue; and while there was practised a retrenchment in expenditure, the charges for interest on public debt was found to swell enormously. In the midst of such a precarious situation the Government of India decided to reduce the hitherto prevailing rate of the income tax in order to silence the outcry raised against it by the richer classes. As a possible method of ways and means to meet the additional deficit of £1,000,000 that was expected to arise from the reduction in the income tax rate, the Government of India issued another Confidential Circular, dated August 17, 1870, in which a much wider scope was given to the contemplated scheme of provincial Budgets. It was stated in this Circular that "If the income tax was to be reduced, the ways and means of government must be otherwise recruited...... preferably...... through the agency of Local Governments, and by adopting such methods of taxation as are considered most suitable to each province and least burdensome to the people."

The method of throwing the burden on Local Governments consisted in making over to them charges of certain departments of the administration more or less local in character with a net grant on them for 1870-1 reduced by a million sterling. It was proposed to distribute this sum among the various provinces in the proportion which the net provincial grant of each bore to the total net grant and leave them free to make up their respective quota of retrenchment either by redistribution, retrenchment, or taxation.

After the concurrence of the Provincial Governments had been obtained to the plan of the Circular, it was announced by the famous Financial Resolution of December 14, 1870, as being adopted for execution from the commencement of the Financial year 1871-2.

We will now proceed to analyse the constitution of the Provincial Budgets as framed by this Resolution. Taking first the expenditure side of the Provincial Budget, it may be noted that the charges for the following Imperial services were incorporated into it :—

1. Jails
2. Registration.
3. Police.
4. Education.
5. Medical services (except Medical establishments).
6. Printing.
7. Roads.
8. Miscellaneous, Public Improvements.
9. Civil Buildings.

To provide the Provincial Governments with funds to meet the above charges incorporated into their budgets the Government of India surrendered to them the receipts which accrued from services handed over to them with an additional assignment from the Imperial fisc to bring about an equilibrium. The receipts surrendered and assignments granted to the Local Governments were as follows:—

Assignments made to Provincial Governments for services incorporated into their Budgets by the Financial Resolution No. 3334 dated December 14, 1870.

Services incorporated into Prov. Budgets.	Imperial Assignments for Services								
	Oudh	C.P.	Bt. Burma	Bengal	N.W.P.	Punjab	Madras	Bombay	Total
	£	£	£	£	£	£	£	£	£
Jails	26,922	27,881	32,777	218,210	88.394	58,204	91,983	73,440	617,811
Registration		3,509		36,609	20,129	11.623	22.970	25,372	120,212
Police	103,269	130,607	139.253	555,757	348.135	289.950	350,730	388,703	2,306,409
Education	26,056	27,864	10.998	234,385	103.528	64.909	90,052	118.271	676,063
Medical services (except Medical establishments)	5,049	11,770	6,460	89,713	27.607	24,935	61,696	74,852	302.532
Printing	7,609	3,640	3,000	41,732	25,302	14,106	25,840	27,050	148,279
Roads and misc. public improvements	32,900	63,403	63,000	157,800	82.636	84.200	123,880	121,900	729.819
Civil buildings	20,090	14,406	23,959	111,370	63,341	39,710	58,506	107,500	438,882
Public Works Establishments	13,777	20.230	22,635	69,984	37,954	32,217	47.421	59,644	303,862
Tools and Plant	1,060	1,556	1.741	5,383	2,920	2,478	3,648	4,588	23,374
Total	237,182	304,866	303,923	1,520,943	799,946	622,332	876,726	1,001,320	5,667.243

Estimated Receipt of the Services

Jails	1,575	6.000	9,420	110,385	11,154		7,300	664	146,498
Registration		5,500		40,000	35.030	20.694	34.000	30,141	165,356
Police	10,586	12,520	18.671	70,363	51.730	41.724	32,350	14,000	251,944
Education	1,482		500	42,012	11,050	5,000	6,900	10,480	77,424
Printing	1,080			2,000	2,160		1,260		6,500
Total	14,723	24,020	28.591	264,760	111,124	67,418	81.810	55.285	647,731
Grand Total of net assignments	222,459	280.846	275,332	1.256,183	688,822	554,914	794,916	946,040	5,019,512

Constructed on the basis of figures given in the resolution of December 14,1870.

These would have been the total assignments to the Provincial Governments for meeting the charges on the incorporated services, had it not been for the fact that the Government of India desired to obtain relief by way of retrenchment of the provincial resources to make up for the deficits expected to follow the reduction in the income tax. The relief originally fixed at £1,000,000 was reduced to £350,000, distributed rateably among the various provinces. Taking account of these retrenchments the permanent assignments made to the provinces were as shown below:—

PROVINCES	NEXT ASSIGNMENTS	PROPORTION OF RETRENCHMENTS	PERMANENT ASSIGNMENTS
Oudh	222,459	15,511	206,948
C.P.	280,846	19,583	261,263
Burma	275,332	19,199	275,332
Bengal	1,256,183	87,591	1,168,592
N.W.P.	688,822	48,030	640,792
Punjab	554,914	38,693	516,221
Madras	794,916	55,428	739,488
Bombay	946,040	65,965	880,075
Total ...	5,019,152	3,50,000	4,688,711

For conversion into Rupees, £1 equal to Rs. 10.

Before the commencement of the time appointed to carry the scheme into practice the Government of India incorporated the following additional services into the Provincial Budgets:—

The Charges for Petty Construction and Repair of Buildings in the Civil Department excepting the Opium Department in Bengal, the Salt Department outside the Lower Provinces of Bengal and Medical Services such as (1) Salaries of Medical Officers of Medical Colleges and Central Jails, and of Lunatic Asylums at the Presidency towns; (2) Extra allowance to Medical Officers for the Medical charge of Lunatic Asylums in the mofussil, and of Colleges, Central Jails, etc., also extra allowances to Medical Officers for the executive charge of jails, and (3) charges for sub-assistant Surgeons and Apothecaries employed in other than civil medical charge of the sudder stations or districts, and for all other subordinate medical establishments. Side by side with these transfers the Government of India withdrew the Calcutta

*Imperial Assignments for 1871—72**

	Oudh.	C.P.	Bt. Burma	Bengal	N.W.P.	Punjab	Madras	Bombay	Total
	£	£	£	£	£	£	£	£	£
Assignment as per Resolution of December 1870	169355	205271	192488	1176406	613095	463727	643271	707693	4171306
Add-									
Official Postings	1551	5093		4893	10840	8031	4163	4311	38882
Transfer from Medical Services	2139	1767	745	6649	5624	2828	7597	8500	35849
Transfer of petty construction and repairs of civil buildings	699	1778	420	6508	2555	1908	1050	4050	18968
Other items net				7866	1485			4600	13753
Deduct									
Transfer of Ajmere charges to Govt.Of India					28714				28714
Total	173744	213909	193653	1202124	604885	476494	656081	729154	4250044

Deduct									
Receipts from Budget of 1870-1	14723	24020	28591	260578	109992	67418	81810	55285	654417
Net charge in Civil Department	159021	189889	165062	941546	494893	409076	574271	673869	3607627
Add budget grant for P. W. as per Res. of 14-12-1870, viz									
Roads and miscellaneous public improvements	32900	63403	63100	157800	82636	84200	23880	121900	729819
Civil Buildings	20090	14406	23959	111370	63341	39710	58506	107500	438882
P.W. Establishments	13777	20230	22635	69984	37954	32217	47421	49644	303862
Tools and Plants	1060	1556	1741	5383	2920	2478	3648	4588	23374
Total public works	67827	99595	111435	344537	186851	158605	233455	293632	1495937
Grand total	226848	289484	276497	1286083	681744	567681	807726	967501	5103564
Deduct									
Proportion of £350,000	15557	19853		88199	46753	38931	55394	66351	331038
Revised permanent assignment	211291	269631	276497	1197884	634991	528750	752332	901150	4772526
Or in round numbers	211300	269600	276500	1197900	635000	528800	752300	901200	4772600
#Add—India	---								26700
								Total	4799300

* Based on the Fin. Dept. Resolution No. 1660 of March 20, 1871.

#The item opposite to "India "in the above table is for the Calcutta University and for Prov. services (not including Public Works) in Coorg, Ajmere and other district under immediate administration of the Government of India.—Sir Richard Temple's Financial Statement for 1871-2.

University from the Provincial to the Imperial Budget. To take account of the revision of charges for Official Postage and Bengal Police, and the additions and withdrawals of services referred to above, the Imperial assignments to Provincial Governments for the year 1871-2 were further altered so that they stood as shown in the table on the preceding page.

Besides these assignments for the fiscal year 1871-2, the Government of India gave the Local Governments a special donation of £200,000 in the year 1870-1 in order that they "may be able to inaugurate the plan successfully, and to have as it were a fair start." Taking round numbers then, the several Provincial Governments had the following resources at their disposal in the year 1871-2 to meet the expenditure incorporated in their budgets:—

Provincial Budget for	Resources		Total
	Receipts surrendered by the Imperial Government	Assignments from the Imperial Treasury	
	£	£	£
Oudh	14,700	211,300	226,000
Central Provinces	24,000	269,600	293,000
Burma	28,600	276,500	305,100
Bengal	264,800	1,197,900	1,462,700
N.W. Provinces	110,000	635,000	745,000
Punjab	67,400	528,800	596,200
Madras	81,890	752,300	834,100
Bombay	55,300	901,200	956,500

Having analysed the constitution of the Provincial Budgets and noted the receipts and charges incorporated into them, we will proceed to inquire into the peculiarity which marks their constitution as framed in 1870-1. No method of ascertaining this peculiarity would be more direct in its approach towards the question raised above than to ask ourselves what problem the framers of the Provincial Budgets were presented with and how it was solved.

From our knowledge of the history of the controversy that raged over the creation of Provincial Budgets we can say that what items of expenditure to incorporate into Provincial Budgets was no longer a prominent question of the time. Long since it was settled that there were charges in the Imperial Budget of a purely local character.

By common consent they were regarded as the most unsatisfactory part of the Imperial Budget. It was admitted on all hands that, knowing nothing about these charges, the Government of India was either obliged to sanction an unnecessary charge which may have been carelessly endorsed by the head of a department having no immediate interest in guarding against the waste of public money, or by a too cautious spirit of a random parsimony, or by parsimony regulated only by the state of public revenue, refuse its sanction and check prudent and profitable expenditure. As either procedure was likely to cause mischief, it was commonly agreed that such matters over which the Central Government by its supreme ignorance was powerless to exercise any control, should be transferred from the direct purview of the Imperial Government to the immediate control and responsibility of the Provincial Government.

One side of the problem had thus been solved by sheer force of circumstances. The matter on which all attention was mainly concentrated was the problem of providing the Provincial Governments with funds sufficient to meet the charges incorporated into their budgets. It was allowed on all hands to be reasonable that the receipts arising from the incorporated services should be appropriated by the Provincial Governments. Two good reasons were advanced for adopting such a procedure. It is laid down as a canon of good finance that tax administration and tax appropriation should go as far as possible together. On this principle it was but proper to have allowed the Provincial Governments to appropriate the receipts from the services which they administered. But there was also another weighty reason which influenced this decision. The main idea in the inauguration of Provincial Budgets was to interest the Provincial Governments in a judicious and economical management of the finances, and one way of sustaining their interest in the same was to have given them the receipts of the services they managed.

The receipts, however, were so small a portion of the total funds necessary to meet the provincialised expenditure that the problem of balancing the Provincial Budgets remained unsolved notwithstanding. Two possible ways of solution were before the Government of India at the time : either to transfer for provincial uses certain sources of Imperial revenue or to give a lump assignment from the Imperial treasury. It was difficult for a time to decide which was the more suitable of the two, for they were not only of unequal merits, but they made different appeals to the different parties concerned. To the Provincial Government assignment of revenues was preferable to fixed assignments as giving greater elasticity to their finances.

To the Government of India, on the other hand, assignment of revenues seemed to be fraught with grave consequences. The past and the existing financial condition of India did not warrant the Central Government to alienate the sources of revenue it then possessed with equanimity and safety for the future. On the other hand, its prospective condition looked as precarious as its past, and it therefore desired to retain its control over the sources the mobilisation of which alone could enable it to stave off any impending crisis. The second alternative, on the other hand, was just such a one as to give the provinces sufficient funds without the Government of India forfeiting its control over its resources. It must not be forgotten that the Government of India by reason of its constitutional position had the sole authority to manage and appropriate the revenues of India. Any solution for financing the provinces had therefore to be in accord with its interests as conceived by itself This being the situation the method of assignments was adopted in preference to that of assigned revenues in solving the principal problem that arose in connection with the constitution of provincial budgets.

It is because assignment of funds from the Imperial treasury was adopted as a method of supply to balance the Provincial Budgets that the system instituted in 1871-2 has been characterised in this study as a system of Budget by Assignments.

This principle on which the Provincial Budgets were constructed in 1871-2 endured till 1876-7. The assignment made to the Provincial Governments for the year 1871-2 had been declared to be fixed and recurring. Recurring they were, but fixed they were not: for, every year, since the start, the Government of India kept on adding to and withdrawing from Provincial Budgets items of charge already incorporated in them.

In accordance with these modifications in the incorporated charges the Imperial assignments had to be either reduced or augmented as necessity dictated. The progressive changes in the assignments from 1871-2 to 1876-7 with the specific purposes for which they were granted are entered in the following tables :—

Statement of Imperial Assignments to the Provinces for the year 1871-72

Purpose of the Assignment	**Amount Assigned**	
	Details	**Total**
	Rs.	**Rs.**
Original Assignment		11979000
Add		
For Cemetery establishments	4000	
For Compensation for		
Agra Brick Factory	28000	114000
For Office and House Rent	82000	
		12093000
Deduct		
For transportation charges for		
convicts	15000	
For fees for licensing cargo-boats	2600	124690
For receipts of public Works		
Departments	107000	
		11968310

Special Grants		
Add ——		
For Calcutta University	60000	
For Midnapore Civil Court Buildings	31680	341680
For Calcutta Small Causes		
Court Building	250000	
		12309990
Total Assignments for 1871-72		**12309990**

Statement of Imperial Assignments to the Provinces for the year 1872-73

Purpose of the Assignment	Amount Assigned	
	Details	**Total**
	Rs.	**Rs.**
Original Assignment		11979000
Add		
Permanent additions in 1871-2 (as above)		114000
For Miscellaneous services	267070	388936
For books and publications	7600	
For ground-rent of Orphan School		
at Howrah	266	
		12367936
Deduct		
Permanent deductions in 1871-2		
(as above)	124680	
For repairing charges of University	5700	130390
		12237546
Special Grants		
Add ——		
For Burdwan Fever Relief	100000	
Compensation for Sudder Court		
Building	400000	966670
Capital value of annual, rent of		
Rs. 21,000 for public offices	466670	
		13204216
Deduct fractions		380
Total Assignments for 1872-73		**13203836**

Statement of Imperial Assignments to the Provinces for the year 1873-74

Purpose of the Assignment	Amount Assigned	
	Details	**Total**
	Rs.	**Rs.**
Permanent additions in 1872-73 (as above)		12237546
Add		
For payment of Medical Officers in charge of Civil stations	385000	
For Land Revenue Sub-divisional establishments	100000	485000
		12722546
Deduct—		
Reduction of rent for public offices	21000	21000
		12701546
Sanctioned for 1873-74		**12701000**
Add for——		
Ground rent for Howrah Orphan School	266	
Charges on account of European vagrants	11500	18066
Ground rent charges	6300	
Deduct		
For pay of medical pupils withdrawn from Provincial to Imperial		5400
For pay of medical officers in charge of civil stations withdrawn from provincial to imperial.	385000	390400
Special Grants		12328666
Add ——		
For rent of Small Cause Court		14400
Total Assignments for 1872-73		**12343066**

Statement of Imperial Assignments to the Provinces for the year 1874-75

Purpose of the Assignment	Amount Assigned	
	Details	Total
	Rs.	Rs.
Permanent additions in 1873-74 (as above)		12328666
Add		
Assignment for encouragement of Mohammedan education.	50000	50000
Sanctioned assignment		12378000
Add—		
Grant on account of Model Farm	7000	8180
Additional grant for ground-rent	1180	
		12386180
Deduct		
Reduction of outlay on account of churches and burial grounds.	14314	
Reduction on account of Assam transferred	1330000	1344580
For ground rent Howrah Orphan School	266	
Total Assignments sanctioned		**11041600**

Statement of Imperial Assignments to the Provinces for the year 1875-76

Purpose of the Assignment	Amount Assigned	
	Details	Total
	Rs.	Rs.
Permanent additions in 1874-75 (as above)		11041000
Add		
Grant for Botanical gardens	52500	
Grant for Ground rents	1180	53680
		11094680

Deduct		
Public Works charges on account of the Salt Department	13683	
Assignments on account of lighthouses and ships withdrawn	1769	33163
Assignment on account of Town Improvement Fund of Assam		17711
Total Assignment		**11061517**

Statement of Imperial Assignments to the Provinces for the year 1876-77

Purpose of the Assignment	Amount Assigned	
	Details	**Total**
	Rs.	**Rs.**
Original Assignments for 1875-76		11041000
Add		
For ground rents	1180	
For Botanical gardens	52500	53680
		11094680
Deduct		
For Form Store Department		13683
		11080997
Deduct		
For Form Store department	8034	
Add—		6034
For Exhibitions and Fairs	2000	
Total		11074963
Assignment as sanctioned		11075000
Add——		
Grant on account of Bankee and Ungool Estates	3271	

Cost of the snake-poison commission, establishments and contingencies.	6000	58753
Grant on account of census registers	49482	
		11133753
Deduct		
Assignment on account of lighthouses and lightships withdrawn.	1769	
Assignment of Town Improvement Fund, Assam	17711	22180
Annual cost of lunatics transferred to Tezpore Lunatic Asylum.	2700	
Total Assignment		**1,11,11,573**

This completes the account of the services incorporated from time to time and the assignments made for them by the Imperial exchequer during the period in which the system of budget by assignments remained in force.

It now remains to consider whether the system under the assignment plan was a success. What constitutes success is a question, which is always open to discussion, for what may seem successful from one point of view may be the reverse of it from another standpoint.

A discussion, however, of this aspect of the question cannot be avoided, for it was on the results of one stage that an advance towards the second was made to depend all throughout the expansion of Provincial Finance. As the definition of success varies with the standpoints, we must first ascertain them for the purpose of our investigation.

Let us therefore inquire into the possible parties whose standpoints counted in the moulding of Provincial Finance, and without whose satisfactory opinion about the results achieved, a new step in advance could not have been taken. The Government of India and the Provincial Governments were obviously the two principal parties.

Naturally their standpoints were different, if not antagonistic. The question prominent in the mind of the

Government of India was how big was the gain to the imperial treasury on the transfer. On the other hand, the Provincial Governments were concerned to know whether the resources offered by the Government of India were adequate enough for their safely accepting the responsibility of managing the incorporated expenditure.

It is obvious the Provincial Governments would not undertake the responsibility of managing the Imperial expenditure within a certain assignment unless they were sure that the assignments were adequate. Similarly, the Imperial Government would see no advantage in making the transfer unless the Provincial Governments undertook to manage the expenditure at a sum less than what it cost under the direct management of the Imperial Government.

Adequacy to the provinces and gain to the Imperial treasury were therefore the two chief considerations, which prevailed in the determination of the continuance and expansion of the scheme.

The people of the Provinces may also be conceived of as a third possible party whose concurrence may have been deemed a necessary factor in the situation. What their viewpoint would have been is not altogether a matter of guess. On the other hand, anyone sufficiently acquainted with the nature of popular demands for political advancement could easily imagine that the most urgent concern of the taxpayers would have been neither the well-being of the Imperial nor that of the Provincial Governments, but the distribution of the money they paid along the different channels of expenditure; and if their approval of the results of the scheme had been made a necessary condition of advance, it is probable that the development of Provincial Finance would have been along different lines.

There was a suggestion even at that time that the people of the country should have some voice in the financial arrangements of the country. In paragraph 19 of its Resolution of December 14, 1870, announcing the scheme of Provisional finance, the Government laid down that

"Each local Government will publish its own Provincial Service Estimates and Accounts in the local Gazette, together with a financial exposition (which should, where possible, be made before the local Legislative Council) analogous to that annually made in the Legislative Council of the Governor-General."

If this suggestion had materialised, the Indian taxpayer would have obtained a voice in determining the financial arrangements between the Government of India and the Provincial Governments.

There were, however, certain legal difficulties in the way of giving effect to this suggestion. If the Budget was introduced in the Council and debate had followed upon it, such a proceeding would have offended against Section 38 of the Indian Councils Act (24 and 25 Vic. C. 67) and would have, therefore, been illegal unless the Budget involved some proposal for tax legislation.

For, that Act had provided that the activity of the legislative Council should not be called into play except for strictly legislative purposes. If, on the other hand, there was to be no debate, there was no advantage in this mode of giving publicity to the Budget which was not equally secured by its publication in the official Gazette. As a solution of these difficulties, the Government of Madras proposed to the Government of India.

"that the Provincial Budget should form a schedule to an Appropriation Bill, the contents of which would, after all the necessary explanation and discussion, be voted section by section."

But the Government of India, which had first broached the subject, was shocked by this suggestion as being revolutionary. In reply it observed:—

"His Excellency in Council does not...... consider that the plan proposed...... for bringing the annual financial statement within the terms of the Indian Council's Act, would be appropriate or possible. The passing of the Appropriation Bill in the House of Commons is a proceeding by which authority is given to carry into effect the Resolutions of the House in Committee of Supply, which till the passing of the Appropriation Bill are not law.

The Bill enumerates every grant that has been made during the whole session, and authorises the several sums voted by the Committee of Supply to be issued and applied to each separate service. It also contains a provision that the various aids and supplies shall not be issued or applied to any other uses than those mentioned.

"Such a proceeding would, His Excellency in council considers, be out of place in India, and might have the effect of transferring from the Executive to the Legislative Council, the power of disposing of all public moneys. His Excellency, therefore does not consider that the introduction of an Appropriation Bill would be advisable."

Against this ruling the Government of Madras appealed to the Secretary of State and pleaded that either the proposal of an Annual Appropriation Act be approved or

"such an alteration in the Council's Act be made as will allow the financial statement to be legally made and discussed in the Local Legislative Council."

But the Secretary of State upheld the decision of the Government of India on the ground that

"such mode of procedure is only applicable in a representative assembly, which has full powers of control over the Executive, and any such powers Parliament has advisedly withheld from the Legislative Council of India."

The suggestion was therefore dropped and was not given effect to till 1921. As the voice of the people did not prevail in the framing of the financial contracts between the Imperial and Provincial Government, it is of no immediate advantage to seek for results that would have interested them to know, if they had been allowed their say in the matter. In so far then the results of the past influenced the policy of the future we have only to lay ourselves out to seek for results in which the two remaining parties to the contract were primarily interested, namely, gain to the Imperial treasury and adequacy to the Provincial Governments. Applying ourselves first to the test of adequacy to the provinces the results of the period may be gauged from the annual surpluses and deficits in the finances of each of the different provinces brought within the pale of the system of Provincial Budgets.

Provincial Surpluses and Deficits

Province	1871-72	1872-73	1873-74	1874-75	1875-76	1876-77
	£	£	£	£	£	£
C.P.	20,988	−8,423	2,268	13,108	8,307	16,800
Bt. Burma	27,634	33,832	−9,922	— 21,889	−5,471	5,100
Assam				5,159	590	9,833
Bengal	180,622	74,622	393,955	271,044	27,397	46,978
N.W.P. and Oudh	31,595	64,036	36,358	11,693	20,945	128,501
Punjab	109,828	28,008	— 33,347	- 117,644	— 92,724	26,908
Madras	40,787	— 19,264	— 56,381	4,303	— 14,210	504
Bombay	65,553	128,805	— 64,373	9,929	— 18,354	— 140,718

Compiled from the annual Finance and Revenue Accounts of the Government of India for the respective years.

It is evident from these figures that the surpluses outnumber the deficits in frequency and magnitude to such an extent that the deficit could have been easily met from the accumulated balances without seriously exhausting them. Care, however, must be taken in explaining the cause of this apparent prosperity of Provincial Governments. Did the province succeed in building up their balances from the savings from the assignments and receipts made over by the Imperial Government is what we have to find out. The answer to this question cannot be given in a categorical form, for the total resources and changes to which the above figures refer include more than the receipts and assignments set apart for provincial management. Besides Imperial assignments and receipts of incorporated services they include a part of what hitherto were known as Local Funds.

It must be recalled that long before the separation of provincial from Imperial Finance there was created since the year 1855 a separation between the Imperial and Local Finance in British India. The Local Funds when separated were under the immediate management of the several Provincial Governments and comprised of two different classes: (a) those which by law or custom were required to be spent within the districts in which they were collected and on the specific objects for which they were collected; and *(b)* those collected all throughout the province and over the disposal of which the Provincial Government possessed unrestricted discretion. When the scheme of provincial Finance was inaugurated it was deemed natural to merge the second class of Local Funds into the Provincial Funds. The total addition made thereby to the provincial resources it is difficult to ascertain. But it was the opinion of Sir John Strachey, the Finance Minister of the time, that such addition was "inconsiderable" and could not therefore have affected materially the financial consequences of the new system.

The question of estimating the gain to the Imperial treasury need not detain us very long. The indirect gain due to the economical management of the services by the Provincial Governments will come for discussion when we come to consider the influences that played a prominent part in bringing about the second state in the evolution of Provincial Finance. The direct gain made by the Imperial treasury was effected throughout the retrenchment in provincial assignments already referred to.

It may be recalled that the Government of India had planned to obtain relief to the extent of one million sterling annually on the services transferred, but the Government of India soon realised that all this retrenchment would necessitate some taxation by the provincial authorities. The burden had already grown since the Mutiny, and being anxious not to add to it directly by Imperial levy or indirectly through provincial levies, it decided to reduce the relief it sought by lowering the retrenchment on provincial assignments from £1,000,000 to £350,000, or more accurately to £350,801 if we deduct, as we must, the sum of £19,199 restored to Burma, being its quota of relief owing to the special circumstances of that province.

Summing up the results of the period, the Government of India, it must be said, realised full share of the benefits it had contrived to obtain by the annual relief of £330,801, though not without causing an insufficiency, however small, in the

Provincial finance. But notwithstanding the burden thrown on the Provinces their position as disclosed by the results cannot by any means be called unhappy.

One unwelcome feature marred the inauguration of Provincial Finance. That feature consisted in the large increase in the levy of rates and cesses for purposes of local improvement.

Receipts from New Resources of Income and Cesses enhanced since *1870*

	1870-1	1871-2	1872-3	1973-4	1874-5	1875-6
	£	£	£	£	£	£
Oudh—						
Ord. cesses on:						
Land Revenue	38,813	29,018	34,354	34,259	33,208	33,146
Margin Fund	7,363	3,461				
Local rate		36,810	42,535	42,883	41,097	41,461
Total	46,176	69,289	76,889	77,142	74,305	74,607
Assam—						
Ord. cess on land:						
Rev. Old Fund	6,506	4,333	711	1,916	*17,149	
New Fund					15,267	16,300
Total	6,506	4,333	711	1,916	32,416	16,300
Bengal— Road Cess Fund:			22,917	59,039	120,128	158,516
N. W. Provinces	168,532	201,548	216,818	213,672	215,968	150,619
Punjab...	58,330	214,441	216,194	208,063	211,862	193,573
Madras-Road Cess	212,813	234,567	377,031	368,031	371,311	369,325
Madras-Tolls Cess			12,144	12,234	14,860	26,531
Grand Total	492,357	724,178	922,704	940,333	1,040,850	980,545

* Balances recovered from Bengal on account of Road and Government Estates Improvement Fund.

For the new resources of income and cesses given above, refer to *Papers, etc., on the extension of the Financial Powers of the Local Governments.*

This shows an increase in 1875-6 over 1870-1 of £488,188, chiefly by raising the cesses in the North-West Provinces, the Punjab and the Madras Presidency to 6 1/4 percent on Land

Revenue in the two last mentioned, to about 5 percent in the North-Western Provinces (after deducting the rural police charge); by a road cess in Bengal and by granting an assignment to Assam, at the Imperial charge, of 6 1/4, percent instead of 3 percent on Land Revenue pending the levy of a cess of a corresponding amount on the ryots. In the Bombay Presidency the 61/4 percent was imposed some years before and hence is not included in the above table. The only province which did not levy any additional cess was the Central Province, though a cess of 6V percent on the Land Revenue was in 1870 considered practicable but not opportune.

Of what benefit, a cynic may say, was the institution of Provincial Finance if it did not obviate the necessity for further taxation ? If further taxation was unavoidable, why did the Imperial Government throw the onus of facing it on the Provincial Government under the garb of Provincial Budgets when it would have done that itself? It must be said in reply that the merits of Provincial Finance are to be looked for in other directions, and it will be shown in its proper place that they justified its institution, even though a certain amount of enhanced taxation followed in its wake. It would indeed be unwise to decry against taxation in general, for no benefit can be obtained without a charge. But it would be equally unjust not to protest against the kind of taxation resorted to, for what really mattered was not the increase of taxation but the inequity of taxation. The method of taxation resorted to make up the deficit in the Provincial Finance was an imposition of rates and cesses on the already over-burdened class of tax-payers, namely the landholders.

Now the services incorporated into the Provincial Budgets, for whose support these rates and cesses were levied, though called local, were not more local in the sense of their being beneficial to the particular localities than those retained by the Imperial Government. On the other hand, the former were from the standpoint of the localities as onerous to them as the latter, and yet they were financed by rates and cesses levied from the localities as though they were directly beneficial to them, which as a matter of fact they were not.

This is all the more lamentable when it is recalled that the necessity for retrenchment which caused the levy of these rates and cesses was occasioned by the abolition of the income tax. As a matter of justice we should have expected the continuance of the income tax to the relief of the State and the ratepayers. But justice was for a long time absent from the Financial Secretariat of the Government of India. A few cared for it in the abstract, but none looked upon it as an element worthy of consideration in providing for the exigencies of provincial or local finance; and as it was unrecognised, its violation by the Provincial Governments was no bar to the development of Provincial Finance.

The scheme of Provincial Budgets, the second stage of which we shall presently study, was launched not without mixed feelings. Boundless hopes were entertained, though not unmingled with a sense of misgiving. Just what was expected of the scheme may be correctly gauged from the remarks of Sir Richard Temple, who, when introducing the scheme in 1870, said :—

"We hope that this concession (of increased control over revenues and expenditure) will give the Local Governments an additional interest in the study and the enforcement of economy in expenditure; will afford them a just inducement to supplement their local receipts from time to time by methods either most acceptable to the people or least fraught with popular objection; will cause a more complete understanding to arise between the executive authorities and the tax-paying classes respecting the development of fiscal resources; will teach the people to take a practical share in the Provincial Finance, and lead them up gradually towards a degree of local self-government; and will thus conduct to administrative as well as financial improvement."

While entertaining these hopes he also took the opportunity of asking the Council to be prepared for disappointment, for he went on to remark:

"the hopes which I am expressing, however sanguinely, or confidently entertained, are after all but hopes, and like all other hopes may or may not be fairly realised. But let all this eventuate as it may, sure I am with certainty free from shade of doubt, that the measure is advantageous to the Imperial Budget of British India. For it will have the direct effect of definitely limiting, for the present, the expenditure from the general Exchequer on certain important branches of civil expenditure, the very branches indeed, where, from the progressive state of the age, the demands for increased outlet have most arisen, and in which from the nature of the case the supreme Central Authority is least able to check the requirements of the local authorities."

Year	Total excess Expenditure on all Transferred Services except Registration over Total Receipts from them inclusive of all Contributions other than those for Bengal Famine under Imperial management		Total excess Expenditure on all Transferred Services except Registration over Total Receipts from them inclusive of all Contributions other than those for Bengal Famine under Provincial management
	£		£
1863-64	5,111,297	1871-72	4,835,238
1864-65	5,606,248	1872-73	4,964,407
1865-66	5,587,779	1873-74	5,329,180
1867-68	5,821,438	1874-75	5,379,509
1868-69	6,030,214	1875-76Est.	5,135,677
1869-70	5,856,310		
1870-71	5,197,250		

Complied from an official volume of Notes on Imperial, Provincial and Local Finance, 1876.

The actual results, however, far surpassed these very moderate hopes and were more than necessary to dispel the misgivings that still lingered in the minds of those who looked upon the institution of Provincial Finance as a project of doubtful utility. Confining ourselves to the issues immediately affecting the Government of India or the Provincial Governments, it was abundantly proved that Provincial management was more economical than Imperial management. If we compare the expenditure incurred upon the services while they were an Imperial charge with the expenditure on them after they were provincialised, the superior economy of provincial management is overwhelmingly proved.

It was therefore with confirmed belief in its utility and even with a sense of relief that the Government of India proceeded to incorporate into the Provincial Budgets additional services local in character or more amenable to local control. But these additions to the incorporated services made the problem of a supply of funds to Provincial Governments assume greater proportions. In the first period the gap between the receipts of incorporated services and the total charges for them was comparatively smaller than what it was found to be the case on the present occasion. The mode of bridging the gap entirely by assignments was deemed to be ill-fitted for the success of the scheme in its enlarged form.

The most radical defect in the system of budget by assignment consisted in its rigidity. The provinces did not favour it as a mode of supply for the reason that while the outlay on the services under their management continued to expand the assignments made to them remained fixed in amount.

Sir John Strachey, to whom belonged the credit of carrying the scheme a stage further, was particularly alive to this weakness of the system. In place of fixed assignments he desired to give the provinces certain sources of revenue, the yield of which largely depended upon good management. His primary object in doing this, no doubt, was to make better and more elastic provision for the growing needs of the provincialised services. But he had also another, and, as he conceived it, a far more important reason in the substitution for assignments of assigned revenues.

That economy was the fruit of good management had by that time become a commonplace, but few were sure as to what good management consisted in. It was Sir John Strachey who, for the first time, defined in unmistakable language his notion of good management, which was since his time applied in an ever increasing degree in the development of Provincial Finance. To him good management of finance was to be had

"not by any action which gentlemen of the Financial Department or by any other department of the supreme Government can take whilst sitting hundreds or thousands of miles away in their offices in Calcutta or Simla; not by examining figures or writing circulars, but by giving to the Local Governments... a direct and, so to speak, a personal interest in efficient management".

And in this he had the strong support of recent experience; for, taking the results of the past stage the provinces not only managed the services at a lesser cost to the revenue than was the case under the Imperial regime, but the services yielded increased revenue under the more immediate and fostering care of the provinces than they did under the remote, uninformed, and therefore impotent vigilance of the Imperial Government.

Sir John Strachey had long held to the view that so long as the Provinces collected the revenues for the Government of India they did not care to check evasion, which they would have surely done if they had collected them for their immediate benefit, or, as he put it,

"when the Local Governments feel that good administration of branches of revenues will give *them,* and not to the Government of India alone, increased income and increased means of carrying out the improvements which they have at heart, then, and not till then, was to be had the good administration that every one desired."

This evidence of the expanding receipts of provincialised services were therefore a pleasant surprise which went a great way in confirming the view he had advocated. It was therefore for a double purpose, of augmenting the revenues and of introducing elasticity in Provincial Finance, that Sir John Strachey substituted assigned revenues for assignments as a mode of supply to the provinces.

Receipts from Incorporated Services

Allocated Services	Under Imperial Management					Under Provincial Management				
	1865-6	1867-8	1868-9	1869-70	1870-1	1871-2	1872-3	1873-4	1874-5	1875-6
	£	£	£	£	£	£	£	£	£	£
Jails	89,260	96,910	141,218	133,806	128,773	149,888	195,755	271,915	297,198	326,023
Police	140,166	231,859	277,179	287,529	270,855	203,624	97,735	90,708	80,509	89,895
Education	53,256	66,869	67,207	72,848	60,740	76,789	80,869	101,306	99,537	101,909
Registration	86,997	127,070	153,488	165,048	147,152	155,262	171,735	121,470	172,111	184,461
Printing	3,333	3,282	2,803	3,718	9,244	10,923	14,383	21,174	18,220	18,066
Medical		---			3,273	20,594	30,649	36,370	43,097	26,583
Miscellaneous	4,070	5,666	4,076	4,489	6,116	20,991	31,345	32,396	39,666	36,234

Compiled from the same source referred to above.

The plan adopted by Sir John Strachey was not new, neither was it brought forward for the first time. It was present in the minds of the people who took part in the discussions of Provincial Finance in 1870, and was actually advocated by Sir John Strachey as early as 1872. That the Government of India did not look upon the plan with favour in 1870 was due to the fact that it was afraid to permanently alienate the sources of revenue on the growth of which its stability depended. By now, however, the financial position of the Government of India had a bit improved, and the six years' trial of provincial management had also engendered a greater confidence in the scheme in the minds of those who had never completely accepted the administrative utility of the project.

To this was added the prospect of the plan being a means of increased productivity in their resources as it had been of increased economy in expenditure. The force of all these factors combined to bring a new stage in the evolution of Provincial Finance which, because of the distinct mode of supply adopted, may be well designated as a stage of Budget by Assigned Revenues.

To be sure, assignments still formed a part of the new system. But that was because of the difficulty of assigning such revenues the yield of which would have been precisely equal to the incorporated expenditure. Under any circumstances there was sure to be some difference. It happened that the normal estimated yield of the ceded revenues fell short of the requirements and the margin of difference had to be made up by some adjusting assignment in the case of each province.

The method of fixing the adjusting assignment for the different Provinces was on the whole a little too complicated, and may therefore be conveniently explained before proceeding to examine the constitution of the Provincial Budgets of the different Provinces as laid down under the second stage of their growth. It must be borne in mind that the total resources of the Provinces were made up under this system of (1) the receipts accruing from the incorporated services, (2) the yield of the revenues assigned, and (3) the adjusting assignment. How to fix upon an adjusting assignment for a particular

Province was a question involving nice calculations. Before arriving at a definite figure for the adjusting assignments it was obviously necessary to have settled the normal yield of the receipts of incorporated services and of the revenues made over.

The assessment of the normal yield was a contentious matter. As a rough and ready method the Government of India took the average yield of each over a series of years as the normal yield, and made it the basis from which to calculate the assignments. Similarly on the basis of the annual growth of the revenues in the past years it assumed a certain normal rate of increase for each of the sources, so that the normal for the succeeding years exceeded the normal for the preceding year at the normal rate of annual progression assumed. And as the normal yield of the assigned revenues increased at their assumed normal rate of growth the assignments fixed for the subsequent years diminished in like proportion. This normal rate of growth assumed for the assigned revenues was sometimes an assumption unjustified by their past productivity. At all events, as a higher rate of increase meant lessened assignments, the Provinces questioned its magnitude.

To pacify the Provinces and to make due allowances for errors of estimating, the Government of India made a very ingenious concession. It agreed that if the actual results showed deviations from the estimated normal yield, either below or above, they should be equally divided between the provincial and Imperial Governments. If the actual yield was greater than the normal the adjusting assignment from the Imperial Government fixed for the year would be reduced by half the excess, and if it were less than the normal the assignment would be increased by half the deficit.

All this very delicate mechanism was adopted primarily for the advantageous manner in which it enabled the Government of India to adjust the assignments without undue hardship being inflicted on either party. But there was also another advantage which, though unperceived at the time, was none the less effective. The consent secured from the Provinces to bear half the burden of a possible deficit in the normal estimate directly put a premium on economical and judicious administration of the ceded revenues. If the Government of India had agreed to bear the whole of the deficit below the estimated normal, it is doubtful whether the Provinces would have exerted themselves sufficiently to develop their resources to such a degree as to bring their yield to the level of the normal. But the fear that their obligation to bear half the deficit might assume a larger proportion, which would undoubtedly be the case if there was a great falling off in the revenue, compelled them to bestow greater vigilance than they would otherwise have done. Whilst an effectual check on relaxation was thus provided the scheme was not wanting in a stimulus to exertion. The prospect of gaining half the excess over the normal gave a more direct stimulus to the Provinces to develop their resources beyond the normal than would have been the case if the total excess had been entirely appropriated by the Imperial Government. In short, the deterrent effect of a deficit to bear and the stimulating effect of a gain to reap made the mechanism of Provincial Finance as perfect as it could be made from the standpoint of economy in expenditure and productiveness in resources.

Having noted the factors that led to the conception and execution of this new step in Provincial Finance and the features which marked its novelty, we may now proceed to the study of the constitution of Provincial Budgets and the revenue and charges that were incorporated into them. Unfortunately it is impossible to present a conspectus of Provincial Budgets as a whole, for the charges were not uniformly incorporated in all the Provincial Budgets. Each Province was treated individually. This compels us to enter upon the analysis of the Provincial Budgets as they were reconstituted in 1877-8 separately for each of the different provinces.

North-Western Provinces and Oudh

The budget of the Province was recast rather than enlarged by additions to the already allocated items, as was the case with regard to some other Provinces. In its new form the budget of the Province incorporated the following heads of expenditure and revenue:—

Heads of Charges	Heads of Revenue
3. Refunds of all Assigned Revenues.	I. Land Revenue— collections from the Terai
4. Land Revenue (excepting settlements, allowances to district and village officers, and Bahbar estates and and special temporary compensations to covenanted civil servants in N.W.P.)	the Dudi estate in Mirzapore and from stone quarries.
6. Excise 10. Stamps.	IV Excise. IX Stamps.
14. Administration (excepting Account and and Currency Officers).	XIII Law and justice.
16. Law and Justice (excepting special temporary allowances to covenanted civil servants in N.W.P.)	
17. Police. 19. Education	XIV Police. XVI Education
21. Medical (excepting the pay of Medical Officers in charge of civil stations).	
22. Stationery and Printing.	
28. Miscellaneous (excepting remittance of treasure and any unenumerated item exceeding Rs. 10,000).	XX Miscellaneous (excepting "Gain by Exchange," "Premium on Bills," unclaimed Bills and unenumerated items exceeding Rs. 10,000 each). Public Works Receipt such as appertained to the Public Works charges incorporated into the Provincial Budget
Public Works Ordinary: Roads and miscellaneous public improvements, civil buildings (except opium, post office and telegraph buildings) and tools and plants; also whole of the Public Works establishment of the P.W.D. excepting that in the Military works and irrigation branches; the imperial government paying towards their cost 20 per cent on the outlay from the imperial funds and works and repairs executed by the establishment.	

In assigning the heads of revenue the Government of India added the proviso that "the Governments of North-Western Provinces and Oudh must surrender to the Imperial treasury half of any sum by which the net revenue from Excise, Stamps, and Law and Justice (omitting Jails and Registration), deducting Refunds under these heads and the charges under 6, Excise and 10, Stamps, exceeded Rs. 83,75,000 " and agreed to reimburse the province with a sum equal to half the deficit if the yield fell below the above sum.

This adjustment was effected by operating upon the balances of the Province so that if the expenditure of the North-Western Provinces and Oudh upon the incorporated services exceeded the enumerated revenues plus any Provincial contribution in support of them by less than Rs. 83,75,000, the difference was to be added to; and if such excess expenditure was more than Rs. 83,75,000 the difference was to be deducted from the balances of the Government of the North-western Provinces and Oudh in the Imperial treasury.

Bengal

Items of Expenditure incorporated in the Bengal Budget	Grant as existing in 1877-8	Retrenchment	Proposed Consolidated Grant
3. Refunds of Revenue from Excise, Stamps, Law and Justice, and of Deposits.	4,91,000		4,91,000
4. Land Revenue (Collectors, Deputy Commissioners, etc. Establishments and charges on account of Land Revenue Collections).	22,62,000		22,62,000
6. Excise on spirits and drugs	2,92,000		2,92,000
8. Customs	6,93,000		6,93,000
9. Salt	39,000		39,000
11. Stamps	2,38,000		2,38,000

15. Administration (excepting Account Office, Allowances to Presidency Banks, Stationery Office at Presidency and stationery purchased in the country).	12,61,000		12,61,000
16. Minor Departments (excepting meteorological and archaeological departments, census and gazeteers).	1,68,000		1,68,000
17. Law and Justice (excepting Law Officers).	63,97,000	1,00,000	62,97,000
18. Marine	10,92,000		10,92,000
23. Political (Govt. House Police Guard).	7,000		7,000
26. Miscellaneous (excepting remittance of treasure).	25,000		25,000
Stationery and Stamps	4,98,000	50,000	4,48,000
27. Provincial allotment as now existing	1,10,59,000	4,40,000	1,06,19,000
Maintenance of Bishop's Palace, etc.	7,000		7,000
Total	2,45,29,000	5,90,000	2,39,39,000

The budget of the Province of Bengal was enlarged rather than recast by additions to the already incorporated heads of revenue and expenditure.

For the second stage of the scheme the Government of Bengal was made responsible for the charges shown in the above table.

To meet these charges the following revenues were handed over to Bengal for its use :—

Assigned Revenues (ooo omitted)

Heads of Revenue	Estimated Yield in 1876-77	Estimated Yield at the assumed Rate of Growth				
		1877-78	1878-79	1879-80	1880-81	1881-82
	Rs.	Rs.	Rs.	Rs.	Rs.	Rs.
IV Exercise in spirits and drugs	6,300	6,400	6,500	6,600	6,700	6,800
VI Customs (see, Customs Misc. and Warehouses and Wharf rents).	3,600	3,600	3,600	3,600	3,600	3,600
VII Salt (Rents of Ware houses, fines and forfeitures and misc.).	220	220	220	220	220	220
IX Stamps }	10,300	10,575	10,850	11,125	11,400	11,675
XIII Law and Justice }						
XIV Marine (pilotage receipts, registration and other fees and misc.).	1,091	1,084	1,084	1,084	1,084	1,084
XVI Misc. (all except premium on bills, unclaimed bills, and any unenumerated item exceeding Rs. 10,000).	771	792	792	792	792	792
Total		22,671	23,076	23,421	23,596	24,171

Complied from statements in the *Gazette of India* referred to above.

But as the revenues assigned were not sufficient for meeting the incorporated charges transferred, after taking account of the excesses over normal to be paid to the Government of India, the Government agreed to make the following assignments from the Imperial treasury to the Government of Bengal :—

Year	**Assignments**
	Rs.
1877-78	48,32,000
1878-79	44,57,000
1879-80	40,82,000
1880-81	37,07,000
1881-82	33,32,000

Central Provinces

In the case of the Central Provinces the following additional items were incorporated in its budget :—

Heads of Charge	Grants as already fixed for 1877-78	Retrenchment	Proposed Net Consolidated Grants
	Rs.	Rs.	Rs.
funds of Excise, Stamp, w and Justice and	47,000		47,000
scellaneous.			
cise	52,000		52,000
mps	14,000		14,000
nd Revenue exclusive of tlement charges	6,66,000		
ministration (exclusive of count and Currency fice).	3,39,000}		
nor Departments clusive of Meteorology	4,000}		
d Archaeology).		90,000	17,74,000
w and Justice	6,91,000}		
tionery and Stamps	69,000 }.		
scellaneous (excepting mittance of	5,000}		
easure and Discount on pply Bills.			
d—			
isting allotment for ovincial services	27,73,000		27,73,000
tal Grant for Services to be ne upon the Central ovinces Budget.	46,60,000		45,70,000

To meet these charges the Government of Central Provinces was authorised to appropriate the yield of the following sources of revenue :—

Heads of Revenue Assigned	Estimated Yield in	Estimated Yield at the Assumed Rate of Growth in		
	1876-77	1877-78	1878-79	1979-80
	Rs.	Rs.	Rs.	Rs.
Excise	13,90,000	14,50,000	15,10,000	15,70,000
Stamps	9,70,000	9,75,000	9,80,000	9,85,000
Law and Justice	1,67,000	1,75,000	1,83,000	1,91,000
Miscellaneous (excepting Premium on Bills, undrawn Bills of Exchange and any unenumerated items exceeding Rs. 10,000 each).	7,000	7,000	7,000	7,000
Total		26,07,000	26,80,000	27,53,000

Compiled from the *Gazette* referred to above.

As these revenues were insufficient the Government of India undertook to supplement them by the following assignments from the Imperial exchequer:—

Year	**Assignments**
	Rs.
1877-78	- 19,63,000
1878-79	- 18,90,000
1879-80	- 18,17,000

These assignments were, however, subject to change because of the proviso applying to the assigned revenues.

By virtue of that proviso the Government of India was to claim half the net increase of their combined annual yield over the estimated normal and was to bear half the deficit if their actual combined yield failed short of the normal.

If there was an increase above the normal the assignments

were to be reduced by a sum equal to half the increase, and if there was a decrease the assignments were to be increased by a sum equal to half the decrease.

Bombay

Coming to the Provincial Budget of the Bombay Government we find the following charges were incorporated in it :—

Heads of Charge	Grant as already fixed for 1877-8	Retrenchment	Consolidated Grant
	Rs.	Rs.	Rs.
3. Refunds	1,10,0001		
4. Land Revenue	65,07,000 }		
6. Excise	80,000		
7. Customs	8,09,000 }		
8. Salt	5,69,000 }		
14. Administration	11,43,0001		
15. Minor Departments	1,13,000 }		
16. Law and Justice	43,12,000 }	5,67,000	2,13,96,000
18. Marine	31,000 }		
20. Ecclesiastical	3,25,000 J		
21. Medical	2,68,0001		
22. Stationery and Stamp	2,29,000 }		
24. Allowances and Assignments	64,81,000 }		
26. Superannuation allowances	8,00,000 }.		
28. Miscellaneous	28,000 J		
Add—			
Existing allotment for provincial services.	1,04,54,000		1,04,54,000
Total	3,24,17,000	5,67,000	3,18,50,000

Besides the receipts accruing from the already incorporated services the Government of India assigned to the Government of Bombay the following sources of revenue :—

Assigned Revenues (ooo omitted)

Heads of revenue assigned	Estimated yield in	Estimated Yield at the Assumed Rate of Growth in				
	1876-77	1877-78	1978-79	1979-80	1880-18	1881-82
	Rs.	Rs.	Rs.	Rs.	Rs.	Rs.
1 Land Revenue (receipts of Inamdari adjustments and service commutations	5,199	6,624	6,624	6,624	6,624	6,624
IV. Excise	3,946	4,000	4,100	4,200	4,300	4,400
Stamps	4,186	4,300	4,350	4,500	4,550	4,600
Law and Justice	277	270	270	270	270	270
Total		8,570	8,720	8,970	9,120	9,270
Miscellaneous (excepting gain by exchange, premium on Bills, and on Money Orders, lapsed Money Orders, Sales, Proceeds of Durbar Presents and unenumerated items—exceeding Rs. 10,000 each).	52	70	70	70	70	70
Total		15,264	15,414	15,664	15,814	15,964

Compiled from the *Gazette of India.*

The adjusting assignments to cover the difference between the expenditure and revenue incorporated in the Bombay Budget were as follows :—

Year	Assignments Rs.
1877-78	- 1,53,20,000
1878-79	- 1,51,70,000
1879-80	- 1,49,20,000
1880-81	- 1,47,70,000
1881-82	- 1,46,20,000

These assignments, it must be noted, were subject to the same proviso as obtained in the case of the Central Provinces.

Punjab

The only remaining Provincial Budget that was framed on the principle of assigned revenues was that of the Punjab. The heads of charge incorporated in this budget were as hereinafter specified—

Heads of Incorporated Expenditure	Grant as Settled for 1877-8	Retrench ment	Proposed Net Consolidated Grant
	Rs.	Rs.	Rs.
Refunds	65,0001		
Land Revenue, exclusing settlement charges	16,21,000 }		
Excise	58,000}		
Stamps Administration (excluding Account and)	72,000}		
Currency Offices and settlement Secretary	9,74,000}		
Minor Departments	16,00,000}	2,24,000	51,38,000
Law and Justice	20,94,000}		
Superannuation and Retired Allowances,	3,38,000]		
Compasionate Allowances and Gratuities.	}		
Miscellaneous, excluding Remittances of	41,000J		
Treasure.	}		
Stationery and Stamps Add—	83,000 }		
Existing allotments for provincial services	54,22,000		54,22,000
Total	1,07,84,300	2,24,000	1,05,60,000

To defray these charges it was proposed to assign the following revenues to the Government of the Punjab :—

Heads of Revenues Assigned	Net Revenue in 1876-7	Estimated Net Yield in		
		1877-78	1878-79	1879-80
	Rs.	Rs.	Rs.	Rs.
Assessed Taxes			12,00,000	12,00,000
Stamps		24,85,000	25,05,000	25,25,000
Law and Justice		4,15,000	4,15,000	4,15,000
Excise		10,30,000	10,50,000	10,70,000
		39,30,000	39,70,000	40,10,000
Miscellaneous ((excluding gain by Exchange, premium on Bills, and unclaimed Bills of Exchange).		60,000	60,000	60,000
Total		39,90,000	52,30,000	52,70,000

In making over these revenues the Government of India had reserved to itself a share of the improvement in the net yield from Stamps, Law and Justice, and Excise. The estimated net yield having fallen short of the estimated expenditure the Government of India agreed to make the following assignments to the Government of the Punjab in order to restore balance in its budget :—

Year	Assignment	Less Share of Improvement in Net Revenue from Excise, Stamp, Law and Justice	Net Assignment
	Rs.	Rs.	Rs.
1877-78	65,70,000	107,000	64,63,000
1878-79	53,40,000	85,000	52,55,000
1879-80	53,10,000		53,10,000

It should be noted that the Government of Madras refused tc undertake the responsibility of a provincial Budget based upon the new principle of assigned revenues. It preferred to remain on the old basis. Provincial Budgets of Assam and

Burma are not included in this chapter. As the principle involved in their constitution appertains to the study undertaken in the following chapter it is deemed expedient not to include them in the present. Before closing the study of the second stage in the development of Provincial Budgets it is advisable to take stock of the results achieved during its prevalence from the standpoint of sufficiency to the Provincial Governments and gain to the Imperial exchequer. The following is illustrative of the results of this stage from the standpoint of sufficiency to the provinces:—

Provinces	Annual Surpluses or deficits				
	1877-78	1878-79	1879-80	1880-81	1881-82
	£	£	£	£	£
C.P.	5,992	7,049	— 28,133	2,956	95,221
Bengal	173,380	158,932	82,523	−11,313	255,189
N.W.P.and Oudh	4,469	237,100	320,729	280,790	667,613
Punjab	18,578	48,195	7,017	59,497	135,979
Bombay	— 609,672	61,249	— 11,201	37,855	418,783

Compiled from the Finance and Revenue Accounts of the Government of India.

From this it is clear that except in Bombay the funds provided by the Imperial Government proved not only sufficient for the purpose of carrying on the services incorporated in the Provincial Budgets, but were such as to afford a safe margin of revenue over expenditure. That the provinces had enough and to spare is clearly proved by the assistance which they gave without much detriment to their finances to the Imperial Government in the years 1879-80 and 1880-1. In the year 1879 the financial position of the Imperial Government had become rather critical. The fall in the value of the rupee and the commencement of hostilities with the Afghans were expected to bring about a deficit estimated in 1879-80 at £1,395.000. As the first line of defence the Government of India urged on the several Local Governments and Administrations the necessity of reducing the ordinary expenditure of the country within the narrowest possible limits and directed that measures for suspending or postponing all optional expenditure, whether Imperial, Provincial, or Local, should be adopted forthwith and that no proposals for increase of salaries or establishments should be entertained without real necessity. As a second line of defence the Government of India ordered that until further—"arrangements could be settled with the Local Governments... no new work estimated to cost more than Rs. 2,500 shall be commenced at the cost of the Imperial or Provincial Funds, even though it may already have received the sanction of the Government" and decided to make large reductions in the expenditure on productive public works. When it was discovered that these restraints on expenditure were not enough to bring about an equilibrium in the Imperial Budget the Government of India adopted a plan of levying benevolences on the provincial balances as a better alternative to increased taxation. It was, of course, an abrogation of one of the most fundamental conditions of Provincial Finance that the Provincial Balances, though in possession of the Imperial Government, were a sacred trust to be released only when required by the provinces. But the solvency of India was deemed to be more sacred than the sanctity of the terms of Provincial Finance. Accordingly the following sums were appropriated by the Imperial Government from the balances of the provincial Governments:—

Province	Contributions to the Imperial Government		
	1879-80	1880-81	Total in Lakhs.
	Rs.	Rs.	Rs.
N.W.P.	10	10	20
N.W.P. .	7 ½	7 ½	15
Bombay	4	4	8
Punjab	3	3	6
Burma	3	3	6
Central	2 1/2	2 1/2	5
Provinces	2	2	4
Madras			
Assam	1 1/2	1 1/2	3
Total	33 1/2	33 1/2	67

These contributions were repaid in 1882-3; but for the time being they were in effect a gain or at least a relief to the Imperial treasury. The real gain to the Imperial treasury consisted in the retrenchments made in assigning allotments for services transferred to provincial management. The amount of retrechment secured in the case of each of the provinces may be summarised as follows :—

Province	Retrenchment	
	Rs.	
N.W. Provinces	3,54,000	5 percent of the total allotment.
Oudh	73,000	"
Bengal	5,90,000	"
Central Provinces	90,000	"
Bombay	73,000	"
Punjab	2,41,000	"

This does not exhaust the total gain reaped by the Imperial Government. Two other ways of gain must also be mentioned along with this. It should be borne in mind that by taking the standard yield of the assigned revenues at a level higher than what was justified by their history, the Government of India was able to assign reduced sums for the provincial services than what it would have been required to do if the standard yield had been fixed at a lower level. This reduction in assignments owing to abnormal estimates of the ceded revenues was a direct gain. The excesses above the standard also opened additional possibilities of gain owing to the clause governing the cessation of revenues, although it must be recognised that under the same clause the Government of India stood to lose in the eventuality of the actual revenue falling below the standard. How much it gained from these conditional channels of gain it is difficult to say. On the whole, it cannot be denied that the gain to the Imperial treasury was substantial.

Thus the results show that the scheme of Provincial Finance on the basis of assigned revenues was a success both from the standpoint of the Provincial and Imperial Governments, so that they agreed mutually to make a further move in the development of the scheme which constitutes its third stage.

4

Budget by Shared Revenues

1882-83 to 1920-21

At every step in the direction of enlarging the Provincial Budgets the crucial question, as has already been pointed out, was with regard to the difficulties of balancing the revenues and charges proposed to be incorporated therein.

The two steps heretofore taken, one in 1871 and another in 1877, in the direction of the evolution of Provincial Finance, were marked by two distinct methods of balancing the Provincial Budgets.

On the former occasion the Imperial Government supplied the Provincial Governments with fixed lump sum assignments from the Imperial treasury. On the latter occasion this mode of supply was partly replaced by assigning certain sources of revenue for the use of provincial Governments.

The plan of assigned revenues, though it went a great way to remove the most serious defect of the measures of 1871-2, which transferred to the Local Governments the responsibility of meeting charges which had an undoubted tendency to increase, with income which, although not quite fixed, had little room for development, fell short of the requirements of Provincial Finance from the standpoint of elasticity.

Superior to those of 1871 though they were, the measures of 1877 were so short of the fullest requirements of elasticity in finance that the Government of Madras refused to accept the enlarged scheme and preferred to abide by the arrangements of 1871. The scheme of 1877 was not offered to Burma or Assam.

But when the Government of India made such an offer in 1879 it was obliged to turn over a new leaf, for, though the difficulty of meeting expanding charges with fixed assignments was overcome in some of the provinces by economy and good management, it was considerably felt by the province of Burma.

The expenditure of the province in the seven years preceding the scheme of Provincial Finance aggregated to Rs. 1,98,45,970, while the assignments for the following seven years, aggregated apart from special additions, Rs. 2,20,22,770, showing an excess of Rs. 21,76,800, in all or about 3 lakhs a year.

But the expenditure during the same period amounted to Rs. 2,40,77,885, being an excess of Rs. 42,31,915 in all or about 6 lakhs a year. The difference therefore between the excess assignment of 3 lakhs, and the excess expenditure of 6 lakhs a year, had to be made good by the Imperial Government by special grants averaging 2 3/4 lakhs every year to maintain the solvency of the Province.

The Government of India while making the supplementary assignments was not unconscious of the demoralising effect of such doles. In fact it was admitted that it would have been much better to have augmented the provincial assignments to Burma by 22 1/2, lakhs at the start had it foreseen the necessity for it, than to have been obliged to grant an equal amount in the form of supplementary aids so detrimental to economy and good management.

The experience of Burma had driven home the fatuity of assignments as a mode of supply and the Government of India had realised that elasticity in revenues was a vital condition for the success of Provincial Finance.

To assign revenues to Burma was therefore inevitable. Being overborne by the needs of the Province and by the fact that the Province yielded a substantial surplus to the Imperial treasury, the Government of India conceded that the Province was "entitled to have its real wants supplied more liberally than heretofore.

It is in the method adopted for the purpose of giving a liberal treatment to the province of Burma that the new step in the method of supply to the Provinces was taken. In the settlements made in 1877-8 with the five Provinces—Central Provinces, N.W.P. and Oudh, the Punjab, Bombay and Bengal—the Heads of Account under Revenue and Expenditure comprising the Indian Budget were grouped under two distinct categories :

(1) wholly Imperial and

(2) wholly Provincial.

But in the case of Burma the Heads of Account were grouped under three distinct categories :

(1) wholly Imperial,

(2) wholly Provincial, and

(3) jointly Imperial and Provincial In so far as items of revenue and expenditure were in the exclusive keeping of the Imperial or the Provincial Government, the settlement did not differ in spirit from that obtaining in other provinces.

The difference consisted in carving out a third category of Account to be made of *jointly Imperial and Provincial.* By it certain revenues and charges were marked off from the rest and were shared between the Imperial and the Provincial in some definitely fixed proportion.

The object of the arrangement was to replace rigidity in the Provincial revenues by elasticity. In the finances of the other Provinces there was elasticity in so far as their assignments were replaced by assigned sources of revenue.

But to the degree in which their revenues were made up of fixed assignments their finances inevitably suffered from rigidity. In the case of Burma, however, the substitution of shares of growing revenues for fixed assignments gave complete elasticity to the Provincial revenues without which it had become so difficult to shoulder the responsibility of meeting expanding charges.

In recasting the framework of the Provincial Budget of Burma on the principle of shared revenues, all the heads of receipts and charges were made wholly Provincial, with the exception of the following, which were treated as wholly Imperial :—

(1) The Army	Receipts and Charges.
(2) Postoffice	"
(3) Telegraph	"
(4) Account Department	"
(5) Meteorological Department...	"
(6) Political	"
(7) Remittance of Treasure and Premium on Bills of Exchange and unclaimed Bills of Exchange.	"

The third category of revenues and charges, namely, jointly Imperial and Provincial, covered the following items :—

(1) Land Revenue, including capitation tax, but excluding Fisheries, with such Land Revenue Refunds, charges of collection and settlement as cannot be attributed to Fisheries only.

(2) Forest revenue. Expenditure and Refunds.

(3) Export Duty on rice, and Refunds.

(4) Salt Revenue, Expenditure and Refunds.

Items comprising the third category were divided between the Imperial and Provincial Governments in the proportion of five-sixths to the former and one-sixth to the latter. By adopting this method of supply Burma, unlike other provinces, secured funds of an elastic character, for, even though the shares remained fixed the amount they brought in any one year varied with the variation in the total yield of the revenues assigned or shared. Of course everything depended upon how Burma nursed the revenues delegated to its control. But if it did its duty, unlike the other provinces, its labours were not to be unrequited.

The same principle of shared revenues was applied to the province of Assam, which had hitherto continued on the old basis of 1871. Although the settlement with that Province had been made after that with Burma had been carried out, the principle of shared revenues as a mode of balancing the Provincial Budget was not adopted on any appreciable scale. The reason for this break in the progressive realisation of the principle is not to be attributed to any spirit of hesitation on the part of the Government of India, but is to be ascribed mainly to the necessity of the case. As it was contemplated to reincorporate the province into Bengal it was deemed expedient to frame the Provincial Budget of Assam on the same plan as that of Bengal so that their financial fusion might be as easy as the administrative. Thus the heads of revenue and expenditure which were provincial in Bengal since 1877 were also made provincial in Assam in 1879, including "Law Officers," which for temporary reasons were reserved as Imperial in Bengal. The only point at which the new principle was applied consisted in making the Land Revenue head in Assam a joint head to be shared by the Imperial and the Provincial Governments in the proportion of four-fifths of its net yield to the former and one-fifth to the latter.

The beneficial results of the new settlement with these two Provinces are easily to be seen from the following comparative table of the estimates of their budgets as prepared on the old basis and as recast on the new :—

000 omitted

	Assam Budget Estimates				Bt. Burma Budget Estimates			
	Old Basis		New Basis		Old Basis		New Basis	
	1878-79	1879-80	1878-79	1879-80	1878-79	1879-80	1878-79	1879-80
	£	£	£	£	£	£	£	£
Revenue	2115	2110	3657	3596	4013	4078	9459	9673
Expenditure	2253	2261	3480	3566	4169	5111	8926	10119
Surplus			177	30			533	
Deficit	138	151			156	1033		526
Closing Balance	206	55	521	555	873	161	1562	1436

From the Resolution of the Government of India in the Department of Finance and Commerce, No. 1249, dated March 13, 1879.

Once the new principle of shared revenues was established in the case of Burma and Assam it was not possible for the

Government of India to withhold its application from the other Provinces. The settlements made in 1877 with the several Provinces were not only of short duration but were also of unequal durations.

It was only in the case of Bengal and Bombay that the settlements were made for five years commencing from 1877-8. In the case of the Central Provinces and the Punjab the period fixed was three years, while in the case of the North-Western Provinces it was as short as two years, from 1877-8.

It is evident from this that the settlements with some other Provinces were to have expired soon after those with Burma and Assam had been completed, and would have required to be reconstituted on the basis of shared revenues.

The Government of India, however, delayed the process, and in that it did wisely, for it was too soon to make the new principle of shared revenues and charges a basis for universal application.

It was nothing but prudent to have regarded it as it were in its experimental stage. Secondly, the disadvantages of the *ex-parte* treatment of the Provincial Budget had come to be realised. It then dawned upon the Government of India that the several provincial Budgets were only parts of an organic whole, viz., the Imperial Budget, and it was manifestly inadvisable to frame the Provincial Budgets each by itself without regard to the claims, needs and exigencies of all others.

But in order that this comparative and compromising operation of judging the claims of one in the light of the needs of others be performed with the desired effect of treating the different provinces in an equitable manner, it was essential that all the Provincial Budgets be dealt with simultaneously.

The importance of this consideration and the desire to gain time in order to profit by the experiences of Burma and Assam led the Government of India with the consent of the Provincial Governments to extend or shorten, as the case may be, the duration of their financial agreements with the Provinces so as to bring about a synchronous expiry of them all on March 31, 1882.

Financial Settlements of 1882-83

The new settlements made with all the provinces with effect from 1882-31. were marked by an extension of the principle applied to Burma since 1878. Certain heads, as few in number as possible, of revenues and charges were wholly, or with minute local exceptions only, grouped as Imperial. Others were classed as wholly Provincial. The remaining were placed in an intermediate category designated as joint and were in most part shared equally between the Imperial and the Provincial Governments.

In those cases, however, where the provincialised expenditure exceeded the resources from the provincialised as well as the shared revenues, the balance instead of being provided as heretofore by fixed assignments from the Imperial exchequer was rectified for each Province by a fixed percentage on its land revenue—a wholly Imperial head of revenue except in the case of Burma, where the percentage was extended to the Imperial rice export duty and salt revenue as well.

Along with the enlargement of the scheme of Provincial Finance in 1882 the Government of India was also anxious to introduce simplicity and uniformity in the matter of grouping the different heads of revenue and expenditure under the three categories now established. It will be remembered that the agreements effected in 1877 were marked by diversity and intricacy.

The same charges were not provincialised in all the Provinces. A charge which was Provincial in one was Imperial in another. Again, in transferring charges a grant was often broken up so that a part was made Provincial and a part reserved as Imperial. On the revenue side the arrangement was not a little intricate.

The computations owing to the proviso in respect of the assigned revenues made the calculations far from simple. Both these defects were, however, removed when the settlements were framed in 1882, and it is to indicate what heads of revenue and expenditure were provincialised, what were imperialised, and what were divided and to what extent, that the following attempt is made.

Revenues—.

	Imperial	Provincial
Land Revenue	The whole except as entered in the Provincial Column	In *Burma,* Fisheries; in the *N.W.P. and Oudh* collections from the Terai, Bhabar and Dudhi Estates, Rents of Water-Mills and Stone Quarries; in *Bombay,* Rents of Resumed Service Lands and Service Commutations. In all Provinces, a fixed percentage on the Imperial land revenue to cover the difference between Provincial Revenue and Provincial Expenditure
11 Tributes	The whole.	Nil.
III Forest	Half.	Half.
IV Excise	Do.	Do.
V Assessed Taxes	Do.	Do.
VI Provincial Rates	Nil.	The whole.
VII Customs	All except as entered in the Provincial Column	All items other than Customs Duties: and, in *Burma* only, the same percentage on Export Duties as on the Land Revenue.
VIII Salt	All except as entered in the Provincial Column	All items other than Duty on Salt and sale of Salt; and, in Burma only, the same percentage on the salt Revenue as on the Land Revenue
IX Opium	The whole.	Nil.
X Stamps	Half.	Half.
XI Registration	Do.	Do.
XIII Post Office	Nil.	The whole.
XIV Minor Departments	Do.	Do.

XVI Law and Justice	Do.	Do.
XVII Police	Do.	Do.
XVIII Marine	As at present.	As at present.
XIX Education	Nil.	The whole.
XX Medical	Do.	Do.
XXI Stationery and Printing.	Nil.	The whole.
XXII Interest	All except as entered in the Provincial Column.	Interest on Government securities (Provincial).
XXIII Pensions	Book transfers from the Military and Medical Funds and subscriptions to these Funds	The remainder.
XXIV Miscellaneous	Gain by Exchange on Imperial transactions, Premia on Bills and unclaimed Bills of Exchange	The remainder.
XXV Railway	As at present.	Whatever is now provincial in each Province.
XXVI Irrigation and Navigation.	Do.	Do.
XXVII Other Public Works	Receipts from Military Works	The remainder.
XXXI Gain by Exchange on Transactions with London	The whole.	Nil.

Expenditure

1. Interest	The whole except as entered in the Provincial Column.	Interest on local Debenture Loans. 4 1/2 percent, on the capital cost to the commencement of the year, and 2 1/2 per cent. on the capital cost during the year, of all Public Works, whether classified as Productive Public Works or not, of which Capital and Revenue Accounts are kept: excepting, always, any portion of their cost supplied from the Provincial Revenues or by Local Debenture Loans. The rate of interest on the cost of Protective Public Works will be the subject of a special agreement.
2. Interest on Service Fund's and other Accounts.	Interest on Service Funds and deposits in Savings Banks.	The remainder.
3. Refunds and Drawbacks	Of the Imperial share of revenues.	Of the Provincial share of revenues.
4. Land Revenues	The same percentage on charges for collection of Land Revenue and on the cost of Surveys (including expenditure hitherto charged in the Accounts of the Central Government) and Settlements elsewhere than in *Bombay* and *Madras*, as is retained of Land Revenue.	The remainder.

5. Forest	Half	Half. Do. Do. The whole. Do. The remainder.
6. Excise	Do.	Nil. Half. Half. The whole. Do.
7. Assessed Taxes	Do.	"
8. Provincial Rates	Nil	
9. Customs	Do.	
10. Salt	In *Madras* the whole. Elsewhere the purchase and manufacture of salt; and in *Bengal* the cost of preventive lines and operations: in *Bombay* charges connected with the administration of Salt Revenue in Portuguese India.	
11. Opium	The whole	
12. Stamps	Half	
13. Registration	Half	
15. Postoffice	Nil	
16. Telegraph	Do.	
17. Administration	Account and Currency Offices and allowances to Presidency Banks.	The remainder.
18.Minor Depts	Archaeological and Meteoro logical Depts., Census Gazetteers and Statistical Memoirs.	The remainder.

19. Law and Justice	Nil.	The whole.
20. Police	Frontier Police and Police employed on Imperial State Railways on Salt preventive duties.	The remainder.
21. Marine	Whatever is now Imperial.	Whatever is now Provincial.
22. Education	Do.	Do.
23. Ecclesiastical	The whole.	Nil.
24. Medical	Nil.	The whole.
25. Stationery and Printing	Stationery purchased for Central Stores.	The remainder, including cost of stationery obtained from Central Stores.
'26. Political	The whole.	Nil.
27. Allowances and Assignment	The whole except as in the Provincial Column.	In *Bombay*, items now Provincial
28. Civil Furlough and	The whole.	Nil.
Absentee Allowances.		
29. Superannuations	Items not provided for in the Al Provincial Column.	pensions and gratuities, except pensions payable from the Military and Medical Funds brought to account in India: each Government being responsible for pensions and gratuities which it now pays, or hereafter grants or recommends, however earned and wherever paid.

30. Miscellaneous	Remittance of treasure, and discount on Supply Bills.	The remainder.
31. Famine Relief	Secondary liability.	Wholly Provincial.
32. Railways	As at present.	Whatever is now Provincial.
33. Irrigation	Do.	Do.
34. Other Public Works	Military Public Works, and except in *British Burma,* Offices of the Supreme Government; Works in the Salt, Opium, Post Office, Imperial Telegraph and Ecclesiastical Depts. And Mint and Currency Offices; and Bengal Surveyor General's Offices.	The remainder.
38. Loss by Exchange	The whole.	Nil.

On the transactions of 1881-82 the Government expected to gain £ 470,000 a year.

Of this sum, however, it returned to the Central Provinces £77,900, for improving the position of the subordinate civil services and other general purposes; to Madras, £ 20,000, for provincial public works; and to the N.W.P. and Oudh, £326,000, of which £ 10,000 was for additional Kanungoes in Oudh, and the remainder, £316,000, for a remission of local taxation.

Besides these benefactions the Government of India gave for a favourable start to Bengal, £ 285,000; Burma, £ 20,000; N.W.P., £ 55,000, to be added to their balances before the close of the year 1881-2. These benefactions, which amounted to £496,000 a year, were expected to turn the annual gain of £470,000 into an annual loss of £26,000 to the Imperial exchequer.

In this connection it must also be recalled that the Government of India reimbursed the Provincial Governments of the amount of the benevolences it had levied on them in the years 1879-80 and 1880-1.

But not long after the revision of 1882 the financial position of the Government of India, which had permitted of such a liberal treatment, suffered a reverse, and the necessity for levying benevolences on the balances of the Provincial governments reappeared in 1886-7. In presenting the financial Statement for that year the Finance Member of the Government of India argued:—

"22. Since the estimates for 1885-6 were presented...... Indian administration and finance have entered on a new phase. The brief period of rest which the country had enjoyed since 1882 had drawn to a close......

By the events of the late years in Central Asia, India finds herself almost in contact with one of the great European Powers, and she cannot hope to escape the necessity which the position imposes on her of increasing her military strength. Events impending have occurred which have changed, as it was known they must change, the face of our estimates, and have thrust us violently out of the peaceful path of internal progress in which we had hoped to have been left undisturbed."

Among the other means employed to weather the storm the Government of India resorted a second time to nibbling at the provincial resources, and gathered a sum of £400,000 in the year 1886-7 by appropriating from their balances the above amount.

The condition of Provincial Finance during this period may be summarised in the following table :—

Provinces	Annual Surpluses and Deficits				
	1882-3	1883-4	1884-5	1885-6	1886-7
	£	£	£	£	£
C.P.	33,775	76,212	18,047	22,080	115,656
Burma	171,207	−90,030	−89,725*	#	71,743**
Assam	13,887	−5,216	−40,577	25,299	28,576
Bengal	539,611	146,027	48,910	26,777	52,911
N.W.P.& Oudh	281,222	357,630	−69,276	−180,060	−12,408
Punjab	−110,966	−15,765	−41,545	42,447	3,106
Madras	108,421	10,820	−87,284	146,692	−78,689
Bombay	−149,894	−2,585	6,006	291,976	−161,369

*No balance left at the dose of the year.

Equilibrium

**Balance obtained by excess of current revenue over current expenditure of the year.

Compiled from the annual Finance and Revenue Accounts of the Government of India.

The settlements entered into with the Provincial Governments in the year 1882-3 not only differed from the preceding settlements in the replacement of fixed assignments by shares in the Imperial revenues, but they also differed in another important respect, namely, their duration. Though the results of the scheme of provincial Finance have been presented in one Table covering the period 1871-7, it must not be supposed that the settlements with the various Provinces were made for the period of six years. On the other hand, the settlements were only annual and lasted up to 1877 by the process of constant renewals.

The results have been presented together for a continuous period not because the settlements were made for that period, but because the principle on which they were based endured for that period. After 1877 the settlements no doubt were made for a longer period.

In two cases they were for five years and for the rest the period ranged between two and three years. The short duration system, like the fixed assignment system, was of immense advantage to the Imperial treasury. The object of these settlements, it will be recalled, was firstly to put a definite limit on the demands of the Provincial Governments on the already too scanty resources of the Imperial Government.

Evidently this object would have been better served had the duration of the settlements been longer than it was. But a longer duration would have deprived the Imperial treasury of its right to profit by an early revision of the revenue side of the contract.

It was this consideration of not remaining too long out of pocket, that had hitherto prevailed upon the Government of India to shorten the duration of contracts as much as possible. But what was an advantage to the Imperial treasury was from the standpoint of the Provincial Government a serious drawback. Owing to the short durations of the settlements the Provincial Governments were not in a position to distribute the funds at their disposal on the incorporated services so as to open a new page in their financial history.

They could not adopt a definite financial policy, for they feared that the new terms on renewal might compel them either to give up the policy or modify it so seriously as to prejudice its results.

A single budget may seem nothing more than the conspectus of financial happenings of the year to which it pertains, yet to the financier who frames them year after year they embody a definite policy running towards its consummation. But a policy, however wisely adopted, may be thwarted by an unwise disturbance of the uniformity of conditions on which its fulfilment depends.

This was just the flaw that deteriorated the sound working of Provincial Finance.

Constant renewals had a general disturbing effect, and the duration between any two of them was indeed too short to give a stable state of conditions. Being impressed by the fact that the advantages of a short-duration-contract to the Imperial treasury were enormously counterbalanced by its disadvantages to Provincial Finance, the Government of India, on the occasion of revising the settlements in 1882-3, made it a definite rule that they shall be quinquennial in duration ; that is, they shall not be subject to revision before the end of the fifth year from their commencement.

Revision of 1887-88

By virtue of this rule the settlements made in 1882-3 expired in 1887. The revision then undertaken, as well as the subsequent ones, left as a rule undisturbed the two categories of revenue and expenditure, namely, those wholly Provincial and wholly Imperial.

It became almost a convention to leave them as they were since the separation in 1882, when the constitution of Provincial Budgets was thoroughly overhauled and consolidated. The only heads of revenue and expenditure that were revised, as revision fell due, were those that were grouped under the third category, namely, jointly Imperial and Provincial, otherwise known as "Divided Heads."

In the revision of 1887-8 the decisive factor was the unsatisfactory position of the Imperial Finances already referred to. To improve its financial position the shares in the joint heads were altered so that each Local Government was allowed to appropriate three-fourths of the stamps and one-fourth of the excise revenue, and required to bear the expenditure under those heads in like proportion.

The proportions of land revenue were also altered so that three-fourths of it was made Imperial, and one-fourth Provincial. But the needs of the Imperial treasury were so great that the Government of India even revised some of the heads of the other two categories, namely, Salt, Customs, Interest, Irrigation and Railways, to its own advantage. The details of the gain to the Imperial treasury are as given below :—

Revenue	*Imperial Share* Increased – Decreased	Net Gain
Land Revenue	437,500	
Stamps (share reduced from 1/2 to 1/4 Excise (share increased from 1/2 to 3/4) Salt revenue of Burma imperialised Customs revenue of Burma imperialised Assessed taxes—divided in moieties	–810,000 947,500 } 5,000 155,000 – 290,000 }	215,000
State Railways gross earnings— Nagpur Chhattisgarh Patna-Gaya }	–310,000	
Cawnpore-Achneyra }		
Eastern Bengal, provincialised	–540,000	
Expenditure	Increased – Decreased	Net Gain
Land Revenue, entire provincialization of survey and settlement	145,000	
Salt in Bombay impērialised	–90,000 {	
Customs in Bombay imperialised	–50,000	
State Railways—		
Working expenses:—		
Provincialised	305,000 {	395,000
Imperialised ...	–215,000 }	
Interest—Provincialised	–70,000	
Imperialised	–65,000 }	
Irrigation—Provincialised. Bengal	65,000 {'	
Irrigation—Provincialised Madras	230,000 }	
Add—Small items of accounts unenumerated		20,000

This gain to the Imperial treasury was distributed in the following proportion among the various Provinces :—

Provinces	Increase of annual resources under the principal Provincial Heads of Revenue as estimated on comparison of 1882 and 1887			Amount by which Annual Provincial Resources were reduced by the Revision of 1887
	Land Revenue	Stamps and Excise	Total	
	£	£	£	£
C.P.	2,200	45,500	47,700	15,600
Burma	4,700	9,200	13,000	
Assam	22,300	21,300	43,600	24,600
Bengal	19,200	171,550 1	190.750	103,600
N.W.P.	8,000	30,150	138,150	100,000
Punjab	32,800	23,100 1	55,900	174,400
Madras	27,750	42,550	150,300	
Bombay	99,000	198,550	297,550	221,900
Total ...	195,950	741,900	937,850	640,100

This would have been the net gain to the Imperial treasury had it not been for the fact that it conceded to Burma the sum of £ 10,000. The net gain was thus reduced to £ 530,100 per annum. The condition of Provincial Finance during the period of 1887-92 may be judged from the following table presenting the annual surplus and deficit of each of the different Provinces:—

	Annual Surpluses and Deficits				
	1887-88	1888-89	1889-90	1890-91	1891-92
	Rs.	Rs.	Rs.	Rs.	Rs.
C.P.	13,148	22,583	−12,322	−31,573	17,540
Burma	77,028	11,560	64,072	106,216	50,598
Assam	7,751	26,343	20,090	−17,871	31,185
Bengal	131,007	−65,792	102,547	−120,377	−11,934

N.W.P. & Oudh.	−53,900	45,949	102,710	−12,544	−4,399
Punjab	12,446	32,142	29,264	31,367	−1,719
Madras	105,371	113,932	144,571	−136,739	−241,770
Bombay	−24,574	18,322	41,361	−123,887	−53,189

Compiled from the annual Finance and Revenue Accounts of the Government of India.

Revision of 1892-3

The next revision of provincial settlements under the rule of quinquennial revisions occurred in 1892-3.

The new settlements to commence from that year did not differ in principle from those of 1887-8.

The shares in the Joint Revenue were so readjusted as to give to the Imperial treasury a larger gain from the growing yield of the provincialised sources.

The amount resumed by the Imperial Government at this revision through readjustments of shares was estimated as follows :—

Province	Increase of Revenue in 1891-92 (Revised Est.) as compared with the Estimate for the Contract of 1887-88 to 1891-92	Amount resumed by the Government of India
	Rs.	Rs.
C.P.	119,200	22,700
Lower Burma	334,900	58,900
Bengal	517,700	51,900
N.W.P.&Oudh	53,300	56,900
Punjab	195,400	41,000
Madras	313,200	103,800
Bombay	399,200	131,100
Assam	99,800	
Total	2,042,700	466,300

But this gain to the Imperial treasury seriously disturbed the equilibrium between the expenditure of the Provinces estimated as normal for the ensuing period and the normal estimated yield of revenues left to them.

To restore equilibrium between their normal expenditure and normal revenue the Government of India reverted to the discarded method of fixed adjusting assignments, so that while the actual revenues and charges deviated from what was estimated as normal for the period of the settlement, the adjusting entry allowed by the Imperial Government to each of the provinces remained fixed throughout the whole period.

The following is a statement of estimated normal expenditure and revenues of the different Provinces with their respective adjusting assignments as fixed for the new period :—

Provinces	Provincial Revenues			Provincial Expenditure
	Ordinary Revenue being a share of certain Receipts	Adjusting Assignments	Total	
	Rs.	Rs.	Rs.	Rs.
C.P.	567,600	220,500	788,100	788,100
Lower Burma	1,427,500	414,300	1,841,800	1,841,800
Assam	657,700	−112,700	545,000	545,000
Bengal	4,249,300	−143,900	4,105,500	4,105,900
N.W.P. & Oudh	3,403,500	−250,000	3,152,900	3,152,900
Punjab	1,370,400	348,500	1,718,900	1.718,900
Madras	2,479,300	325,400	2,804,700	2,804,700
Bombay	3,123,900	771,400	3,895,300	3,895,300

The evil effect of large resumptions and fixed assignments will be clearly seen in the condition of Provincial Finance as indicated by the annual surpluses and deficits over the period of the settlement:—

Province	Annual Surpluses or Deficits				
	1892-93	1893-94	1894-95	1895-96	1896-97
	Rs.	Rs.	Rs.	Rs.	Rs.
C.P.	−21,798	−60,772	−105,108	19,653	−37,408*
Burma	66,642	−90,653	−272,319	226,505	780
Assam	9,336	28,532	−27,422	30,507	−25,421
N.W.P.&Oudh	−16,752	−25,155	−165,987	−139,798	−164,740
Bengal	−9,826	36,887	169,796	149,808	−186,558
Punjab	−106,050	−22,699	−24,811	−7,156	−64,073
Madras	−159,081	33,636	92,328	44,118	−200,579
Bombay	−23,888	19,443	−102,472	100,690	−221,119

*No closing balance left.

Complied from the Annual Finance and Revenue Accounts of the Government of India.

It must, however, be admitted that the financial arrangements of the Provinces during this period were considerably disturbed by the outbreak of plague and famine towards the close of the settlements.

The expenditure which the Provinces were obliged to incur to meet these two calamities depleted the resources of all and brought the Central Provinces and the North-West Provinces to the verge of bankruptcy, from which they were rescued by the following contributions made by the Government of India in aid of their balances in the year 1896-7 :—

To Central Provinces	Rs. 526 lakhs.
To N.W.P. and Oudh	Rs. 1,609 lakhs.

This depression in Provincial Finance was alleviated to some extent at least in the revised settlements of 1896-7 by allowing a higher standard of expenditure and of revenue to the Provinces than was granted to them in 1892.

The following table presents the old and the new standard of expenditure with the percentage difference between them :—

Provinces	Standard Net Expenditure		Increase
	1892	1897	per cent.
	Rs.	Rs.	
Central provinces	653,300	710,700	8.8
Lower Burma	1,064,600	1,206,100	13.3
Assam	467,600	564,900	20.8
Bengal	2,816,700	3,125,500	10.9
N.W.P.	2,215,400	2,428,700	9.6
Punjab	1,384,600	1,537,300	11.0
Madras	2,054,800	2,238,600	8.9
Bombay	2,049,500	2,544,100	5.6
Total	13,066,500	14,355,900	9.9

This new and enhanced standard of expenditure called for a revision of the shares of the Imperial and Provincial Governments in the joint revenues. But the revision had to be so devised that while it gave larger resources to the Provinces it obviated the necessity of making fixed assignments as much as possible; for the Government of India had learnt to its cost that fixed assignments on a large scale tended to make the resource side of the Provincial Finance rigid to such an uncomfortable degree that, if the variability of expenditure surpassed the expandability of the revenue incorporated in the Provincial Budgets, it was perforce obliged to distribute benefactions to ease what would otherwise be a difficult situation. Secondly, these fixed assignments also created a certain degree of inequality as between the backward and the more advanced Provinces.

In the advanced Provinces the fixed assignments formed a comparatively smaller part of their resources than they did in the case of the relatively backward Provinces, and, as larger expenditure could be undertaken by the Provinces only when their revenues expanded, the advanced Provinces, a larger part of whose resources were of an expanding nature, obtained a more favourable treatment than the relatively backward Provinces, a large part of whose resources were of a frozen character. This was rightly conceived by the Government of India as the reverse of what ought to have been, having regard to the fact that the needs of the backward Provinces were relatively more imperious than those of the advanced Provinces.

To obviate this injustice the Government of India enhanced the shares of the backward provinces in the joint revenues by reducing *per contra* the fixed assignments made at the last revision. To the Punjab it gave .4 and to the Central Provinces .5 of the Land Revenue instead of .25 only. The share of Burma in the Land Revenue was raised to .66, and to make provision for the enhanced expenditure due to the addition of Upper Burma, and in lieu of the railway revenue withdrawn from it, Burma was allowed to appropriate .5 of the Excise instead of .25 only. The financial condition of the North-Western Provinces was not very happy. Its revenue had proved so very unprogressive that it advanced only 2 percent.

The treatment of the North-Western Provinces at the revision of 1892 was also a little unjust. The revision had left its revenues short by 5 lakhs of its standard expenditure, to be made up by reduction of its balances. To make amends for this the Government of India re-distributed the shares in the Land Revenue to the advantage of the North-Western Provinces. In addition to this the Government of India gave to that Province a grant of 4 lakhs for the year 1897-8, to enable it to establish district funds on a financially independent footing, a result accomplished long ago in every other Province in British India.

To give an equitable treatment to the backward as well as to the advanced Provinces, it realised that an unequal treatment was the only proper way. It therefore adopted a less liberal attitude in revising the terms of the settlements with the more advanced Provinces of Bengal, Madras and Bombay. It allowed them a proportionately smaller increase of expenditure than the backward Provinces, as may be seen from the figures given above, and reduced slightly their shares in the revenues.

On the occasion of this revision the gain to the Imperial exchequer was practically negligible. In 1877 its total gain by retrenchment amounted to 40 lakhs a year; in 1882 the Imperial Government was so very prosperous that instead of contriving for a gain it surrendered to the Provinces 26 lakhs of the annual imperial revenue. But in 1887 it resumed 63 lakhs and in 1892,46 lakhs. On this occasion however its gain was nil, for what it got from the advanced Provinces it gave to the backward ones. Just and liberal as the terms of the settlement were, the abnormal circumstances which disturbed the entire period of the settlement made such heavy demands on the Provincial resources that, ample though they were, they fell far short of the requirements of the Provinces.

The famine of 1896 and 1897 affected all the Provinces, although in unequal degree. In the North-Western Provinces and Oudh, the Central provinces, and Burma the effect was most severely felt. In Madras, Bengal and the Punjab it was serious, and in Burma it was slight. On the other hand, the famine of 1899 and 1900 affected Bombay and the Central Provinces most severely, the Punjab very seriously and the rest of the Provinces slightly.

And Assam, though unaffected by either of the two famines, suffered very severely from the great earthquake of June, 1897. Besides famine the plague was also making its ravages and taking its toll. As a result of these unforeseen calamities ail the Provinces were forced to incur extraordinary expenditure on preventive measures, for which no provision was made in the standard of revenue fixed for the period of settlement. The expenditure on these unforeseen calamities being of an extraordinary nature was treated as imperial and defrayed from the Imperial exchequer, but even this much succour did not prove equal to the necessity and the Government of India was obliged to make special grants-in-aid of the Provincial Revenues as shown on page 168.

Thus the Government of India was not only obliged to pay for the cost of the famine, but to grant funds to restore equilibrium and to provide for useful public services held up or curtailed by the Provincial Governments owing to the extraordinary circumstances of the time. All this aid from the Imperial Government was made available because of the very prosperous condition of the Imperial finances throughout this period. While it is better that governments in general should always be in penury, the surpluses in the Imperial Finance proved a timely resource, the utility of which was doubled by the commendable way in which they were spent. Besides giving them grants for useful public works the superfluous funds of the Imperial Government were utilised in carrying out the following additional measures to the relief of the Provinces:

(1) Remission of Imperial Land Revenue Rs. 50,94,000 and reimbursement to the Provinces for their share remitted Rs. 59,81,000; in all Rs. 1,10,75,000.

(2) The abolition of the pandhari tax in the Central Provinces, costing Rs. 7,000 a year.

(3) The reduction of the patwari rate in Ajmere, from 10 percent on land revenue to 6 1/4percent.; the amount of the local revenue remitted was—Rs. 13,000, but the contribution paid to the local fund was Rs. 23,000. Taking into account these various contributions in aid of Provincial Revenues, the following table is presented as indicative of the condition of the Provincial Finances during this period of settlement :—

Provinces	Provincial Surpluses or Deficits						
	1897-98	1898-99	1899-1900	1900-01	1901-02	1902-03	1903-04
	Rs.	Rs.	Rs.	Rs.	Rs.	Rs.	Rs.
C.P.	(a)	12.286	−1,22,883	(a)	22,42,408	−705	-7,40,742
Burma	1.69,435	4.11,494	26.14,312	15,16,220	7,55.285		
Assam	−45,580	86,742	−8,15,488	−86.829	1,47,353	10.08,393	11,40.517
Bengal	-3.03.250	2,19,449	7,01,899	4,43,224	6.44.170	6,23.640	87,23.496
N.W.P.	(a)	3,28,562	7,53,815	8,04.789	---	---	---
Punjab	−2,278	1,15,379	-16,53,794	(a)	14,96,350	10.28.770	6.74,880
Madras	-1.57,707	1,60,706	-17.58.029	-3,21,013	40,41,297	-15,810	52,40,809
Bombay	-1.29.663	1,00,427	-15,04,271	(a)	58,23,235	-24,23,235	-1,23,000
U.P.of Agra and Oudh	---	---	---	---	-9,63,788	-64,372	37,11,281

(a)No closing balance left because of Budget equilibrium.

Compiled from the Annual Finance and Revenue Accounts of the Government of India. .

Imperial Special Grants-in-aid to Provinces*

Year		India	C.P.	Assam	Bengal	N.W.P. and Oudh	Punjab	Madras	Bombay	Burma
		Rs.	Rs.	Rs.	Rs.	Rs.	Rs.	Rs.	Rs.	Rs.
1897-98			7,72,000	8,00,000		10,27,000			12,18,000	
1898-99			5,00,000	18,00,000	17,00,000	10,00,000	5,00,000	16,96,000	48,75,000	
1899-1900			19,32,000				95,000	3,49,000	34,37,000	
1900-01			34,15,000				5,98,000		64,79,000	
1901-02	{		26,89,000	2,00,000			12,40,000	32,14,000	91,00,000	4,00,000
			6,50,000				4,00,000	10,00,000	19,50,000	
1902-03 ...	{1		2,00,000	1,00,000	10,00,000	5,00,000	4,00,000	8,00,000	6,00,000	
	{2	A 70,000	2,00,000	2,80,000	6,00,000	4,50,000	5,00,000	5,50,000	5,50,000	
	{3	B 1,00,000	2,00,000	1,50,000		3,50,000	3,00,000	3,50,000	3,50,000	
1903-04	{1		2,00,000	1,00,000	10,00,000	5,00,000	4,00,000	8,00,000	6,00,000	4,00,000
	{2		5,00,000	5,00,000	2,00,000	3,00,000	10,00,000	5,00,000	10,00,000	
	{3		1,90,000	1,11,000		2,26,000	2,76,000	3,50,000	3,50,000	

1. For education (recurring)
2. For use Public Works.
3. For improving district and Other establishments.
   A. Allotment for Public Work s in Baluchistan, Rajputana and Central India.
   B. Amount taken the "India" estimates for subsequent distribution to the provinces.

* Complied from the annual Financial Statements of the Government of India.

Revision of 1902-03

Settlements made with the Provinces in 1897 should have ended in the ordinary course of time in 1902-3. The central operation in the periodic revision of the settlements was to arrive at the standard provincial expenditure for the ensuing quinquennium and as a rough and ready method of decision the average expenditure during the expiring quinquennium was taken as a standard expenditure for the opening quinquennium. There is nothing grossly erroneous in such a procedure, provided the preceding and succeeding quinquenniums are equally normal with respect to the course of their events. But as we have seen, the events of the past quinquennium were entirely abnormal and could not have been made the basis of any calculations worthy of trust.

To be on the safe side the Government of India thought it desirable to await the return of normal times before undertaking wholesale revisions of provincial settlements. The occasion of 1902-3 for revision was therefore postponed save in the case of Burma. For, the last settlement had become unduly favourable to that Province in comparison with the other Provinces, notwithstanding the very nice and equitable calculations on which the settlements of 1896-7 were based. The extent to which the revenues had exceeded its expenditure is indicated in the following table:—

Burma	Estimated Standard for the Settlement of 1897-98 to 1901-02	Estimates for 1902-03	Difference
	Rs.	Rs.	Rs.
Revenues	2,93,81,000	3,73,86,000	80,05,000
Expenditure	2,93,81,000	3,31,86,000	38,05,000
Surplus		42,00,000	

The continuance of such an outcome was deemed unfair to the Imperial and unjust to the other Provincial Governments. The financial settlement of the Province of Burma was accordingly revised notwithstanding the established canon of simultaneous revision, when the occasion presented itself in 1902-3. The revision resulted in the resumption by the Government of India of this surplus by readjusting the shares of the Province in the joint revenues. The share in the Land Revenue was reduced from two- thirds to one-half and that in the Excise from one-half to one-third, and a few minor heads were added to the already provincialised heads of expenditure. By these changes the standard revenue and expenditure of Burma for the new settlement of 1903 to 1906 assumed the following totals :—

Adjusting	Total Revenues	Total Expenditure	Assignment
Rs.	Rs.	Rs.	Rs.
2,78,31,000	53,02,000	3,31,33,000	3,31,33,000

Another province whose settlement was revised was the Punjab; but the reason of it was different. The territory covered by the North-Western Provinces was divided into the North-Western Frontier Provinces and the United Provinces of Agra and Oudh, usually styled U.P. Along with this some of the districts of the Punjab were separated from it and joined to the newly created North-Western Frontier Province. This caused a readjustment of the provincial revenues and expenditure, but not any wholesale revision of the settlement. The changes were confined to the necessary alterations in the adjusting assignment.

Quasi-Permanent Revision 1904-05

With the exceptions noted above the settlements of 1897 were extended up to the end of the year 1904. The primary cause of the postponement of the revision as explained above was the abnormality of the conditions prevailing in the year 1901-2. But there was also another reason why the Government of India was so very anxious for the return of normal conditions before taking any steps towards revision. It was about this time that the Government of India contemplated to introduce permanency in Provincial Finance.

The five-year budget system which in 1881 replaced the annual budget system as the basis of Provincial Finance, though a marked improvement in the direction of continuity and stability, was not deemed to be quite sufficient. Under it the Provincial Governments were left free to enjoy the fruits of their economy in expenditure and of the successful nursing of their resources for the period of five years. Beneficial as far as it went, this time-bar was found to exercise a most pernicious influence on Provincial Finance. Under the quinquennial budget system it so happened that the provincial Governments as the result of feeling their way under the new conditions were parsimonious in the first few years lest their expenditure should prove too much for their revenues, and extravagant in the last few years lest their expenditure should shrink below the standard and leave large margins to be cancelled by the Government of India on revision of their settlements. No Local Government could be expected to put into execution any carefully matured and well-thought-out scheme of improvement within the short span of a quinquennium. All that it could do was to spend the first two or three years in working out a scheme and utilise the last two or three years in rushing it through, as was done by most of the Provinces.

This tendency to undertake such schemes, the only merit of which was that they could be carried through before the revision, and mainly in order to reach the standard expenditure, was a direct consequence of the quinquennial budget system. This is by no means an a priori conclusion. A glance at the annual surplus of the provinces will indicate how they tend to rise in the beginning of the quinquennium and fall at the end of it. To obviate these evils of parsimony and extavagance the only remedy was to do away with the principle of quinquennial revision, and this the Government of India courageously undertook to effect. The right to revise was a much cherished right, and the Government of India had not failed to exercise it in the teeth of ail opposition from the Provinces. It was abandoned only because its exercise was deemed to be mischievous.

Taking the year 1903-4 as the normal one, the Government of India decided to revise the provincial settlements of all the different Provinces. The idea was to adjust the revenues between the Imperial and the Provincial Governments on the basis of the total expenditure they respectively controlled. It was found that the aggregate provincial expenditure represented less than one-fourth of the whole, while the Imperial expenditure, which included Army and Home Charges, aggregated in excess of three-fourths. These proportions of expenditure were taken as the basis of the division of revenue between the Imperial and the Provincial, and the following standard shares of revenue and expenditure under the joint heads were agreed upon :—

	Imperial	Provincial
Bengal, U.P., Bombay, Madras	3/4	1/4
Punjab, Burma	5/8	3/8
C.P., Assam	1/2	1/2

The reasons for adopting different standard rates of division in the case of the Punjab, Burma, C.P. and Assam was to give the backward provinces opportunities of development in the same proportion as lay within the reach of the advanced provinces. Of the settlements made in 1904-5 the Government of India declared that those made with the Provinces of Bengal, Madras, Assam and U.P. were to be permanent and not subject to revision in future, except when it was found that the financial results were unfair to a Province or to others by comparison, or to the Government of India when it was confronted by an extraordinary calamity. Owing to this proviso their settlements were termed quasi-permanent. To obviate the recrudescence of unfairness during the currency of the settlements the Government of India felt it necessary to enter certain modifications in the standard ratio of division of the joint-heads of revenue and expenditure with regard to the Provinces brought under the quasi-permanent settlement.

Revenue	Provincial Share		
	Bengal	Madras	U.P.
Excise Stamps	7/16	---	---
Registration	1/2	1/2,	½
Irrigation	Wholly	Wholly	---
	---	---	Wholly

Expenditure	Provincial Share		
	Bengal	Madras	U.P.
Excise	7/16	---	---
Stamps	1/2	½	½
Registration Land	Wholly	---	---
Revenue	Wholly	Wholly	Wholly

Compiled from the Financial Statement of the Government of India for 1904-5, p. 67.

Besides these modifications the Government of India gave them the following grants :—

Bengal	Madras	United Provinces
1. Addition of 4 lakhs to The assessment to Improve the pay of Ministerial establish ments.	1. Grant of 20 lakhs for Survey and settlements	1. Irrigation revenue guaranteed up to 40 lakhs.
2. Further addition not Exceeding 2 1/2 lakhs for For strengthening the staff of Deputy Collector.	2. Grant of Rs. 75,000 a year recurring for relief of certain local bodies.	2. Grant of 2 1/2, lakhs a 1/2, lakhs a year in relief of local bodies.
	3. Rs. 50,000 a year for agricultural experiment.	3. Half a lakh a year to reform District Board Finance.
	4. Undertaking to bear charges for reorganising district administration	

Compiled from the same Financial Statement of the Government of India.

The standard revenues and expenditure of the quasi-permanently settled provinces, after taking into consideration the alterations in their respective shares in the joint revenues, were as follows:—

Standard Revenues and Expenditure (in Thousands of Rupees)

Province	Expenditure	Revenue		
		Revenues	Assignments	Total
Madras	3,50,48	2,90,82	5,966	3,50,48
Bengal	4,98,87	4,49,84	4,903	4,98,87
U.P.	3,66,64	3,62,64	400	3,66,64
Assam	72,07	60,07	1,200	72,07

The gain to the Imperial treasury on the revenue side brought about by the revision of the quasi-permanently settled Provinces was Rs. 2,06,000. But the revision also over-burdened the Imperial Government with a total charge of Rs. 36,000 hitherto borne by the Provincial Budget. Thus its net gain was only Rs. 1,70,000 a year on the normal.

As in the beginning of the scheme of Provincial Budgets, the government of India thought it advisable to make to the quasi-permanently settled Provinces the following initial grants so as to give them a fair start :—

To Bengal	Rs. 50 lakhs. (Exclusive of 50 lakhs for Calcutta University.)
To Madras	Rs. 50 lakhs. (Inclusive of 20 lakhs for survey settlement
To U.P	Rs. 30 lakhs. (Exclusive of 1 1/4 lakhs to compensate for expenditure on the purchase of encumbered estates.)
To Assam	Rs. 20 lakhs.

Of the remaining Provinces, Bombay and the Punjab were the next to obtain quasi-permanent settlements with effect from 1905-6.

In recasting their settlements the Government of India departed a little from the standard rate of division as applied to the Provinces quasi-permanently settled in 1904-5. With certain exceptions mentioned below the joint heads of revenue and expenditure were divided half and half, including Irrigation in Bombay, instead of three-fourths and one-fourth between the Imperial and the Provincial. The exceptions to this rule were the following :—

Revenue	Provincial Share		Expenditure	Provincial Share	
Heads of			Heads of		
Account	Bombay	Punjab	Accounts	Bombay	Punjab
Land Revenue	Guaranteed Up to 189 1/4,	3/8	Land Revenue	Wholly	Wholly
	Lakhs				
Registration	Wholly	Wholly			
Irrigation	½	3/5 Guaranteed up to 28 lakhs			

Compiled from the Financial Statement of the Government of India

The standard revenue and expenditure of these two provinces under the quasi-permanent settlement was as follows:—

Province	Expenditure	Revenue		
		Revenues	Fixed Assignments	Total
	Rs.	Rs.	Rs.	Rs.
Bombay	4,91,75,000	4,48,98,000	42,77,000	4,91,75,000
Punjab	2,49,50,000	2,46,50,000	3,00,000	2,49,50,000

The raising of the shares and the fixing of assignments on a liberal scale with respect to these famine and plague-stricken Provinces left the Imperial Government a loser on the transaction. On the basis of the new standard of revenues the Government of India lost Rs. 5,95,000 on the two Provinces together. The corresponding increase in the provincial shares of the joint heads of expenditure, however, lessened the Imperial expenditure by Rs. 2,21,000 a year. On the whole, therefore, the Imperial Government sacrificed a normal gain of Rs. 3,74,000 to give permanency and stability to the finances of these two Provinces. This was over and above the initial grant of Rs. 50,00,000 to each of them in order to enable them to set their sails in smooth waters.

A year after, the settlement of the Central Provinces was made quasi-permanent with effect from April 1, 1906. The shares in the joint heads of revenue and expenditure were raised, as they were in the case of Bombay and the Punjab, and particularly because of the addition of Berar, which was hitherto administered directly by the Imperial Government, from three-fourths and one-fourth to one-half between the Imperial and the Provincial, the share in the land revenue being guaranteed up to 82 1/2 lakhs.

The only exception to this rule of even division was the Registration revenue, which was made wholly provincial. To balance the revenue with the expenditure an assignment of Rs. 27,07,007 a year was fixed and an initial grant of Rs. 30,00,000 was given for a fair start.

Along with the settlement of the Central Provinces it became necessary to reorganise the budgets of the quasi-permanently settled Provinces of Bengal and Assam owing to certain administrative changes. The two Provinces were reconstituted into (1) Bengal and (2) Eastern Bengal and Assam.

In the revision of its financial settlement the new Province of Bengal was accorded the same proportionate share in the joint revenues as were granted to Bombay and the Punjab—namely, a share of a half in all the joint heads. Registration and that portion of the Land Revenue which was derived from Government Estates under the direct management of the Imperial Government were, however, made wholly provincial. In lieu of this favoured treatment the fixed assignment of the Province was reduced from 49.03 lakhs to 5.72 lakhs.

In the new Province of Eastern Bengal and Assam the principle of even distribution was applied to all joint heads of revenue and expenditure with the exception of Registration, which was made wholly provincial. This enhancement of shares so greatly augmented the resource side of the Provincial Budget that the balance had to be restored by a negative operation of a fixed adjusting assignment from the Provincial to the Imperial funds. The following figures show the standard expenditure and the standard revenue for the three provinces brought under the quasi-permanent settlements:—

		Revenue		
		Revenues	Assignments	Total
	Rs.	Rs.	Rs.	Rs.
C.P.	1,76,43,000	1,49,36,000	27,07,000	1,76,43,000
Eastern Bengal and Assam	2,12,19,000	2,18,42,000	6,23,000	2,12,19,000
Bengal	4,72,73,000	4,67,01,000	5,72,000	4,72,73,000

Some modifications were later on introduced in the settlement of the Province, so that a positive adjustment had to be made by an assignment from the Imperial to the Provincial of Rs. 60,000 a year. The only Province which was outside the pale of the quasi permanent system was Burma. The last quinquennial settlement made with it in 1902-3 having expired, the Government of India decided to bring it in uniformity with the other Provinces by giving it a quasi-permanent settlement from April 1, 1907. In a spirit of perfect impartiality it was also given an even share in the principal joint heads of revenue and expenditure, salt being imperialised as in other provinces. It was given an adjusting assignment of Rs. 90,68,000 a year to cover the deficits in its standard expenditure and an initial grant of Rs. 50,00,000.

By the year 1907 all the Provinces were brought within the pale of the quasi-permanent settlement, and we would have expected the scheme of Provincial Finance to run its course undisturbed by any further changes. But it so turned out, as must have been noticed, that the quasi-permanent settlements made with Madras and U.P. in 1904 had become a little unfair to them in comparison with the terms offered to the Provinces subsequently dealt with. To remove this ground of injustice, which was one of those recognised for subjecting the quasi-permanent settlements to revision, the shares of the two Provinces in the joint heads were raised with effect from April 1, 1907, to one-half, with the following exceptions :—

Madras

Revenue

I. Registration. Wholly Provincial.
  1. Land revenue. Minimum receipt of 308 lakhs guaranteed if the provincial share fell below that amount.

II. Expenditure
  1. Registration. Wholly provincial.
  2. Land Revenue. Wholly provincial.

United Provinces

Revenue

I. Land Revenue, 3/8 Provincial. Minimum of 240 lakhs guaranteed.

II. Irrigation. Minimum receipt of 60 lakhs from major irrigation works guaranteed, if the provincial share fell below that amount.

The fixed assignments to cover the difference between the excess of standard expenditure over standard revenue were :—

To Madras	- Rs. 22,57,000
To U.P.	- Rs. 13,89,000

Thus the scheme of Provincial Finance in British India had advanced by gradual but distinct steps of assignment budgets, assigned revenue budgets and shared revenue budgets to a stage the terms of which were regarded by the parties concerned as sufficiently final. How far their expectations were fulfilled may be judged from the annual surpluses and deficits in Provincial Finance and from the range in their deviations as indicated in the following table:—

Provincial Surpluses and Deficits

Province	1904-05	1905-06	1906-07	1907-08	1908-09	1909-10	1910-11	1911-12
	Rs.	Rs.	Rs.	Rs.	Rs.	Rs.	Rs.	Rs.
C.P.*	-701000	3235000	1750607	-930617	-3097865	721755	280556	1214573
Burma	-1591796	-2613890	1890516	-129590	-2060678	2515371	1900297	-1260040
Assam**	-269316	-3720027	-200140	-2596682	-2357687	549270	5539698	5218802
Bengal	-1252818	-1952312	-1877455	-2256994	-1330371	3274065	3960612	8296233
U.P.	-869099	-2879192	795600	-3587066	1007260	2045221	3635904	144240
Punjab	4794387	-2796052	-661214	-2408818	-1576981	1300559	4199121	3398055
Madras	-1402344	220328	1217745	—44992	2025109	1266326	2316383	2938502
Bombay	4396000	-42892	1752202	-308925	-2618926	7137996	7585460	-541411

*Indudes Berar since 1906.
**Eastern Bengal d Assam since 1906.
Compiled from the Annual Finance and Revenue Accounts of the Government of India.

In judging of these results account must also be taken of the various benefactions made by the Government of India to the Provinces by way of grants-in-aid during the same period. These grants were as follows :—

Imperial Grants-in-aid to the Provinces

Province	1904-05	1905-06	1906-07	1907-08	1908-09	1909-10	1910-11	1911-12
	Rs.	Rs.	Rs.	Rs.	Rs.	Rs.	Rs.	Rs.
C.P.*	2853710	6957793	110500	2752010	2903668	3588270	3465500	2080845
Burma	567500	1845000	7219000	682000	215253	1820952	4232742	3605164
Assam		3362916	327294	280030	2358947	4464435	4608965	6100732
Bengal	24794	4806984	475548	1362634	4157393	5753692	6137013	11131276
U.P.	136600	4036307	7641697	9879667	8770345	1624329	4513729	3136107
Punjab	7526436	2467579	4209531	5541529	6037990	5839014	9592844	3101681
Madras	700946	4430714	9980400	9473304	704885	612941	3691426	5008889
Bombay	10312928	3427325	4024512	4574284	5726162	5797603	12009360	4935159
Total ...	22122914	31334618	34982982	34543458	30874643	29502286	15475360	39099853

*Includes bearer since 1906.

Compiled from the Annual Finance and Revenue Accounts of the Government of India.

But in taking account of these benefactions it must not be supposed that, barring a solitary case or two, they were necessary in order to preserve the solvency of Provincial finance as it was defined by the terms of the settlement made with the different provinces. Far from being insufficient, the revenues settled upon the different Provinces proved quite ample for their needs if we take the last years, and they are the most typical years, into consideration.

Permanent Settlements of 1912

Soon after the series of quasi-permanent settlements were concluded with the different provinces, the subject of Provincial and Central Finance in British India among others of a like nature was investigated by the Royal Commission on Decentralisation. In its Report issued in 1909 the existing method of allocating revenue and charges between the Imperial and Provincial Governments was upheld in principle.

Of the many adverse criticisms passed by witnesses who appeared before the Commission only two were regarded by it as worthy of consideration: (1) The adjusting assignment and (2) Grants-in-aid, or doles as they were cynically termed. It was urged, and with some truth, that the adjusting assignments impaired the elasticity in provincial revenues by reason of the fact that while charges grew, that part of the provincial resource, which was made up by assignments, and in some cases it formed quite an appreciable part, remained unaltered. Secondly, it was argued that doles were demoralising and that it would be better to replace them by shares in growing revenue.

The Commission seems to have been completely impressed by the disadvantages of large adjusting assignments, but it demurred, and rightly so, to the criticisms with regard to the doles.

Every one extolled the benefits of decentralisation to the Provinces, but few realised the anxieties that it involved to the Government of India. It must have been clear that by the process of decentralisation the Government of India had given the Provinces more or less complete freedom in distributing their funds in any way they liked upon the services delegated to their management, while it had remained responsible for their efficient upkeep by the provisions of the law which governed its constitution.

But the freedom which the provinces had obtained in carrying on the financial management of the services made over to their particular control, involved the possibility of their fostering certain services deemed to be of immediate utility to the people of the Provinces, and neglecting others the utility of which, though remote to the Provinces, was nevertheless real to the country as a whole. Neglect of nationally important services such as Education, Sanitation, Police, was especially to be avoided during periods of plague and famine. But the Government of India could not enforce distribution of provincial funds on such services; for one of the vital conditions of Provincial Finance was freedom of appropriation on provincialised services, which were not distinguished into obligatory and optional as is the case in the continental system of local finance.

The Government of India was indeed not as powerless as the Central Government in England which, as is well known, cannot rectify cases of neglect by local authorities without resort to a writ of *mandamus*. But the way to bring a recalcitrant province to order, if easier, was not pleasant.

For, the only way to mend such a situation was to end it by suspending the operation of Provincial finance. Rather than resort to such a grave measure the Government of India happily hit upon grants-in-aid of particular services as a powerful and well-tried corrective to the negligence of the Province, and require it to maintain a" national minimum "in those services which it regarded as onerous rather than beneficial.

Convinced of the virtue of grants-in-aid as a brake on decentralisation degenerating into disintegration, the Commission only recommended that measures be taken to give Provincial Finance the greatest elasticity possible by diminishing the assignments to the smallest magnitude possible.

Following the recommendations of the Commission the Government of India decided to make certain modifications in the existing allocation of revenue and charges and to make the quasipermanent settlements permanent settlements from the year 1912. The permanent settlements did not differ from the quasipermanent settlements which they superseded in any material point so far as the principle of allocation was concerned. The only point of difference between them in that respect was a partial replacement of the fixed adjusting assignments by increased shares in the following joint heads of revenue and expenditure :—

Modifications in Shares

Revenues	
Heads of Account	Provincial Share
1. Land Revenue including the portion credited to Irrigation	5/8 to Burma 1/2 Punjab
2. Excise	Wholly in Eastern Bengal and Assam, Bombay. In C.P Bengal and U.P.3/4
Assessed Taxes	
3. (P.W.D.)	1/2
4. Forest	Wholly.
5. Major Irrigation works (excluding portion of Land Revenue credited to it).	1/2 in Punjab, minimum of 4 lakhs guaranteed.
6. Major and Minor Irrigation.	1/2 in Bengal

Expenditure	
Heads of Account	Provincial Share
1. Land Revenue	5/8 Burma ½ Punjab
2. Excise	Same as in revenue Column.
4. Forest	Wholly
5. Major Irrigation	½
6. Major and Minor Irrigation.	1/2/ in Bengal

The effect of these modifications in the shares in the joint heads of revenue and expenditure was to reduce the adjusting assignments to the following figures :—

Province	Assignments in Lakhs of Rupees from Imperial to Provincial	From Provincial to Imperial
Central Provinces...	21.40	
Burma...	13.12	
Eastern Bengal and	13.55	
Assam... Bengal...		18.40
U.P.		19.26
Punjab...	6.77	
Madras...		21.43
Bombay...		9.38

During the permanent as during the quinquennial and quasi-permanent settlements the grants-in-aid of specific services, unobjected to as they were by the Decentralisation Commission, were continued to be given to the different Provinces throughout the period although, as may be seen from the following figures, in a continually diminishing magnitude:—

It was natural that the results of the permanent settlement should have been more anxiously awaited for with great interest by the Provinces, for the permanent settlement had the potentiality of a permanent gain or a permanent loss.

That their anxiety on that score could not but have been completely allayed is amply supported by the repeated surpluses that meet the eye as it passes over the following figures of annual additions to and deductions from their balances during the period of its currency :—

Special Grants-in-aid (in Rupees)

Provinces	1912-13	1913-14	1914-15	1915-16	1916-17	1917-18	1918-19
C.P.	4790480	2643264	5138256	4407802	3795784	3817540	2726008
Burma	8536948	2263939	38497G3	3869472	216979	2478482	2490
Assam	5530991	3283011	7533878	6577619	2497661	1922252	2444730
Bengal	15401885	6480800	7594894	7186436	6538732	7074773	9669717
Bihar & Orissa	6379420	4761028	3526567	4278654	3262214	4235205	4179425
U.P.	11470603	8542279	3842624	3229924	2453969	2706164	3590530
Punjab	6700924	2424404	3988117	5908923	4925830	4862616	5563665
Madras	12277591	5066343	1697803	1220785	1099165	1483708	1577446
Bombay	11192723	3996729	1468837	1200254	1065964	1154725	2479510
Total	82283565	39461797	38640739	37880069	25856498	24778501	35453521

Compiled from the Annual Finance and Revenue Accounts of the Government of India.

Provincial Surpluses or Deficits (in Rupees)

Provinces	1912-13	1913-14	1914-15	1915-16	1916-17	1917-18	1918-19
C.P.	5085246	1881245	-3544416	-13836	4235704	4870517	920121
Burma	8874174	914026	-3729808	1896621	9427702	12067708	4873587
Assam	3610494	-2217691	-4550789	658812	6044904	2800634	435872
Bengal	14705270	480842	-3967607	1028156	3708838	5280082	732237
Bihar & Orissa	7022199	-920062	-1870264	1133562	5919907	7176786	3643564
U.P.	9588749	50704	-4611080	-973090	3427808	-2268311	3686945
Punjab	7411069	—692512	-3730641	-1133541	500995	-695216	1185930
Madras	4330275	-5298411	-1207754	318508	2571241	1042303	-972354
Bombay	7083281	1558566	-2639924	-951099	122434	611321	1681066

Compiled from the Annual Finance and Revenue Accounts of the Government of India.

While the condition of Provincial Finance was thus undoubtedly prosperous, the erratic movements in the provincial balances do not quite bear out the hope of orderly progress that was entertained of the permanent settlement.

It should be noted, however, that the period during which the permanent settlement was current was not wholly a normal period.

Part of the permanent settlement was no doubt a peace period, but it was not even as long as a quinquennium, and it should not on that account detract from the merits of a permanent settlement if it disclosed the faults of the quinquennial settlements.

Most of the period covered by the permanent settlement was, however, a period of the Great War, the abnormal events of which could not have had any but disturbing effects on Provincial Finance.

Whether the permanent settlements would have been adequate for the purpose in view if sufficient length of time had been allowed for conditions to have become settled it is not given to us to say.

For, from April 1, 1921, provincial Finance in British India entered on an entirely new phase. That phase of it will be dealt with in another part.

Here the study of the growth of Provincial Finance as it developed stage by stage under the old phase comes to an end. But this study will not be complete until we deal with the mechanism which inter-related the finances of the Central and Provincial Governments under the old phase.

But before we proceed to do so it might be of interest as well as of value that the study of the final stage in the development of Provincial Finance were to close with the following retrospect of provincial revenue and expenditure which shows, as nothing else can, the small beginnings, the large strides and the vast proportions that Provincial Finance had reached during the half century over which it had been allowed to run its course.

Growth of Provincial Finance

Provinces	Provincial Revenues As a percentage of the total Revenues of India						Provincial Expenditure As a percentage of the total Expenditure of India					
	1871-2	1882-3	1892-3	1904-5	1912-3	1918-9	1871-2	1882-3	1892-3	1904-5	1912-3	1918-9
C.P. ...	.655	1.055	.863	.905	2.52	1.715	.652	1.008	.87	.984	2.19	1.685
Burma ...	.572	1.66	2.256	3.023	4.73	3.57	.592	1.914	2.16	3.31	4.14	3.15
Bengal ...	2.8	5.9	4.72	4.12	5.56	4.00	2.7	6.68	4.52	4.26	4.56	3.84
N.W.P.andOudh	1.99	4.16	3.6				2.04	4.4	3.32			
Punjab ...	1.66	1.59	1.888	2.08	3.96	3.11	1.55	2.165	2.03	1.83	3.47	2.81
Madras ...	1.595	3.32	3.3	2.88	6.27	4.75	1.61	3.24	3.4	3.09	6.1	4.53
Bombay...	1.8	4.9	4.49	4.05	6.17	5.45	1.836	5.08	4.4	3.77	5.7	5.00
Assam ...		.61	.738	.597	1.38	1.00		.505	.617	.618	1.13	.857
U.P. ...				2.99	5.5	4.15				3.01	4.87	3.94
Bihar and Orissa					2.6	1.9					2.11	1.775
Total Provincial	11.11	22.8	21.75	20.4	38.6	29.2	10.8	25.00	21.3	20.8	34.3	27.6

Complied from the Annual Finance and Revenue Accounts of the Government of India.

5

Provincial Finance: Its Mechanism

The Limitations of Provincial Finance

To those who might be expected to have a knowledge of the anomaly—unparalleled in the annals of administration—involving the existence of provincial Government without there being the necessary complement of Provincial Finance, the study could not but have been of profound interest as disclosing the manner in which the anomaly created in 1833 was rectified or seemed to be rectified in 1870.

There, however, prevails the idea that Provincial Finance existed tong before 1870, But this is undoubtedly an error which may as well be corrected in this place by briefly recalling the history of financial decentralisation prior to 1870. The year 1855 will always stand pre-eminent in the history of decentralisation of Indian Finance. It is from that year that local Finance dated its origin. It must not, however, be supposed that prior to 1855 there were no local revenues. On the contrary, there were very small funds such as Ferry Funds, Toll Funds, Cesses, etc., in existence and were spent on improvements of local utility, but the important point to note is that the balances from such funds were not carried to a separate account but as a rule merged in the general balances of the country, with the exception probably of Bengal and North-Western Provinces, where it seems that such balances were carried to separate local Fund Accounts (of. *Calcutta Review,* 1851, Vol. 16, pp. 464 and 466).

It was by the Financial Resolution of May 11,1855, that local Funds were completely separated from Imperial Funds and were treated as "Deposits "—a sub-division of the Account Head "Debt "(cf. *Accountant's Manual,* by Y. Venkatramaiah, Part I, Madras, 1866, p. 79) and by the Resolution of September, 1863, local Finance was established on a separate footing by the institution for each of the different provinces of a distinct local Fund Budget as separate from the Imperial Budget. It so happened that in the absence of local authorities the Government of India entrusted the task of the preparation and execution of the local Funds Budget to the respective Provincial Governments as being more in touch with local wants. It is this accident that has betrayed many into the supposition that this was essentially Provincial Finance. But nothing can be a greater blunder. What existed before 1870 was local Finance, pure and simple, although under the supervision of the Provincial Government, in whose hands the local Funds were essentially a kind of trust.

The mere bringing together by the Provincial Governments of the receipts and charges pertaining to the local Funds into a local Fund Account for the whole Province can hardly be interpreted to mean the amount to be at their disposal—and that is the only sense in which Provincial Finance can be a reality—any more than the bringing together of the local Rates levied in the United Kingdom in the budget of the Chancellor of the Exchequer can give an indication of its financial position. The local Funds were not at the disposal of the Provincial Governments, for they could not be disposed of on purposes other than those which attached to them. In this sense they constituted local Finance and not Provincial Finance. Some people mistake it for Provincial Finance probably because the term "local Government" is used as a synonym for Provincial Government. But, while local and Provincial Governments are often used as interchangeable terms, it must be remembered local and Provincial Finance cannot be so used.

As a matter of fact, there was a period in the history of Financial organisation in India during which there was local Finance without local Government to be precise, and there was no Provincial Finance, even though there were Provincial

Governments. It is probable that, as tong as the habit of speaking of Provincial Government as local Government continues, this confusion of ideas will not entirely vanish. While some have insisted that Provincial Finance had its being tong before 1870, the Resolution of December 14, 1870, which instituted the scheme of Provincial Finance, is called * Resolution on local Finance "as though it gave rise to local and not Provincial Finance. Such absurdities can be avoided only by insisting upon precision of terminology.

On a purely a priori consideration of the matter, nothing could have been more natural than to suppose that the system of Provincial Finance thus established in British India was independent in its organisation. Indeed it is difficult to imagine how one could emerge from the study of its origin and development without such a faith having silently grown upon him. But if Provincial Finance was independent in its organisation, we should find the Provinces in possession of financial powers which are commonly associated with the functioning of independent States. For the immediate purpose of finding out whether or not Provincial Finance was an independent system of finance, we may take the freedom of budgeting and everything that is involved in it as an evidence of the existence of these powers. Independent budget powers would involve the power to determine the services which, according to the needs of the country, a good government should undertake, and to decide upon the mode of raising either by taxation or loan sufficient money to meet the expenditure upon those services. Alongside these powers the budget system entails the obligation of keeping accounts and submitting them to independent audit.

Applying these tests to the Provincial Budget, the origin and growth of which have been treated in the foregoing parts of this study, we cannot predicate a tithe of the independence which characterises the budgets of sovereign States. On the contrary, the budget system introduced into India with regard to the different Provinces was accompanied by the most stringent limitations. They were given a budget *without its powers,* and they bore the obligations of accounts and audit just because they were left free within the limits of their budgets. Why these limitations were imposed will be explained when we come to scrutinise the ways of enlarging the scope of Provincial Finance, it must, however, be emphasised that these limitations formed an integral part of the scheme, and the stringency of the former had grown *pan passu* with the scope and proportions of the latter. In fact they defined the law of the Constitution of Provincial Budgets. A complete comprehension of the operation of Provincial Finance in British India is therefore not possible without a thorough knowledge of its rules of government. Such being the importance of these rules it cannot but be to our advantage to analyse them at this stage.

These rules were laid down on various occasions during the interval between 1870, when the scheme of Provincial Finance came into being, and 1912, when the scheme reached through an evolutionary process its final and permanent stage, in the form of Resolutions of the Government of India in the Department of Finance. The rules framed in 1870 were few and simple. Nor was there any necessity for a complex code to govern the operation of the very meagre budgets which were then constituted. Many supplementary rules were issued afterwards to dispose of unforeseen cases of order and procedure; but it was not till 1877 that we come across a most elaborate set of rules and regulations governing the financial transactions of the provincial Government.

The Rules of 1877 were the basis of all those that were subsequently issued. With very small addenda or corrigenda they remained in force for a period of fifteen years, when they were superseded by a new series of Rules promulgated in 1892. But only within a short span of a quinquennium this series was replaced by another issued in 1897, and the latter formed the governing body of Rules till the year 1912, when a new series was brought out to regulate the working of the permanent settlement made in that year.

The same was reissued in the Financial Department Resolution No. 361 -E-A. dated July 24, 1916. But as the alterations therein were not in any sense consequential, the series of 1912 may be taken as laying down the final regulations of Provincial Finance.

Recognise as we must the necessity for analysing the rules, we must determine beforehand the point or points of view from which to conduct the analysis. It must be premised at the outset that the object of entering upon the examination of the Rules is twofold : (1) to know what limitations there were and (2) why they were placed. Our immediate interest, it is true, is to state what limitations there were, but this is only a preliminary, if not a minor, object. The second is really the more important of the two. It is only as an aid to the proper understanding of the causes of the necessity for these limitations that knowledge of them is to be sought. While keeping in our mind the immediate object of stating the limitations, it will be unimaginative not to foresee that in the following chapter, in which we shall be presently engaged, we will learn that the necessity for these limitations arose from the very peculiar nature of Provincial Finance itself.

On the other hand, it is important to anticipate this conclusion, and instead of producing the Rules *seriatim* as they occur, arrange them in such a way that they shall be an external register of the internal conception of Provincial Finance which particularly pervaded the minds of its promoters. For the consummation of this end, the labours of the officials in charge of Provincial Finance who have laid down these rules are of no avail.

To them these rules were only instruments of financial control, and it did not therefore matter in what order they were grouped. On the other hand, to get at the conception behind these rules it is necessary to classify and group them according to the purposes they were calculated to subserve. But the cardinal point in the matter of classification lies in defining the likely purposes which the originators of such an interrelated scheme of Provincial Finance as obtained in India must have had in view.

Without being at all dogmatic, it may be said that for a successful working of such a scheme rules would have to be laid down for the purposes of defining (1) the Administrative and (2) Financial Powers of the Provincial Government. Each of the two categories may be further subdivided for a clearer understanding of the nature of Provincial Finance. Thus the Rules relating to Administrative Powers may be further subdivided into those pertaining to (i) Services and (ii) Staff. Similarly the Rules defining the Financial Powers may be conveniently grouped under the following subsidiary categories : Those (i) of a general nature and those pertaining to (ii) Provincial revenues; (iii) Provincial Expenditure, (iv) Budget Sanction and (v) Audit and Account.

Taking purpose as the *fundamental divisions,* the above categories may be supposed to exhaust the possible purposes that the framers of the scheme may be said to have had in mind. On the basis of these categories we may therefore proceed to reduce the amorphous mass of Rules into a digest which, it may be hoped, will be convenient and instructive at the same time.

Limitations on Administrative Powers

Rules of Inter-Provincial Services

For regulating the inter-provincial or inter-departmental relations affected by the creation of separate budgets for the different

Provinces, it was ordained that:

(i) No inter-provincial adjustments were to be allowed.

(ii) No service previously rendered to other Departments at the charge of the Department made over to the control of the Provincial Governments was to be abolished, and no service previously rendered to these departments at the charge of other departments was to be increased.

(iii) No line of through communication was to be abandoned or allowed to fall out of repair.

Rules Pertaining to Staff

As to the staff engaged in the execution of the provincialised services the Provincial Governments were enjoined *not to:*

(i) Create a permanent appointment or augment the pay and allowance of any appointment.

Prior to 1912 this applied to appointments with a pay of Rs. 250 a month and above. But after 1912 it applied only to appointments ordinarily held by a Gazetted Officer or by an officer of the Imperial Service as defined in Article 29-B of the Civil Service Regulations.

(ii) Create a temporary appointments or deputation for an Officer.

Prior to 1912 this applied to appointments with a pay of Rs. 250 a month and above. But after 1912 it applied to such of the appointments the remuneration of which exceeded Rs. 2,500 a month, or Rs. 800 a month, if the temporary appointment or deputation was expected to last for more than two years'.

(iii) Abolish a permanent appointment or reduce the pay and allowances of such an appointment.

This rule was in the beginning applied to such appointments the remuneration of which exceeded Rs. 250 a month. After 1912 it was confined to such appointments as were held by Gazetted Civil Officers recruited in England or as were defined by Article 29-B of the Civil Service Regulations.

(iv) Grant to a Civil officer in Government employ or in receipt of a service pension.

(a) Land, except where the grant was made under the ordinary revenue rules of the Province concerned without involving any special concession in money or its equivalent beyond the fact that the grantee received the grant in preference to others or

(b) An assignment of Land Revenue when the amount exceeded Rs. 600 a year, or the assignment, though within that amount was not limited to three lives and reduced by one-half on each succession. All grants as assignments of Land Revenue made by Provincial Governments to civil officers were to be confined to cases in which the services were of a very distinguished and exceptional character.

(v) Revise

(a) permanent establishments which involved additional expenditure exceeding Rs. 50,000 a year; or (*b*) rates of substantive pay of any one branch of the service at a cost to that service alone of more than Rs. 25,000 a year, or

(*c*) the average pay of a service of which the maximum pay exceeded Rs. 500 a month and raise it above the average rate approved at the last revision of the service by the Secretary of State or the Government of India, or (d) the local allowances as compensation for dearness of living or for increase of rents in any locality.

Limitations on Financial Powers

General

Before actually detailing with the limitations on the financial powers of the Provincial Governments it is necessary to recall that the financial settlements made with the Provinces consisted in handing over to them certain *heads* of revenue and expenditure. From this accidental feature it is not to be supposed that the settlements were a collection of separate settlements for each head of revenue and expenditure incorporated into the Provincial Budget. To obviate such a construction by the Provincial Governments and the consequences thereof, it was ruled that:

(1) The Provincial Governments were to understand that the funds assigned to them formed a consolidated grant for all the services *en masse* entrusted to their respective administration and that no claim could therefore lie against the Imperial treasury on the ground that the actual cost of any service exceeded the amount at which it was estimated in the calculations of the consolidated grant.

(2) And they were not to make any extra demands on the Imperial treasury, but were bound to maintain from the funds given to them all the services entrusted to their management in a state of administrative efficiency. With regard to the powers of the Provincial Governments concerning the custody of their funds it was ruled :

(3) That the funds allotted for their use were to be lodged in the Imperial treasury, and were not to be removed for investment or deposit elsewhere; nor were the provincial Governments competent to withdraw such money except for expenditure upon the public services.

Revenue Rules

Turning from the general limitations to those pertaining to the revenues of the provinces, it should be noted that they were required to maintain themselves within the funds allotted to them by the Central Government at each settlement.

The provinces could not *augment* their resources beyond the yield due to their natural growth by any possible means, for it was provided that Provincial Governments were:

(i) Not to impose any additional taxation or make any change in the existing system of revenue management.

(ii) Not to alter or augment within its area the rates of discount upon the retail of Stamps, Court Fee labels, and duties on spirits and drugs.

(iii) Not to raise *for its own* finances any loans in the open market. Powerless in the matter of augmenting their resources, the Provincial Governments were not free to will them away to any other authority subordinate to them. To guard against such eventualities it was ruled that Provincial Government were

(iv) Not to alienate any item credited to the general revenues, Imperial or Provincial, so as to form an asset of a local or Special Fund. This provision as regards the non-alienation of the resources of revenue made over to the provinces was a little relaxed by the Rules of 1912 so that it was permissible for them to assign to a local body or special fund, as defined in Article 33 of Civil Service Regulations, constituted by law, petty items of Wholly Provincial Revenue of a recurring character, not derived from the proceeds of general taxation and not yielding on an average more than Rs. 25,000 a year.

(v) Not to make grants, subventions or assignments from

the funds at their disposal to local or Municipal bodies so as to create a permanent charge on the revenues of India.

This by no means prevented grants, subventions or assignments from being made to local or municipal bodies by the Provincial Governments from their funds although the Government of India had sounded to them a note of warning by declining to bind itself to continue the grants after the expiration of the settlements or to provide for them in the succeeding settlements. By the Rules of 1912, however, the power of making such grants was more clearly circumscribed so that a Provincial Government could not make (1) recurring grants to local bodies from provincial revenues exceeding Rs. 1,00,000 a year in any one case, or (2) non-recurring grants to local bodies exceeding Rs. 10,00,000 in any one *case* or (3) a grant to a charitable or religious institution other than educational, not being outside India, in excess of Rs. 10,000 a year if recurring, and Rs. 50,000 if non-recurring.

(vi) Not to make any grants to non-official (1) on political considerations of (a) land, either free of revenue, or on favourable terms, or (b) of assignment of land revenue, if the value of the land or land revenue exceeded Rs. 1,000 a year. (2) on the consideration of injury to himself or to his family in the event of his death during or in consequence of service rendered to Government, or (3) on the consideration of exceptional services to the Government of a pension exceeding Rs. 1,000 a year or a gratuity. exceeding Rs. 3,000 in any one case.

Rules of Expenditure

The powers of sanctioning expenditure granted to the Provincial Government were as limited as their revenue powers. While they were free to spend their funds on the services entrusted to them, certain limitations were laid down for the purposes of expressly ruling out certain objects and subjects of expenditure from the provincial domain.

With regard to the *objects* of their expenditure Provincial Governments were required:

(i) Not to sanction any expenditure from public money on anything outside the category of objects of expenditure recognised by the Government of India.

(ii) To confine themselves to the carrying on of the services particularly entrusted to them by the terms of the settlement.

Prior to 1912 they could undertake a "new general service or duty" only if they satisfied the Government of India that they could provide the necessary funds temporarily if it was temporary, and permanently if it was permanent. This provision was altered in 1912 so that a Provincial Government could undertake a new general service or duty provided it was not *(a)* of an unusual nature, or *(b)* devoted to objects outside the ordinary work of administration, or (c) likely to involve at a later date expenditure beyond its powers of sanction.

(iii) Not to spend;

(a) On State ceremonies and assemblies, and on the entertainment at the public charge of distinguished visitors to India more than Rs. 1,00,000.

(b) On Railway Carriages especially reserved for the use of high officials otherwise than in connection with the maintenance of the carriage.

(c) On the purchase of a Motor-car or Motor-cycle for the use of an official, or on the maintenance of it otherwise than from the "Contract Grant" with the Head of the province.

(d) On the increase of the "Contract Grant" to the Head of the province.

(e) On the construction or purchase of a vessel required for inland navigation and for use at ports, the cost of which exceeded Rs. 1,00,000.

(f) On an Irrigation or other Public Works projects of which the estimated cost chargeable to the general revenues exceeded Rs. 20,00,000 inclusive of establishments, tools and plants. It was however competent for a Provincial Government to spend up to an amount 10 percent in excess of the original sanctioned estimate provided such excess was not more than Rs.12 1/2 lakhs inclusive of establishment, tools and plants.

As to the limitations respecting the subjects of provincial expenditure, it was ruled that in virtue of the application of the general condition precedent to the delegation of all authority to disburse public money, that it shall be bona fide for a public purpose, Provincial Governments could not spend from their funds for benefiting:

(i) Any individual or body of private persons unless in accordance with some declared or established rule or principle recognised by the Government of India.

(ii) Native States, directly beyond Rs. 10,000 a year on any one project or Rs. 50,000 if non-recurring.

Budgetary Rules

Besides being subject to the ordinary rules of the Budget System introduced into India for the first time by Mr. Wilson in 1860, by which they were required to submit their budget estimates for sanction to the Government of India, and to observe the rules of appropriation in the execution of the grants, Provincial Governments were further given to understand that without the previous consent of the Government of India they:

(i) Could not exhaust their balances in the Imperial Treasury.

Prior to 1887 a Provincial Government could propose in its budget estimates to draw upon the whole of its balance. But by the Rules then framed the Provincial Government was required to maintain at all time a certain minimum balance in the Imperial treasury, the amount of which varied with each successive settlement.

(ii) Could not budget for a deficit, that is for provincial expenditure in excess of the provincial revenues of the year.

The stringency of this rule was a little softened, so that a Province could after 1912 budget for a deficit, if it satisfied the Government of India that the cause was exceptional and non-recurring but it was at the same time provided that, if this drawing upon the balances to make up the deficits resulted in reducing the balance below the prescribed minimum, the budget for a deficit would be sanctioned only if the Government of India was able to allow the Provincial Government in question an overdraft to the extent necessary to restore the balance to the required minimum from the general balances to be repaid in such rates of interest and instalments as may be prescribed.

(iii) Could not exceed during the currency of the year the expenditure on any head of account as finally sanctioned for it, for that year, by the Government of India.

It could increase the expenditure only if the increase was counterbalanced by re-appropriation, that is, reduction by the amount of the excess of the sanctioned grant under some other head of account under its control. The powers of reappropriation of Provincial Governments were very extensive, for it could sanction re-appropriation between the grants for provincial expenditure included in its budget, whether under a Wholly Provincial or a Divided Major or Minor Head provided that the aggregate grant of provincial expenditure was not exceeded.

Rules of Audit and Account

Though the Provinces were allowed considerable powers of reappropriation within their budgets there was imposed upon them the obligation of audit and accounts of the money they spent. The important point to note in this connection is the fact that this obligation of the keeping of accounts and submitting them to audit was an obligation which the Provinces did not owe to their legislatures, but was an obligation which they owed to the Government of India, who had conferred upon them the financial power they exercised. Moreover, the Government of India did not leave the Provinces to discharge this obligation according to their own sweet will by employing their own audit and account staff. On the contrary the responsibility of realising this obligation was entrusted to the imperial officers of audit and account stationed in the different Provinces, who acted as the critics and guides of Provincial Governments in the matter of administration and interpretation of the Rules discussed above. To facilitate their task Provincial Governments were instructed;

(i) Not to make any alterations in the form of procedure of public accounts or direct the division of a charge between two or more heads of account. In all such matters they were to abide by the decision of the Comptroller General—an officer of the Imperial Government.

(ii) To transmit the objection of the Imperial audit officer against its appropriation or sanction with regard to expenditure with the explanation of the Provincial Government concerned to the Government of India for final disposal.

Such were the limitations on the Financial Powers of the Provincial Governments. Apart from these specific limitations the Provincial Governments were not altogether the free architects of their own destiny within the sphere allotted to them; for it was provided that the power of supervision and control in any Department still rested in the Governor-General in Council, and that the Provincial Governments should keep him fully informed of their executive and financial proceedings so as to enable the former to discharge its obligations for peace, order and good government. Their general effect on the financial freedom of the Provinces could hardly have been concealed. It must therefore have been a most impervious mind which in face of these paralysing limitations had not lost its faith in the independence of the system of Provincial Finance and had not asked, what was after all the nature and advantage of this illusive institution ?

6

The Nature of Provincial Finance

The study of Provincial Finance cannot be said to be complete unless it furnishes a true answer to the question which is bound to be asked in the end, What was the resulting financial relationship under the old scheme between the Central and Provincial Governments in British India? The question is an important one, for the validity of the criticisms and proposals with regards to Provincial Finance, or any subject for that matter, depends entirely upon a correct understanding of its nature. Unfortunately it had not received the attention that its importance demanded, and consequently we find the rather distressing fact that no subject was so confidently discussed, and yet none was so grossly misunderstood, as that of the nature of the old system of Provincial Finance in British India. It therefore becomes necessary to explain what was the exact nature of the system of Provincial Finance established in British India.

In an inter-related system of politics, such as is composed of Central and Provincial Governments in British India, it is always difficult to grasp the exact nature of their financial relationship; for, what may appear on the surface may be very different from what it may really be. None the less, the view was commonly held that the Indian system was based on a separation of sources between the Provincial and the Central Governments, and contributions from the yield by the former to the latter, much the same as was found in the federal system of finance which obtained in the German Empire. Whether such a view was wrong or right there were various incidents of the relationship between the Central and Provincial Governments in India, which, there can be no doubt, went a tong way to strengthen that view.

Among such incidents must be mentioned the division of functions between the Central and Provincial Governments. An onlooker could not fail to observe that in this distribution of functions the former controlled matters pertaining to Military Affairs, Foreign Affairs, General Taxation, Currency, Debt, Tariffs, Posts and Telegraph, Railways and Adult and Accounts; while the latter administered matters of ordinary internal administration, such as Police, Education, Sanitation, Irrigation, Roads and Buildings, Forests, and the control over local Bodies.

If this incident encouraged the view that there was a separation of services, there was another incident of the relationship which encouraged the view there was also a separation of revenues between the Central and Provincial Governments in British India. That incident was the collection of most of the taxes in India by the agency of Provincial Governments. As observed by the Royal Commission on Indian Expenditure.

"in the United Kingdom the Revenue Administration is centralised..... under the Chancellor of the Exchequer in London. In India the administration of some branches of revenue is centralised, though not always under the Finance Minister (of the Government of India). That of other branches is decentralised. The Land Revenue is under the control of the Central Department at Calcutta, but that department is subject not to the Finance Minister but to the Minister in charge of the Home and Revenue Departments. The Telegraph Department is under the Minister of Public Works.

The Central Government controls the collection of part of the Salt duty and of part of the opium revenue, of Post Office revenue and of other revenues..... The remainder of the revenue is collected by the Provincial Governments.... As regards..... a large portion of the revenue, the Provincial Governments are units of administration and are efficiently equipped for their duties." As a third incident supporting the same view, reference must be made to the peculiar mode of presenting Indian Accounts adopted in official Blue Books. As might have been noticed, to the General Accounts of the Government of India is attached a supplementary account professing to show the distribution of the different heads of receipts and expenditure among the various Provinces into which British India has been divided. This mode of showing the accounts is beyond doubt misleading.

It appears as if the aim was to show the financial position of the Provinces. But as a matter of fact the figures given in the columns in which the revenues and charges are shown in their provincial distribution do not represent the respective claims and responsibilities of the different Provinces. Far from showing the financial position of the Provinces, the figures in the columns merely represent the geographical distribution of the different agencies through which the financial business of the Government of India is conducted, and through which the revenues are collected and the expenditure is defrayed.

The revenue and expenditure, for instance, shown under "Bombay" represent the income and out go which pass through the books of the Accountant General of the Government of India stationed at Bombay, and the same is true of entries under the heads of other Provincial Governments. The figures really represent the transactions of the Government of India distributed geographically, and there is nothing provincial about them in the least. However, such a system of account bears the impression that the system of finance in India is primarily Federal.

With these three incidents before one's mind it was easy to fall into a federal line of thinking in reasoning about the financial relationship between the Central and Provincial Governments in British India. So deep seated was the view that the Indian system was one of separation of sources and contributions from the yield, that many witnesses giving evidence before the Royal Commissions on Indian Expenditure

(1892) and on Decentralisation in British India (1909) sallied forth to assail the Commissioners with the criticisms on the inequity of the system and proposals for amending it according to what they considered to be the requirements of justice. Nowhere have they stated the reasons for their assumptions in explicit terms. Yet their proposals are an unmistakable proof that they held that view.

Unless they had taken for granted that the Provinces had separate revenues and separate services, they could not be expected to have wasted their energies in directing as they did their efforts to getting redressed what appeared to them as a piece of injustice embodied in the unequal contributions made by the different Provinces form their revenues to the support of the Central Government.

If their view of the financial relationship between the Central and Provincial Governments was acceptable, then a good deal could not but have been conceded in favour of their criticisms and their proposals. Contributions, if the Imperial share could have been conceived of in such a light, as between the different Provinces whether in ratio to their revenues or population, were certainly unequal if calculated on the somewhat questionable but generally accepted hypothesis that all the revenues collected within a Province belonged to the Province.

Similarly, whatever may be said of the relative merits of the proposals of changing the system of divided heads of revenue into one of complete separation supplemented in favour of the Central Government by contributions from the Provinces in the form of (1) a fixed sum revisable every few years, or (2) a lump percentage on provincial revenues, or (3) a fluctuating contribution from the provinces on their population, revenues or wealth, there can be no doubt that they were all aimed at reaching some such intelligible basis of distributing the burden of the Imperial exchequer as equality of payment or ability to pay. No one who had cared to scrutinise the true nature of Provincial Finance could have been expected to take these proposals with the same seriousness with which they were offered by their authors. However, strange as it may seem, none of the two Commissions questioned their propriety.

Provincial Contributions to the Imperial Government

Province	Ratio of Amount Surrendered to the Government of India to the Total Revenues raised in the Province.					Ratio of Amount Surrendered to the Government of India per Head to the Population of the Province.				
	1871-72	1882-83	1892-93	1904-05	1912-13	1871-72	1882-83	1892-93	1904-05	1912-13
C.P.	.655	.464	.615	.297	.204	.9	.69	1.3	.55	.59
Burma	.728	.575	.598	.497	.38	3.4	.39	.7	4.37	3.08
Assam		.438	.390	.376			.75	.75	.87	
Bengal N.W.P.and	.903	.746	.761	.742	.596	2.4 1.5	1.99	2.9 1.4	2.29	2.39
Oudh	.785	.617	.435				1.24			
Punjab	.768	.648	.726	.512	.391 .479	1.7 2.3	1.5	1.4	1.57	1.64
Madras	.828	.664	.667	.638			2.0	2.3	2.34	1.79
Bombay	.845	.648	.66	.614	.58 .381	5.0	4.1	5.4	4.75	5.6
U.P.				.567					1.48	93
Bihar and Orissa					.220					.17

Compiled from the Finance and Revenue Accounts of the Government of India and the Decennial Census Reports.

The Royal Commission on Decentralisation did make it clear, though not quite forcibly, that equal contributions were not necessarily equitable contributions, but neither it nor the Royal Commission on Indian Expenditure challenged the language which spoke of the Provinces as surrendering *their* revenues to make contributions to the Imperial treasury after paying for their services.

It therefore becomes all the more necessary to examine at some length the grounds which supported that view which argued that the system was based on the principle of separation of sources and contributions from the yield. Indeed the question of equity of contributions would hardly be worth discussion until it is settled that the Provinces had revenues which they could call their own and services for the efficient discharge of which they were primarily liable.

What is the criterion by which to judge whether the provinces had revenues and services which they could call their own? There is, of course, the administrative criterion by which it would be possible to say that anything which a Province administered was provincial. But that criterion cannot be a final criterion. For, whatever may be the view regarding the origin of administrative polities or regarding what their position should be in an ideal organisation, yet all regional rights of an administrative polity are in modern times exercised in the main, not in virtue of any social compact or the mere discharge of certain functions, but in virtue of a general law. The question must therefore be decided with reference to the law which defined the status of the Provincial Governments in British India.

Did the Provinces have a legal title to the revenues? Although it is uncertain whether or not those who spoke of Provincial revenues invested the term provincial with a legal status there is no doubt that it had acquired such a connotation in ordinary parlance. Even the Provincial Governments, who ought to have known better, thought and argued that by the provincialisation of revenue what the Government of India passed on to them was not the mere usufruct but a title to the revenue.

But the Government of India had always been prompt in suppressing such pretences. The facts are patent that provincial settlements were revisable every five years, that the usufruct was not perpetual and that the Government of India could resume it at the end of five years if it wanted. This is made quite clear in answer to the pretensions advanced by the Government of Bengal in a letter No. 284 of January 14, 1882, from which the following is extracted :—

"For the sake of diminution of friction and other well-known objects which need not be specified, the Imperial Government delegated a share in its administration to local Governments.

It makes a rough calculation that a certain portion of the general income, together with the increment thereon, will suffice to meet the expenditure which it retains under its own control, and it hands the rest over to local Governments, with the obligation to meet out of it certain necessary expenditure.... But it cannot bind itself to this proportion for ever, because the calculation must necessarily be a rough one, and is liable to be vitiated by unforeseen failure of resources, or growths of charges, whether in the share of financial administration which it retains or in that which it delegates. An examination of the appropriation and a readjustment of it in any particular found necessary are indispensable. A surrender of the right to this would be analogous in its nature and effects to the Permanent Settlement of Bengal."

Although anxiety was expressed for the provinces the revisions were primarily conducted in the interests of the Imperial Government as the resumption incontrovertibly proved, and the Permanent Settlement was delayed because the Government of India did not desire to relinquish its control over its revenues.

Under the quinquennial settlement the usufruct was permitted to be undisturbed for five years only. But how tentative was this surrender, which, even for five years, was looked upon as highly impolitic by the Secretary of State, was proved by the Government of India, which did not take back to exercise its inherent right to resume the usufruct of its revenues at any time it liked as is indicated by the not too uncommon levies or benevolence, as they were called, which it forced upon the provincial balances.

Not even the Permanent Settlement can be interpreted to mean that the revenues settled upon the different Provinces became their revenues in anything like a legal sense, for in the eye of the law all revenues including those provincialised still remained the constitutional possession of the Government of India. Whether the Government could have effected a legal separation by investing itself of the revenues of India in favour of the Provinces is doubtful. The Parliamentary enactment which vests the revenues of India in the Government of India had limited the legislative powers of the Government of India by a clause which prevented it from

"making any laws or Regulations which shall in any way repeal, vary, suspend or affect any of the provisions of this Act (of 1833).... or the Prerogative of the Crown or the Authority of Parliament."

At least it is significant that it has required an Act of Parliament to do so. But the Government of India had not made any legal separation of the title to the revenues, and if it could have done that by its own law it could have undone it as well. Nor can it be said that the separation of Provincial revenues involved separate possession. If the Provincial Governments had been allowed to establish their own treasuries to receive the collections from Provincialised revenues, then Provincial revenues in the sense of separate possession could have had a meaning. But by the rules, Provincial Governments were not to deposit their funds elsewhere than in the treasury of the Imperial Government.

Consequently the possession of the revenues remained in the hands of the Government of India and the disbursement from the provincial revenues was carried out from the Imperial Treasury by the officers of the Imperial Government. None the less, the view was hard to die. But such an erroneous view was never more confidently stated than by the Honourable Mr. Sayani, and never more forcibly controverted than by Sir James Westland in a passage-at-arms between the two on the occasion of a Budget debate in the Council Hall of the Government of India from which the following is reproduced :—

The Honourable Mr. Sayani said :—

"The whole theory underlying the system (of Provincial Finance) is that the revenues of the country, far from belonging to the Provinces which raise them or being available for their own requirements.... constitute a common fund to be absolutely at the disposal of the Central Government, out of which it is to dole out what amount it pleases for provincial services."

Catching the condemnatory tone of these comments, the Finance Minister, Sir James Westland, rose to say :—

"The Honourable Mr. Sayani, if I correctly followed him, stated that the arrangements of the Government of India were made upon the theory that the revenues were not the revenues of the separate Provinces and were not applicable to the expenditure of the several Provinces, but were the revenues of a common fund, the local Governments being merely the agents of the Government of India for their realisation. I think he mentioned the theory in some words like these, only for the purpose of condemning it. Well, I wish to assert that theory in the most positive manner I can. The revenues are the revenues of the Government of India—its Constitutional Possession. The Government of India is a body created by Act of Parliament, and if reference be made to that Act of Parliament it will be seen that the revenues of India are the revenues of the Government of India and of that Government alone. Every action that the local Government takes in respect of them must be justified by a specific order of the Government of India; the local Governments derive their powers entirely from the Government of India, and apart from that Government they exercise no financial powers whatsoever.

Again, if the financial relationship between the Central and Provincial Governments in India were based upon the principle of separation of sources and contributions from the yield, what ought to have been shown was the existence of legal responsibility of the Provinces for the services they administered. It is true there was a certain division of functions between the Central and Provincial Governments in India analogous to what existed between the Central and State Governments in most of the federal countries. But it must, however, be remembered that this division of functions had no sanction in law and no legal responsibility attached to the provinces for any of the services, not even for those Provincialised.

The entire responsibility by law rested on the shoulders of the Imperial Government and it could not absolve itself of that responsibility by transferring it on to any of the Provinces. That the Provinces accepted the financial responsibility for some of the Imperial services was their choice.

That they could not be compelled to undertake them was proved in a singular manner by Madras refusing to accept such responsibility in 1877. By law it was thus the Government of India which was responsible for peace, order and good government in the country. All services were therefore necessarily Imperial in status undertaken by the Government of India in discharge of its constitutional obligations.

It is therefore obvious that the view which posited that the relationship between the Central and Provincial Governments in British India was one of separation of sources and contributions from the yield was an untenable view.

The Government of almost every country in these days is carried on by an inter-related group of polities operating in specific areas and discharging specific public functions ; and it may well be that in any two given countries the number of polities engaged in carrying on the work of government is the same. But it is quite erroneous to argue from that fact that the nature of their inter-relationship must have been alike.

It is therefore as well to invite attention to the point that the ordered relationship between such inter-related polities depends upon which of them is the law-giving polity. It will be granted that in such group of polities there is one that is supreme in the sense that from a variety of reasons mostly historical it is competent to give law to the other polities. In federal countries it is the State Governments which are the law-giving polities.

They occupy a pivotal position. They are the depositories of sovereign powers original as well as residuary. They can claim independent existence, have their own resources and discharge their own functions. The Federal Government, on the other hand, is the creature of the State Governments. It can have no powers and no functions other than those which the States have been pleased to transfer to it by an act of self-abnegation. It is therefore truthful as well as becoming to speak of the financial relationship between the State and Federal governments as one of separation of sources and contributions from the yield.

For there the States have their separate resources which they lawfully own and can therefore be spoken of as surrendering their revenues to make contributions to the Central Government after paying for their own services. But the same was inconsistent with the position of the Provincial Governments. Far from pivotal, the Provincial Governments formed the weakest entities in the group of administrative polities functioning in India. Up to 1833 the Provinces had separate rights to surrender in a *foedus* and had the government of India been then organised on a federal basis the position of the Provinces would have been very much the same as those of the States in federal countries.

But with the establishment of the Imperial system by the Act of 1833 the last chance of creating a federation in India vanished. By that Act the sovereignty of the Provinces was so entirely crushed that no trace was left of it to permit of a truly federal element ever to enter into their relationship with the Central Government.

Since that Act the government of the country has been entrusted to a single authority charged with the sole responsibility for the good government of the country. As no single administration could support the Atlantean load of governing such a vast country with the help of central bureaux, great powers were delegated to the Provincial Governments. But this must not obscure the fact that they were literally the "agents of the Government of India." Common usage had elevated the term "Provincial" to a proud position. Along with

Provincial Revenues it had been usual to speak of Provincial Services, Provincial Civil Servants, Provincial Courts, etc., as if all these and other things constitutionally belonged to the Provincial Governments. But the usage was full of irony.

For, when one recalls the provisions of the constitutional law of the land, so far from thinking of them as Sovereign authorities one felt inclined to say that notwithstanding their high-sounding apparatus of Governors and Councils it was not appropriate to call them Governments. In any case the Provincial Governments had no legal powers or functions which polities designated as Governments have been known to possess. The fact is the Indian system of polity was diametrically opposed to the federal system of polity. It was a centralised system in which there was nothing Provincial; what appeared to be Provincial was but the regional aspect of the Imperial. It was therefore untruthful and over becoming to speak of the financial relationship between the Provincial and Central Governments in India as being one of separation of sources and contributions from the yield.

For here the Provinces had no separate resources which they lawfully owned, and could not therefore be spoken of as surrendering their revenues to make contributions to the Central Government after paying for what may be supposed to have been their own services—a supposition rigorously excluded by the law of the constitution.

If the complex code of limitations discussed in the last chapter had the effect, which it was not unreasonable to expect, of revealing the true nature of Provincial Finance, such a view as the one herein criticised could never have prevailed. That notwithstanding the existence of these limitations there should have been men who instead of wondering as to what remained of Provincial Finance when it was regulated by such limitations, argued with the confidence of the ignorant that the system was independent in its organisation, is itself a proof that in their study of Provincial Finance the study of its limitations formed no part.

Otherwise a reference to that code would have shown that if the Provinces had separate revenues and separate services they would have had powers of alienating whatever revenues they liked, of spending on any service they desired, of framing their Budget Estimates with a view to any particular policy they decided to adopt, and of arranging for supplementary grants in any manner they chose. But such powers they never had. Indeed no greater proof could be furnished in support of the view that everything had remained imperial in status after 1870, as it was before 1870, than is afforded by these limitations on the working of Provincial Finance.

If separation of sources and contributions from the yield as a theory of the financial relationship between the Central and Provincial Government in India was incompatible with the facts of the case, what theory was there which could be said to have been compatible with the position as defined by law? We may at once proceed to state that the only theory of financial relationship between the two governments which accorded with facts and agreed with law was that of aggregation of the sources and distribution of the yield.

It may seem fallacious to speak of aggregation of sources when what the Government of India gave to the Provinces was assignment of revenues and shares of revenues. To this the reply is not difficult. It has already been made clear that Provincial Finance did not involve a *de jure* separation of sources. Nor was there a *de facto* separation either. For as has been remarked before, all revenues whether assigned or reserved were collected into the Imperial treasury and were thence paid out on all approved Government transactions. Obviously, when all the revenues are thrown into a common pool, it cannot be said without unduly straining the imagination that what the Provinces were given were revenues.

The collections from all sources of revenue being inextricably mixed up, the only proper view is to say that what was given to the Provinces were funds. The expressions Budget by Assignments, Budget by Assigned or Shared Revenues are in a certain sense all fictitious phrases. In all the stages of Provincial Finance what the Provinces were supplied with were funds. Under the assignment stage the supply granted was a definitely fixed sum and the only difference made as a consequence of the replacement of Assignments by Assigned or Shared Revenues was that the supply, instead of being a fixed sum, was a sum which varied in amount with variations in the yield of the Assigned or Shared Revenues.

But all the same it was a supply of funds and nothing more. It is even incorrect to say that the Government of India *gave* funds to the Provincial Governments for meeting the expenditure on the services the responsibility for which was undertaken by them. As a matter of fact, the receiving as well as the disbursing of all public money, including the provincial portion of it, remained in the hands of the Government of India. The only proper expression, if it is to be true to facts, would be to say that Provincial Finances simply meant that the Government of India opened a Provincial Services Account in its Treasury books which varied with the yield of the Assigned or Shared Revenues and on which and to its extent only the Provincial Governments were permitted to draw.

Thus there was a complete aggregation of the sources of revenue in the hands of the Government of India. From this fact it follows that instead of the Provinces contributing from their funds it was the Government of India which distributed the yield of its taxes among the Provinces. The situation could not be otherwise. For it should be recalled that in virtue of the Act of 1833 the financial responsibility for the services undertaken to subserve the ends of peace, order and good government rested upon the Government of India. While some of the services were administered directly by the Government of India, owing to the well-nigh impossibility of managing directly from a central bureau the affairs of a country as vast as the continent of Europe minus Russia, many of the services attaching to the Imperial Government were left to be administered under its supervision by the Provincial Government.

The weak point of the situation, as has been remarked, consisted in the fact that the administrative and financial responsibility did not rest on one and the same authority as should have been the case. On the other hand at the end of every financial year all Provincial Governments sent in their estimates of the charges for the services they administered to the Government of India in the Financial Department, leaving the obligation of refusing, curtailing or granting the supply asked for to the Government of India to discharge as best it could. Not having the obligation to find the money, the Provinces tended to make extravagant demands.

And the Government of India, not being in possession of the details, was unable to judge of the true requirements of each service. Being afraid of failure of its responsibility as much by too little trust as by too much trust in the estimates sent to it, it was often obliged to submit to extravagance of the Provinces, which as we saw brought on the crisis of 1859. To avoid this fatality there was instituted the system of Provincial Finance under which the Government of India distributed its funds among the Provinces, and the Provinces in their turn undertook to manage *some* of the services which they administered for the Government of India *within* the sum which came to them severally out of this distribution.

This being the nature of the financial relationship, the criticisms of the system of Provincial Finance on the ground of inequity were quite inapplicable. Contributions must be according to ability, but distribution must be according to needs in order to make it equitable. If the system of Provincial Finance was to be impeached on the ground of inequity, then it was necessary to have shown that the distribution was unfair. Even here it may perhaps be shown that the different Provinces got different amounts if measured by their population or their area. But it must be remembered that the distribution was not primarily among the Provinces, but among the various departments, whether controlled by the Government of India or by the Provincial Governments.

This could make a considerable difference in the equity of the distribution; for, the needs of the areas within the jurisdiction of the different administrative polities must be very different and cannot certainly be held to be coterminous with the needs of the departments maintained under them. The distribution of funds by the Government of India was not based upon the principle of each Province according to its needs but upon the principle of each department according to its needs. It was therefore futile to criticise the equity of the system on any other principle.

Thus interpreted, the system of Provincial Finance must strike as of the nature of what may be called Departmental Finance, something quite different from Decentralised Finance or Federal Finance. This view cannot be far wrong from the true view as supported by the facts of the case. As in the case of Departmental Finance every Department of the State has a certain grant fixed for it in the Budget and it then draws upon the Treasury to the extent of the grant. In the same manner Provincial Governments were given a certain consolidated grant for the departments they managed and for the expense of which they were to draw upon the Imperial Treasury to the extent of the grant. Notwithstanding Provincial Finance, nothing was provincial in its status.

The revenues, the services, the Civil Service, were as strictly Imperial in status after 1870, when Provincial Finance came into being, as they were before 1870, when there was no such thing as Provincial Finance in existence. It is therefore no exaggeration to say that Provincial Finance, instead of being an independent system of Finance involving freedom to tax and freedom to spend, was only a matter of accounts, the operations on the debit and credit side of which were subject to stringent control on the part of the Government of India.

This means that there was no change in the nature of the financial relationship between the Central and Provincial Governments as a result of the introduction of the scheme of Provincial Finance. The relationship of aggregation of sources and distribution of the yield was not a new one but was as old as 1833. It was a financial counterpart of the Imperial system then established.

It was because there was no alteration in the relationship that Provincial Governments, even with Provincial Finance, far from becoming separate clocks, each with its own mainsprings in itself, remained as before the departments of the Government of India. Such a conclusion is bound to be regarded as somewhat of a startling character.

There can, however, be no doubt that it is true and that no other conclusion is possible, given the legal relationship of the Provincial and Central Governments in British India. But if Provincial Finance is only a matter of accounts then, were there no changes that followed in its wake, in the financial organisation of the Imperial system? It would be idle to deny that any change took place in the financial organisation of Imperial system owing to the introduction of the scheme of Provincial Finance, and equally idle to assert that some fundamental change had taken place in consequence thereof.

To be just, only two changes worth speaking of may be said to have resulted from the introduction of Provincial Finance:

(1) Before 1870 balances on *all* services lapsed to the Government of India at the close of the financial year. After 1870 all unspent balances on the services delegated to the management of Provincial Governments remained at their disposal and formed a part of their resources for the ensuing year.

(2) Before 1870 Budget estimates on ail services had to be sanctioned by the Government of India and the Provinces could not undertake any reappropriations between the different grants for the year, even if it was found necessary, without the previous sanction of the Government of India. After 1870 the Provinces were left to a greater extent free to distribute their expenditure in any way they thought proper among the various services delegated to their management, provided their total expenditure did not exceed the funds lying in the Imperial treasury to their credit respectively.

But by the rules they were required to maintain all the services under their management in a state of administrative efficiency. Similarly after 1870 the Provincial Government had complete freedom which they never enjoyed before to carry on reappropriations between the grants under their management without the sanction of the Government of India, provided their total expenditure did not exceed the amount budgeted for the year.

For the purposes of visualisation the financial relationship between the Provinces and the Government of India may be likened to the Hindu Joint Family System with the Patria Potestas vested in the latter. Before 1870 the similarity between the two was more or less exact. Like the family property of the Hindus the revenues of India were jointly enjoyed by all the departments whether under Central or Provincial management without metes and bounds being fixed to the shares of any one of them. After 1870 the only change that took place consisted in the cesser of commensality and the fixing of metes and bounds to the shares of each in the common property according to their respective needs. The system remained a joint family system, although separate accounts were opened by the head of the family, namely the Government of India, to guard against any member overdrawing the amount placed to his credit.

Were these results worth striving for? On the results achieved in consequence of Provincial Finance a variety of opinion has been expressed. But if we judge of the results as we ought to in the light of the antecedents that gave rise to the system in 1870, it cannot be said that the hopes entertained were in any way belied. It is only when critics, solely because of their misunderstanding of the nature of Provincial Finance, sought for results which were never intended by its promoters that an adverse pronouncement came to be made. But if we keep clear of these misunderstandings and never lose sight of the fact that in 1870 what the Provinces wanted was freedom and the Government of India stability, none can assert that this compromise between Imperialism and Federalism was tried in vain.

How great was the freedom gained by the provinces can be appreciated only when it is realised that before 1870 the Governor of Bengal could make "no alteration in the allowances of the public servants.... establish a new school or augment the pay of a daroga (watchman) to the extent of a Rupee"

nor could the Governor of Bombay have. a lock made without a vote of the Council of India. Nor can the importance of the large measure of stability derived from it be fully realised unless it is borne in mind how before 1870 the Government of

India was left between the devil and the deep sea by having to refuse or to accept the bewildering demands ranging from dustbins for a Department to education for the people made by the Provinces on its not too large resources. The Provincial Governments had been saved the delay and the indignity in having to depend upon the Government of India for sanction of the meanest of their wants.

The Imperial Government on the other hand was saved the fumbling task of scrutinising the most trivial of demands and grant or reject it, but always under the apprehension of having done wrong by acting either way. The system not only gave freedom to the Provinces and stability to the Government of India, but had replaced the irresponsibility and extravagance which had proved the bane of the Imperial System by economy and responsibility, for by setting bounds to the funds of the Provincial Governments the Government of India had ended in setting bounds to itself.

These results, it is true, did not satisfy the critics of Provincial Finance. More in other directions was expected of it, but that could have been possible only if Provincial Finance was a system independent in its organisation. So tong as Provincial Finance was a part of Imperial Finance, inseparably linked to it, it could have yielded no greater results than have followed from it, and those that have followed are by no means slight.

There, however, remains the question that, although it was not possible to alter the nature of Provincial Finance, whether it would not have been feasible to enlarge its scope by relaxing the limitations imposed upon it by the Government of India without in any way interfering with the due discharge by it of its own responsibilities. That aspect of the question will be examined in the next chapter.

The Enlargement of the Scope of Provincial Finance

It used to be made a matter of complaint that the system of Provincial Finance was unjust in that under it the Government of India conscripted, at every revision of the financial settlement, the increases in the revenues given over to the management of the Provinces, either for its own benefit on the pretext of meeting the requirements of the Central Exchequer or for the benefit of such of the Provinces as had by inertia not cared to improve their resources on the pretext of tempering the wind to the shorn lamb. There was a good deal of truth in this complaint in the early period of Provincial Finance. Being the custodian of the funds, the Government of India did often put the consideration of Imperial Services above that for the Provincialised Services.

In the early period of Provincial Finance the prevailing idea in the distribution of funds was not how much of the revenues assigned under the expiring settlement could be continued to be usefully spent on heads of expenditure controlled by Provincial Governments, but how much of the general revenues consistently with its obligations, and having regard to the growth of demands upon its resources during the currency of the settlement, could the Government of India surrender for a further period to the Provincial Governments in order to enable them to meet whatever expenditure was essential to the conduct of their administration. This attitude of the Government of India, justifiable as it was by the financial stringency of the period, changed as the financial condition became easy, so that in the latter period

"the distribution of revenues between the Provincial and Central Governments was made, except on occasions of grave emergency, with direct reference not to the needs of the Central Government, but to the outlay which each Province might reasonably claim to incur upon the services which it administered. The first step taken in concluding a settlement was to ascertain the needs of the Province and assign revenue to meet them; the residue only of the income of the Province coming into the Imperial Exchequer."

With the shifting of emphasis on the competing needs of the Central and Provincial Governments the complaints on the score of unfair distribution of funds ceased, and no fear of an adverse revision remained when the settlements were declared permanent. There, however, remained the other main objection to the system of Provincial Finance, namely, that the limitations imposed upon it tended to reduce the Provincial Government to a nonentity by restricting the scope of their activity within the field allotted to it.

It was said that if the system of Provincial Finance was inaugurated on the understanding by which the Government of India said to the Provinces

"Take what we are able to give you, and for the residue take certain powers of taxation and raise it yourself.... for there are subjects which can be dealt with far better by local than by imperial taxation,"

there was no reason why the Provinces should not have been allowed the freedom to tax. Again, if certain resources had been made over to the Provinces, what justification was there in not allowing them to raise loans for promoting purposes of local utility? This restriction was particularly resented; for , it was pointed out that even the humblest local Authority in India enjoyed the power to raise loans to effect improvements in its respective jurisdiction, while such an important polity as a Provincial Government was deemed unworthy of shouldering such a responsibility.

Indeed it was felt as a most galling restriction, for under it it happened that a Provincial Government which was deemed to have enough credit to be accepted as security by the Government of India against loans to other local bodies subordinate to it, was ruled to have no credit to pledge in its own behalf!

What, again, was the justification for limitations on the spending powers of the Provincial Governments in the matter of staff and establishments? If the administration of certain services had been entrusted to the Provincial Governments, why should they have been circumscribed in the matter of creating new or abolishing old appointments or revising the establishments of their departments? If under the system of Provincial Finance the Provinces were responsible for the services they managed, why should they not have been trusted with powers to make needful changes in the agencies which carried out those services?

Further, it was asked, what justification was there for the limitations on the preparation and execution of the Provincial Budgets? If separate Budgets had been carved for each of the Provinces out of what once formed an Imperial Budget for the whole of India, why should the Provinces have been required to submit their Budgets to the Government of India? Merely as a matter of conveying information the requirement was comparatively of a trifling character. But why should the Government of India have claimed to alter their estimates and compel them to abide by the grants as fixed by it? Was such a scrutiny of Provincial Budgets a cover for dictating a policy to the Provincial Governments? If this was so, what was the scope for initiative and freedom left to the Provinces which it was the primary object of Provincial Finance to promote and of the permanent settlements to ensure? Again, why should a Provincial Government have been required to come to the Government of India for a supplementary grant as it had to do where the excess over estimates could not be met by reappropriations, even when it had balances to its credit so sufficient as not to be reduced below the required minimum by a draft to meet the excess?

For each of these limitations which fettered the Provincial Governments and contracted the scope of Provincial Finance, the Government of India was of course ready with abundant excuses. In the matter of revenue restrictions it urged that the revenues of India were its constitutional possession for the proper disposal of which it was responsible to the Secretary of State and Parliament. That being the case it was fair that the Government of India should require that the sources assigned to the Provinces should not be alienated nor spent on unauthorised grants or unapproved services. Again, being responsible for all services it followed that the Government of India could not have afforded to weaken its position as to managing the resources of the country by partitioning the taxing or borrowing powers.

The field for taxation in India being considerably limited, an indiscriminate levy of taxes by a competing authority, it was feared, would have led either to discontent by additions to the Imperial imposts or to a retrenchment of the field for Imperial taxation. The concentration of borrowing powers in its hands, the Government of India urged, was a natural corollary of the statutory hypothecation of all India revenues to all-India needs. The Government of India could not allow its revenues to be mortgaged by a Provincial Government for its own needs. Besides it was afraid that if this freedom to borrow were granted

"the temptation to hypothecate revenues in advance might become inconveniently strong, and the future administration of a Province might be starved because a former Government had been in a hurry to proceed with some costly ambitions and non-productive project."

Moreover, the loan market in India, it was said, was as limited as the taxable capacity of the country. Therefore "if many buckets are dipping into one well and drought cuts short the supply of water, obviously the chief proprietor of the well must take it upon himself to regulate the drawings." In the matter of specific restrictions on spending powers with respect to staff and establishments, the defence of the Government of India was that such restrictions were necessary in the interest of uniformity and economy. It was urged that if each province was allowed the freedom to regulate the remuneration of the Public Service which carried on the actual work of administration the result would probably have been unequal pay for equal work. Such a consequence would have engendered discontent in the servants of the State which it was desirable to prevent in the interest of good administration. Again, if the Provinces had been given full freedom to revise establishments it might have resulted in considerable additions to the recurring expenditure of the Provinces, thereby jeopardising the stability of the Provincial as well as of the Imperial finance, for in the last resort the Government of India was responsible for maintaining the Provincial Governments.

In the matter of control over the preparation and execution of Provincial Budgets the Government of India urged that the scrutiny was not motivated by a desire to control an unwelcome policy, but was inevitable because of the three important ties by which the Provincial Budgets were bound up with the Budget of the Government of India. These were (1) the incorporation of the income and expenditure of the Provincial Governments into the Budget and the Annual Accounts of the Government of India as an integral part thereof; (2) the system of divided heads of revenue and expenditure, and (3) a common treasury involving a combined "ways and means" for the transaction of the Central and Provincial Governments.

The first two points of inter-relation required that the Government of India should examine the Budget Estimates of the Provincial Governments.

It was urged that the power to make such alterations was rendered specially necessary by the inveterate tendency of local Governments to over-estimate their expenditure and under-estimate their revenue.

Estimates which departed widely from actuals meant bad finance and also a provision of larger ways and means for the working of the Treasury. But even if this tendency was absent it was incumbent on the Government of India to scrutinise the Provincial Estimates in order to preserve accuracy in the combined accounts.

Besides the interests of accuracy, the Government of India had to ascertain by a scrutiny of their estimates that a Province did not impair the stability of its finances by (1) including in its budget expenditure on schemes which had not received due administrative sanction, or was not likely to receive such sanction in time to be incurred during the year; or (2) by entering on an enhanced scale of expenditure a Province was not unduly depleting its balances.

But by far the strongest reason why the Government of India needed to scrutinise the Provincial Estimates consisted in the fact that in so far as some of the Heads of Accounts were shared, the ultimate result of the Central Budget, whether there was to be a surplus or deficit, depended upon the accuracy of the estimates.

The Government of India, it was urged, was thus directly interested in the Provincial Budgets, and could not have abandoned its right to scrutinise them without exposing its budgetary system to serious derangement. The third point of inter-relationship necessitated that the Provincial Governments should work within the grants as fixed finally by the Government of India.

To have allowed the Provincial Governments the liberty to exceed the grants because they had ample balances to their credit would have been incompatible with the responsibility of the Imperial Government to provide the ways and means for the whole administration of the country.

A provincial balance, it was pointed out, was not a separate balance locked up in a separate provincial chest. It was a part of the general balances on which the Government of India operated daily. If a sudden demand uncontemplated in the Budget were to be made upon these balances, as would have been the case if the Provincial Governments had exceeded their budget grants, it would have disturbed the ways and means transaction and would have involved the Government into insolvency by causing insufficiency of cash.

All these defences of the restrictions on Provincial Governments were plausible defences and could have been decisive if the centralised system of administration in favour of which they were urged could be deemed to have satisfied the ends of good government.

But it was not unreasonable to argue as was done by the Provincial Governments that modern tendencies were all moving in the direction of forms of government which placed fullest powers as tow down in the administrative scale (i.e. as near the section of population immediately affected) as could be safely arranged.

It is reasonable to centralise such powers as could not be efficiently exercised otherwise. But it is equally unreasonable to centralise powers where central control or uniformity is not clearly essential or is impracticable. By centralisation all progress tends to be retarded, all initiative liable to be checked and the sense of responsibility of local Authorities greatly impaired. Besides, centralisation involves and must involve a serious sacrifice of elasticity, for it is naturally disagreeable to a central department to have to deal with half a dozen different ways of managing the same branch of administration, and which therefore aims at reducing all types to one.

Further centralisation conflicts with what may be regarded as a cardinal principle of good government, namely, that when administrative business reached an authority fully competent to deal with it, that authority should deal with it finally. Even when there is a higher authority equally competent, to pass the business on to it would at best help to transfer power to the hands of the tower ranks of the official hierarchy, by causing congestion of business in the Central Department. Thus centralisation, unless greatly circumscribed, must lead to inefficiency.

This was sure to occur even in homogeneous states, and above all in a country like India where there are to be found more diversities of race, language, religion, customs and economic conditions than in the whole continent of Europe. In such circumstances there must come a point at which the higher authority must be less competent than the tower, because it cannot by any possibility possess the requisite knowledge of all local conditions.

It was therefore obvious that a Central Government for the whole of India could not be said to possess knowledge and experience of all various conditions prevailing in the different Provinces under it. It, therefore, necessarily became an authority less competent to deal with matters of provincial administration than the Provincial Governments, the members of which could not be said to be markedly inferior, and must generally be equal in ability to those of the Central Government, while necessarily superior as a body in point of knowledge.

To these arguments the only reply the Government of India could make was that it concentrated all power in its hands, not from principle but from necessity.

That necessarily arose out of its constitutional obligations. The law had invested it with the superintendence, direction, and control of the civil and military government and the ordering and management of the revenues of the country. It could not therefore relax its control over the powers it had delegated to the Provincial Governments. It was, of course, impossible to deny the force of this argument. So tong as the Government of India remained the authority solely responsible to Parliament it was reasonable to hold that it should be the controlling authority in all matters pertaining to the administration of the country.

But it was equally reasonable to ask whether it would not have been possible in the interests of cordiality between the Central and Provincial Governments to have relaxed such of the restrictions on the financial powers of the Provinces as would not have been incompatible with the due discharge by the former of its own responsibilities. That it was possible so to enlarge the scope of Provincial Finance by a relaxation of the limitations without injury to the position of the Government of India must be said to be evident from the following analysis of the suggestions made by the Provincial Governments.

These suggestions were:

(i) Power of taxation and borrowing on the security of Provincial Revenues.

(ii) Power of sanctioning expenditure on Staff and Establishments up to a limit higher than that allowed by the Government of India.

(iii) Separation of Provincial Estimates from the Imperial Budget and Accounts.

(iv) Abolition of the system of divided heads of revenue and expenditure and the replacement of it by a system of separation of sources and contributions from the yield.

(v) Power to spend part of their balances up to a defined amount, without the previous sanction of the Government of India in meeting an excess of expenditure over Budget Estimates.

What objections were there, from the standpoint of the constitutional responsibilities of the Government of India, to the grant of these demands? Clearly it was possible for the Government of India to have marked off certain sources of taxation best suited for provincial levy and unconnected with the imperial imposts. Similarly it was possible to have permitted the Provincial Governments to borrow to a limited extent on the security of the revenues assigned to them. To suggest as did the Government of India, that the Provincial Governments would abuse these powers to the extent of causing discontent or jeopardising the stability of their financial system, was to believe that such legally recognised polities as the Provincial Governments were run by incompetent administrators unmindful of their obligations.

The second demand could have been granted with greater ease. It is to be noted that the Civil Service of the country which deals with revenue and general administration has been divided into:

(i) The "Indian Civil service "recruited in England by competitive examination, at which natives of India, like other subjects of His Majesty, can compete; and

(ii) The "Provincial" and "Subordinate" Civil Services, recruited in India, and, as a rule, only open to persons who are natives of the country or domiciled therein.

Each Province has had its own separate "Provincial" and "Subordinate" Services, but while it has a free hand in recruiting for the latter, appointments to the former have been regulated by rules laid down by the Government of India.

That being the case it would have been only logical that the Government which had the power of recruiting for an appointment should also have the power of regulating the salary. There can be no reason why the salaries of posts of similar grades should be equal in all Provinces; nor can they be equal having regard to the differences in the economic conditions of the Provinces.

A local Government knows better the economic value of a local man, and should therefore have been trusted with powers up to a limit covered by the Provincial and Subordinate Services. The suggestion of the Government of India that the grant of such powers would have resulted in heavy additions to the recurring expenditure of a Province must be said to be too ungracious to be taken seriously. The acceptance of the third recommendation could not have in any conceivable way affected the responsibility of the Government of India. The only objection which the Government of India urged was that such a separation would have been unwise.

To have published accounts or estimates of the Imperial Government which excluded the accounts of the Provincial Governments, when the items excluded covered such a large magnitude, would have misled the public and rendered a wholly incomplete idea of the financial position of the Government of India.

Now it must be granted that if such a separation of accounts could have avoided the scrutiny and the consequent restraint on budget-making by the Provinces, not to have done so was to have put the supposed convenience of the student of Accounts above the administrative convenience of the Provincial Governments. Besides, it is to be pointed out that the suggestion was not a novel one. It was only a revival of the old practice which obtained between 1871 and 1877. During that period of financial decentralisation Provincial figures did not appear in the Imperial Budget.

The Provincial Budget as framed by the Accountant General was passed by the Provincial Government and no more reference was required to the Government of India except to inform it that the estimate was a probable one and that it was within the limits of the revenues assigned to the Province. It is therefore obvious that there could not have been any constitutional objection to the granting of the demand for a separation of accounts.

The fourth recommendation was of the same class as the third, in that it too could not be said to have involved any infringement of the constitutional responsibilities of the Government of India. The abolition of the divided heads of revenue would have clearly eliminated the interference of the Government of India in the preparation of the Budget Estimates by the Provinces. Similarly the abolition of the divided heads of expenditure would have given the Provinces greater freedom in the matter of spending the revenues assigned to them.

Under that system a Provincial Government could not spend more on a particular service if it was a divided head unless the

Government of India consented to increase its figure for expenditure under that service. If the Government of India reduced its figure the Provincial Government was perforce obliged to reduce its own. The substitution of a system of separation of sources and contributions from the yield for the system of divided heads would have clearly resulted in a greater freedom to the Provincial Governments, without any evil consequence to the Government of India.

The objections which the Government of India was able to oppose to this demand was far from convincing. It was urged that the Provincial Governments under complete separation may cease to take such interest as it took in respect of revenues which were divided. But it is evidently a mistaken view that a Provincial Government could not have been trusted to administer a tax efficiently unless it had a financial interest in the result.

This view supposed that the people engaged in the collection of revenue really knew whether it went to the Imperial or the Provincial credit. As a matter of fact the ultimate credit could in no way have affected the collection of the revenue. And even if that view were true the difficulty could easily have been met by each government having its own staff to collect its own revenues. The employing by one Government to execute its functions the agencies of another, as has been the case in India, is obviously a complicated and awkward system.

If separation of agencies had resulted from the separation of sources it would have been a reform all to the good. Besides it was overlooked that the fact that the divided heads gave a personal interest to the Provincial Governments was indeed a point against the system rather than in favour of it. A system which created a vested interest in a revenue apart from the interest of the public was a bad system, for such an interest was sure to lead to harshness and rigidity in collection.

As an instance of this may be cited the notorious unwillingness of Provincial Governments in the matters of remitting taxation. If humanising the Provincial Governments was a desirable end, then the abolition of divided heads was a good means. The other objection which the Government of

India was able to oppose was that such a change would have given the share of the Government of India from the revenues raised in the provinces the character of a tribute, and the Government of India would have appeared to be the pensioner of the Provincial Governments, depending upon them rather than controlling them. This objection must be ruled out as being sentimental.

The fifth and the last suggestion for the enlargement of the scope of Provincial Finance was least obnoxious to the responsibility of the Government of India.

There is no reason why there should have been a single-treasury system for both the Governments, Provincial and Central. It is true that a common treasury permits a high state of economy in the cash balances of the country, which it is the duty of every Government to effect, just as any business firm looks upon it as its duty to economise its till money or floating cash. But if a common treasury hindered the use of the balances the gain in freedom would have more than compensated the toss involved by the increase in the cash balances that would have followed the institution of separate treasuries and separate ways and means.

But the demand of the Provincial Governments did not ask for a complete separation of Provincial balances from the balances of the Central Government involving separate treasury system and separate ways and means, probably because they anticipated that as such a proposal meant separate possession of provincial revenues the Government of India would raise a constitutional objection to such a demand. All they asked for was a power to spend part of their balances up to a defined amount without reference to the Government of India. The suggestion was accepted as "reasonable," for its consequences, provided it was not a big amount, would have been not a deprivation of the Government of India's power of control over nor a disturbance in the ways and means, but only a slight increase in the cash balances of the country.

Thus it is clear that the scope of Provincial Finance was unduly restricted by a too narrow and too legalistic an interpretation of the constitutional obligations of the

Government of India. From the above analysis of the suggestions made by the Provincial Governments it is clear that without making any breach in the constitutional position of the Government of India it would have been possible, with a more charitable view of their sense of responsibility, to effect the changes they desired. Such concessions would have made Provincial Finance as self-sufficient and as autonomous as it was capable of being made. The system would no doubt have rested on pure convention: none the less its benefits would have been as real as though it was based on law.

But the time had arrived when the financial arrangements could no longer be looked upon as a matter which concerned the Central and Provincial Governments. There arose a third party whose counsels were rejected in 1870 but which now insisted on having a voice in the disposition of the financial resources of the country. It was the Indian taxpayer, and his clamour had grown so strong that it compelled the powers that be to alter the system so as to permit him to take the part he claimed to play.

7

Provincial Finance under the Government of India Act of 1919

The Necessity for a Change

As two types of governmental systems, the Presidential and Parliamentary are often contrasted to the advantage of the latter.

For the Parliamentary type of government it has been claimed that no other arrangement seems able quite so effectively to place the centre of authority under the control of those who are supposed to represent the popular will : that it means government by consent : that it ensures the exercise of the functions of government by a body of persons who are amenable to and whose views are in accord with those of the majority of the Legislature : that it is the only form of government which provides for a powerful Executive so very necessary for a stable government without rendering it so irresponsible as to endanger the essentials of a good government: that it throws upon the holders of high office the onus of vindicating their acts or, failing, suffer dismissal : it renders the Legislature supreme both in legislation and administration so that it forms a government not only to make life possible but also to make life good.

No other form of government, it is urged, can so effectively prevent order degenerating into tyranny or progress blocked in the name of peace. So eminently has Parliamentary Government demonstrated its supreme virtue in securing orderly progress that, though originally developed as an accident in the evolution of the British Constitution, it has been most eagerly adopted as the most fundamental institution by many countries whose political convulsions have required them to prepare anew or alter the existing framework of their governmental systems. If the fact of the Executive being a part of the Legislature be a sufficient indication of the Parliamentary type of government, then the system of government in India since 1853 may be said to be analogous to the Parliamentary system. Indeed it would hardly be possible to deny this characteristic to the Indian constitution, for the provision of the constitutional law has since then been that the additional (i.e. the Legislative) members *and* the ordinary (i.e. the Executive) members shall *together form* the Legislature for the making of the laws and regulation for the peace, order and good government of British India.

But judged in the light of its *de facto* consequences the Indian system falls lamentably below the *de jure* connotation of the class of governmental systems to which it belonged. If in other countries the record of Parliamentary government is one of submission of the Executive to the Legislature, in India it had been one of the Executive thwarting, often of flouting, the legislature. In vain may one search the proceedings of the Legislature to find the Executive ever paying deference to the wishes of the people Reforms have been incessantly, asked for by the legislature only to be denied with equal tenacity by the Executive.

The following table from N. C. Kelkar's *The Case for Indian Home Rule, p.* 81, is illustrative of the fact :—

Legislative Council	No. of Resolu-tions moved	No. of Resolu-tions with-drawn	No. of Resolu-tions rejected	No. of Resolutions accepted
Supreme	3	2	1	0
Madras	32	26	6	0
Bengal	38	26	12	0
U.P.	22	10	12	0
Bihar and Orissa	5	5	0	0
C.P.	4	2	2	0

The reason why the Indian parliamentary system was but an empty form is to be found in the fact that it was a Parliamentary system without a Parliamentary Executive. In other words, the Executive under the system was not responsible to the legislature and was not removable by it. The Indian Legislature could neither make nor unmake the Indian Executive. The Indian Executive made peace or war as it liked without being afraid of dismissal by the Legislature. It taxed as it pleased and spent as it liked, without the slightest compunction as to the wishes of the Legislature, it undertook acts or refused to undertake them according to its own sweet will, but had no fear of a vote of censure from the legislature. The nearest approach to the Indian system of parliamentary Government is to be found in the position of the Irish Parliament which existed from 1782 to 1800. The peculiarity of the case lay mainly in the fact that while this Irish Parliament, commonly known as Grattan's Parliament, was during the period it lasted admittedly a sovereign Legislature, the Irish Executive of the time was as regards the Irish Parliament in no sense a Parliamentary Executive. The Irish Executive, instead of being appointed and dismissed by the Irish Legislature, was in reality appointed and dismissed by the Crown on the advice of the English Ministry. In the same manner the Indian Executive was appointed and dismissed by the Crown on the advice of the Secretary of State for India who is a member of the English Ministry and was in no way responsible to the Indian Legislature.

It is true that the Executive in India was ultimately responsible to the Secretary of State for India and through him to the British Parliament. But it must not be forgotten, said Mr. Fisher, that "the affairs of India are in the hands of the Government of India.... Proposals may come from the Indian Government to London and be vetoed by the Imperial Government. The large lines of Indian policy may be shaped by a Secretary of State in the India Office, and a powerful Secretary of State may make his influence felt strongly on the direction of Indian affairs if he encounters no serious opposition from the Government of India. But in reality the last word lies with the Indian official opinion (i.e. the Executive in India), that a measure would not be forced upon India against the united opposition of the Indian bureaucracy."

As a matter of fact neither was the Secretary, though all-powerful in Indian affairs, inclined to restrain the Executive in India from doing what the people regarded as evil nor to constrain it to do what he thought to be for the good of the people. Hardly can it be said that the British Parliament, wherein every member has been supposed to be a member for India, has made the acts of the Indian Executive a matter of anxious scrutiny.

The salary of the Secretary of State for India being paid out of the revenues of India, Parliament, had no occasion, as it had in the case of the Colonial Secretary, to annually review his actions in the full activity of the parliamentary Session. At the end, generally after the Appropriation Bill had been read a second time, the Indian Budget used to be submitted to Parliament which, after a somewhat desultory discussion, used to pass a Resolution proclaiming in solemn terms that the Indian Accounts show certain totals of income and expenditure ! Many attempts were made to improve the control of Parliament on Indian affairs. But Parliament never cared to increase its control. In 1873 Mr. R. N. Fowler moved" that in the opinion of this House it is desirable that the Statement of the financial affairs of India should be made at a period of the Sessions when it can be fully discussed." Again in 1883 the same motion was brought forward by Mr. Fowler. Both of these attempts to furnish the House with a better opportunity to review Indian affairs fell to the ground. In 1899 the same Resolution was moved by Mr. Cladwell, M.P., with the addition that the Salary of the Secretary of State for India be placed on the British Estimates. It was opposed by Mr. Fowler, who was then the Secretary of State for India, and was in consequence lost. By the provision of the Government of India Act of 1919 the House has a better opportunity to criticise Indian affairs owing to the salary of the Secretary of State having been placed on the British Estimates.

On the other hand, its interference in Indian affairs has on some occasion been positively harmful to the interests of the Indian people. Indeed, there can be no doubt that the interest of Parliament in Indian affairs since the assumption of the Government of the country by the Crown instead of increasing has considerably diminished as compared with the interest it took when the affairs of the country were in charge of the Company. Nay, the influence of the British Parliament over Indian affairs, it may be said, has undergone a decided change for the worse, inasmuch as all its influence is exerted to strengthen the Executive in India against popular clamour rather than restraining it from flying in the face of public opinion.

It is therefore evident that the control of the Secretary of State and of Parliament over the Executive in India was only a nominal control, and the Indian Executive was in reality an uncontrolled body of bureaucrats in the exclusive charge of Indian affairs. How was this trust discharged by this irresponsible Executive ?

The answer to this question may be summed up in the statement that the Indian Executive has sacrificed progress to order. Whether we examine its actions in the field of legislation or finance, the truth of this statement becomes painfully evident.

There are very few countries in the world where there may be said to prevail so many social evils as has been the case in India. Law is a means by which society from time to time repairs its ills in order to effect its conservation. But with very few exceptions the rule of *personal* law of a most pernicious character has been allowed to govern the social relations of the citizens, notwithstanding the fact that enlightened public opinion has long since raised its voice of protest against its perpetuation. So religious has been the regard of the Executive for the preservation of the personal law, notwithstanding the fact that it has disabled millions of its subjects from enjoying the most elementary rights of citizenship, that it has been careful not to allow in cases of conflict the rational provisions of the civil law to override or chasten the irrational rulings of that archaic *code*. Judged by the modern standard of legislation the Executive must be pronounced to be extremely conservative. In the matter of securing economic rights its response was of a very halting character, and the legislation it has been persuaded to undertake for giving security or fixity of tenure to the agricultural or ease and comfort to the industrial population sank in comparison to what it refused to undertake for liberating the rest from a species of industrial slavery notwithstanding incessant demands for its abolition.

Its financial system was similarly characterised by the desire to preserve peace and order by taxing the masses and exempting the classes. It has been urged that the revenue system be so altered as to give relief to the poorer classes. Indirect taxes are justified as a method of making the poorer classes pay their share of the burden of the State without their being sensible of the fact. But there is a limiting principle which forbids the imposition of certain kinds of indirect taxes.

It may be said to be agreed by students of public finance that indirect taxes be such that the poor on whom they impinge rather heavily relatively speaking, must be able to adjust the burden of such taxes to their means. When such indirect taxes fall on luxuries it is possible for them to apportion for themselves the burden they need must bear by regulating their purchases.

But in those cases where they fall on necessaries of life this elasticity is not possible. The pernicious character of the salt tax in India was urged as a sufficient ground for its elimination from the revenue system of India. But not only did the Executive refuse to accept the demand, it actually increased the salt tax whenever a deficit has occurred instead of tapping some other source of revenue, which it could have done with equal ease and greater justice. In 1886, to cite one example, it was admitted that

"There can, after all is said and done, be no manner of doubt, but that one great fact remains established, one great blot not only unremoved but aggravated by the course of events in recent years..... It is that..... the classes in (India) which derive the greatest security and benefit from the British Government are those who contribute the least towards it." But in the Budget of 1887-8 the Executive eschewed its own conviction and increased the salt duty to make up for the deficit caused not by any extraordinary measure of internal improvement but by an enormous act of external aggression, namely the conquest of Burma, as though the income tax of 1886 which left untouched the incomes of the Bengal zamindars, the Assam Tea planters and the Talukdars of Oudh, in making the richer classes pay, made them pay, at the very moderate rates it levied, all they could be made to pay.

But the salt tax is not the only instance of inequity under which the masses paid for the classes. The land revenue as it has been levied in India may be cited as another example of inequity in the Indian Tax System. The sources of inequity are various. There is first of all the glaring fact that in some cases the amount of the tax is permanently fixed, while in other cases the amount of the tax payable in respect of land revenue is periodically revised. Now there is no justifying circumstance why some citizens should be exempted from contributing their quota to the growing needs of the State when the same is rigorously exacted from their fellows. This is, however, only one point of injustice to those whose taxable capacity in respect of land revenue is subject to periodical revisions.

There is another which consists in the adoption of a wrong measure of capacity to pay. The cardinal feature of this revisable part of the land tax in India is to be found in the basis of the tax which, as is well known to every student of Indian Finance, is a certain unit of land. Now nobody has ever suspected the pernicious effect of the system which bases the tax on a unit of land held ; but surely there can hardly be a system more mistaken in thought or more mischievous in practice. It ignores the commonplace of economists which asserts that taxes are paid not by things but by persons and if it is persons who ultimately pay the taxes then it is manifest that they must be required to contribute not according to the land they hold but in proportion to the total income derived. On the contrary the system, in undertaking to tax per unit of land, taxes the poor peasant with only one acre to cultivate and the landlord owing hundreds of acres at a *uniform* rate without realising that as the total incomes of the two must be vastly different this uniformity of taxation must produce a glaring inequity of treatment as between the rich and the poor. If the revenue thus raised by sacrificing equity to the dictates of order had been spent on services promoting progress there would have been some compensation. But such was not the case.

All the revenue that was collected was spent on Services such as Police, Military and Administration which are calculated to maintain order. Such services as Education, State aid to industries, hardly found any place in the scheme of public expenditure as managed by this irresponsible Executive. But it may be asked as to why the Executive, sovereign as it was, should have stood for order and against progress ?

Percentage of Expenditure

(Excluding expenditure on commercial services, i.e., Post Office and Telegraph Dept., Railways and Irrigation). In thousands of rupees.

Periods	District Administration	Forest	Other Heads, including Opium	Debt Sources	Civil Depts.	Civil Changes	Civil Works	Army (Including Military Works and Special Defence Works)	Famine Relief and Insurance	Total
1877-78 to 1881-82	5.2	.8	5.6	8.9	18.7	6.8	5.8	39.2	2.6	93.6
1882-83 to 1886-87	6.0	1.2	6.6	8.2	21.4	7.5	7.6	35.6	2.3	96.4
1887-88 to 1891-92	6.0	1.3	5.4	7.6	22.1	7.5	7.3	37.7	2.8	95.7
1892-93 to 1896-97	6.1	1.3	4.9	6.4	22.5	8.4	6.9	38.5	1.6	96.6
1897-98 to 1901-02	5.8	1.4	5.5	4.3	22.6	7.8	6.8	35.2	4.8	94.2
1902-03 to 1906-07	5.9	1.6	8.2	3.1	23.2	7.3	9	37.1	1.8	97.2
1907-08 to 1911-12	6.3	1.8	7.1	3.5	25.7	7.7	8.5	35.6	2.1	98.3
1912-13 to 1916-17	6.0	1.9	6.2	2.1	28.2	7.3	9.3	35.1	1.5	97.6

From the statistics of British India, Vol. II, Financial Statistics, 1920.

The answer is that an irresponsible government, however sovereign, is incapable of progress, for in the exercise of its sovereign powers it is hampered by two very serious limitations. There is first of all the internal limitation which arises from the character, motives and interests of those who are in power.

If the Sultan does not abolish Mahomedanism, Pope ban Catholicism, the Brahmin condemn caste, or the British Parliament declare the preservation of blue-eyed babies illegal, it is not because they *cannot do* things, but it is because they will not do these things.

In the same way if the Executive in India did not do certain things most conducive to progress it was because by reason of its being impersonal** and also by reason of its character, motives and interests it could not sympathise with the living forces operating in the Indian Society, was not charged with its wants, its pains, its cravings and its desires, was inimical to its aspirations, did not advance Education, disfavoured Swadeshi or snapped at anything that smacked of nationalism, it was because all these things went against its grain. But an irresponsible government is powerless to do even such things as it may like to do.

For its authority is limited by the possibility of external resistance. There are things which it would do but dare not do for the fear of provoking thereby resistance to its authority. Caesar dare not subvert the worship of the Roman people, a modern parliament dare not tax the Colonies, however much they would.

For the same reason the Government of India dared not abolish the caste system, prescribe monogamy, alter the laws of succession, legalise intermarriage or venture to tax the tea planters. Progress involves interference with the existing code of social life and interference is likely to cause resistance.

**Impersonal because the higher and controlling grades of public services are devoid of Indian element. Although the eligibility of the natives of India for employment in public services was proclaimed as far back as 1833, the regulations made by the Secretary of State for admission to the Public

Services in India has had the tendency to exclude them from the employment of the right granted to them by statute. Under the regulations made by the Secretary of State for War, candidates for Commission in the Army were to be of pure European descent and a similar regulation was adopted by the Admiralty for cadetship in the Navy, thereby excluding Indians. As to the Civil Service the Statute (Government of India Act, 1858, s. 32) laid down that all "natural-born subjects" of the Crown be admitted for examination, thereby including the natives of India.

But the ruling of the Secretary of State that examination should be held only in London had indirectly debarred many natives of the country from benefiting themselves under the statute. Regulations for admission to other public services varied.

For the Indian Medical Service, candidates were to be natural-born subjects of European or East Indian descent ; for the Indian Police Service they were to be British subjects of European descent ; for the Forest Service they were to be natural-born British subjects ; for Public Works Department one-tenth might be natives of India who are British subjects.— Cf. in this connection Halsbury, *Laws of England,* Vol. X, pp. 588-9.

None the less a government which is of the people and is not detached from them can venture on the path of progress, because it is in a position to know where obedience will end and resistance will begin.

But the Indian Executive not being of the people could not feel the pulse of the people. The gist of the matter is that the irresponsible Executive which had been in power in India was paralysed between these two limitations on its authority and much of what went to make life good was held up. Part of the programme it would not undertake and the other part it could not undertake.

As a result of this, so far as the moral and social life of the people was concerned, the change of government by the Moghuls to a government by the British was only a change of rulers rather than a change of system. Owing to the adoption of the principle of non-interference partly by preference and partly by necessity by the British

"the natives of India found themselves under a government distinguished in no vital respect from those under which they had toiled and worshipped, lived and died through all their weary and forgotten history. From a political standpoint, the change was but the replacement of one despotism by another. It accepted the arrangements as it found them and preserved them faithfully in the manner of the Chinese tailor who, when given an old coat as a pattern, produced with pride an exact replica, rents, patches and all.

That there was some advancement in material progress is not to be denied. But no people in the world can long remain contented with the benefits of peace and order, for they are not dumb brutes.

It is foolish to suppose that a people will indefinitely favour a bureaucracy because it has improved their roads, constructed canals on more scientific principles, effected their transportation by rail, carried their letters by penny post, flashed their messages by lightning, improved their currency, regulated their weights and measures, corrected their notions of geography, astronomy and medicine and stopped their internal quarrels.

Any people, however patient, will sooner or later demand a government that will be more than a mere engine of efficiency. Under the influence of Western ideas of representative government the Indian people had for some time been demanding a change in the form of the government. A Parliamentary form of government with a Parliamentary Executive was the goal they had laid before themselves.

The popular agitation for achieving this end assumed such proportions that, in the course of time, there was presented a serious issue for the consideration of the Executive in India. How was the government of the country to be carried on ? By force or by consent, Power seldom commits suicide of its own accord. Rather, when it fails to secure the willing compliance of the people, it resorts to force. That was the resource adopted by the Executive in India. Not satisfied with the aid of the power with which the Executive was endowed by the provisions of the Criminal and Penal Codes to anticipate offences by preventive acts, it besmeared the Indian Statute Book with a set of repressive laws hardly paralleled in any other part of the world.

The Criminal Law Amendment Act XIV of 1908 empowered a magistrate with special sanction of the Government to hold an *ex-parte* inquiry without the presence of the accused or of his legal representative and commit him for trial to be conducted without a jury. Under another provision of the same Act the Executive could declare unlawful any association which in its view interfered with the maintenance of law and order.

The State Prisoners Regulations and Acts authorising the Executive to place under restraint any person whom it suspected but against whom it had no proof, constituted by themselves a perpetual suspension of the Habeas Corpus Act: while under another Act the Executive was empowered to proclaim "a State of Siege" or martial law in any area and suspend therein the jurisdiction of the civil courts in favour of the military courts.

The Indian Press Act of 1910 put a complete muzzle on the Press. So wide were its provisions that in the opinion of a learned judge of one of the Indian High Courts it was "difficult to see to what length its operation might not be plausibly extended by an ingenious mind "and" that they would certainly apply to writings that might even command approval "and" much that is regarded as standard literature might undoubtedly be caught."

The right of public meeting was suppressed in the same manner and with the same sterness as was the right to personal freedom and the right to freedom of discussion; for, over and above the restrictive provisions contained in the ordinary law of the land, the executive armed itself with discretionary powers under a special enactment to prohibit any public meeting on the excuse of what it regarded as the interest of the public.

The rigour of this regime of *lettre de cachet* and the *Bastille* was quite untempered by any fear of responsibility on the part of the Executive for any excesses committed in putting these repressive laws into operation.

For it is to be noted that the Executive had, coupled with the large grants of these discretionary powers to suppress the liberties of the people in order to preserve law and order, the gift of an equally generous measure of immunity to its agents in carrying out those powers. The Police Acts and the Press Act *all* contained provisions which barred all action in a civil court against these agents for damages to be done in pursuance of these Acts.

Officers and soldiers taking part in the suppression of riots were not criminally responsible for acts done in good faith and were not to be prosecuted for other acts without the sanction of the government. In like manner superior Executive officers could not be prosecuted for crimes committed in discharge of public functions except with the permission of the government and then only in the manner prescribed by government. There is no wonder then if such discretionary powers, exercised extra-judicially, substituted a reign of terror in place of a regime of peace.

But it was soon found out that force was not a sure means of carrying on the government of a country. The verdict of history was well summed up by Burke when he said :

"The use of force alone is but temporary. It may subdue for a moment, but it does not remove the necessity of subduing again: a nation is not governed which is perpetually to be conquered. (The) next objection to force is its uncertainty. Terror is not always the effect of force, and an armament is not a victory.

If you do not succeed, you are without resource ; for conciliation failing, force remains, but force failing, no further hope of reconciliation is left. Power and authority are sometimes bought by kindness, but they can never be begged as alms by an impoverished and defeated violence. A further objection to force is, that you impair the object by your very endeavours to preserve it. The thing you fought for (to wit the loyalty of the people) is not the thing which you recover, but depreciated, sunk, wasted and consumed in the contest......"

Government by consent was indeed long ago accepted by the Indian Executive as a principle of political wisdom, and the changes introduced from time to time in the constitution of the Indian Legislature were avowedly for the purpose of making it reflect the popular will. The result for a time was an astonishing degree of accord between the Indian Executive and the Indian Legislature ; so much so that the regime of *lettre de cachet* and the *Bastille* had the sanction of the majority of the *Indian legislature.*

But all this government by consent or conciliation was a camouflage. On the other hand, an analysis of the changes introduced from time to time into the constitution of the Indian Legislature clearly shows that the motive behind these changes was to make it an impotent body or a willing tool in the hands of the Executive. A Legislature as distinct from the Executive was first inaugurated in 1853. But in 1861 the constitution of the Legislature then established was altered. The ground urged was that Legislature was not a body representative of the Indian people.

Its members were drawn from the official class representing the several Provincial Governments. In order to make the Legislature representative of the people, the Act of 1861 directed that it should be composed of *nominated* members chosen by the Governor-General from among the public, of course on the advice of the Executive.

Again, by the Act of 1892 the Governor-General was directed to nominate such persons to the Legislature as were selected by public bodies in the country. These changes in the constitution of the Legislature appear to be aimed at liberalising it. But was this tendency towards making the Legislature representative accompanied with a tendency to make it more powerful as regards the Executive ? Quite the reverse. As the legislature gained in its representative character it lost in its controlling power.

The powers exercised by the Legislature under the Act of 1853 were far vaster than anything possessed by the Legislature under the Act of 1861. Under the former the Indian Legislature modelled itself on the procedure of the House of Commons in

England, and not only dealt with matters of legislation, pure and simple, but also with matters of administration. In the words of Sir C. Ilbert, it showed an inconvenient degree of independence by asking questions as to and discussing the propriety of the measures of the Executive Government—deeming itself competent to inquire into abuses and grievances, calling for reports and returns from local administrations, debating long on questions of public interest and introducing motions and resolutions independent of the Executive Government.

In a despatch of Lord Canning at the time, he pointed out that the Legislature had become invested with forms and modes of procedure closely imitating those of the House of Commons, that there were 136 standing orders to regulate the procedure of a dozen gentlemen assembled in council, that in short, in the words of Sir Lawrence Peel, they had assumed jurisdiction in the nature of that of a grand inquest of the nation. This was deemed to be a very grave defect (!!) in the Legislature as constituted by the Act of 1853. Its reform was therefore looked upon as very necessary for maintaining the supremacy of the Executive, and its non-popular character was made the ostensible excuse for its reconstruction. Under the pseudo representative system introduced in 1861 the Legislature was a meek body entirely in the hands of the Executive.

Being composed of *nominated* members, division in the Legislature was directly influenced by that fact. In every legislative body a man must sit, unless he has a hereditary right, by what in modern parlance is called a mandate. That mandate usually proceeds from the authority to whom he owes his seat.

The nominated members, official as well as non-official, owed their elevation to the legislature to the pleasure of the Executive, and as such were bound to support the Executive on any measure on which a division was taken. The Executive had always at its command the official block of nominated members, who gave implicit obedience to its mandates either because of its convictions or by reason of its being a part of the same.

The nominated non-officials, who may be said to be opposed by conviction to the Executive, were not men of independent character and were largely concerned to make themselves agreeable to the Executive rather than make themselves reckoned with. But had they been men of independent character they could not have made themselves masters of the Executive, for by the provisions of the Constitutional law and the rules of procedure made under it, the Legislature was rendered entirely powerless to compel the Executive to do anything against its wishes.

From 1853 to 1861 the Legislature dealt with both legislative and administrative questions. From 1861 the legislature met only for legislative purposes.

As a consequence of this limitation the Legislature was debarred from asking a question, moving a resolution or dividing on the Budget. During the first thirty years of its existence the legislature did not even discuss the annual budget on more than sixteen occasions, and that too because some new tax legislation had been called for, and which the Executive could always carry through with the help of the nominated official block as it did every other kind of legislation it deemed necessary. The right of discussing the annual financial statement and the right of asking questions in regard to matters were first conceded to the legislature by the Rules of Procedure framed under the Indian Councils Act of 1892.

But it may be doubted whether these concessions of powers to the Legislature amount to a restoration of the position which it occupied and dominance it exercised under the Act of 1853.

Even the reforms of Lord Morley fell short in the matter of according a real measure of independence and power to the Legislature over the Executive. In the reforms which he introduced in 1909 nomination, directly or after selection, was in principle replaced by election as a basis for the constitution of the legislature.

At the same time the procedure of the legislature was liberalised so as to give power to the members to put supplementary questions along with interpellations, to move resolutions on the Financial Statement and on matters of general public interest. But a little analysis is enough to show that even this attempt was of a piece with the old endeavour of liberalising the Legislature without impairing the supremacy of the Executive.

This supremacy of the Executive was maintained (1) by means of a permanent majority of officials of the government nominated to the legislature, and (2) by controlling the rules of procedure. Although election was admitted by the Act of 1892 as a basis of the composition of the Legislature, the elected members were in a minority, so that they could not give effect to the wishes of the people whom they represented. They were entitled to move resolutions if permitted by the Executive but the Executive was not bound to carry them out.

They served only as recommendations, and were not binding upon the Executive. This direct thwarting produced irritation between the Executive and the elected members of the Legislature. In a certain sense the reforms of 1909 were a bad piece of engineering. Before 1909 whatever conflict there was manifested outside the Legislature.

For by the rules of election and procedure the Legislature was entirely muzzled : it could do no mischief. By the reforms of 1909, however, an attempt was made to make the Legislature independent and at the same time to muzzle it.

This attempt, ingenious as it was, only served to bring to the surface the deep-seated conflict between the Executive and the forces agitating the minds of the people. Election procedure or business procedure governing a legislature is, in the words of Prof. Redlich, as it were a political pressure gauge, indicating the tension in the parliamentary machine and thence in the whole organism of the State.

It is possible that this pressure gauge in the first instance may either be badly constructed or may become worn out so as to give a false reading of the actual tension. But there can be no doubt that in the case of India the Executive, in the alterations which it introduced from time to time and particularly in 1909 in the election and business procedure of the legislature, had all along constructed it badly of purpose and had attempted to conceal thereby dangerous pressure of the steam in the political machine, so as to cause it to give a false reading of the situation. So long as the members of the legislature derived their mandates from the Executive, owing to the fact that all of them were nominated members, such an artifice worked well, with the entry of the elected members holding their mandates from the people, the weakness of the artifice became evident.

The mortification of the elected members led them to obstruct and challenge the great fundamental principles recognised as the theoretical basis of procedure.

Now if a party complained of inequality among members, of the rules of conducting proceedings, of freedom of speech or of the majority principle, it is a danger signal indicative of the existence of some serious defects in the life of the State. When such a conflict arises it is for a political statesman to judge whether he has to face a reform of the procedure of the representative assembly or a reform in the constitution of the State.

While inside the Legislative Assembly there were signs of hardening opposition and weariness which comes from sterile efforts, outside the Legislature the tide of feeling was rising more quickly, for, all the time the sense of national consciousness and the desire for political power were growing rapidly in the minds of educated Indians, no doubt, because the Legislature with its limited powers was found to be an insufficient safety valve. As a result of the realisation of this fact those who had given their thoughts to the political reconstruction of the country agreed that a mere reform of the procedure will not do. Only a reform of the constitution will save the state from anarchy.

There was, however, a considerable diversity in the reforms suggested for effecting an alteration in the constitution of India. One scheme may here be noted in passing and that was the scheme propounded by the Indian National Congress and the Moslem League, shortly known as the Congress-League-Scheme.

The scheme demanded a four-fifths majority of elected members in the Central Legislature. As to the Executive, it demanded that one-half of the total number of the Executive members should be Indians and that they should be elected by the elected members of the Legislature. The Legislature was to have complete financial and legislative powers. Nay, its recommendations, passed in the form of resolutions, were to be binding on the Executive. Such "was the latest, most complete and most authoritative presentation of the claims of the leading Indian political organisations" on behalf of the Indian people. But when we come to analyse the scheme it speaks poorly of the political genius of the Indian politicians.

The scheme was formulated as a fulfilment of *responsible* government in British India. But in practice it was not only not a measure of responsible government, but it was deficient even to subserve the ends of good government. The scheme did not ask that the legislature should have the power to make or unmake an Executive as it pleased. If it had asked that, then the scheme would have been a scheme for responsible government. But what it asked for was to compel an Executive, which was irremovable, to conduct the administration of the country according to the orders of the Legislature. The Scheme was of a piece with that of Lord Morley in an enlarged form.

He had introduced an Indian element into the Government so that Indian opinion and Indian advice might have some weight with the Executive in addition to what it exercised through the legislative organ of the Government. Those who framed the Congress-League-Scheme merely increased the Indian element in the Executive and the Legislature, and added provisions aimed at converting advice into control without realising what was to happen if the Executive refused to be bound by the wishes of the Legislature.

The essence of the project was an Executive with a divided mandate legally responsible to Parliament, and practically to an elected Legislature. Such a separation of mandates, it was obvious, would have enabled the Legislature to paralyse the Executive without having power to remove it.

Being without any constitutional means to change the Legislature in cases of conflict by an appeal to the Electorate it would have been obliged to carry on the Government even where it did not respect the wishes of the Legislature. The scheme was unsound, like all previous attempts at the reform of the Indian Constitution, because in it the Executive and the legislature derived their mandates from and were responsible to different powers.

It was unsound because it overlooked the possibility that two mandates may not agree, in which case there would be a conflict. That conflict is inherent in a non-parliamentary executive. Some form of a Parliamentary government with a Parliamentary executive was the only way of avoiding it.

It is from this standpoint that the announcement of August 20, 1917, forms a landmark in the annals of the development of the Indian Constitution. On that date the Secretary of State for India announced in the House of Commons that—

"The policy of His Majesty's Government, with which the Government of India are in complete accord, is that of the increasing association of Indians in every branch of the administration and the gradual development of self-governing institutions, with a view to the progressive realisation of responsible government in India as an integral part of the British Empire. They have decided that substantial steps in this direction should be taken as soon as possible......" "I would add that progress in this policy can only be achieved by successive stages. The British Government and the Government of India, on whom the responsibility lies for the welfare and advancement of the Indian peoples, must be judges of the time and measure of each advance, and they must be guided by the co-operation received from those upon whom new opportunities of service will thus be conferred and by the extent to which it is found that confidence can be reposed in their sense of responsibility."

This momentous announcement marks the end of one epoch and the beginning of a new one. It definitely abandoned the old conception under which the Executive might, as it saw fit, consult the wishes of the legislature, which were only given an increasing share in the administration of the country and increasing opportunities for influencing and criticising, but never for controlling, the Government. Under the new conception the aim was to endow the Legislature with the power to make or unmake the government, so that it would be not only a government of the people and for the people, but by the people. The adoption of such a change of policy in the basis of the political institutions of the country involved far-reaching changes in their relations with one another, administrative, legislative and financial.

The changes in the system of Provincial Finance introduced in consequence of the Reforms Act of 1919 were not caused by any inherent defects in the system as it stood at that date. On the other hand, the system was eminently workable. They were effected because the system as a whole was inconsistent with the great revolution which that Act had sought to effect in the governmental system of that country.

The nature of the changes, their extent and their adequacy will form the subject-matter of the two following chapters.

8

The Nature of a Change

The announcement of August 20, 1917, spoke of progressive realisation of responsible government as the goal of the future British policy in India, and the Montague-Chelmsford Report on Constitutional Reforms surveyed the ways of giving effect to that announcement. One of the merits of that Report consisted in showing that the Congress-League-Scheme of political reforms did not embody the principle for the recognition of which they were agitating so long.

Instead of inaugurating a responsible government in India, the scheme would have saddled the country with a non-parliamentary executive under a parliamentary system of government. Being convinced of their error the Congress-League politicians, be it said to their credit, abandoned their scheme in favour of the proposals contained in the Joint Report. But in their turn they demanded the introduction of a more or less complete responsible government in most of the political institutions at one stroke. But the framers of the new constitution pointed out that the emphasis on the word progressive in the announcement was as great if not greater than the emphasis laid on the word responsible.

In consonance with this view it was decided to introduce, as a substantial step in the progress towards the realisation of the goal laid down in the announcement, a responsible government of a limited character in the Provincial Governments. The Provincial Governments in India, like the Central Government, were irresponsible governments. The changes made in the constitution of Provincial Legislatures were of the same nature as the changes in the Central Legislature, in that both were calculated to enable the Executive to consult the Legislature without being amenable to its control. Only on one occasion were the frameworks of the two machines of governments, the Provincial and the Central, constructed on a slightly different basis, and that was in the Morley-Minto Reforms of 1909.

Under those reforms the Central Legislature was dominated by *official* members who with the members of the Executive formed a standing majority in the chamber. In the Provincial Legislatures this principle of a standing majority of official members was dispensed with.

The second point of departure in the constitution of the Provincial Legislatures as compared with that of the Central Legislature consisted in the Budget procedures in the two governments. In the Central legislature the Finance Member early in each calendar year presented to the Legislature his preliminary estimates accompanied by an explanatory memorandum.

On a subsequent day he made such further explanations as he thought necessary. Members of the Legislature could thereupon move resolutions regarding (a) any proposed alteration in taxation, (*b*) any proposed loan, or (c) any additional grant to a Local Government. The first stage in the discussion of the Budget of the Government of India was over when once these resolutions were voted upon. The second stage commenced when the estimates were taken into consideration by groups.

At this stage also it was open for members to move resolutions on any heads of revenue and expenditure, except those that were declared by rules of procedure to be not open for discussion to the legislature. After the resolutions had been moved and voted upon the Finance Member took the whole discussion into consideration and made such changes as were agreeable to him and then presented his final Budget. At this, the third stage, the Finance Member explained his reasons for the acceptance of some and the non-acceptance of other suggestions made during the course of the Budget debate. A general discussion of the Budget then followed, but no resolution was allowed to be moved upon the final Budget or a vote taken.

The Budget procedure in the Provincial Legislatures was a little different. There the first stage commenced with the preparation of a rough draft of the provincial estimates, accompanied by a schedule including in it all projects involving an expenditure of over 5,000 rupees, divided into two parts, the first containing all allotted, i.e. obligatory, items of expenditure and the second containing unallotted, i.e. non-obligatory, items of expenditure.

The Government of India to whom this draft Budget was submitted corrected the estimate of the revenue and determined in consultation with the Provincial government the aggregate expenditure for which the latter should provide, and if need be, altered or added to the items in the first part of the schedule. When the figures of the altered revenue and the aggregate expenditure as fixed by the Government of India were communicated to the Provincial Government it marked the close of the first stage of a Provincial Budget.

The second stage commenced when this draft Budget was submitted by the Provincial Government to a committee of the Provincial Legislature. The Committee was composed of officials and non-officials in equal number, the former nominated by Government and the latter elected by their fellows. It was presided over by the member of the Executive in charge of Provincial Finance; the proceedings of the committee were informal and private and decisions were by majority votes.

The Committee concerned itself only with the second part of the Schedule containing non-obligatory items of expenditure and, provided it did not exceed the aggregate expenditure fixed by the Government of India, it was free to make variations and even to insert new items occasionally. On the conclusion of its labours the Committee reported the changes it made to its Government. With this ended the second stage in the Provincial Budget. The third stage began when the Provincial Estimates as a whole were presented to the Provincial Legislature by the member in charge of finance.

The Budget was then considered in a committee of the whole House and resolutions moved on each group of estimates discussed. When all resolutions were debated and voted upon the result of the discussions was communicated to the Provincial Government.

But the resolutions were not binding. The fourth stage commenced when the Provincial government introduced the final budget and explained its reasons for the acceptance of some and the non-acceptance of the rest of the suggestions made by the Legislature. A debate followed, but no resolutions were in order at this stage ; nor did the Legislature divide upon the Budget. It was adopted as passed by the Executive.

From these differences in the constitution and procedure of the Central and Provincial Governments, it must not be supposed that the provincial Governments were less irresponsible with regard to their Legislatures than the Central Government was with regard to its own Legislature.

The fact that since 1909 there was no majority of official members in the Provincial Legislature as there was in the Central Legislature was a matter of no moment so far as its practical consequences to the Executive were concerned ; for it is to be remembered that in practice the difference between nominated members from among the non-officials and the official members was only superficial.

Both had their mandate from the government who gave them their seats in the Legislature, and as nominees of the Government they voted for the Government, so that, though not in theory, in practice the Provincial Government had as much a standing majority in Legislatures as the Central Government had in theory as well as in practice.

Nor did the budget procedure of the Provincial Government mark any decided improvement over that adopted in the Central Government in the matter of giving greater control to the Legislature over the Executive. In both cases the aim was to give the members of the Legislature the privilege of discussing *beforehand* the question of such alteration with reference to the necessities of the Budget, only in the case of the Provincial

Budget this privilege was allowed to be exercised at an earlier stage than in the case of the Imperial Budget.

But in view of the fact that the Resolutions of the Legislature on the Provincial Budget, as those of the Central Legislature on the Imperial, were only recommendations to their respective Executives, this difference between the Budget procedure of the two Governments did not impose any greater control over the one Executive than it did on the other. Again, the provision that a committee of the Provincial Legislature had been allowed the privilege of framing the non-obligatory portion of the Provincial Budget did not give the Legislature any appreciable control over the Executive.

First of all, the Provincial Government could always restrict the scope of this Budget Committee by transferring any head from the class of non-obligatory expenditure to the class of obligatory expenditure. Besides this, the operation of certain other rules of Budget procedure based upon general principles of public finance tended directly to restrict the powers of the committee to put forth schemes of alternative or additional expenditure.

It was rightly provided that schemes involving recurring expenditure could only be proposed with due regard to the rate of growth of recurring revenues and recurring expenditure. Owing to this rule, the committee had to drop proposals which involved recurring expenditure, but which were desirable from its standpoint.

On the other hand, similar proposals made by the Executive could be easily carried through by the device freely adopted of obtaining previous sanction of the Government of India. The consequence was that in all the Provincial Budgets presented under the new rules the amount of this "unallotted" fund left to the discretion of the committee bore too insignificant a proportion to the total expenditure in the budget to make the Provincial Executive in any real degree amenable to the Provincial legislature.

No really responsible government could, however, be introduced in the provinces without first of all making a complete change in the mutual relations between the Central Government and the different Provincial Governments in India. The relation between the two which existed before the passing of the Act of 1919 was one of complete subordination of provincial Governments to the Central Government. In this bond of subordination we can discern three strands—legislative, financial, and administrative.

Of these three we have seen how tight was the financial strand. The Government of India's control over revenues and expenditure was derived from Parliamentary Statutes which treated the revenues of India as one and applied them to the purposes of the Government of India as a whole.

It is true that this provision was not so strictly construed as absolutely to prevent the appropriation of particular sources of income to specific purposes all-India or provincial. Or else the development of the provincial system of finance would have been impossible.

But it certainly had the effect of denying to Provincial Governments any inherent legal right to the revenues which they raised. The Government of India completely controlled taxation imposed in British India, apart from the local taxes which were raised by local bodies. Taxation could only be levied by law, but the law had forbidden a Provincial Legislature, without the previous sanction of the Government of India, to consider

"any law affecting the public debt of India or the customs duties or any other tax or duty for the time being in force and imposed by the authority of the Governor-General in Council for the general purposes of the Government of India."

This is the natural corollary of the statutory hypothecation of all-India revenues to all-India needs. The law would not inhibit a provincial legislature from exploiting for provincial purposes any new source of taxation which it had the ingenuity to discover. But even in that case the project would, before being translated into action, have to secure the assent of the Finance Department of the Government of India, which would not give its sanction without considering closely if it trespassed on the Central Government's sources of taxation. Again, the provision of the law which required that

"no governor or governor in council (of a province) shall have the power of creating any new office or granting any salary, gratuity or allowance without the previous sanction of the Governor General of India in Council" had given the Government of India a right of control over expenditure in the Provinces which was exercised through the instrumentality of a series of codes of instructions, such as the Civil Service Regulations, the Civil Account Code, the Public Works Code and the like.

These codes partly dealt with the mechanism of finance such as the maintenance of a uniform system of audit and accounts, the custody of public money, remittances, economy, and such matters ; but they also imposed definite restraints upon the powers of Provincial Governments, to create new appointments or raise emoluments and other matter such as recruitment, promotions, leave, foreign service and pensions upon which the codes really constitute a digest of the case-law laid down from time to time by the Government of India which the Provincial Governments must strictly obey.

If their powers of taxation and expenditure were strictly controlled the power of borrowing was never conceded to the provinces. It will be recalled that Port Trusts and Municipalities might raise loans within defined limits, but because the revenues of India were legally one and indivisible and were liable for all debts incurred for the purposes of the Government of India, Provincial Governments possessed no separate resources on the security of which they could borrow.

Even within the prescribed limits of Provincial Finance the Provincial Governments were not free from the control of the Central Government. Because the provincial settlements were based not on provincial revenues but on provincial needs, a central control was inevitable.

The Government of India could not allow a Province to go bankrupt. But if the Government of India were responsible for provincial solvency they must be in a position to control provincial expenditure. Again, as regards revenues, so long as the Government of India took a share in the proceeds they had a strong motive not only in interfering in the Budget estimates of the provinces, but also in interfering in details of administration.

Their interest in land revenue, for example, inevitably led them to close supervision over revenue settlements, and the control tended to become tighter in cases where expansion and development of a source of revenue, such as irrigation, depended on capital outlay.

The legislative powers of the Provincial Governments had in the same manner been made subject to statutory restrictions. There was no doubt an extensive field in which, so far as the substantive provisions of the Statute were concerned, the legislative competence of the provincial Legislatures was legally unfettered.

Actually, however, the power of the local legislatures was curtailed in two ways. In the first place, owing to the fact that in their existence all the Provincial Legislatures were younger, and most of them much younger, institutions than the Central Legislature of the Governor-General, a great part of the field that would have otherwise been open to them was covered by acts of that body, which had always retained a concurrent power of legislation for the country at large.

But the field yet remaining open for Provincial Governments in the matter of legislation was further restricted by the fact that the power of the Secretary of State and Parliament to control all-Indian legislation was made operative by means of executive directions, which had made it incumbent on Provincial Governments to submit for the previous sanction of the Government of India and the Secretary of State all their projects for legislation before introduction.

It is true that these directions did not apply to private members' Bills ; but inasmuch as a Bill could only be introduced with the leave of the Legislature, and the Provincial Government was in most cases in a position if it chose to do so to oppose such a motion successfully, the Government of India by directions to the Provincial Governments were in a position to control all private provincial legislation almost as effectively as the Provincial Government's Bills.

In carrying on the actual work of administration every Provincial Government was by law required to obey the orders of the Government of India and keep that Government constantly and diligently informed of its proceedings and of all matters which ought, in its opinion, to be reported to that Government, or as to which that Government required information. That was because in law every Provincial Government was placed under the superintendence, direction and control in all matters relating to the Government of its Province.

This administrative control of the Government of India was exercised by that Government in the interest of uniformity. It is obvious that in many respects India is one single and undivided country, in which much work had to be carried on uniform lines.

The Civil servants who executed the orders of Provincial governments having been recruited from England on terms guaranteed by the Secretary of State, many questions affecting them could not be determined by any Provincial Government. Again, the development of trade, industry and science throughout India similarly favoured the formulation and pursuit of uniform policies by the Government of India.

Even with one law for the whole of India business and industry might have been left to their discretion to administer such matters as statistics, patents, copyright, insurance, income tax, explosives and mining, etc. Not only were the provincial Governments subordinated to the Central Government to follow established lines in the matters of administration, but they were not free to initiate any new policy.

It was the Government of india which regarded itself as distinctly charged with the duty of framing policy and inspiring reforms for the whole of India by issuing new orders. To make them effective these orders were often accompanied by handsome grants to Provincial Governments strictly earmarked for the purpose of pushing on some particular feature of the new policy. Not seldom did the Government of India appoint new advising or inspecting officers whose task it was to see that the new energy suddenly infused into the system was well maintained and well directed to the chosen ends.

So long as the provincial Governments continued to be bound by such strands to the Government of India there could be no responsible government in the Provinces. No government can be made to serve two masters at one and the same time.

To keep the Provincial Governments subordinate to the Government of India and also to make them responsible to popular Legislature would have been inconsistent in theory and vicious in practice. It is quite conceivable that under such a double government the wishes of the Provincial Legislature on certain matters may not coincide with those of the Government of India.

On such occasions a Provincial Government may not know whom to obey. If it deferred to the wishes of the Legislature it would be failing in its duty towards the Government of India. Indeed there is on record a case of such a conflict.

There was an occasion during the currency of the Morley-Minto Reforms when the Government of Bombay were unsuccessful in their endeavours to persuade the Government of India to sanction certain charges affecting the educational staff. The proposals were locally popular and were again put forward for adoption in a resolution moved in the Bombay Legislature by an elected member.

The Bombay Government thereupon accepted the resolution which was carried unanimously, and once more put forward their proposals to the Government of India on the ground that they had the Legislature's entire support. But the Government of India and the Secretary of State held that these tactics were out of order and that it was "the duty of the Local Government in dealing with the resolutions to uphold with all their authority the decision of the Government of India," i.e. to have opposed the resolution even if it agreed with the Legislature in the principle thereof.

The strong ties of subordination which bound the Provinces to the Central Government were therefore the chief obstacles in the path of Provincial autonomy. In order that the Provincial Government be made subject to Provincial Legislatures, the first thing to do was to curtail the powers which the Government of India possessed of interference in provincial finance, provincial legislation, and provincial administration. As was well observed by the authors of the Report on Constitutional Reforms:

"We have to demolish the existing structure, at least in part, before we can build the new. Our business is one of devolution, of drawing lines of demarcation, of cutting long-standing ties. The Government of India must give and the Provinces must receive ; for only so can the growing organism of self-government in the Provinces draw air into its lungs and live."

The path to provincial independence therefore lay through a satisfactory division of functions and finances between the Provincial and Central Governments. Of the two, the task of dividing the functions was comparatively an easier one. For facilitating the necessary division of functions the following principles were laid down by the Government of India.

"There are certain subjects which are at present under the direct administration of the Government of India. The Government of India maintain separate staffs for their administration and the Provincial Governments have no share in it.

The category is easily recognisable, and for the most part there will not be much room for doubt as to the subjects to be included in it. At the other end of the line are matters of predominantly local interest which, however much conditions must vary between Provinces, will, generally speaking be recognised as proper subjects for provincialisation.

"Between these extreme categories, however, lies a large indeterminable field which requires further examination before the principles determining its classification can be settled. It comprises all the matters in which the Government of India at present retain ultimate control, legislative and administrative, but in practice share the actual administration in varying degrees with the Provincial Governments. In many cases the extent of delegation practised is already very wide.

The criterion which the Government of India apply to these is whether in any given case the Provincial Governments are to be strictly the agents of the Government of India, or are to have (subject to what is said below as to the reservation of powers of intervention) acknowledged authority of their own. In applying this criterion the main determining factor will be not the degree of delegation already practised, which may depend on mere convenience, but the consideration whether the interests of India as a whole (or at all events interests larger than those of one Province), or on the other hand the interests of the Province essentially preponderate.

"The point is that delegation to an agent may be already extensive, but that circumstance should not obscure the fact of agency or lead to the agent being regarded as having inherent powers of his own."

These principles, in which it was stated that "where extra provincial interests predominate the subject should be treated as central," while "all subjects in which the interests of the provinces essentially predominate should be provincial, and in respect of (which) the Provincial governments (to) have acknowledged authority of their own," were accepted by the Functions Committee appointed to make a division between all-India and Provincial subjects.

The recommendations made by the Committee were with minor amendments embodied in what are called Devolution Rules under section 45A of the Government of India Act of 1919, which gave effect to the policy of responsible government and are made a part of the constitutional law of the land, so that the subjects thereby devolving upon the Provinces became the services over which the Provinces gained an *acknowledged authority of their own* such as they never had before 1833.

Provincial Subjects

Local Self-government, that is to say, matters relating to the constitution and powers of municipal corporations, improvement trusts, district boards, mining boards of health and other local authorities established in a Province for the purpose of local self-government, exclusive of matters arising under the Cantonments Act, 1910 ; subject to legislation by the Indian Legislature as regards:

(a) The powers of such authorities to borrow otherwise than from a Provincial Government, and

(b) the levying by such authorities of taxation not included in schedule II to the scheduled Taxes Rules.

Medical administration, including hospitals, dispensaries and asylums, and provision for medical education.

Public Health and Sanitation and Vital Statistics; subject to legislation by the Indian Legislature in respect of infectious and contagious diseases to such extent as may be declared by any Act of the Indian Legislature.

Pilgrims within British India

Education, provided that:

(a) The following subjects shall be excluded, viz.

  (i) The Benares Hindu University, and Aligarh Muslim University, and such other universities constituted after the commencement of these rules, as may be declared by the Governor-General in Council to be Central subjects, and

  (ii) Chiefs' Colleges and any institution maintained by the Governor-General in Council for the benefit of members of His Majesty's Forces or of other public servants or of the children of such members of servants; and

(b) the following subjects shall be subject to legislation by the Indian Legislature, namely:

  (i) The control of the establishment, and the regulation of the constitutions and functions, of universities constituted after the commencement of these rules; and

  (ii) The definition of the jurisdiction of any university outside the Province in which it is situated, and

(iii) For a period of five years from the date of the commencement of these rules, the Calcutta University, and the control and organisation of secondary education in the presidency of Bengal.

Public Works included under the following heads, namely:

(a) Construction and maintenance of provincial buildings used or intended for any purpose in connection with the administration of the Province; and care of historical monuments, with the exception of ancient monuments as defined in Section 2(i) of the Ancient Monuments Preservation Act, 1904, which are for the time being declared to be protected monuments under Section 3(i) of that Act; provided that the Governor-General in Council may by notification in the *Gazette of India,* remove any such monuments from the operation of this exception ;

(b) roads, bridges, ferries, tunnels, ropeways, and causeways, and other means of communication, subject to such conditions as regards control over construction and maintenance of means of communication declared by the Governor-General in Council to be of military importance, and as regards incidence of special expenditure connected therewith, as the Governor-General in Council may prescribe;

(c) tramways within municipal areas; and

(d) light and feeder railways and extra-municipal tramways in so far as provision for their construction and management is made by provincial legislation ; subject to legislation by the Indian Legislature in the case of any such railway or tramway which is in physical connection with a main line or is built on the same gauge as an adjacent main line.

Water Supplies, irrigation and canals, drainage and embankments, water storage and water power ; subject to legislation by the Indian Legislature with regard to matters of inter provincial concern or affecting the relations of a Province with any other territory.

Land Revenue administration, as described under the following heads, namely:

(a) Assessment and collection of land revenue;

(b) Maintenance of land records, survey for revenue purposes, records of right ;

(c) Laws regarding land tenures, relations of landlords and tenants, collection of rents ;

(d) Courts of wards, incumbered and attached estates;

(e) Land improvement and agricultural loans;

(f) Colonisation and disposal of Crown lands and alienation of land revenue ; and

(g) Management of Government estates.

Famine Relief

Agriculture, including research institutes, experimental and demonstration farms, introduction of improved methods, provision for agricultural education, protection against destructive insects and pests and prevention of plant diseases ; subject to legislation by the Indian Legislature in respect of destructive insects and pests and plant diseases, to such extent as may be declared by any Act of the Indian Legislature.

Civil Veterinary Department, including provision for veterinary training, improvement of stock, and prevention of animal diseases ; subject to legislation by the Indian Legislature in respect to animal diseases to such extent as may be declared by any Act of the Indian Legislature.

Fisheries

Co-operative Societies

Forests, including preservation of game therein ; subject to legislation by the Indian Legislature as regards disforestation of reserved forests.

Land acquisition; subject to legislation by the Indian Legislature.

Excise, that is to say, the control of production, manufacture, possession, transport, purchase and sale of alcoholic liquor and intoxicating drugs, and the levying of Excise duties and licence fees on or in relation to such articles, but excluding in the case of opium, control of cultivation, manufacture and sale for export.

Administration of Justice, including constitution, powers, maintenance and organisation of courts of civil and criminal jurisdiction within the Province; subject to legislation by the Indian Legislature as regards High Courts, Chief Courts, and Courts of Judicial Commissioners, and any courts of criminal jurisdiction.

Provincial Law Reports

Administrators-General and Official Trustees ; subject to legislation by the Indian Legislature.

Non-Judicial Stamps, subject to legislation by the Indian Legislature, and Judicial Stamps, subject to legislation by the Indian Legislature as regards amount of court fees levied in relation to suits and proceedings in the High Courts under their original jurisdiction.

Registration of deeds and documents; subject to legislation by the Indian Legislature.

Registration of births, deaths, and marriages ; subject to legislation by the Indian Legislature for such classes as the Indian Legislature may determine.

Religious and Charitable Endowments

Development of Mineral resources which are Government property; subject to rules made or sanctioned by the Secretary of State, but not including the regulation of mines.

Development of Industries, including industrial research and technical education.

Industrial matters included under the following heads, namely:—

(a) Factories;

(b) Settlement of labour disputes;

(c) Electricity;

(d) Boilers;

(e) Gas;

(f) Smoke nuisance ; and

(g) Welfare of labour, including provident funds, industrial insurance (general health and accident) and housing : subject as to heads (a), (b), (c), (d), and (g) to legislation by the Indian Legislature.

Stores and Stationery ; subject in the case of imported stores and stationery to such rules as may be prescribed by the Secretary of State in Council.

Adulteration of food-stuffs and other articles ; subject to legislation by the Indian Legislature as regards import and export trade.

Weights and Measures; subject to legislation by the Indian Legislature as regards standard.

Ports, except such ports as may be declared by rule made by the Governor-General in Council or by or under Indian legislation to be major ports.

Inland Waterways; including shipping and navigation thereon so far as not declared by the Governor-General in Council to be Central subjects, but subject as regards inland steam-vessels to legislation by the Indian Legislature.

Police; including railway police ; subject in the case of railway police to such conditions as regards limits of jurisdiction and railway contributions to cost of maintenance as the Governor-General in Council may determine :

a) Regulation of betting and gambling ;

b) prevention of cruelty to animals;

c) protection of wild birds and animals;

d) control of poisons, subject to legislation by the Indian Legislature;

e) control of motor vehicles, subject to legislation by the Indian Legislature as regards licences valid throughout British India; and

f) control of dramatic performances and cinematographs, subject to legislation by the Indian Legislature in regard to sanction of films for exhibition.

Control of Newspapers, Books, and Printing Presses ; subject to legislation by the Indian Legislature.

Coroners, Excluded Areas

Criminal Tribes: subject to legislation by the Indian Legislature.

European Vagrancy: subject to legislation by the Indian Legislature.

Prisons: prisoners (except State prisoners) and reformatories ; subject to legislation by the Indian Legislature. Pounds and prevention of cattle trespass.

Treasure Trove

Libraries (except the Imperial Library) and Museums (except the Indian Museum, the Imperial War Museum and the Victoria Memorial, Calcutta) and Zoological Gardens.

Provincial Government Presses

Elections for Indian and provincial legislature, subject to rules framed under section 64 (i) and 72A (4) of the Act.

Regulations of medical and other professional qualifications and standards; subject to legislation by the Indian Legislature.

Local Fund audit, that is to say, the audit by Government agency of income and expenditure controlled by local bodies.

Control as defined by rule 10, of members of all-India and Provincial Services serving within the Province, and control, subject to legislation by the Indian Legislature, of public services within the province, other than all-India services.

Sources of Provincial revenue, not included under previous heads, whether:

(a) Taxes included in the schedules to the scheduled taxes Rules, or

(b) Taxes, not included in those schedules, which are imposed by or under provincial legislation which has received the previous sanction of the Governor-General.

Borrowing of money on the sole credit of the Province, subject to the provisions of the Local Government (Borrowing) Rules.

Imposition by legislation of punishment by fine, penalty, or imprisonment, for enforcing any law of the Province relating to any provincial subject; subject to legislation by the Indian Legislature in the case of any subject in respect of which such a limitation is imposed under these rules.

Any matter which, though falling within a Central subject, is declared by the Governor-General in Council to be of a merely local or private nature within the province.

Matters pertaining to a Central subject in respect of which powers have been conferred by or under any law upon a Local Government.

The second task that of allocating the revenue resources between the Central and provincial Governments was a comparatively difficult one. As the problem was conceived in the main as one of making the Provinces independent of the Government of India in matters in which it was proposed that they should acquire an authority of their own acknowledged by law it was natural for the authors of the Report on constitutional Reforms to hold that

"Our first aim...... has been to find some means of entirely separating the resources of the Central Government from those of the Provinces."

The first step in that direction was therefore to abolish the system of "divided heads" or budget by shared revenues, for there was a consensus of opinion that this coparcenary system, in so far as it gave a handle to the Central Government to interfere in the domestic affairs of the Provinces, was a source of friction and was incompatible with provincial independence. But such a system of complete separation was fraught with two main difficulties. The first difficulty was in connection with the disposal of dividend heads. To whom should they be handed over ? At the time the scheme of complete separation was contemplated the heads of revenue which were divided in all or some of the Provinces were land revenue, stamps, excise, income tax and irrigation. The authors of the Report on Constitutional Reforms proposed.

"......that the revenue from stamp duty should be discriminated under the already well-marked sub-heads *General* and *Judicial* ; and that the former should be made an Indian and the latter a provincial receipt. This arrangement will preserve uniformity in the case of commercial stamps where it is obviously desirable to avoid discrepancies of rates ; and it will also give the provinces a free hand in dealing with court-fee stamps and thus provide them with an additional means of augmenting their resources.

Excise is at present entirely a provincial head in Bombay, Bengal, and Assam, and we see no valid reason why it should not now be made provincial throughout India...... Land revenue, which is far the biggest head of all, is at present equally shared between the Indian and all the provincial Governments, except that Burma gets rather more than one-half and the United Provinces get rather less...... Now land revenue assessment and collection is so intimately concerned with the whole administration in rural areas that the advantages of making it a provincial receipt are obvious.......

Moreover, famine expenditure and expenditure on major irrigation works are for obvious reasons closely connected with land revenue, and if the receipts from that head are made provincial it logically follows that the Provinces should take over the very heavy liability for famine relief and protective works...... We were told that in the days of dawning popular government in the Provinces it would be well that the provincial government should be able to fall back on the support of the Government of India (as, if the head were still divided, it would be able to do) when its land revenue policy was attacked.

But it is just because divided heads are not regarded as merely a financial expedient but are, and so long as they survive will be, viewed as a means of going behind the provincial government to the Government of India, that we feel sure that they should be abolished. We propose therefore to make land revenue together with irrigation wholly provincial receipts. It follows that the Provinces will become entirely liable for expenditure on famine relief and protective irrigation works...... The one remaining head is income tax. We see two very strong reasons for making this an Indian receipt.

First, there is the necessity of maintaining a uniform rate throughout the country. The inconveniences, particularly to the commercial world, of having different rates in different Provinces are manifest. Secondly, in the case of ramifying enterprises with their business centre in some big city, the Province in which the tax is paid is not necessarily the Province in which income is earned.

We have indeed been told that income tax is merely the industrial or professional complement of the land revenue ; and that to provincialise the latter, while Indianising the former, means giving those provinces whose wealth is more prominently agricultural, such as the United Provinces and Madras, an initial advantage over a Province like Bombay, which has very large commercial and industrial interests.

Another very practical argument is that the tax is collected by provincial agency and that if Provincial Governments are given no inducement, such as a share of the receipts or a commission on the collections which is only such a share in disguise, there will be a tendency to slackness in collection and a consequent falling off in receipts.

We admit that these arguments have force ; but we are not prepared to let them stand in the way of a complete separation of revenues. Equality of treatment as between one Province and another must be reached so far as it is possible in the settlements as a whole, and it is not possible to extend the principle of equality to individual heads of revenue.

If it should be found that receipts fall off, it may be necessary to create an all-India agency for the collection of the tax, but this we should clearly prefer to retaining it as a divided head. To sum up : we propose to retain the Indian and Provincial heads as at present, but to add to the former income tax and general stamps, and to the latter land revenue, irrigation, excise and judicial stamps. No head will then remain divided."

However, when all the existing sources of revenue were completely distributed between the Central and Provincial Governments as proposed, it was inevitable that there should be a deficit in the Budget of the Government of India. How to make up this deficit was therefore the second difficulty that was involved in replacing the system of divided heads by a system of separate heads of revenue. The authors of the Report on Constitutional Reforms were presented with many a plan for the solution of this knotty problem. In the course of their survey they observed :

"One way of meeting it would be to maintain the basis of the present settlements, but to allot to the Government of India a certain proportion of growing revenue instead of its share of the divided heads. But this device would stereotype all the existing inequalities between the Provinces which by reason of the permanent settlement in some of them are considerable ; while it would also introduce an element of great uncertainty into the Indian Government's finance.

A second was that we should take an all-round contribution on a *per capita* basis. But this expedient also would not obviate very undesirable variations between Provinces in the rate of levy owing to the inequality of provincial resources and of provincial needs.

A third plan was to take an all-round percentage contribution based on gross provincial revenue. This is open, *inter alia,* to the objection that it would leave several of the Provinces with large deficits. Fourthly, we considered but rejected the proposal that Provinces which had a surplus should temporarily help others as being cumbrous and impracticable."

The plan recommended by the authors of the Report was "to assess the contribution from each Province to the Government of India as a percentage of the difference between the gross provincial revenue and the gross provincial expenditure ";

in other words, a levy on the surplus of the estimated gross revenue of the Province when all divided heads are separately allotted over its estimated normal expenditure, including

expenditure on famine relief and protective irrigation. On the basis of the Budget figures for 1917-18 it was found that it would require a levy of 87 percent on the provincial surpluses to make up the deficit of Rs. 1363 lakhs in the Budget of the Government of India found likely to be caused by the abolition of the system of divided heads.

The way in which the proposed plan would have worked out in practice can be gathered from the following figures given in the Report, Cal. Ed., and based on the Budget figures for 1917-18—

(In Lakhs of Rupees)

Province	Gross Prov. Revenue	Gross Prov. Expenditure	Gross Prov. Surplus	Contribution (87 per cent. of Col. 4)	Net Prov. Surplus
1	2	3	4	5	6
Madras	13,31	8,40	4,91	4,28	63
Bombay	10,01	9,00	1,01	88	13
Bengal	7,54	6,75	79	69	10
United Provinces	11,22	7,47	3,75	3,27	48
Punjab	8,64	6,14	2,50	2,18	32
Burma	7,69	6,08	1,61	1,40	21
Bihar and Orissa	4,04	3,59	45	39	6
Central Provinces	4,12	3,71	41	36	5
Assam	1,71	1,50	21	18	3
Total	68,28	52,64	15,64	13,63	2,01

N.B—The Punjab figures in column 5 should be reduced and those in column 6 raised by 3 1/2 lakhs in each case to allow for the continued compensation which the province is entitled to receive for the cession of a crore of its balances to the Government of India in 1914.

In making these recommendations the authors of the Report were careful to observe. "One caveat we are bound to make. Emergencies may arise which cannot be provided for by immediate raising Government of India taxation ; and in that case it must be open to the Central Government to make a special supplementary levy upon the provisions. We must add that inasmuch as our proposals are based on war figures they should be open to revision hereafter, but not subject to change for a period of say six years, and to avoid intermediate discussion the scheme should in the meantime be regarded as part of the constitutional agreement with the Provinces. It should also be one of the duties of the periodic commission which we propose should be appointed to examine the development of constitutional changes after ten years' experience of their working or of some similar body at that time, to re-investigate the question of the provincial contributions to the Government of India."

These proposals were put before the Provincial Governments, for their opinion. The objections to a plan which appeared to make some Provinces bear a greater burden of the cost of the Central Government than others readily suggested themselves. Madras and the United Provinces seemed to pay 47.4 percent and 41.1 percent of their surpluses to the Government of India, while Bombay and Bengal appeared to escape with a sacrifice of no more than 9.6 percent and 10.1 percent of their respective surpluses. The inequity of this treatment seemed to be so very apparent that the Provinces against which a greater burden was set down raised loud protests. So impressed was the Government of India with the justice of this clamour that in its letter to the Secretary of State it observed :

"We recommended that the initial contributions should be recognised as temporary and provisional, and that steps should be taken as soon as possible to fix a standard and equitable scale of contributions...... The whole question...... requires skilled investigation ; (the difficulty of the position was foreseen in the

Report and investigation by the first statutory commission was promised, but) we propose that a Committee on Financial Relations be appointed, either by you or by us, to advise fully upon the subject, so that each province may know exactly how it stands before the new regime starts." And this recommendation was endorsed by the Joint Select Committee of Parliament which sat on the Reform Bill. Accordingly the Secretary of State appointed a Committee under the chairmanship of Lord Meston to advise on:

a) The contributions to be paid by the various provinces to the Central Government for the financial year 1921-22;

b) The modifications to be made in the provincial contributions thereafter with a view to their equitable distribution until there ceases to be an all-India deficit ;

c) The future financing of the provincial loan accounts and

d) Whether the Government of Bombay should retain any share of the revenue derived from income tax.

After about seven weeks of investigation the Committee produced its Report. In advising on clause (a) of its terms of reference the Committee expressed its dissatisfaction of the plan set forth in the Joint Report of taking from the Provinces a fixed uniform proportion of their respective surpluses as their contributions to the Central Exchequer. The principal objection urged against the plan was that in some Provinces it left no surplus and in others no adequate surplus after the payment of their respective quotas of contributions. The Committee held, and rightly too, that

"in no case may a contribution be such as would force the province to embark on new taxation *ad hoc,* which to our minds would be an unthinkable sequel to a purely administrative rearrangement of abundant general resources."

The Committee felt itself bound by a limiting consideration in providing the contribution, as a result of which it felt itself obliged "to leave each Province with a reasonable working surplus"— a surplus which it preferred "to calculate, so far as possible, with some relation to the general financial position of the Province and the more imminent claims upon its resources."

"To be able to comply with the requirements of leaving each Province with a surplus, and of inaugurating the new Councils without the necessity of resort to fresh taxation," the Committee deemed that the most equitable plan to be to take, not *equal* contributions as the Joint Report advised, but *unequal* contributions from the surpluses of the Provinces liable to make them.

For the consummation of its plan the Committee held that the augmentation of Provincial Surpluses was an essential step. Without it, it deemed its task to be futile. The only way to augment the provincial surplus was to allocate some other source of Imperial revenue in addition to those already provincialised. To the provincialisation of the income tax, a matter which was included in clause (d) of its terms of reference so far as Bombay was concerned, the Committee being impressed by the reasoning of the Joint Report, felt bound to oppose.

As an alternative it recommended that *General Stamps* should be provincialised, as means of augmenting provincial surpluses, along with *Judicial Stamps.* The effect of this transfer of *General Stamps* from the all-India list to the provincial list was to increase the provincial resources and diminish those of the Central Government.

That deficit the Committee accepted as amounting in the year 1921-2 to ten crore, composed of six crores previously estimated by the Government of India *plus* four crores for the loss of *General Stamps,* the revenue from which the Committee gave to the Provinces.

This amount subject to certain adjustments, which when made resulted in a clear deficit of 9,83.06 lakhs net. In strict adherence to the limiting consideration which it felt bound to respect, the Committee proceeded to fix the following ratios in which each of the nine Provinces were to contribute to make up this amount of 9,83 lakhs in the year 1921-2 —

Initial Contributions (In Lakhs of Rupees)

Provinces	Increased spending power under new distribution of Revenue	Contributions as recommended by the Committee	Increased spending power left after Contributions are paid
Madras	5,76	3,48	2,28
Bombay	93	56	37
Bengal	1,04	63	41
United Provinces	3,97	2,40	1,57
Punjab	2,89	1,75	1,14
Burma	2,46	64	1,82
Bihar and Orissa	51	*nil*	51
Central Provinces	52	22	30
Assam	42	15	27
Total	18,50	9,83	8,67

This ratio of initial contributions was not intended in any manner by the Committee "to represent the ideal scale on which the Provinces should have in equity to be called upon to contribute." Indeed in making its recommendations as to initial contributions the Committee paid less attention to equity of contributions and more to "established programmes of taxation and expenditure and legislative and administrative expectations and habits, that cannot without serious mischief be suddenly adjusted to a new and more equitable ratio of contributions widely different (as an equitable ratio must admittedly be) from that of the past.

It is accordingly inevitable, if such mischief is to be avoided, that the ratio for initial contributions should bear little relation to that which would be ideally equitable." But the Committee also recognised that "an initial ratio of this nature can only be defended as a measure of transition. It is necessary, but it is necessary only in order to give time to the provinces to adjust their budgets to a new state of affairs; and we are clearly of opinion that no scheme of contribution can be satisfactory that does not provide for a more equitable distribution of the burden of the deficit within a reasonable time."

The Committee therefore proceeded next to consider the question of *standard* contributions as distinguished from *initial* contributions, which were only transitional. As to what should be the ideal basis for such an equitable distribution of the burden the Committee felt quite certain ; for it stated that,

"to do equity between the provinces it is necessary that the total contribution of each to the purse of the Government of India should be proportionate to its capacity to contribute."

Two questions were involved in translating this principle into practice. What is the total contribution of a province to the purse of the Government of India ? Secondly, what is the measure of the capacity of a Province to contribute ? With regard to the first the Committee observed that,

"the total contribution of a Province to the purse of the Government of India will consist in future of its direct contributions towards the deficit, together with its indirect contribution (as at present) through the channels of customs, income tax, duties on salt, etc." in other words, the pressure of the taxes from within its jurisdiction for the benefit of the Central Government. With regard to the second the Committee held that, "the capacity of a Province to contribute is its taxable capacity, which is the sum of the incomes of its taxpayers, or the average income of its taxpayers multiplied by their number."

The Committee was frank in its avowal of the fact that the data available was not sufficient for a direct quantitative evaluation either of the total net contribution which a Province made to the Government of India or of its capacity to contribute, and held that it was "useless to attempt to state a formula, to serve as a basis for a standard ratio of contributions, capable of automatic application from year to year by reference to ascertained statistics."

None the less the Committee did not abandon the ideal basis it had selected for fixing the standard contributions. For it observed :

"We are able, after surveying such figures as are available and after close inquiry into the circumstances of each Province, to recommend a fixed ratio of contributions which in our opinion represents a standard and equitable distribution of the burden of any deficit.

In arriving at this ratio we have taken into consideration the indirect contributions of the Provinces to the purse of the Government of India, and in particular the incidence of customs duties and of income tax.

We have inquired into the relative taxable capacities of the Provinces, in the light of their agricultural and industrial wealth and of all other relevant incidents of their economic positions, including particularly their liability to famine.

It should be observed that we have considered their taxable capacities not only as they are at the present time, or as they will be in the immediate future, but from the point of view also of the capacity of each Province for expansion and development agriculturally and industrially, and in respect of imperfectly developed assets such as minerals and forests.

We have also given consideration to the elasticity of the existing heads of revenue which will be secured to each Province, and to the availability of its wealth for taxation."

After estimating, to the best of its ability, the weight which should be given to each of these circumstances, the Committee recommended the following fixed ratio as representing an equitable basis for the relative contributions of the Provinces to meet the deficit in the Budget of the Government of India:—

Standard Contributions

Province	*Percent. Contribution to Deficit.*
Madras	17
Bombay	13
Bengal	19
United Provinces	18
Punjab	9
Burma	61/2
Bihar and Orissa	10
Central Provinces	5
Assam	2 1/2
Total	100

The Committee agreed that there should be an interval of time sufficient to enable the Provinces to adjust their budgets to the new conditions before they should in equity be called upon to contribute according to this standard ratio.

But the Committee thought that the interval allowed for adjustment should not be unduly prolonged.

"The initial ratio which," the Committee said, "we have proposed is a practical necessity, but the Provinces which will be called upon to pay thereunder more than they should pay in equity, ought not to be required to bear that burden for a longer period or to a greater extent than is required to prevent dislocation of the provincial budgets."

The Committee therefore proposed "that contributions should be made on the standard ratio to any deficit that there may be in the seventh year of contribution, and that the process of transition from the initial to the standard ratio should be continuous beginning in the second year of contribution, and proceeding in six equal annual steps."

The following table shows the initial, intermediate, and ultimate ratios of contributions for the seven years in accordance with the recommendations of the Committee :—

Percent, Contributions to Deficit in Seven Consecutive Years Beginning with the First Year of Contribution

Rounded off to even Halves

Province	1st Year	2nd Year	3rd Year	4th Year	5th Year	6th Year	7th Year
Madras	35 ½	32 ½	29½	26 ½	23	20	17
Bombay	5 ½	7	8	9½	10½	12	13
Bengal	6 ½	8½,	10½	12 ½	15	17	19
United Provinces	24 ½	23 ½,	22 ½	21	20	19	18
Punjab	18	16½,	15	13½,	12	10½	9
Burma	6 ½	6½,	6½	6½	6 ½	6½	6½
Bihar and Orissa	*nil*	1 ½	3	5	7	8 ½	10
Central Provinces	2	2½	3	3½	4	4½	5
Assam	1 ½	1 ½	2	2	2	2	2 ½
Total	100%	100%	100%	100%	100%	100%	100%

These recommendations were accepted by the Government of India and the Secretary of State. But when the rules in which they were embodied came before the Joint Select Committee of Parliament appointed to revise the draft rules made under the Government of India Act, for consideration, the Committee made some important alterations in the allocation of revenues and contributions from the Provinces. In its Report the Joint Committee recognised "the intricacy of the problem with which the Financial Relations Committee had to deal, and the difficulty, amounting almost to impossibility, of arriving at any solution which was likely to be acceptable to all Local Governments...... They believe that such dissatisfaction as the proposals have aroused is inevitable in distributing resources between a Central and Provincial Governments, and that the impossibility of removing by a stroke of the pen inequalities which are the result of long-standing and historical causes have been overlooked." "None the less," the Committee desired, "on grounds of policy, to alleviate the disappointment caused by the restraints which the system of contribution laid on the employment by the provinces of their revenues. As a means of alleviating the burden the Committee suggested:

(1) That there should be granted to all provinces some share in the growth of revenue from taxation on incomes so far as that growth is attributable to an increase in the amount of income assessed."

(2) That in no case should the initial contribution payable by any province be increased, but that the gradual reduction of the aggregate contribution should be the sole means of attaining the theoretical standards recommended by the Financial Relations Committee." Accordingly it is provided in the Devolution Rules that:

(15) There shall be allocated to each Local Government a share in the income tax collected under the .Indian Income Tax Act, 1918, within its jurisdiction. The share so allocated shall be three pies on each rupee brought under assessment under the said Act, in respect of which the income tax assessed has been collected. The number of pies to be specified shall be so calculated as to yield at the outset to the Local Governments collectively a sum amounting as near as may be to 400 lakhs and that

(17) In the financial year 1921-2 contributions shall be paid to the Governor-General in Council by the Local Governments mentioned below according to the following scale:—

Name of the Province of the Province	Contributions (in lakhs of rupees)
Madras	3,48
Bombay	56
Bengal	63
United Provinces	2,40
Punjab	1,75
Burma	64
Central Provinces and Berar	22
Assam	15

(18) From the financial year 1922-3 onwards a total contribution of 9,83 lakhs, or such smaller sum as may be determined by the Governor-General in Council, shall be paid to the Governor-General in Council by the Local governments mentioned in the preceding rule. When for any year the Governor-General in Council determines as the total amount of the contribution a smaller sum than that payable for the preceding year, a reduction shall be made in the contributions of those Local Governments only whose last previous annual contribution exceeds the proportion specified below of the smaller sum so determined as the total contribution ; and any reduction so made shall be proportionate to such excess:

Madras	17/90 th
Bombay	13/90 th
Bengal	19/90 th
United Provinces	18/90 th
Punjab	9/90 th
Burma	6 ½ /90 th
Central Provinces and Berar	5/90ths
Assam	2 ½ /90 th

In cases of emergency the Local Government of any Province may be required by the Governor-General in Council, with the sanction of the Secretary of State, to pay to the Governor-General in Council a contribution for any financial year in excess of the amount required by the preceding rules in the case of that year. Two more matters had to be settled in order to make the separation between Provincial and Central Finance as complete as possible. Both were connected with capital transactions. One was the question of the Provincial Loan Account.

This Account represented the fund from which a Provincial Government advanced agricultural loans, loans to indebted landholders, to municipalities and other local bodies, etc. The capital was provided by the Government of India as required and was returned to it as it was repaid. The province paid the Government of India interest on the average capital outstanding in each year, recouping itself by higher rates of interest which were supposed to compensate it for bad debts. It was commonly agreed that it was the natural result of the Reforms Scheme that the Provinces should for the future finance their own loan transactions, and that joint accounts of this nature between them and the Government of India should be wound up as quickly as possible. The matter was referred to the Financial Relations Committee and on the basis of its recommendations in that behalf it was provided by Rule 23 of the Devolution Rules that :

"Any moneys which, on the 1st day of April 1921, are owed to the Governor-General in Council on account of advances made from the provincial loan account of any Province shall be treated as an advance to the Local Government from the revenues of India, and shall carry interest at a rate calculated on the average rate carried by the total amount owed to the Governor-General in Council on this account on the 31st March 1921. The interest shall be payable upon such dates as the Governor-General in Council may fix. In addition, the Local Government shall pay to the Governor-General in Council in each year an instalment in repayment of the principal amount of the advance, and this instalment shall be so fixed that the total advance shall except where for special reasons the Governor-General in Council may otherwise direct, be repaid before the expiry of twelve years. It shall be open to any Local Government to repay in any year an amount in excess to the fixed instalment."

The other was the question of responsibility for capital expenditure on irrigation works. In this as in the matter of Provincial Loan Account it was agreed that it would be incompatible with the scheme of complete separation of Provincial Finance to hand over to the former the control of irrigation works and to make the latter responsible for the capital transaction incurred thereon. Hence the rule that:

(1) The capital sums spent by the Governor-General in Council upon the construction in the various Provinces of productive and protective irrigation works and of such other works financed from loan funds as may from time to time be handed over to the management of

Local Governments shall be treated as advances made to the Local Governments from the revenues of India. Such advances shall carry interest at the following rates, namely: (a) In the case of outlay up to the end of the financial year 1916-17, at the rate of 3.3252 *percentum. (b)* In the case of outlay incurred after the financial year 1916-17, at the average rate of interest paid by the Governor-General in Council on loans raised in the open market since the end of that year.

(2) The interest shall be payable upon such dates as the Governor-General in Council may fix. Thus was broken the financial and administrative strand which tied the Provincial Governments to the Central Government and prevented the introduction into them of responsible government. As the Provinces thereby acquired "an acknowledged authority of their own" over the services and sources allocated to them it followed that they should have the freedom to borrow in their own name, which was denied to them heretofore. Consequently the Local Government Borrowing Rules made under the Reforms Act provided that subject to certain conditions:

"A Local Government may raise loans on the security of the revenues allocated to it for any of the following purposes, namely:

a) To meet capital expenditure on the construction or acquisition (including the acquisition of land, maintenance during construction and equipment) of any work or permanent asset of a material character in connection with a project of lasting public utility, provided that :

   I. the proposed expenditure is so large that it cannot reasonably be met from current revenues, and

   II. if the project appears to the Governor-General in Council unlikely to yield a return of not less than such percentage as he may from time to time by order prescribe, arrangements are made for the amortisation of the debt;

b) to meet any classes of expenditure on irrigation which have under rules in force before the passing of the Act been met from loan funds;

c) for the giving of relief and the establishment and maintenance of relief works in times of famine or scarcity ;

d) for the financing of the Provincial Loan Account ; and

e) for the repayment or consolidation of loans raised in accordance with these rules or the repayment of advance made by the Governor-General in Council."

With the cutting off of the financial and administrative strand there remained only the legislative strand which had so far debarred the growth of provincial autonomy. This legislative strand, as was pointed out before, operated through the principle of requiring previous sanction and subsequent assent of the Government of India.

By the rules made under the Reforms Act a field has been marked off for the free exercise of the Legislative powers of the Provinces in which that principle has been dispensed with. So far as the field of tax legislation was concerned it was provided that:

"The Legislative Council of a Province may, without the previous sanction of the Governor-General, make and take into consideration any law for imposing for the purposes of the Local Government any tax included in Schedule I."

This schedule comprises the following heads of taxation: —

1. A tax on land put to uses other than agricultural.
2. A tax on succession or acquisition by survivorship in a joint family.
3. A tax on any form of betting or gambling permitted by law.
4. A tax on advertisements.
5. A tax on amusements.
6. A tax on any specified luxury.
7. A registration fee.

8. A stamp-duty other than duties of which the amount is fixed by Indian legislation.

In the matter of non-tax legislation the procedure adopted by the rules has been slightly different. In tax legislation the rules stated in what cases previous sanction was not necessary. In non-tax legislation the rules required in what cases previous sanction was necessary. The effect of this difference in the requirements of the rules of previous sanction was that while in matters of tax legislation a Provincial Government could only levy certain named taxes, in the matter of non-tax legislation it could do anything provided it did not infringe certain laws.

The reasons for this difference are obvious. A widening of the basis of provincial taxation means a narrowing field for imperial taxation. Such a detrimental effect could not flow to the Government in the matter of non-tax legislation, be the non-tax legislative powers of the Provinces howsoever large. The taxing power to be granted to the Provinces had therefore to be more strictly circumscribed than the grant of legislative power. None the less it cannot be denied that the rules regarding previous sanction sufficiently loosened the legislative strand as to permit of the Provinces being autonomous in theory as well as in practice.

This autonomy is well reflected in the new Budget Procedure in the Provinces. Under the old regime the Provincial Budgets had to be passed by the Finance Department of the Government of India, the Provincial Accounts to be supervised by the Accountant-General and audited by the Controller and Auditor-General of the Government of India and appropriation reports submitted to the Finance Department of the Government of India. All this is changed under the new regime. The Provincial Budget, instead of being passed by the Finance Department of the Government of India, is framed by the Finance Department constituted in each Province under the Reforms Act and is voted item by item by the Provincial Legislature.

The accounts of the Provinces still continue to be supervised and audited by the officers of the Government of India, but the important point under the new regime which is the hall-mark of provincial independence is that the appropriation reports, instead of being sent to the Government of India for action, are now sent to the Committee of Public Accounts constituted from amongst the members of the Provincial Legislature which sanctioned the Budget for report that the money voted by the Legislature was spent within the scope of the grants made by the Legislature.

Thus is effected the demarcation of the field for the governance of. India into Central and Provincial. Such a demarcation of administrative and financial matters was the dream of many an Indian politician and statesman. It was urged before the Royal Commission on Decentralisation and was also urged by the late Mr. Gokhale in his political testament which he left before he died. But all these projects were ill timed and could not be given effect to until the law of the Indian constitution had been altered. Now that such an alteration has been made the ideal of Provincial autonomy bids fair to become real. But before closing this study it may be useful to evaluate the changes of its successful working.

9

A Critique of the Change

It is obvious that good administration depends upon good finance; for finance is "the fuel of the whole administrative machine." No aspect of the scheme of Reforms therefore demands a closer and more anxious study than the financial arrangements with which the new system of administration starts. The necessity for such an examination is all the greater because this aspect of the Reforms Scheme has received comparatively little intelligent criticism at the hands either of the public or the expert.

The first question to consider is, can the new financial arrangements be said to be *administratively* workable ? To make administrative polities independent by requiring them to finance themselves entirely out of their own respective resources without having to depend upon one another must always be regarded as a very important end to be kept in view in devising a new financial arrangement. It is true that it is not always possible to realise this end, and it may in some cases be actually helpful to their working that the polities should be made mutually dependent; for interdependence, at least in matters of public finance, instead of being an impediment might conceivably furnish a basis for co-operation and strength. None the less independence in finance for each administrative policy is to be sought for wherever possible. There can be no doubt that from this standpoint the system of contributions is better than the system of divided heads. This is not to condemn the system of divided heads. The existence of several concurrent or overlapping tax jurisdictions must always be a source of difficulty whenever an attempt is to be made to distribute the different sources of revenue among the competing tax jurisdictions so as to allow each a sufficiency of funds. The reason is that this distribution of the sources of revenue must not only be governed by considerations of adequacy, but must also be governed by considerations of suitability. "The problem of efficiency of taxation," as Prof. Seligman observes, "is naturally of vital importance. No matter how well intentioned a scheme may be, or how completely it may harmonise with the abstract principles of justice, if the tax does not work administratively it is doomed to failure."

Whether among the sources of revenue to be partitioned there are any which are naturally more suitable for utilisation by one tax jurisdiction rather than by another depends upon what is the basis of the tax. If the basis of the tax is narrow then the argument in favour of its utilisation by a narrower tax jurisdiction will be correspondingly stronger. If its basis is wide then the scales would weigh in favour of its utilisation by the broader tax jurisdiction. But as a result of following the dictates of suitability it is not always possible to make a partition such as to give each administrative polity revenues adequate for its purposes. For it may happen that a particular tax is suitable for one jurisdiction while its yield, instead of being necessary for that jurisdiction, may be required for another jurisdiction which is unfit to levy it, or may be partially necessary for both. In such a case, how are the ends of adequacy to be subserved ? Two remedies suggest themselves. One is the adoption of the system of divided heads, and the second is to apportion the deficiency among the several component states and require them to make a definite contribution towards meeting it.

The system of divided heads was by no means peculiar to the Indian fiscal system. It has been adopted in some form or other by many other countries. In England, for instance, the inheritance tax is assessed by the Central Government, but a part of the proceeds is allotted to the Local Government. The same is true of some other taxes in England. In Germany, under the Empire, the proceeds of certain indirect taxes were divided between the federal and state governments. In Canada it is well known that a large part of the provincial revenues is derived from proceeds of taxes that are levied by the federal government. The prejudice in India against the system of divided heads of revenue is particularly regrettable because it is founded on the view that it is opposed to the principle of separation of revenues. People who opposed it said that it involved divided heads of expenditure which fettered the spending powers of the Provinces and enabled the Government of India directly to interfere in their Budget estimates and "to have its finger in every pie" of theirs. The system of divided heads was no doubt characterised by these objectionable features. But division of expenditure is not a necessary accompaniment of division of revenue. Nor is it a necessary incident of it that a polity which shared in the yield of a tax but did not administer it should interfere in calculating the estimates of the yield.

Chipped of its evil features, the system of divided heads of revenue is simply another name for what Prof. Seligman calls the system of segregation of source and the division of the yield. The essence of the system consists in the exclusive assessment of a particular source of revenue by one tax jurisdiction, coupled, however, with an apportionment of a part of the proceeds to another tax jurisdiction. The system of divided heads of revenue does not cease to be a system of separation of sources merely because there is the division of the yield. In such a system of divided heads there is a separation because the assessment of the tax is segregated—which is the essence of separation—exclusively in the hands of one tax jurisdiction, and the division of the yield can be so regulated that it need not be incompatible with real separation.

The system of contributions does what the system of divided heads aims to do. Like the system of divided heads it answers the tests of suitability as well as of adequacy by allowing the tax to be administered by the jurisdiction most competent to do it, and also of adequacy by making the taxing jurisdiction hand over a sum to the non-taxing jurisdiction. Essentially the system of divided heads and the system of contributions are alike. The only difference between the two is that so far as the apportionment of proceeds are concerned the one is an itemised arrangement while the other is a lump-sum arrangement. There is therefore really nothing much to choose between them. But this is not altogether a case of merely giving a different name to a discredited system in the hope that it might smell more sweet. For the system of contributions has one real point of superiority as compared with the system of divided heads. It does not merely permit of separation of assessment, but it also makes for a greater separation than does the system of divided heads. Under the system of divided heads the receiving party has still an anxious concern in the assessment and collection of the tax for any laxity in the administration of a divided head of revenues is bound to affect its interests adversely, and may therefore claim a hand in the administration of the tax. But under the system of contributions there is no room for such a possibility. Its quota being assured it is out of the business of assessing and collecting the tax.

There is thus a greater separation under the system of contributions than there can be under the system of divided heads. When we come to analyse the equity of the new financial arrangements we find that great objections are raised to the system of contributions. But many of these objections are misconceived. It will be recalled that the contributions from the Provinces to the Central Government in India are regulated according to their spending powers. In other words, it is the apportionment by expenditure method of dealing with the deficit.

That the method subserves the ends of adequacy is of course obvious. But what does not seem to be so obvious, but which all the same is a great virtue of the system of contributions, is that it promotes economy in the giving as well as in the receiving tax jurisdiction; for extravagance in the contributing tax jurisdiction immediately increases its burden, while extravagance in the receiving tax jurisdiction is directly reflected in enhancing the contributions. None the less, the contributions, it is protested, are iniquitous, for they are held to be based not on population, nor on area, nor on wealth, nor on the capacity of the Provinces. It is also complained that the system of contributions according to spending powers is unwise, for it tends to check desirable expenditures in the more progressive Provinces.

The latter is, of course, a real objection to the apportionment by expenditure method of contributions in its general form. But it may be said, on the other hand, that in the first place if a jurisdiction is willing to undertake the burdens of a larger expenditure for desirable aims, it will scarcely be deterred by the slight additional burden which might result from the increase in the contribution. Secondly, if it were found that the contribution did produce such a result it would be possible to obviate it by adopting the simple expedient of exempting certain kinds of expenditure which might be deemed to be necessary. What these expenditures should be would be a matter of adjustment, which might differ in different provinces. The virtues of the system of apportionment by expenditure method of levying contributions would still be conserved intact, and its automatic features would work equally well if certain expenditures only, instead of all expenditures, were selected as the basis of calculations. This objection cannot, however, be urged against the Indian system of contributions. In the first place, the contribution is not a varying sum as is the case in the financial systems of other countries. Because the Provinces are made contributory towards the deficit of the Central Government it is to be remembered that they are not liable to the whole of the central deficit whatsoever it may be from year to year. On the other hand, in ordinary years the Provinces are only liable to make contributions towards meeting what is called the Standard Central Deficit of Rs. 9.83 lakhs.

That being the case the contributions do not form an element of uncertainty in the Provincial Budgets. Secondly, the contributions are not a permanent feature of the financial arrangements between the Central and Provincial Governments. The levy of the contributions is contemplated to be only transitional, to allow the Government of India to work out its financial salvation, and the Government of India has promised that they will adopt such a policy as to bring about the extinction of the contributions in as short a time as possible. Lastly, the ratio of the contributions to the standard revenues or expenditure of any of the Provinces is not so great as to place a heavy incubus on their financial system, and not being a varying quantity cannot be said to check useful expenditures by Provinces which propose to incur them.

As a matter of fact whatever may be said against the flaws in the apportionment by expenditure method of levying contributions it would be difficult to deny that the system eminently answers the requirements of equity. It certainly brings about a more equitable distribution of the burden than is possible under other systems. For it may fairly be assumed that expenditures very nearly correspond to the actual abilities of the communities concerned more than do population or area.

Not only is the principle equitable in itself, but care has been taken to do equity in its application as between the different Provinces. For we know that the contributions are so regulated as to leave to the Provinces, rich as well as poor, a reserve of spending power in order to enable them to meet such of their pressing needs as may not have been covered by the figure for standard expenditure. The main purpose of rejecting equal in favour of unequal contributions was to see that the burden of the contributions did not prevent any of the Provinces from meeting such extra expenditure as may be absolutely necessary. Indeed, no system of contributions can be said to be calculated to produce greater equity than the Indian system.

So far we have examined whether the new financial arrangement is administratively workable and equitable. What we have now to see is: Has the arrangement proved itself to be financially adequate? It will be recalled that the Financial Relations Committee held that the general resources of the country were abundant, and that it required only a wise plan of distribution in order to leave each Province with a sufficiently large "spending power" or surplus.

(In Thousands of Rupees)

Province		Standard Figures	Revised 1921-2	Budget 1922-3
	Revenue	14,98,02	15,58,59	16,76.50
Madras	{ Expenditure	14,07,20	17.15.93	17,18,55
	{ Surplus and Deficit	90,82	—1,57,34	—42,05
	Revenue	12,09,70	13,67,13	14,93,06
Bombay	(Expenditure	11,55,03	16,52,80	15,42,17
	Surplus and Deficit	54,67	—2,85,67	—50,11
	Revenue	8,55,28	8,86,53	10,55,86
Bengal	{ Expenditure	8,61,13	11,10,60	10,36,90
	Surplus and Deficit	—5,85	—2,24,07	18,96
	Revenue	12,29,88	13,34,31	13,58,67

United Provinces	{ Expenditure	12,06,56	14,59,87	13,85,65
	L Surplus and Deficit	1,23,32	—1,25,56	—26,98
	/ Revenue	9,73,51	10,73,76	11,38,26
Punjab	{ Expenditure	9,10,69	62,82	12,23,24
	{ Surplus and Deficit	—1,49,48	12,68,44	—1,30,18
	/ Revenue	8,24,28	9,99,33	10,00,57
Burma	/ Expenditure	7,84,78	10,27,51	11,90,70
	{ Surplus and Deficit	39,50	—28,18	—1,90,13
	/ Revenue	4,30,39	4,46.15	4,62,65
Bihar and	{ Expenditure	4,20,70	4,85,97	5,13,80
Orissa	{ Surplus and Deficit	90,69	—39,82	—51,15
	/Revenue	4,35,37	5,14,80	5,35,23
Central	{ Expenditure	4,38,80	5,41,76	5,72,17
Provinces	{ Surplus and Deficit	—3,43	—26,96	—36,94
	{ Revenue	1,81,46	2,01,12	2,08,06
Assam	{ Expenditure	1,78,25	2,19,45	2,22,58
	{ Surplus and Deficit	3,21	—18,33	—14,52

That the plan recommended by the Committee was calculated to bring about such a result must of course be taken for granted. But when we analyse the Budgets of the different Provinces since the introduction of the Reforms the result appears to be entirely disappointing.

Thus, taking the estimated revenue and expenditure of the nine Provinces for 1922-3, equilibrium between current revenue and expenditure is only to be found in two of them, Burma and Bengal, and in the latter this result could not have been attained but for the temporary remission of its annual contribution to the Central Government, and a programme of taxation calculated to bring in Rs. 140 lakhs. In the rest of the Provinces the deficits of the year aggregated to the large figure of Rs. 7,74 lakhs. This huge deficit was financed by new taxation to the extent of Rs. 3,52 lakhs, and for the rest by drawing on balances and by raising loans from the public and from the Central Government. But as the Secretary of State in his despatch pointed out, this"process of financing provincial deficits in part from the accumulated revenue balances of the past will now practically come to an end, as such balances will be generally exhausted by the end of the current financial year............ If the financial stability of the Provinces is not to be undermined, with ultimate jeopardy to the Government of India itself, it is impossible to contemplate the continuance of a series of Provincial deficits financed by borrowing either direct from the public or from the Central Government."

What is to be the remedy ? At the Conference held in Simla in April, 1922, "to consider various matters connected with the financial arrangements between the Central Government and the Provinces," it was disclosed that the Government of India and the Provinces were divided as to the proper solution for the rehabilitation of Provincial Finance on a stable and secure footing. The Provinces proposed an increase in their resources by revising the financial arrangements made by the Reforms Act. On the other hand, the Secretary of State as a mouthpiece of the Government of India urged that "Equilibrium can only be achieved by reduction of expenditure and the adoption of measures which will lead to an increase of revenue"

The Provinces were not, however, unanimous in the suggestions they made for the revision of the arrangements effected by the Act. Some like the Government of Bombay suggested a return to the system of "divided heads" while others were opposed to it. But the majority was for securing relief through the abolition of contributions. This attitude of the Provinces towards the new financial arrangements is on the face of it a very unreasonable attitude. They are opposed both to the system of divided heads and the system of contributions as well. This is to have things both ways, and they could certainly have had it if the existing resources of the country had been properly husbanded.

Inadequacy of finance is not always the result of a paucity of revenue resources. National prosperity may be great and growing and the increase of national wealth may be proceeding unchecked. If under such circumstances enough revenue is not obtained the fault does not lie with the social income. Rather it is a fault of the government which must be said to have failed to organise and marshal the national resources for fiscal purposes. The same is to some extent true of the Indian Government.

Surveying the national resources of the country, it becomes evident that there are two sources which the Government has not been able to marshal properly. One is the land revenue. It is notorious that land revenue has been the biggest resource to the Government of India. In the collection of the land revenue every landholder is laid under contribution, but the rate of assessment is not periodically enhanced for every one of them. On the other hand, in Bengal and in other parts of India the rate of assessment is permanently settled.

Consequently in such parts of India which by the long period of settled government enjoyed by them, and by the consequent influx of capital, have attained to a greater advance in prosperity than any others, the land revenue yields practically no increase; the land-owners, with enormously increased incomes, contribute nothing to the increase in the financial burdens of the State. Permanent Settlement has ever since the days of Lord Canning been suggested as a panacea for improving the financial condition of the people. After the severe famine of 1860, Lord Canning, then Viceroy and Governor-General of India, recommended the extension of the Permanent Settlement to all parts of India.

Sir John (afterwards Lord) Lawrence supported the recommendation, and the two Secretaries of State for India, Sir Charles Wood and Sir Stafford Northcote, approved of the proposal. Fortunately for the country the proposal for making the Permanent Settlement universal was finally rejected in 1883. Some no doubt regarded the decision as unfortunate, and continued the agitation in favour of the permanent Settlement long after. But the real force, if there was any in the agitation, was derived from the motive of putting a limit on the financial resources of an alien and an irresponsible bureaucracy.

Those who then agitated in favour of the Permanent Settlement probably did not realise that some day this irresponsible bureaucracy would give place to a responsible government of the people and the Permanent Settlement which it was desired to be instituted as a curb on the unchartered licence of a bureaucracy would result in placing a fetter on the freedom of a popular government to enter upon the path of orderly progress.

A bad government may abuse its financial powers, but a government cannot be a good government if there is a serious limitation on its financial powers. It was therefore a good thing that this evil of a permanent settlement was not allowed to spread to the whole of India. But it would have been better if the new financial arrangements had contrived to replace the permanent settlement system of land revenue by a periodical settlement system. That was one important way of augmenting the general resources of the country and thereby giving adequacy to all the governments concerned. Instead of this the financial arrangements were so conceived as not to "subject the permanently settled provinces to financial pressure which would have the practical result of forcing them to reconsider the permanent settlement." If this had been done it would have augmented the general resources to the benefit of all. As it was, not only provision was made favouring the retention of the Permanent Settlement, but the Bengal Government, which has the largest number of permanently settled holders of land, was later on exempted from contributing to the Government of India which was compelled to meet its deficit in other ways.

Land Revenue therefore is one source which the Government could have marshalled in the interest of giving adequacy to the new financial arrangements.

The other source which the Government refuses to tap is the customs revenue. The kind of fiscal policy that was adopted during the pre-Mutiny days, was, as we know it to be, of a suicidal character. The same is true of the post-Mutiny fiscal policy. From the Mutiny up to the present time, the Government of India has never looked upon the customs revenue as a resource to be used to meet the exigencies of the State, and when it has used it, it is only very reluctantly, and never to the fullest, not to mention the circumstances when it has actually reduced its revenue from this source in spite of the crying needs of the exchequer.

While the ostensible reason given in favour of such a fiscal policy is that the customs revenue is wrong in principle, everybody knows that the customs revenue is not raised in India because it is feared that under it Indian industries would be protected against English industries. That the whole policy of India has been dictated by the interests of English manufactures is beyond dispute, and the reason for it is not far to seek. The Secretary of State for India, the supreme executive for India, is directly amenable to the English voters, whose primary concern has been to see that their markets are not closed against them. Whether a protectionist policy is good or bad is another question. For the present it is sufficient to note that the Government of India has been subjected to a pernicious kind of limitation on its fiscal powers which prevents it from using a source of revenue which has everywhere else proved to be most elastic and abundant of financial resources.

If these limitations were not there the present financial inadequacy in all probability might not have ensued at all, and there would have been no necessity either for adopting the system of divided heads or for imposing contributions. As it is, owing to these limitations on the taxable resources of the country, a deficit in the Budget of the Central Government is inevitable. Given this fact, the adoption of some method of meeting that deficit was imperative, and there is no doubt that the system adopted is better than the system it replaced. In the present circumstances of the finances of the Central Government, contributions must be taken as a settled issue. Nor can it be said that the abolition of contributions would restore stability to Provincial Finance. Such no doubt is the prevalent view of the Provincial Governments and also of non-official politicians.

The Resolution moved in the Indian Legislative Assembly on the 14th September, 1922, rested on the same view that if the Government of India were only to dispense with the contributions it would immediately restore equilibrium in the financial position of the Provinces. This belief was strengthened by the assumption that the aggregate estimated deficit of all the Provinces disclosed itself to be 352 lakhs of rupees for the financial year 1922-3; and as the total contribution to the Imperial Government by the Provinces aggregated to the sum of 983 lakhs, a remission of this amount would more than wipe off the deficit in the Provincial Budgets.

It must, however, be said that the deficit of 352 lakhs of rupees does not disclose the true position of the Provinces as derived from the financial arrangements made by the Act. If we are to deduce the true position of the Provinces as following from the new arrangement we must take note of the new taxation imposed and of the gain to Bengal through the remission of its contribution to the Imperial exchequer. Making adjustments for these, the position of the Provinces as it would have been without contributions may be seen from the following:—

Financial Position of the Provinces 1922-23

(In Thousands of Rupees)

Provinces or	Revenue	Expenditure	Surplus Deficit
	Rs.	Rs.	Rs.
Madras	15,99,00	17,18,55	—1,19,55
Bombay	14,32,06	15,42,17	—1,10,11
Bengal	9,15,86	10,99,90	—1,84,04
U.P.	13,58,67	13,85,65	—26,98
Punjab	11,38,26	12,68,44	—1,30,18
Burma	10,00,57	11,90,70	—1,90,13
Bihar and Orissa	4,62,65	5,13,80	—51,15
Central Provinces	5,35,23	5,72,17	—36,94
Assam	2,05,06	2,22,58	—17,52
Total deficit			—8,66,60

According to this calculation the aggregate deficit of the Provinces would have been about 867 lakhs. But we must make some further adjustments to this account. It has not been possible to deduct from the revenues of the Central Provinces the sum derived from the enhancement of the Excise duty in the Provinces. Secondly, the revenues of the Central Provinces for the year 1922-3 include collections of suspended revenue of previous years.

If these adjustments were made the aggregate deficit of the Provinces would give rise to a figure which would be barely covered by the remission of contributions. We must therefore conclude that remission of contributions would have at best been a very inadequate measure for removing the financial stringency of the Provinces, even if the problem of financing the extra deficit caused by such remission in the budget of the Central Government were to be ignored.

But if remission of contributions cannot improve the difficult situation that has arisen with regard to Provincial Finance, we must go to the root of the matter and inquire what are the causes which have brought on that situation. Is it due to the normal expenditure of the Provinces being under-rated ? Or is it due to the normal revenues of the Provinces being over-estimated ? For this purpose we must first ascertain whether the resources allocated to the Provinces were really inadequate to their normal needs. The following table compares the standard receipts and expenditure and shows the margin left between them for covering a probable advance in expenditure.

Standard Revenue and Standard Expenditure

Provinces	Standard Revenue	Standard Expenditure	Excess or Defect of Standard Revenue over Standard Expenditure
	Rs.	Rs.	Rs.
Madras	14,98,02	14,07,20	90,82
Bombay	12,09,70	11,55,03	54,67
Bengal	8,55,28	8,61,13	—5,85
U.P.	12,29,88	11,06,56	1,23,32
Punjab	9,73,51	9,10,69	62,82
Burma	8,24,28	7,84,78	39,50
Bihar and Orissa	4,30,39	4,20,70	9,69
C. P.	4,35,37	4,38,80	—3,43
Assam	1,81,46	1,78,25	3,21

From this it is obvious that except in the case of two Provinces the standard revenue has left a sufficient margin over standard expenditure. Only in Bengal and Central Provinces there was no margin, owing to the fact that the standard expenditure was slightly in excess of the standard revenue. But this defect was more than remedied in the case of Bengal by the remission of the contributions to the Central Government, and the excess of standard expenditure over standard revenue in the case of Central Provinces was indeed very small.

Barring this, in the rest of the Provinces the margin allowed was substantial. Let us now turn to the actual figures and compare them, with the standard figures. First of all, let us take the revenue side of the Provincial Budgets. Has the realised revenue fallen short of the standard revenue ? The following table compares the realised receipts of the Provinces with the standard figure assumed to be the normal in the financial allocation made under the new Act :—

Provincial Revenues

Provinces	Standard	Increase over Standard:— Revenues Decrease from Standard.	
		For 1921-22	For 1922-23
	Rs.	Rs.	Rs.
Madras	14,98,02	60,57	40,41
Bombay	12,09,70	1,57,47	2,22,36
Bengal	8,55,28	31,25	60,58
U.P.	12,29,88	1,04,43	1,28,79
Punjab	9,73,51	1,00,15	1,64,75
Burma	8,24,28	1,75,05	1,76,29
Bihar and Orissa	4,30,39	15,76	32,26
C. P.	4,35,37	79,43	99,86
Assam	1,81,46	22,60	23,60

The above table brings out very clearly the fact, not readily admitted, namely that the realised revenue has in no case fallen short of the standard revenue. It may, however, be asked : Has the increase in the realised revenue been equal to the margin allowed under the allocation between the standard revenue and of the Provinces ?

As throwing some light on that aspect of the question the following table is interesting:-

Expansion of Provincial Revenues

Provinces	Standard Margin	Excess or Defect of Realised Margin over Standard Margin	
		For 1921-22	For 1922-23
Madras	90,82	—30,25	—50,41
Bombay	54,67	1,02,80	1,68,19
Bengal	—5,85	25,40	54,73
U.P.	1,23,32	—18,89	5,47
Punjab	62,82	37,33	1,01,93
Burma	39,50	1,35,55	1,36,79
Bihar and Orissa	9,69	6,07	22,57
C. P.	3,43	76,00	96,43
Assam	3,21	19,39	20,39

From these figures it is obvious that except in the case of Madras the realised margin has in no case fallen below the standard margin. The excess of the realised over the standard margin is enormous. It cannot, therefore, be said that the financial deficit in the Provinces is due to provincial revenue having failed to reach the assumed normal. On the other hand, the revenues were more than necessary to cover the normal expenditure of the Provinces. The only conclusion that can fairly be drawn from the facts of the case is that the provincial deficits are due to an extraordinary increase in the expenditure of the Provinces. The following figures furnish enough evidence in support of this view:—

Provinces	Standard Expenditure	+ Increase over Standard: — Decrease from Standard.	
		For 1921-22	For 1922-23
Madras	14,07,20	3,08,73	3,11,35
Bombay	11,55,03	2,97,77	3,87,14
Bengal	8,61,13	2,49,47	1,75,77
U.P.	11,06,56	3,43,31	2,79,09
Punjab	9,10,69	3,12,55	3,57,75
Burma	7,81,78	2,42,73	4,05,92
Bihar and Orissa	4,20,70	65,27	93,10
C. P.	4,38,80	1,02,96	1,23,37
Assam	1,78,25	41,20	44,33

We are, therefore, led to the view held by the Secretary of State that reduction of expenditure and increase of taxation is the only remedy for placing provincial finance on a sound footing.

What chances are there that the Provinces will undertake the reduction of expenditure and increase of taxation so very necessary for their safety ? In this connection it is well to recall the dictum of that great financier, Mr. James Wilson, who once said:

"Finance is not mere arithmetic; finance is a great policy. Without sound finance no sound government is possible: without sound government no sound finance is possible." If there is any truth in this, then whether or not the Provincial Governments will undertake economy or face increase of taxation depends upon whether or not the system of government established in the Provinces by the Reforms Act is a sound system. Now, what is the nature of the government that is established in the Provinces under the Reforms Act ? In common parlance the system is known as dyarchy. Under it the Executive of the Province, instead of being composed of the Governor in Council as before, is now divided into the Governor in Council and the Governor in Ministry.

Under it the subjects marked off as Provincial from the Central are further divided into "Reserved" and "Transferred" subjects. The former are in charge of the Governor in Council, and the latter in that of the Governor in Ministry. Of these parts of the Provincial Executive the Council in charge of the "reserved" subjects still remains as before irresponsible to the Provincial Legislature, is unremovable by it, and in that sense is a non-parliamentary executive. The other part of the Provincial Executive, namely the Ministry in charge of the "transferred" subjects, is recruited from the elected members of the Provincial Legislature, which is made responsible to the Provincial Legislature which is based on a more or less popular franchise, and is removable by it, and in that sense is a Parliamentary Executive.

The Provincial Legislature is supreme with regard to both the parts of the Provincial Executive. It has not only full powers of legislation, but has also full and unfettered powers of interpellation. Its powers of sanctioning and voting upon the Provincial Budget are complete, although provision is made in the Reforms Act, which allows that

"the Local Government shall have power in relation to any such demand (for a money grant) to act as if it had been assented to, notwithstanding the withholding of such assent or the reduction of the amount therein referred to (by the Provincial Legislature), if the demand relates to a reserved subject (which is assigned to the charge of the Governor in Council) and the Governor certified that the Expenditure provided for by the demand is essential to the discharge of his responsibility for the subject."

Can such a government tackle the problems of sound finance? It is obvious that of the two parts of this dyarchical Executive, one, i.e. the Governor in Council, need have very little anxiety for reduction of expenditure or for the increase of taxation.

It derives its mandate from Parliament, and as such is free to adopt any policy—backed up as it is by the certification power of the Governor without any regard for the best interests of the taxpayer. The authors of the Joint Report had seen that this certifying power to override the wishes of the Legislature might lead to irresponsible extravagance on the part of the Governor in Council, and had proposed to endow the Governor in Ministry with a countervailing power which was to act as a curb on the former. That power was to have consisted in the Proviso which laid down that no taxation even in the interests of the ".reserved" subjects should be imposed in any Province without the consent of the ministry.

The Extremists—a class of politicians in India who were bent upon minimising the reforms as being inadequate—disliked the proviso as calculated to make scapegoats of ministers and to bring them into discredit with the people. But their rivals, the "Moderates," now calling themselves "Liberals "—one does not know why—saw clearly what the proviso meant. If this had materialised, there can be no doubt that the ministry would not have been a mere outsider tendering advice to the Council which might be accepted or rejected, but would have obtained a powerful voice in the settlement of the budget.

Having regard to the fact that no minister unless he was in a position to justify the budget proposals, including even those which pertained to the reserved subjects, would have hoped to persuade the Legislature to agree to a proposal of new taxation, the influence of the ministry on the "reserved" subjects, i.e. on the Council, would have inevitably been in the direction of thrift and retrenchment. The moderates were entirely right in their interpretation of the proviso and also in their insistence upon acquiring power, even at the cost of burdening the country with new taxation.

But in the heat of the controversy and their desire to convince the public of the substantiality of the Reforms, they drew some very amusing pictures of how the ministers working under the aegis of the proviso would be able to hold the Council at bay. This alarmed the bureaucracy, which raised the cry that it was dangerous to leave the provision for the "reserved" subjects to the tender mercy of ministers who bore no responsibility for the consequences of refusing adequate Budget provision for those subjects. The authors of the Joint Report had realised the force of this argument, and had confessed that the success of the arrangements depended upon their being worked by reasonable men who would conduct themselves in a reasonable manner.

They were probably right in refusing to assume that the ministers would not co-operate, either by reducing their own claims or by imposing taxation, in order to meet expenditure which the Council considered essential for the proper administration of the "reserved" subjects. But the bureaucracy, which had been frightened by the tactless jubilations of the Moderates, insisted that even reasonable men would at times, in all good faith, differ vitally from other reasonable men when it was a question of providing supply for work which one party was responsible for safeguarding and developing, while the other was only concerned in getting a share of the money.

In its opinion circumstances could well be imagined in which reasonableness might not prevail. Let us suppose, it was argued, that the Governor in Council finds new and heavy expenditure imperative on some reserved subject, but that he cannot induce ministers to consent to accept less for their subjects or impose taxation for it. The Governor then, under his exceptional powers, insists on the expenditure being provided for in the next budget, and the result is to leave ministers with inadequate funds for their transferred subjects. What is to happen ? Are ministers to be compelled to raise a tax which is apparently for their own need, but a need which has been created against their will by the Council refusing to curtail their demands ? Such a procedure, it was pointed out, would be tortuous, provocative, and indefensible.

Again, let us suppose that ministers consented to raise the necessary money, but the legislature refused to pass their revenue measures. Are the ministers to resign as having lost its confidence? The bureaucracy placed another dilemma before the authors of the Joint Report. Ministers have raised a new tax for some purpose of their own. In the next budget the Governor finds himself compelled to add substantially to the reserved provision for some new necessity, and thus to curtail the provision for "transferred" subjects. Ministers virtually see their new taxation receipts going to finance some development for which they are not responsible, and of which indeed they may disapprove. What are they to do? To avoid these difficulties the proviso was dropped and in its place the following changes were made in the Devolution Rules:—

Taxation and Borrowing

All proposals for raising taxation or for the borrowing of money on the revenues of a Province shall in the case of a Governor's Province be considered by the Governor with his Executive Council and ministers sitting together, but the decision shall thereafter be arrived at by the Governor in Council, or by the Governor and Minister or Ministers, according as the proposal originates with the Governor in Council or the Governor and Ministers.

Preparation of Budget in Default of Agreement of Order of Allocation

35. If at the time of the preparation of any budget no agreement or allocation such as is contemplated by these rules has been arrived at, the budget shall be prepared on the basis of the aggregate grants respectively provided for the reserved

and transferred subjects in the budget of the year about to expire.

Thus rather than depend too implicitly on reasonableness when circumstances must often be provocative effective precaution is taken by these rules against the ministry disapproving the allocation of funds to the "reserved" subjects by allowing the Governor to make such an allocation which is to be binding on both parts of the executive and also by arming him with the power of veto over the Provincial Legislature by allowing the Governor, should he deem it necessary, to restore a Budget grant on a reserved subject if it were refused or reduced by the Provincial Legislature which has the right to determine the Provincial Budget, and thirdly by allowing the Governor in Council equally with the Governor in Ministry to raise new taxation or new loans for the development of the subjects in its own charge.

The result is that one part of this dyarchical Executive, namely the Governor in Council, can have little reason to be interested in economy or be over-weighed by considerations of taxation. Its supply being assured its concern in the stability of provincial finance must be deemed to be somewhat remote. The whole burden of meeting the problem of restoring sound finance, therefore, falls upon the Governor in Ministry in charge of the "transferred" subjects.

For, under the distribution and certification powers it is the "transferred" subjects which must go without the funds they need, and it is those in charge of them, namely the Ministers, who must bear the brunt of economy or resort to new taxation to bring about an equilibrium in the finances of the Provinces. For it is doubtful that the Governor in Council will choose the onerous task of raising new taxes or practise economy when there are open to them other ways of amply providing themselves for the subjects they have under their control.

Will the other half of the Government, namely the Governor in Ministry, consent to practise economy, or if need be undertake the burden of new taxation ? That obviously depends upon the temper of the Legislature.

At the outset it is to be noted that the Legislature will not readily favour projects of increased taxation. It is true, as

Burke remarks, that "To tell the people that they are relieved by the dilapidation of their public estate, is a cruel and insolent imposition. Statesmen, before they valued themselves on the relief given to the people by the destruction of their revenue, ought first to have carefully attended to the solution of the problem: Whether it be more advantageous to the people to pay considerably, and to gain in proportion; or to gain little or nothing, and to be disburthened of all contribution?"

Whatever may be the philosophers' answer to this question, there can be no doubt that in a poor country like India with a very low capacity for bearing the burden of taxation, it is always very unpleasant, if not cruel, to propose an augmentation of that burden. Besides, any proposals for extra taxation would be shunned as likely to prejudice the chances of the legislators at the polls. So long as nomination was the general mode of obtaining a seat in the Legislature it was unnecessary to mind the prejudices of the electors. But when a seat is in the gift of the elector a candidate to the Legislature who proposes to touch his pocket has a small chance of success, even though the new taxes are to result in more than proportionate benefit. Besides, a political party which has won power from a bureaucracy by accusing it of heavy taxation cannot easily consent to disgrace itself by continuing the same policy.

This innate aversion to taxation on the part of the Legislature is strengthened by the peculiar attitude of the Legislature towards the "reserved" and "transferred "subjects. The reserved subjects are those which mostly pertain to peace and order, while the transferred subjects are those which largely pertain to progress. But as has already been pointed out, the policy of the bureaucracy before the Reforms was calculated to sacrifice progress to order. It is therefore obvious that under the revised constitution the popular Legislatures should aim at turning the scales in favour of subjects tending towards progress. Their aversion to increase of taxation and their partiality for the transferred subjects will favour them to welcome proposals on the part of ministers making drastic reduction in the funds allotted to the reserved subjects.

Their attitude towards the ministers will be largely governed by the amount of economy they will be able to effect in the reserved subjects for the benefit of the transferred subjects. Thus in the absence of any very large chances of increase of revenue the two halves of the Executive, the Governor in Council backed by the distribution and certification power and the Governor in Ministry backed by the general Budget powers of, a popular Legislature, will compete in the matter of developing their subjects by forcing economy on each other. The Legislature being unwilling to tax, the Governor in Council being in a position to resist retrenchment and the Governor in Ministry anxious to expand, the chances of an early equilibrium in Provincial finance are very small.

It is, therefore, evident that if there is no sound finance in the Provinces it is because dyarchy is not a good form of government. Now, why is dyarchy not a good form of government ? The answer to this question is very simple. Dyarchy is a bad form of government because it is opposed to the principle of collective responsibility. An administrative machine must work smoothly and harmoniously. But in order that it may do so it must recognise the principle of impartibility of governmental work and a collective responsibility of the administrators in the execution thereof.

That the work of government is by its nature impartible may not seem to accord with facts : for, in practice the functions of government can be and commonly are partitioned, as they are between local bodies and between departments. Nevertheless it is true that a common thread runs through them all : that no function of government acts *in vacuo* ; that each reacts on some other function, and that the various functions cannot act at all to produce orderly progress unless there is some force to harmonise them. Otherwise a policy enunciated in one department may fail to fructify for want of helpful action on behalf of other departments. That harmonising force can only be found in the principle of collective responsibility. This is so because under it, as Hearn points out.

"Each minister acts in his own department as the recognised agent of his colleagues in that particular department, subject, however, to inquiry and control by the whole body. But in all cases on which any difficulty is likely to arise each minister, from motives not merely of prudence but of honour, takes the opinion of the Cabinet. When the precaution is taken the measure becomes the common act of the Ministry."

Right or wrong there is a common co-ordinated policy which guides a unified government based on collective responsibility. But having made a partition of governmental work, dyarchy must be said to have introduced an element of divided responsibility in the Executive. It is true that the partition is not horizontal but vertical. It is also true that in setting the two parts to work it has not been provided that there should be two separate Legislatures for two separate executives ; or that each should make its own laws, control its own finance, frame its own budget, impose its own taxation, and raise its own loans ; or that each should have its separate staff for the administration of subjects allotted to it and have its own methods of recruitment, pay and pension for its services ; so that the two authorities might in fact have clearly defined spheres of their own exclusively within them.

The Government of India had indeed suggested that some, if not all, of these concomitants of a typically dual executive should also be made a part of the dyarchical system adopted to carry on the government of the Provinces. Fortunately for the country the framers of the new constitution held.

"that wisdom lies not in equipping each of the different elements with a complete paraphernalia of its own, and trusting to their orbits lying sufficiently apart for collision to be avoided; but in taking every opportunity of bringing the two elements into contact so as to induce the habits of joint action." "It is our intention," wrote the authors of the Joint Report; "that the Government thus composed and with this distinction of functions shall discharge them as one Government," and that "the Provincial budget should be framed by the Executive Government as a whole."

It was no doubt well to have modified the working of dyarchy by subjecting it to the interplay of two principles, one of division in order to give as clear a definition as possible of the several responsibilities of the two parts of the government and of union, in order to get association in aims and policy between those parts. For to have equipped each part of the Executive with a separate paraphernalia would have been nothing short of a calamity. But because there is an understanding that when ministers will act in matters of transferred subjects the councillors will advise them, and that when councillors will act in matters of reserved subjects the ministers will advise them, it does not alter the fact that dyarchy is a system of divided responsibility.

It is not a system which ensures the work of government being conducted in harmony and in accordance with a common policy. On the other hand, it is a system fraught with organised quarrel. The dividing line between dyarchy and anarchy is very narrow. If such a system is not rent in practice it is because of two transient circumstances. One such circumstance consists in the Provincial Legislature being a weakling sapped of its vitality by political dissensions.

The other consists in the tenure of the Ministers not being at the will of the Legislature, but for the duration of the Legislature's existence, and are to hold office during the pleasure of the governor. To allow a governor to choose ministers from among the elected members of the Legislature instead of requiring him to accept ministers who are elected by the Legislature is a grave derogation from the principle of responsible government which was avowedly the object of the Reforms Act. A minister who has the confidence of the governor, and a minister who has the confidence of the Legislature, are two entirely different things.

How great is the difference between the two in so far as good government is concerned is writ large in the pages of English political history of the eighteenth and the nineteenth centuries. That such a system should have been adopted against which the whole English constitutional history is a grand protest cannot of course be without some reason. The ostensible reason advanced is that the Legislature

"had had no experience of the power of dismissing Ministers, or the results attending the exercise of such power. Nobody in India is yet familiar with the obligations imposed by tenure of office at the will of a representative assembly.

It is only by actual experience that these lessons can be learned...... By the device of appointing the ministers from the elected members of the (Legislature) and making their tenure of office conditional on the retention of their seats (there is) established at once some measure of responsibility, in the form of responsibility to their constituents and thus (is) put an end to the condition of affairs in which those entrusted with the administration are wholly irresponsible to the constituents who elect the (Legislature)."

It is difficult to believe in the cogency of this piece of reasoning. To argue that nothing can be learned without experience is simply absurd. What is necessary for a proper conduct on the part of an individual or a group is to understand the meanings and values of things. For that it is unnecessary to undergo actual trial. A Legislature composed of responsible persons may be trusted to know the consequences of dismissing a Minister at the start without having to wait to learn it by experience. Again, to argue that the system is not the less responsible because ministers are responsible to their constituents is a shallow piece of pedantry.

Bibliography

Ambedkar, Bhimrao Ramji: *Thus Spoke Ambedkar: selected speeches*, Jullundur City, India: Bheem Patrika, 1964.

Anant, S. S.: *Changing Caste Hindu Attitudes Towards Harijans: A Follow Up After Four Years*, Vikas, New Delhi, 1979.

Bagchi, Reeta: *Mahatma Gandhi and Dr. B.R. Ambedkar on Islam and Indian Muslims*, Delhi: B.R. Pub. Corp. 1998.

Bailey, F. G.: *Caste and the Economic Frontier: A Village in Highland Orissa*, University of Manchester, Manchester, 1957.

Bakshi, S. R.: B.R. *Ambedkar: His Political and Social Ideology*. New Delhi: Deep & deep publications, 2000.

Barill, C.: *Social and Political Ideas of B.R. Ambedkar*, Aalekh Publishers, Jaipur, 1977.

Bhave, S.: *Pan on Fire: Eight Dalit Women Tell Their Story,* Indian Social Institute, New Delhi, 1988.

Bondurant, Joan V.: *Conquest of Violence; The Gandhian Philosophy of Conflict*, University of California Press, Berkeley, 1965.

Chatterjee, Partha: *Caste and Subaltern Consciousness*, Oxford University Press, Delhi, 1994.

Das, Bhagwan: *Revival of Buddhism in India and role of Dr. Baba Saheb B.R. Ambedkar*, Lucknow: Dalit Today Prakashan, 1998.

Dubois, Abbe: *Hindu Manners, Customs and Ceremonies*, AES, New Delhi, 1983.

Epstein, T. S.: *Economic Development and Social Change in South India*, Manchester University Press, Manchester, 1962.

Fisher, F.B.: *Touching the Untouchables, India's Silent Revolution*, MacMillan, New York, 1920.

Ganesan, L.: *Relevance of Reservation*, Valentina Publications, Madras, 1991.

Gautam, C.: *Babasaheb Ambedkar*. London, Ambedkar Memorial Trust, 1993.

Goyal, Bhagat Ram: *Educating Harijans*, Academic Press, Haryana, 1981.

Halbar, B. G.: *Lamani Economy and Society in Change: Socio-Cultural Aspects of Economic Change Among the Lamani of North Karnataka*, Mittal Publications, Delhi, 1986.

Ishwaran, K.: *Shivpur: A South Indian Village*, Routledge, London, 1968.

Jadhav, N.: *Dr. Ambedkar's Economic Thought and Philosophy*, Popular Prakashan, Bombay, 1993.

Jaffrelot, Christophe: *Dr. Ambedkar and Untouchability: Fighting the Indian Caste System*, New York, Columbia University Press, 2005.

Joshi, B.R.: *Untouchable! Voices of the Dalit Liberation Movement*, Zed and MRG, London, 1986.

Kamble, N. D.: *Deprived Castes and their Struggle for Equality*, Ashish Publishing House, New Delhi, 1983.

Khairmode, C.B.: *Dr. Bhimrao Ramji Ambedkar*, Pratap, Bombay, 1978.

Khan, Mumtaz Ali: *Human Rights and the Dalits*, Uppal Publishing House, New Delhi, 1995.

Kshirsagar, R. K.: *Dalit Movement in India and Its Leaders (1857-1956)*, MD Pub. Pvt. Ltd., New Delhi, 1994.

Kuber, W.N.: *Dr. Ambedkar: A Critical Study*, People's Publishing House, New Delhi, 1973.

Lannoy, Richard: *The Speaing Tree*, Oxford University Press, London, 1971.

Majumdar, D. N.: *Caste and Communication in an Indian Village*, Asia Publishing House, Bombay, 1958.

Mallik, Suneila: *Social Integration of the Scheduled Castes*. Abhinav, New Delhi, 1979.

Maw, Martin: *Visions of India*, Vertag Perer Lang, London, 1990.

Mohan, P.E.: *Scheduled Castes: History of Elevation, Tamil Nadu, 1900-1955*. New Era Pub., Madras, 1993.

Nagaraj, D. R.: *The Flaming Feet: A Study of the Dalit Movement*, South Forum Press, Bangalore, 1993.

Narain, A.K. & Ahir, D.C.: *Dr. Ambedkar, Buddhism and Social Change*, BR Publishing, Delhi, 1993.

Nath, Trilok: *Politics of the Depressed Classes*, Deputy Publications, Delhi, 1987.

O'Malley, L. S. S.: *Indian Caste Customs*, Vikas Publishing House, Delhi, 1974.

Omvedt, Gail: *Ambedkar: towards an enlightened India*, New Delhi, Penguin, 2004.

Parmaji, S.: *Caste Reservations and Performance*, Mamata Publications, Warangal, 1985.

Parvathamma, C. *New Horizons and Scheduled Castes*. Ashish Publishing House, New Delhi, 1986.

Rajasekharaiah, A.M.: *B.R. Ambedkar: the Politics of Emancipation*, Sindhu Publications, Bombay, 1971.

Raju, G.G.: *The Life of B.R. Ambedkar*, Babasaheb Dr. Ambedkar Memorial Society, Hyderabad, 1979.

Ramaiah, P., and K. Sateesh Reddy: *Dr B.R. Ambedkar's Economic Philosophy,* New Delhi, Delta Publishing, 1994.

Rao, Hemlata and Babu, M. Devendra: *Scheduled Castes and Tribes: Socio-Economic Upliftment Programmes*, Ashish Publishing House, New Delhi, 1994.

Rao, M. S. A.: *Social Movement and Social Transformation: A Study of Backward Class Movement*, MacMillan Press, New Delhi, 1978.

Rege, Sharmila: *Sati: A Critical Analysis,* University of Poona, Poona, 1989.

Robb, Peter: *Dalit Movements and the Meanings of Labour in India*, Oxford University Press, New Delhi, 1993.

Sangharakshita: *Ambedkar and Buddhism*, Glasgow, Windhorse Publications, 1986.

Sarkar, J.: *Caste, Occupation and Change*, B. R. Publishing Co., Delhi, 1984.

Shah, Ghanshyam: *Caste Association and Political Processes in Gujarat*, Popular Prakashan, Bombay, 1975.

Sharma, Kusum: *Ambedkar and Indian Constitution*, New Delhi, Ashish Pub. House, 1992.

RURAL MARKETING

Pallavi Bahuguna

CENTRUM PRESS
NEW DELHI-110002 (INDIA)

CENTRUM PRESS
H.O.: 4360/4, Ansari Road, Daryaganj,
New Delhi-110002 (India)
Tel: 23278000, 23261597, 23255577, 23286875
B.O.: No. 1015, Ist Main Road, BSK IIIrd Stage,
IIIrd Phase, IIIrd Block, Bangalore-560085 (INDIA)
Tel: 080-41723429
Email: centrumpress@gmail.com
Visit us at: www.centrumpress.com

Rural Marketing

First Edition, 2011

ISBN 978-93-80921-08-2

PRINTED IN INDIA

Printed at Balaji Offset, Delhi.

Contents

Preface

Rural Markets are growing at faster rate in Asian region. All the companies at national and international level are eyeing on the rural sector. India being predominately agrarian based economy and large part of its population living in rural areas is attracting all national and multi national firms to rural sector. But the consumers and market space in rural space is different than urban set up.

This book covers all the aspects of Rural Marketing right beginning from introduction to the concept, challenges in rural marketing, rural scenario of India, Rural consumers and their features, different marketing techniques to be adopted in rural sector of India for marketing the products and services. The book will prove helpful to all the students, practitioners and management faculty in understanding the pulse of rural marketing. Technology is the one important aspect that has been touched in this book with special reference to rural people. Agriculture has much talked about in this book because of its high importance in the development of rural markets for industry.

The book contains live examples of rural marketing in different states of this country. It has largely covered all the programs launched by different multinationals in the field of rural marketing whether it is Gram Sewa, ITC e choupal, etc. I am sure that this book will give good insight of rural markets to its readers. The book has comprehensively covered all the aspects related to rural marketing in its chapters.

Author

1

Introduction

DEFINITIONS OF RURAL MARKETING

Marketing: Identifying needs of customers and potential customers, providing products/services that satisfy these needs and developing efficient processes or systems to deliver your product/service to the market when, where and how consumers want it.

Rural marketing: Can be defined in terms of the location (villages) and occupation (mainly farming) A large variety of transactions are considered a part of rural marketing

These are marketing of:

- Agricultural inputs like fertilizers. Pesticides, farm equipment.
- Products made in urban centres and sold to rural areas like soaps, toothpastes, TVs etc.
- Products made in rural areas sold to urban centres like khadi cloth, handcrafted products etc.
- Products made and sold in rural areas like milk and milk products. Locally manufactured toothpowder, cloth etc.

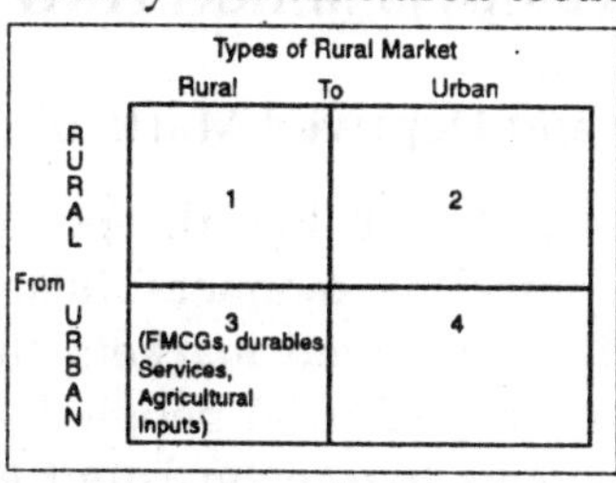

*We are going to concentrate only on point numbers 1. And 2.

*We are concentrating on Block 3

Definition of a Rural Area (*by planning commission, Insurance Regulatory Development Association {IRDA}*):

" That which is not urban"

- Population of less than 5000
- At least 75% of the male workforce is engaged in agricultural activities
- Absence of a municipality/ corporation
- Density of population is less than 400 per sq km

It is important to remember that a definition for a rural area does not exist, so the definition that is used is the exact opposite, of the definition of an urban area.

Rural Population

Table. Population of India – Rural v/s Urban

	Population In Crores	% To Total	Population In Crores	% To Total	Population In Crores	% To Total	Population in Crores	% To Total
Year	1971	1971	1981	1981	1991	1991	2001	2001
Rural	43.9	80	50.2	76.3	64.1	76	74	73
Urban	10.91	20	15.62	23.7	20.3	24	29	27
Total	54.8	100	65.82	100	84.4	100	103	100

A perspective

Total world population: 6 Billion

Rural population in India: 740 million, which is 12.6% of world population.

Urban population in India: 290 million, which is 4.4% of world population.

HURDLES AND CONSTRAINTS VIS-À-VIS MARKETING

Deprived People and Deprived Markets

The number of people below the poverty line has not decreased in any appreciable manner. Thus, poor people and consequently under developed markets characterize rural markets. A vast majority of rural people is tradition bound and they face problems like inconsistent electrical power, scarce infrastructure, and unreliable telephone system, politico-business associations that hinder development efforts.

Lack of Communication Facilities

Even today most villages in the country are inaccessible during the monsoons. Moreover 3 lakh villages in the country have no access to telephones. Other communication infrastructure is also highly under developed.

Transport

- Many rural areas are not connected by rail transport.
- 50% of the roads have been poorly surfaced and majority are severely damaged by the monsoons
- The use of bullock carts is inevitable even today
- Camel carts are used in Rajasthan and Gujarat in both Rural and Urban sectors
- Out of the 15 million carts 12 million are estimated to be in the rural areas transporting as much as 6 billion ton KM of freight per year

Many Languages and Dialects

The number of recognized languages is 16; the dialects are estimated to be about 850. The languages and dialects vary from state to state, region to region and probably from district to district. Since messages have to be delivered in the local language it is difficult for marketers to design promotional strategies for each of these areas. Facilities such as phone, telegram and fax are less developed in villages adding to the communication problems faced by marketers.

Dispersed Markets

Rural populations are scattered over a large land area. And it is almost impossible to ensure the availability of a brand all over the country. 7 Indian states account for 76% of the countries rural retail outlets. District fairs are periodic and occasional in nature. Manufacturers and retailers prefer such occasions as they allow greater visibility and capture the attention of the target audience for larger spans of time.

Advertising in such a highly heterogeneous market is also very expensive.

Low Per Capita Income

Even though about 33% to 35% of the GDP is generated in rural areas it is shared by 74% of the population. Moreover demand in rural markets depends on the agricultural situation, which in turn depends upon the monsoons. Therefore the demand is not stable or regular. Hence, the per capita income is low in Villages compared to urban areas.

Low Levels of Literacy

The levels of literacy are lower compared to urban areas. This again leads to a problem of communication in these rural areas. Print medium becomes ineffective and to an extent irrelevant since its reach is poor.

Prevalence of Spurious Brands and Seasonal Demand

For any branded product there are a multitude of local variants, which are cheaper and hence more desirable. Also due to illiteracy the consumer can hardly make out a spurious brand from an original one. Rural consumers are cautious in buying and their decisions are slow they generally give a product a trial and only after complete satisfaction do they buy it again.

Different Way of Thinking

There vast difference in the lifestyles of the people. The choice of brands that an urban customer enjoys is not available to the rural customer, who has usually 2 – 3 choices. As such the rural customer has a fairly simple thinking and his decisions are still governed by customs and traditions. It is difficult to make them adopt new practices.

Distribution Problem

Effective distribution requires village level shopkeeper, taluka level wholesaler/ dealer, district level stockist/ distributor and company owned depot at state level.

- So many tiers increase the cost of distribution.
- Rural markets typically signify complex logistical challenges that directly translate into high distribution costs.
- Also there is relatively slower growth of demand and lack of adequate institutional mechanism for retail operations.
- Bad roads, inadequate warehousing and lack of good distributors pose as the major problem to marketers.

AREA UNDER CULTIVATION

- 70% for food crops
  - Food security
  - 50% retained for self consumption by farmer
- 30% for non- food crops *(cotton, sugarcane etc.)*
  - Entirely marketed
  - Generates disposable income

The above pattern shows that the Indian farmer is extremely food security oriented and is not willing to allocate more than one-third of his land to growing cash crops, which generates additional income for him. Whereas in countries of America and Europe the farmers use most of their land for cash crops and hence they have greater incomes.

Table. Monsoon and Food Grain Production

Year	Rainfall (% of normal)	Food-grain output (million tones)
1992	93	179
1993	100	184
1994	110	191
1995	100	180
1996	103	199
1997	102	192
1998	105	203
1999	96	209
2000	92	196
2001	98	212
2002 (drought year)	81	184

It is observed that in the drought year along with low rainfall food grain output has also decreased. 2003-projected 96% rainfall, the normal figures are between 98% and 102%

Grain Pain:

- Public investment i ι agriculture has been stagnant for the past 10 years
- Indian farmers are grappling with problems of declining soil fertility and water salinity and the rise of complex pest pathologies.

Poor agricultural growth leads to:

- Fall in rural incomes
- Higher food prices reduce consumers purchasing power
- Even Non-agricultural GDP falls (due to last years drought, non-farm GDP decelerated)

CHARACTERISTICS OF RURAL MARKETS

- Out of the total 6,30,000 villages in India less than 500 people live in 50% of these villages
- 40% (300 mn) live in 7% (50,000) villages
- Only 1% (6300 villages) have more than 5000 people
- Owner/ farmers constitute 34% of the house hold sectors in rural India and they account for 65% of TV purchases
- Even though literacy levels are on the rise in rural India it is of limited meaning in terms of marketing as by definition literate people can only sign their names

ECONOMIC STATUS

- The average household income of the urban population (Rs.36,000p.a) is thrice that of the rural (Rs.12,000p.a).
- According to NCAER (National Council of Applied Economic Research) the lower income group (<70,000) will shrink by 55% in 2006-2007 and upper income groups (>1,40,000) will double in 2006-2007

- The aspirants, lower middle and middle class are the largest segment and are the largest base for durables and FMCG goods
- The well off segment like the wheat farmers in Punjab are as of today a negligible base
- The destitute i.e. the lowest income group have a very low purchasing power.
- % Of per capita expenditure on food in the rural area is 61% as compared to urban which is 50% For other items it is:

  FMCG 15% (Urban) 10% (Rural)
  Durables 5% 3%

DEMAND

- The demand for goods is irregular as it is seasonal and agriculture dependant
- It depends on the harvest periods. Their cash flows are better after harvest.
- It is festival and marriage linked. For e.g. The demand for sweets would go up during Durga pooja in villages in Bengal. Companies like Heinz use festivals to sponsor "pandals" at various pooja sites and indirectly promote their products.

Changing Scenario

Table. Indicative of a Move from an Agrarian to a Service Economy

Component	1981	1992	1995	2000
Agriculture	38%	32%	29%	26%
Industry	21%	27%	29%	22%
Services	41%	41%	42%	52%

- Aspirations to improve lifestyles with increased purchasing power and disposable incomes
- Growth in demand for durables, services
- Bank branches, schools, primary health centres at nodal points
- Government focus on rural development (outlay of

Rs.45,000 cr in 9 five-year plan from Rs. 14,000 cr. In 7th five year plan)

- Rural markets growing at five times the rate of urban market especially category III durables.
- Marketer's efforts
- New employment opportunities (IRDP :Integrated rural development programme, Banks)
- Green, white revolution, WTO removals of quantitative restriction for exports of food produce.
- Improved penetration of mass media has resulted in creation of awareness among rural consumers.

INCREASED FOOD GRAIN PRODUCTION

- Green revolution
- Scientific methods, increased crop yields
- 200 million tones if food grains P.a.
- Increased exports of Indian agricultural produce because of WTO support
- Increased rural purchasing power

Government Initiatives

- Self sufficiency (Operation Flood, white revolution; blue revolution)
- Integrated Rural Development Programme (IRDP); TRYSEM (Training Rural Youth for Self-Employment); REP (Rural Electrification Programme)
- REP gave impetus to consumer durables industry, it also aims at having electricity in almost all villages by 2010
- PSU and Co-op banks lend farmers (with 'Kisan' credit card by Canara & Andhra bank, a person can borrow up to 50,000 with these credit cards.)

Co-operatives and Corporate Support

- Amul, Campco (initiated co-operative movements)
- Contract Farming: companies give High Yielding Variety HYV seeds and tied up with farmers to cultivate crops and sell them back to the company.

$ 2billion World Bank loans in this fiscal year

- The World Bank's first loan of $ 150 million for 2003-04 will go to the Andhra Pradesh rural poverty reduction project – it is expected to benefit 2million Households.
- District poverty initiative started in 2000 includes an expansion of the geographical area from six districts to the entire state and a sharper focus on poorer and more vulnerable rural consumers for sectors like power, road, and poverty reduction.

DISTINCTIVE FEATURES OF RURAL MARKETS VIS-À-VIS URBAN MARKETS

Features	Rural	Urban
Demand pattern	Seasonal	Uniform
Spread	Scattered	Concentrated
Literacy level	Low	Moderate
Per Capita Income	Low	Moderate
Awareness of needs	Not entirely known	Known
Infrastructure	Poor	Moderate
Sources of information, communication	Word of mouth personal/ direct selling, TV, radio, unconventional media	All
Supply	Erratic, untimely	Timely
Product info guidance	Needed	Adequate
Consumer Protection	No awareness	Increasing awareness

ARE RURAL MARKETS AN OPPORTUNITY?

- Green revolution has highly increased the disposable income of farmers, there are many farmers in high income group

- Purchasing power has increased tremendously (Administered price mechanism APM) ensures that the farmers get the correct/fixed prices for their produce through the government.(usually for cash crops) In addition to this when the farmer wants to buy inputs like fertilizers, the govt. gives it to him at a fixed price.
- Vast size- Majority of India's population still lives in villages (Demand Base)
- A growth rate of 3-4% adds 1 million rural consumers every year
- Steep rise in support price of paddy, wheat
- 10 consecutive good monsoons (except 2001-2002) – so increased income

RURAL DEMAND PATTERN

Table. Rural Product Portfolio

Category I	**II**	**III (Items costing more thanRs.6,000)**
Pressure cookers	2 in 1 (mono_	CTV (S)
Pressure pans	2 in 1 (stereo)	CTV (R)
Mono cassette recorders	B & W TV (S)	VCRs
Bicycles	B&W TV (R)	VCPs
Wrist watches (mech)	Instant geysers	Scooters
Wrist watches (Quartz)	Storage geysers	Mopeds
Radio/ transistors	Sewing machines	Motorcycles
Electric Irons	Vacuum cleaners	Refrigerators
Ceiling fans	Mixer/ grinders	Washing machines
Table fans		

Source: NCAER (Economic Times)

- CTV sales – 65% in rural India

- Rural share of durables about 60% (esp. bicycles, wrist watches, radios/ transistors)
- Share of category I is declining and II and III is increasing.
- Purchase of goods under category III has increased by 25 % over the previous year, category II has increased by 15% and category I by 3%

Table. Preference for brands

Segment % of consumers who preferred branded items	< 40%	40 –80%	>80%
Necessity/ popular	Coconut oil	Iodized salt Tea Washing cakes Biscuits Blues (*neel*)	Toilet soaps Washing powder Analgesics Toothpaste Razor blades
Premium	Refined oil	Hair oils Bulbs	Shampoo Batteries Rubs, balms Skin cream Toothbrushes Antiseptics Chyavanprash Digestives Mosquito repellents Shaving creams Tube lights

Of The 740 Million rural consumers realistically about 200 million have the propensity to spend. However, it is claimed that disposable incomes in higher income classes in rural areas is higher than in urban areas since many services such as housing, health and education (leaving quality issues aside) cost far less.

This chapter analyses the spatial distribution of rural services in selected regions of three states in India (Andhra Pradesh, Maharashtra, and Tamil Nadu), based on data collected over three decades. In spite of economic disparities between regions, Christaller's Central Place Theory provides a framework in which to examine demographic, functional and spatial characteristics of settlements in these regions. In all regions, there has been a tremendous improvement in rural service provision, since the late 1960s, especially in smaller sized settlements.

Over time, more complex services in particular, have become more widely available. In Andhra Pradesh and Tamil Nadu, the introduction of new agricultural technologies was largely responsible for simulating such improvements, whereas in Maharashtra they were a consequence of urban industrial development in a metropolitan city. The government played a critical role in this process during the earlier stages of development of the regions, which facilitated greater involvement of the private sector at later stages.

The changes in rural service provision are further examined in the context of decentralized service centre planning in India. The analysis suggests how the concepts and methodologies employed in this study might provide the basis for a more integrated regional approach to planning and policy formulation for rural service provision at the district level in India. Investments in infrastructure, and the associated provision of services, are integral to the process of development. Hard infrastructural investments in the agricultural sector in particular, have played a key role in improving agricultural production, and have facilitated the growth of 'soft' infrastructure in developing countries. Among the more tangible benefits observed, are increased accessibility to these services, and the dissemination of new technologies.

Although interest in rural infrastructure and its impact on agricultural and regional development in developing countries is growing, infrastructure is not easy to define. Generally, when the research community refers to infrastructure, it means hard infrastructure such as roads, telecommunications, electrification and irrigation. But focusing only on hard infrastructure provides a partial picture; other types of infrastructure, notably institutional and 'soft' infrastructure, are equally important. The absence of this institutional infrastructure can lead to unsound agricultural development planning. For example, local data on climate, physiographic, soils, water, vegetation and population need to be collected, stored and analysed by government agencies before planning agricultural development activities.

Similarly, soft infrastructure includes various services such as those related to transport bus and truck), finance (credit and banking), input distribution (of seeds, fertilizers, pesticides, and agricultural machinery), animal husbandry and marketing (of agricultural produce) which are also necessary for development.

Also included in this category, are those services related to production and consumption activities that influence rural populations. Soft infrastructure services such as these, are the subject of this chapter. The economic and spatial features of the distribution systems for these services need to be studied. Services are often available in only a few settlements, but are used by a larger number of settlements, resulting in economic transactions across a greater geographical area.

These spatial aspects influence access of the rural population to services and affect the prospects for agricultural and economic development. In this chapter, the spatial distribution of rural services is analysed, and based on empirical evidence from three different geographical regions in India, the implications for rural development are noted. The important roles of both government and private sector in the provision of services are also examined.

PLANNING FOR THE PROVISION OF RURAL SERVICE INFRASTRUCTURE

Planning for the provision of rural service infrastructure is an exercise that in India is entirely conducted at the state level and, since the mid-1960s, increasingly at the district level. By the early 1970s, district level planning efforts were becoming the norm. Broadly speaking, these district level planning efforts are a component of state development plans for which the state government makes resources available. These resources are to be allocated to different heads of development at the district level over a given period. The main institution at the district level that is responsible for rural service infrastructural planning and implementation is the Zilla Parishad (district council) which is an elected body. These planning efforts, whether at micro (village), meso (district), or macro (state) levels, have tended to exhibit two characteristic components:

1. The schematic budgets for different sectors of development; and
2. The period during which the targets, aggregated at the state or district levels, are to be achieved.

Both these components tended to be shaped at the state government level, and substate units such as the districts were left to plan the process of implementation in their respective administrative territories. Although the district had been accepted as a unit of planning and development administration, not much thought seemed to have been given initially to the spatial matrix within which all developmental activities in the district took place.

As a consequence of a lack of empirical studies that would indicate how to weave the spatial aspect of planning with the budgetary and time horizon aspects at the district level, and to address the question of spatial inequalities that had emerged between states and within states regarding the provision of rural service infrastructure, the Government of India, through its Planning Commission, decided in the late 1960s to evolve a policy for securing spatial balance of activities and functions through their appropriate 'clustering' or 'dispersal'.

In evolving this policy, it soon became apparent that it was not possible to do everything nor to act everywhere at once. In all regions or areas there tended to appear certain rural and urban centres around which the rural socio-economic life revolved. In most cases, this rural socio-economic life consisted of agricultural and agriculture-related operations undertaken by the population in these regions, which required related production and consumption activities. A major objective of planning for the provision of rural service infrastructure, was to provide a facilitating environment in which these agricultural and agriculture-related operations could be undertaken efficiently in the rural areas of India. Therefore, it was felt that understanding the demographic, functional and spatial characteristics of the settlement system of the region would greatly assist in either providing or strengthening the facilitating environment in which agricultural and agriculture-related operations could be conducted in rural India.

A basic task was to develop a methodology to identify these centres and make use of them to facilitate the process of rural socio-economic interaction and transformation. One spatial theoretical concept that has helped in analysing the Indian rural environment was that of growth and service centres. This concept, it was argued, has tended to influence a number of development policy decisions in different developing and developed countries and 'the Planning Commission had, therefore, new dimensions of regional development uncovered'. An earlier report prepared by the Ford Foundation, New Delhi, and the Council for Social Development, New Delhi, stated that: As a part of studies on area planning, a centrally sponsored scheme of pilot research projects in growth centres is being launched. The aim of the pilot projects would be to evolve a broad research methodology for identifying emerging growth centres, to indicate how the growth potential of these centres could be promoted through comprehensive and scientific study of overall development needs, and how these centres could be meaningfully woven into the framework of the district plans and thus help in the process of planning from below.

THE FORD FOUNDATION AND COUNCIL FOR SOCIAL DEVELOPMENT, 1969

Many examples of how methodologies derived from central place theory can be used for planning for provision of rural service infrastructure are presented in this chapter.

Service Provision and Agricultural and Regional Development

Over the last two decades, and since the Ford Foundation

sponsored studies in the early 1970s in particular, there has been increasing decentralization of planning responsibilities and power to the district level. Several studies were conducted in India to observe the nature and scope of these growth and service centres in rural India, as a consequence of the initiative taken by the Ford Foundation, New Delhi. In this chapter, methodologies and results from such exercises with particular reference to methodologies for planning of rural service infrastructure are noted.

Planning processes for rural service provision have often been similar across different states in India. However, the existing levels of economic development in each state have been important determinants of the outcome of such service centre planning activities and of subsequent rural service infrastructural development. The findings of this chapter, however, are primarily based on methodologies adopted in studies for planning for rural service provision in Maharashtra, Andhra Pradesh, and Tamil Nadu. At the outset, it should be noted that there are some peculiar characteristics of the overall economic development of these study areas that are responsible for the differences in the implications of their respective settlement systems for regional development.

For example, Nagpur Metropolitan Region of Maharashtra, which is economically more developed and urban relative to Miryalguda taluk of Andhra Pradesh and the North Arcot region of Tamil Nadu, has enjoyed a sustained level of infrastructural investment over the last five decades. In Miryalguda taluk and North Arcot region, on the other hand, there has been a spurt of development in rural service infrastructure mostly over the last two decades, whereas in Nagpur Metropolitan Region this was a consequence of the development of the urban economy.

It should also be noted that a majority of the rural services in Nagpur Metropolitan Region and Miryalguda taluka were planned. But other factors have been instrumental in stimulating investment in rural service infrastructure in these latter two states. In Miryalguda taluk, the development of a canal irrigation system transformed a largely rainfed agricultural system into an irrigated one. In the North Arcot region, which already enjoyed the benefits of river, tank, and canal irrigation, the introduction of green revolution technology (high-yielding varieties of paddy) transformed the agricultural production system from one based on traditional varieties, to one based on high-yielding varieties.

Thus, the introduction of canal irrigation in Andhra Pradesh, and green revolution technologies in Tamil Nadu were responsible for structural changes in the demographic, functional, and spatial characteristics of these study areas in which much of the ensuing development of rural service infrastructure took place.

Service Centre Planning

The concept of service centre planning is almost 25 years old and it would be appropriate to review how it has unfolded over this period. Service centre planning is defined for our purposes, as an exercise where the socio-economic needs of a district are assessed based on factual information from the households, villages or towns of that district or region. The service centres are defined as those focal points around which rural life revolves, and which provide socioeconomic services such as trade, transport, communications, agricultural inputs, finance, administration, education and health.

There could be a series of service centres offering varying ranges and complexities of the services mentioned which would facilitate the economic development of the district. Ever since this work began in India in the late 1960s, a number of studies have been conducted in different parts of the country, both at the national and sub-national levels, on aspects of supply, demand, impact and dynamics of rural service provision. Most numerous are the studies on the aspects of supply; with those of demand, impact and dynamics being very limited in number.

This is because data collection at the household level, in order to assess the demand for, and the impact of, access to rural service infrastructure is a very time-consuming task. Similar difficulties are also encountered, or perceived to exist, when trying to collect the data on service provisions at two points in time for the same villages in the same district. These actual or perceived difficulties in data collection have resulted in only very few attempts to address the issues of demand for, and dynamics of, rural service provision in the Indian literature on service centre planning.

The following discussion is, therefore, based on three studies conducted in three districts from three states of India, where the data was collected from two points in time in order to understand the processes that explain the dynamics of rural service provision in India. In two instances, data was also collected from sample households to understand the patterns of demand that exists for these kinds of services in rural India.

Lessons from Work on Service Centres

Notwithstanding the limited number of studies on which the process observations made in this chapter are noted, some lessons could be drawn from a large body of these studies to identify the patterns involved. In essence, these studies attempted to identify the characteristics of rural service provision in the settlement systems of the study areas. The analysis of the demographic, functional and spatial characteristics of the settlement system, as was noted above, can help in understanding the set of relationships that describe the mutual interplay and interdependence between centres, whether of the same or of different orders of service complexity.

Such an approach is considered essential for formulating an integrated plan of rural service provision in India, as it is almost impossible to understand these characteristics of each centre separately for each service in a region.

Research and Associated Aspects

Descriptions of the Study Areas

The analyses noted below are based upon studies of three regions in India see which were conducted at two different points in time:

1. Miryalguda taluk, Nalgonda district, Andhra Pradesh in 1968 and 1978;
2. Nagpur Metropolitan Region, Nagpur district, Maharashtra in 1969 and 1978/79;
3. North Arcot region, North Arcot district, Tamil Nadu, in 1982/83, and 1990/91.

In the discussion that follows, Nagpur Metropolitan Region and Maharashtra, Khryalguda taluk and Andhra Pradesh and North Arcot region and Tamil Nadu are used interchangeably to mean the study areas of Nagpur Metropolitan Region, Miryalguda taluk, and North Arcot region respectively.

The three regions were chosen because each was unique in terms of its level and stage of development, and because the impetus for development in each region was provided by different exogenous factors, as noted earlier. The studies took Christaller's central place theory as a major point of reference and departure, given its relevance to understanding demographic, functional, and spatial characteristics of service centres in the study areas.

Central place theory attempts to explain the spatial and functional distribution of settlements in a region and their interlinkages. The theory recognizes the importance of demand for central functions (services) as the driving force behind the emergence of central places (service centres), as well as the importance of access (transport) to these central places and the functions they provide. In brief, what emerges is a hierarchy of central functions (services) that underlie and explain the hierarchy of central places (service centres). There are different orders of service centres, with higher order centres providing all those services found at lower order centres as well as more sophisticated services.

Thus, central place theory has three main elements:

1. Urban centres;
2. Their hexagonal marketing areas; and
3. Transport networks.

Certain theoretical modifications were necessary in order to address the variations in conditions in India as compared to those in the theory. These were replacing rural centres for urban centres, service areas for hexagonal market areas and movement patterns for transport networks. The relevance of the framework discussed has been applied in other developing countries, but particularly in South Asia.

However, the basic concepts remained unviolated and yielded significant results after the data was analysed. These concepts are related to: hierarchy of settlements; spatial interaction among settlements; entry population threshold and clustering of services; service areas; service score ratios; index of service provision; median population threshold of services; locational priorities for removing regional disparities; and spatial organizational form for regional development. Each of these concepts will be explained in further detail in the relevant sections below. It would be difficult to note the details of the outcome of each study in this short chapter, but certain general features, in keeping with the basic postulates of central place theory, tended to emerge despite differences in agroecological and socio-economic features in the study areas.

Hierarchy of Settlements

In all three study areas, there existed an underlying scale of service hierarchy that explained the settlement hierarchy. Neither all settlements have all services, nor are all components of service groups necessarily available in each settlement. For example, in the education category, the various components are primary school, middle school, high school, higher secondary school or junior college and college. Not all these services were available in all settlements of the study areas; as some (e.g. primary schools) are more rudimentary than others (e.g. higher secondary schools) which are considered to be more sophisticated.

Thus, services can be classified according to their level of complexity or sophistication (also see section entitled 'Entry population threshold and clustering of services'). One way to rank services, in terms of their sophistication or complexity, is based on their entry population thresholds. This is the lowest population level at which a service is first observed to 'enter' a settlement in a particular study area. Basic services have a lower entry population threshold than 'higher' or more complex services. Depending upon its entry population threshold value, each service has a weight assigned to it to help arrive at a score for a settlement's service provision.

This score is referred to as the centrality score, which is itself a measure of a settlement's importance. (The quality or scale of service is not considered in determining centrality scores. Rather the primary concern, and that of rural dwellers, is that a service is present and that people have access to it. For example, as long as people have access to a bus stop, the score is not concerned about whether there are seats or a roof provided at the bus stop. Clearly, quality or scale of service is important with regard to many of the other services, but to rate services according to quality or scale would have required a subjective assessment and ranking of services, which was well beyond the scope of the exercises conducted.)

For example, in 1990/91, in North Arcot, a family planning centre which has the lowest entry population threshold of 610 is assigned a weight of 1.00. A private hospital, however, which has an entry threshold of 1098, is assigned a weight of (1098/610) = 1.8. By considering the variety, hierarchy and number of services available in a settlement and multiplying the number by the appropriate weight, it is possible to arrive at an indicator of the settlement's centrality. An important observation made in all three study areas, is that over time, the population thresholds at which services first enter' a settlement system have, for most services, declined, thus indicating a more widespread availability of services in the later time periods in all regions.

Since entry population thresholds are used to determine weights, and subsequently, centrality scores, service score ratios, and the index of service provision, strict comparisons cannot be made between differing periods and regions because the entry population thresholds differ slightly for each of these. Were the same weights used over both periods for any given region, researchers would be better able to make comparisons regarding improvements in service provision relative to a base period, but any dynamic changes would be masked; as weights change over time, they are indicative of a reordering of services in terms of importance and availability within the region, at a particular point in time. Nevertheless, it is still valid and useful to make comparisons between time periods in some instances, as the statistics provide a broad indication of the general trends in service provision.

Centrality scores were calculated for all settlement in each study area to understand the basic service structure of the settlement system. In each study area, it was seen that this structure consists of a major group with the most numbers of settlements having rudimentary services, dominated by another group consisting of few settlements with a more complex set of services.

In each case, at the top of the regional settlement system there existed only a few settlements (one or two at the most) which had the most complex functions available in that study area. There are different levels service hierarchy, corresponding to different ran of centrality scores in the Nagpur Metropolitan Region in 1969. Even though the number of service may increase only marginally at each level of functional hierarchy, their complexity (as measured centrality scores) tended to increase quite markedly.

For lower order services, the distance travelled was not much, and frequently there was little interaction between different villages for such services. But for complex services, the distance travelled was quite substantial. Further, the initial distance travelled to services was greater in less economically-developed study areas such as Miryalguda taluk, than in more economically-developed study areas such as Nagpur Metropolitan Region.

For example, in the relatively developed Nagpur Metropolitan Region in 1969, village inhabitants tended to travel 4.8 kilometres to the bus stop and secondary school, 6.44 kilometres to the weekly market, 8.0 kilometres to the post office and 9.65 kilometres to the more complex services, such as the primary health centre and cooperative bank. In relatively underdeveloped Miryalguda taluk of Andhra Pradesh in 1968, the distances travelled to all these services were far greater: 12.8 kilometres to the bus stop, 11.26 kilometres to the secondary school, 27.36 kilometres to the weekly market, 9.65 kilometres to the post office, 20.9 kilometres to the primary health centre, and 33.8 kilometres to the cooperative bank.

Entry population threshold and clustering of services Services of different functional complexities tended to 'cluster' within certain population size groups. This phenomenon is closely related to the concept of 'entry population threshold' which can be explained as a population size above which all settlements tend to have the service in question and below which the service in question is absent.

In Nagpur Metropolitan Region, services tended to 'enter' the settlement system at different population thresholds. For example, for primary school, middle school, high school, and college, the thresholds were 350, 800, 2100 and 15 000 respectively. This also illustrates, as noted earlier, that more complex services tend to be located in centres with larger populations and less complex services tend to be located in centres with smaller populations. Services also have a tendency to duster in identifiable population size groups in study areas. This spatial characteristic is illustrated by analysing data from Andhra Pradesh, which also applies to Maharashtra and Tamil Nadu. Services of different kinds were observed to 'cluster' in Miryalguda taluk within particular population size groups as follows:

- Primary school, centre for medical check-up and preventive medicine, branch post office, regular bus stop, primary credit society, retail market, and seeds, fertilizers and agricultural implements distribution centres, tended to occur in settlements with a population size 250-950;
- The middle school, the secondary school, centre for allopathic treatment and hospitalization, sub-post office, bus station, block level cooperative bank, pesticides distribution centre, animal husbandry centre and the weekly market tended to occur in settlements with a population size 1250-3500;

- Junior (pre-degree) college, centre for surgery and hospitalization, centre for maternity care and family planning, post and telegraph office, telephone exchange, bus junction, scheduled bank, land mortgage bank, animal husbandry centre and regulated market tended to occur in settlements with a population size 15 000+.

Each of the three service groups, with their associated population sizes were identified as belonging to low, middle, and high order of service hierarchy respectively. Following from this, the high order services have a more extensive zone of influence (service area) than the low order services. Thus, by looking at the complexity of services offered by centres, it was possible to identify their zones of influence, the number of persons served and the extent of area served.

An interesting empirical observation is that in North Arcot region of Tamil Nadu, in 1982/83, services of different kinds also tended to 'cluster' in population size groups of less than 1000; 1000-3500; and 3500+ respectively, for low, middle, and high order of service hierarchy. As in the case of Miryalguda taluk of Andhra Pradesh, the more complex services were found in larger population size groups, but the size of the larger population settlement group in North Arcot region was one-fifth of that in Miryalguda taluk. This clearly denotes the impressive extent of the development of rural infrastructural facilities in North Arcot region as compared to those in Miryalguda taluk.

Service areas As noted above, the availability of services is not uniform among the settlements of a study region. This means people need to travel in order to avail themselves of some services. Noted below are the functional and spatial characteristics of the range of services provided by different service centres and the extent and nature of service (market) areas they serve.

For this purpose, it is useful to distinguish between settlements that provide services to rural populations and those that do not. Settlements that provide at least half their own used services and serve another settlement are called service centres, whereas settlements that depend on other settlements for more than half their services are called dependent settlements. The same classification of services can be applied separately to the provision of low, middle, and high order of services.

Once the service centres and their service areas are delineated, it is seen in the study areas that there emerges a hierarchy of service centres from high to low order with specific spatial and functional connotations associated with it. For example, analyses of Nagpur Metropolitan region, Miryalguda taluk and North Arcot region, show that the most important service centres in these study areas, have the greatest number of services, the highest service population and the most extensive service area.

It can, therefore, be said that service area and population of other less important service centres in these study areas 'nest' under the influence of the most important service centre. Further, even individual service centres display this nesting pattern for different levels of service hierarchy. What is true with regard to the nesting pattern of service centres and service areas, is even more true of the services themselves. For each type of service, the service area and service population tend to increase with the order of service complexity.

This neat vertical organization of services becomes somewhat obscure when viewed in terms of their provision by service centres, because at the level of service centre, one is concerned with the patterns of availability and use of all services, and not just one service, provided by that centre. Service score ratios It is possible to identify areas within a given study region which exhibit a lack of services or a surplus of them. Such indicators are useful to policy planners and development administrators as they suggest areas and services that need urgent attention.

The service score ratio is calculated by dividing the score values of service provision by the area for the subregion and for the district as a whole, and then obtaining the ratios of the two values. For example, if the subregion has an area of 50 square kilometres and a total service provision score of 50, and if the district has an area of 1000 square kilometres and a total service provision score of 2000, then the service provision score per square kilometre would be 1.00 for die subregion and 2.00 for the district. The ratio value would be 0.50 for the subregion. In the studies conducted in Maharashtra, Andhra Pradesh, and Tamil Nadu, whenever the value of the ratio is more than 1.00, the service provision is considered above average for the subregion (consisting of service centres and their service areas) in that service.

This helped in identifying parts of the study areas that were deficient in the provision of both individual and all services. When the ratio values below 1.00 are divided further into four equal parts, as was done in Tamil Nadu for example, those with the following values were categorized: 0.750 to 0.999 - least poorly developed; 0.500 to 0.749 - poorly developed; 0.250 to 0.499 - more poorly developed; and 0.000 to 0.249 - most poorly developed in terms of provision of rural services. Nevertheless, all are 'poorly developed' subregions in Tamil Nadu, because their ratio values are less, than 1.00, though to different degrees.

Since the subregions consist of service centres and their service areas, the gaps identified are indeed the gaps in the provision of rural infrastructural services in the settlements of the subregion. In all the study areas, the existence of such gaps in the provision of rural service infrastructure was identified.

Index of Service Provision

The index of service provision is the mean service score per square kilometre for a study region. As noted earlier, it should be emphasized that index values are not strictly comparable because of differences in weights, and hence in service scores, across study areas over the two periods. However, the figures still highlight some differences in service provision among the study areas, and over time.

Miryalguda taluk initially has the lowest index, which is indicative of its 'late start', as discussed earlier, compared with Nagpur Metropolitan Region. North Arcot region, which already enjoyed the benefits of a more developed agricultural system initially, as compared to Miryalguda taluk, has a higher index of service provision. Nagpur Metropolitan Region, in contrast, has existed as an urban industrial region since the beginning of the century and, therefore, has the highest index value, indicative of its prime position among the three study areas.

MEDIAN POPULATION THRESHOLD OF SERVICES

The search for a quantitative estimate of entry of various services in a regional settlement system is important for settlement studies. The logic of central place theory suggests that such thresholds must exist but their exact definition remains elusive. One major reason for this is the complexity of locational decisions; services are established in a given settlement for a variety of reasons of which population size is an important but not necessarily an overriding factor. As a result, the simple concept of 'entry level' is replaced by 'entry zone', at the lower limits of which all settlements lack the service and at the upper limit an settlements possess it.

Median population thresholds for rural infrastructural services were calculated for all the three study areas in Maharashtra, Andhra Pradesh, and Tamil Nadu. Settlements that had the required population threshold for a service, but did not have the service in question, were considered to exhibit a gap in their structure of service provision, even though at the median population threshold, there is only a 50 per cent chance of it having that service.

This identification of a gap in geographic space tended to provide the development administrators with a set of 'locational priorities' for the development of rural service infrastructure in the study areas. The gaps were also seen as a potential that needs to be developed in order to strengthen the system of service delivery in the study area. It was expected that once these gaps were filled, the delivery system itself would be better articulated and be better equipped to serve the study areas. Locational priorities for removing regional disparities It was observed that when the locational priorities noted with the help of median population thresholds are followed while implementing a development plan for rural service provision, then the disparity between more developed and less developed parts of a study area would be reduced. As an example, the standards of service provision for Kalmeshwar subregion in the Nagpur Metropolitan Region were recalculated, 'assuming that the development of social and economic facilities had taken place according to the new set of locational priorities' as identified by the analysis.

Figures nearer the value of 1.00 indicate improvements in service provision. As can be seen, based on the locational priorities identified, improvements are noted in the provision of all services, but especially in the cases of education, communication, finance and trade, thus reducing disparity within the subregion substantially.

SPATIAL ORGANIZATIONAL FORM FOR REGIONAL DEVELOPMENT

The lowest order service centre with its service area, was identified as a spatial organizational form that could initiate the strengthening of a rural service system from the grassroots level upwards within a district. This facilitates the establishment of a functionally-integrated system of service centres, where the dependent villages are provided with basic infrastructural services that are complemented by more complex service provision at the central village and service centre levels.

For example, in Miryalguda taluk in 1968, at the dependent village level, a primary credit society was proposed to be located at the dependent village level; at the central village level, a cooperative bank was proposed to be located; and at the service centre level, a scheduled bank and a land mortgage bank were proposed to be located. In Miryalguda taluk, a form of 'spatial organization' was thus observed, where a focal point with a population of between 1500 and 2500 tends to serve an area of not more than 77.7 square kilometres and about 6000 - 8000 population. This was identified at the lowest level of a settlement hierarchy where this focal point served about seven to ten dependent villages. All other centres tended to serve larger areas, a greater number of people and more villages than this form. Similar such spatial organizational forms were also identified in Nagpur Metropolitan Region and in North Arcot Region.

Agro-based Industries and Service Centres

Two other spatial characteristics were also studied in all three study areas. These were related to the locations of agro-based industries around the service centres thus identified, and to the transportation network that would make the subregion a more compact spatial organizational form.

These characteristics are briefly noted below. The study of land use around all the service centres, with a view to establishing agro-based industries that would utilize the resource base, was another aspect of service centre planning that was investigated in the initial studies in Maharashtra and Andhra Pradesh.

A detailed study of the land use pattern around each service centre indicated the type of crop grown, the amount produced, the link between the service centre and its service area, the agricultural production that would facilitate the location of resource-based industries at the service centre, and the fink between factor and product markets. Such industries were weight losing' and had an advantage if located as near the resource base as possible.

Further, the rural service infrastructural content for these resource-based industries is very high. With 'clustering' of the necessary services at the centre, the advantages of economies of scale emanating from such 'clustering' could easily be availed of. Thus, it was observed in Miryalguda taluk that to establish a two metric-ton rice mill working in eight-hour shifts at a service centre, the service area of the centre should produce at least 12 500 metric tons of paddy per year.

A centre was, therefore, recommended for location of a rice mill after ascertaining that it had good access to its dependent villages which produce the paddy in required quantities.

Transportation Networks and Small Centres

An important area neglected in the studies on service centre planning, was the type of transportation network appropriate for rural spatial interaction. It was observed, for example, in Miryalguda taluk and also in North Arcot Region, that a poor farmer travels by poor means of transport over short distances, with greater frequency of visits per year, for monofunctional trips; whereas the rich farmer travels by better means of transport over long distances, with less frequency of visits per year, form multifunctional trips.

This pattern immediately offered several possibilities in transportation planning, such as a combination of cart tracks/ village roads between the lowest order service centre and its dependent territory, and a combination of village road/other district road or major district road between that centre and other centres of equal and higher importance. This conscious approach to transportation networks also facilitates the movement of other goods and services both in and out of the area served by a service centre.

Household Use of and Access to Services

In the initial studies, no attempt was made to analyse the pattern of use of these services from the point of view of households in rural areas; nor was any attempt made to assess the, impact of access to existing rural service infrastructure on consumption (demand) of these services. As discussed below, this aspect has been studied only recently in Andhra Pradesh and Tamil Nadu. Household use of services is influenced by a variety of factors. Among these are: distance to services; ease of access to services; importance of services; and economic status of the household.

Frequently, these factors interact to influence household use of services. Two studies focused more specifically on this aspect of service use in Miryalguda taluk of Andhra Pradesh in 1983, and North Arcot region of Tamil Nadu in 1982/83. In the first study, it was found that with increasing distance from the household, the frequency use of services declines. However, distance was a less important factor for economically-advantaged households who presumably were able to spend more on travel. The importance of a service, and, therefore, its frequency of use, also depended upon whether it was production or consumption oriented and the extent to which it needed to be 'replaced' given the consumption pattern of that service in the household.

Neither income nor distances were found to be significant in influencing frequency of use for most food and personal services. Income, however, was found to be significant for use of consumer durables and distance was significant for agroservices. In the North Arcot region in 1982/83, the relationship between access to services and household expenditure on consumption and production services was examined. These consumption and production services are a part of die total rural infrastructure system of the study region. As might be expected, greater distance from households entailed less expenditure on services.

DYNAMICS OF SERVICE PROVISION

The above spatial characteristics of service provision in Andhra Pradesh, Maharashtra, and Tamil Nadu have changed since the initial studies were conducted. In order to analyse this change and understand the underlying processes influencing it, the study areas of Nagpur Metropolitan Region, Miryalguda taluk, and North Arcot region were resurveyed in 1978, 1978/79, and 1990/91 respectively.

The results of these analyses emphasize mostly the dynamics of service provision in rural India as it related to changes in the settlement systems. Changes in the structure of service provision in the study areas It was seen from the Maharashtra studies that the overwhelming changes that took place in the study area between the two periods were a consequence, of the development of the urban-industrial economy of Nagpur city and its subsequent impact on the surrounding rural region.

The studies of Andhra Pradesh and Tamil Nadu showed, however, that the major changes that took place over the two time periods were a consequence of the development of the rural economy of the study areas. In all instances, the population that was influenced by these changes was mostly rural and not urban. This is because the changes in the metropolitan and agricultural sectors of the study areas tended to influence business establishments and services in the rural sector.

Changing demographic patterns in the study areas From the analyses of the demographic data, clearly there has been an increase in the number of settlements having higher service scores and the more complex services offered by these settlements have generally been associated with higher population levels. These changes are better understood if placed in the context of demographic transformations that have taken place in the study areas.

In Miryalguda taluk, most of the growth between the two time periods took place in settlements of 2000 to 4999 which accounted for about 36 per cent of the population in the second period as compared to about 15 per cent a decade earlier. In Nagpur Metropolitan Region, the percentage of the population in settlements of 5000 to 9000, increased from about four per cent to 12 per cent between the two periods. In the earlier period in North Arcot, settlements of 2500 to 9999 accounted for about 30 per cent of the population but by the second period, these accounted for almost 50 per cent of the total population.

However, within this group, smaller sized settlements of 2500 to 5000 in particular, have grown in importance, accounting for about 36 per cent of the population in the latter period compared to 22 per cent in the earlier period. So in all three regions, an increase in the number of mid-sized settlements, particularly at the lower end of the 2500 to 10 000 range in population, is observed.

Also, settlements smaller than this have declined both in size and importance. Similarly, settlements larger than 10 000 have not increased in number, but in fact have declined in importance particularly in Miryalguda taluk and in North Arcot region. The rapid growth and development of mid-sized settlements is indicative of their increasing ability to provide a broader and more complex range of services to a larger percentage of the population, which in turn is escalating competitiveness with large urban centres that have declined in importance over the two periods.

Changing patterns of service provision in the study areas Service provision has also become more balanced in Maharashtra, Andhra Pradesh and Tamil Nadu, with a remarkable increase in the percentage of services provided by the middle segment of the settlement system consisting of larger villages and small towns. Thus larger towns and cities are not the only major providers of services to the rural areas, many small towns and larger villages are assuming that role in the study areas. This is in part due to the demographic changes that have been noted in the previous paragraphs.

In the North Arcot region, the number of settlements offering a greater number of services, as well as more complex ones (as indicated by service score groups), decline rapidly at higher service score categories, particularly in the first time period. Interestingly, it was observed that in the second time period there was both a tremendous increase in the number of settlements with scores above 70, especially in those with scores greater than 130. Thus the settlement system of North Arcot region has improved vastly since 1982/83 in terms of service provision.

This relationship between service and settlement hierarchy is also observed in Miryalguda taluk, Andhra Pradesh. As in North Arcot region, there has been a great improvement in the level of services available. The decline in the number of settlements that offer no services at all is apparent in both regions. Most increases in services provision are in the basic services category. In this connection, it is noted that the first public sector service to appeal is usually a primary school and the first private sector service to appear is a retail general provision store.

Particularly notable is the improvement in the provision of retail services by the private sector in settlements in both regions over time, relative to the provision of services by the public sector. The level of involvement of the government and private sectors in service provision in rural areas depends on the level of agricultural development in these areas. Heavy government involvement in policy planning and service provision typifies earlier stages of development. Later, at a more advanced stage of development, the service provision is characterized by greater involvement of the private sector than of the government sector. Investments by the private sector at this stage tend to be more demand-driven.

Changes in the levels of service centres in the study areas In all the study areas, whilst in the first period there were very few low-order service centres, in the second period their numbers increased quite impressively. Also, in the first period, large parts of the Andhra Pradesh and Tamil Nadu study areas were provided with services by centres outside the study areas, whilst in the second period only a very small fraction of the study areas was thus serviced, and for only one or two services.

In Miryalguda taluk and Nagpur Metropolitan Region, new centres have emerged, mostly at the low order of service hierarchy. In all three study areas, the middle and high orders of service hierarchy have also become stronger over the two periods. Thus, quantitatively and qualitatively, there has been an impressive improvement in the service provision system of all the study areas.

Changes in the composition of service areas in the study areas In all three study areas, with the emergence of new centres and the strengthening of the old ones, the extent of service areas covered by a typical service centre has generally declined and the service population served by each centre has either increased or decreased. Various kinds of new spatial relationships are identified in the study areas based on the location (establishment) of a new service.

The mere location of a new service in a service centre or a settlement does not necessarily mean that it will immediately start to serve the surrounding villages. The location of a new service needs to be seen in its regional context. If the service is so new that it is the only one of its kind in the region, then there are bound to be associated changes in the region. This, for example, has happened in the establishment of regulated markets for agricultural produce, which is a new service in the study areas. However, if the location is new only at a particular service centre or settlement, but not in the region, then it is quite possible that the service centre within which it is established will begin to evolve new regional relationships with the introduction of that particular service.

Service areas and serviced populations have declined when new services are introduced in settlements of an the study areas for animal husbandry, rural banks, allopathic treatment centres, medical clinics, general provision stores, retail cloth stores, hardware stores, weekly markets, fertilizer and pesticide shops and medical stores.

Changes in the locations of services in the study areas Over both time periods in Andhra Pradesh and Tamil Nadu, an increase in the number of services in a service centre was reflected in both the total area and population served by the centre in various ways. In Andhra Pradesh, the number of services, the centrality scores, the extent of service area and the size of service population have all changed, if rather selectively.

Those service centres that exhibit low values, in all the above variables, in both periods in Andhra Pradesh are located either in the dry tract or in areas away from the Left Bank Canal or in areas that have been provided with gravity or lift irrigation more recently. There is also some evidence that the service centres in close proximity to the more important service centres have also grown slowly. In Tamil Nadu, service centres that were headquarters of development administration have grown more rapidly than those that perform no such development administrative function.

Changes in index of service provision in the study areas In Miryalguda taluk the index increased from 1.79 to 3.84 between 1968 and 1978, in North Arcot region it increased from 8.44 to 14.10 between 1982/83 and 1990/91, and in Nagpur Metropolitan Region, it increased from 60.29 to 97.25 between 1969 and 1978/79. It can also be seen that the direct role of the government in rural service provision tends to get reduced as the level of overall economic development rises; the private sector starts playing a more direct role in rural service provision. Thus, in Andhra Pradesh although the public sector was a major service provider over both time periods, the percentage share of the service index generated by the private sector increased over the decade. In Maharashtra, however, the private sector has primarily been responsible for most of the improvements in service provision over the decade.

Changes in median population thresholds of services in the study areas Over time, one would expect the median population threshold to fall as improvements in service provision occur in the study areas. A good example of this is in North Arcot Region. Between 1982 and 1990, the median population threshold for almost all services fell. In 1990/91, for example, there would have been a 50/50 chance that settlements with at least 2490 inhabitants would have a middle school, whereas in 1982/83, one would have been surprised to find these in settlements with fewer than 3180 inhabitants.

Table. Median Population Thresholds for Selected Services in North Arcot Region

Service	Median Population Threshold	
	1982/83	1990/91
Middle school	3180	2490
High school	5400	2820
Private hospital	6960	5290
Shop selling vegetables	6510	4050
Shop selling sweetmeats	6990	3540

Note: Median population thresholds are rounded to the nearest ten. Services selected are from those for which median population thresholds were calculated with only minor modification of the assumption in 1982/83, and which also existed as services in the 1990/91 survey.

Government Policies and Regional Development in the Study Areas

The state governments have tended to follow policies formulated on the basis of the above types of studies in India.

The details of how this has taken place are given elsewhere; the findings of the studies in Andhra Pradesh and Maharashtra, for example, have become part of substate development plans for the provision of rural infrastuctural services in these two states. Noted below are experiences from Andhra Pradesh.

Regional development policies followed by the Government of Andhra Pradesh to correct the imbalances in rural service provision, led to the establishment of new services in selected centres of the settlement system of the study region. It was hoped that once provided, the services would be used by the residents of the surrounding villages. It was also hoped that once the government introduced services under this policy, more private businesses would feel encouraged to locate their services in the study area. These new establishments, it was felt, would tend to concentrate initially in that part of the region that had such structural advantages as: assured irrigation facilities; a diversified cropping pattern; more double cropping; more wealth; a higher demand for these services; and a higher concentration of rural population.

A significant feature of the regional development reality of Andhra Pradesh is that most of these changes took place in the study area during 1968-83. Service areas defined by government regulation are a common feature of development administration at the district level in all the study areas.

There are cooperative banks, regulated markets for agricultural produce, centres for seed and fertilizer distribution and veterinary hospitals normally located at the headquarters of a community development block, which serve only the settlement of its jurisdiction. The second survey of 1978-79 in Andhra Pradesh shows that below the community development block level there are also regulated or controlled service areas for all the above services.

The more practical and direct implications of the regional development policy in Andhra Pradesh can be seen in the provision of such rural services as: primary credit-society; secondary school; centre for medical checkup; bus service; centre for allopathic treatment; animal husbandry centre; and rural services in both irrigated and dry tracts. In the study area, by 1978, it is possible to discern a small locational bias in their provision. For example, although secondary school, centre for medical checkup, bus service, and centre for allopathic treatment are provided in selected settlements throughout the study area, new agricultural services such as primary credit societies, animal husbandry centres, rural banks, and regulated markets for agricultural produce are only provided in the irrigated tracts of the study area.

Such a locational bias does not appear to exist in an already irrigated study area of Tamil Nadu. Similarly, in the study area of Maharashtra, which is an urban-metropolitan region, there is no such locational bias in the distribution of services except for the fact that all new services are emerging in the rural sector of the metropolitan region.

The early studies have, whether inadvertently or for reasons unknown, treated the community development block or the district as a 'closed system', which is a rather inappropriate course of action. All regions for one purpose or another are 'open systems' and, therefore, extra regional linkages and flows need to be studied in detail before any inter-regional recommendations are made for the study areas. In the case of North Arcot region of Tamil Nadu, such extra regional linkages have indeed been studied and are also reported elsewhere.

This comparative analysis has shown that in spite of inherent disparities due to the different stages of development observed in the three study areas, the extent of urbanization and the nature and scope of innovations - especially in irrigation and agriculture - that have initiated the existing rural service infrastructural development patterns, there are similar processes at work that help explain the changes observed across the three different study areas and over two points in time.

Concepts derived from central place theory, such as spatial and service hierarchy, clustering of services, population thresholds, scores of service provision and gaps in the service provision, have provided a common foundation from which to make recommendations for the future provision of rural service infrastructure in the study areas. In all cases, an improvement in the availability of services, particularly in the case of low-order services, has been observed across all sizes of settlements over time.

Notably, there has been a tremendous improvement in the capacity of larger villages and small towns to provide these services. In addition, more sophisticated services are increasingly available within the study areas, though only in a few settlements, obviating the need to go 'outside' the region for these services.

Each study area is at a different stage of development. As such, development targets will be different for each of the three areas and will be dynamic rather than static, given the rapid improvements observed over the two periods. Closely related to this is the extent to which the public and private sector is involved in provision of rural service infrastructure.

In the earlier stages of development, the government appears to play a major role in establishing the necessary rural service infrastructure. At this stage in particular, research, planning and implementation activities under-taken by the government authorities are of paramount importance. In spite of the increasing evidence of the role of the private sector in providing services, the analysis indicates that the government still has a seminal role to play in the provision of basic rural service infrastructure, especially in underdeveloped areas in which the private sector is reluctant to invest.

In this respect, the role of the government as a facilitator of development, which encourages demand-driven private sector involvement in the long run, will remain critical. The potential for collaboration between the public and private sector in order to strengthen rural service provision merits further exploration.

Treating systems as 'closed', a lack of coordination between researchers and development administrators and creating a false dichotomy between urban and rural systems, are just three of the many problems that can adversely affect the investment levels and provision of rural service infrastructure, which may also influence adversely the subsequent involvement of the private sector in the study areas. Strategies for rural service infrastructural development will, therefore, have a chance of some success, only if demographic, functional and spatial characteristics of rural settlement systems are considered by researchers, planners and administrators while preparing plans for rural development. Furthermore, the linkages between rural and urban systems and other sectors of the regional economy and rural service infrastructure will need to be clearly identified, and delineated, in order to develop a functionally integrated system of rural service provision.

The state governments, right from the beginning, actively supported the establishment of rural institutions below the district level, and planned for the diffusion of public-sector rural service infrastructure in all regions. The result has been improved access to goods and services and, also, a widespread decentralization of previous urban functions to the rural areas.

Given that planning of rural service delivery systems is a state concern in India, the implications of the methodology adopted in the studies noted above assume great importance. These studies show how to approach planning of rural service provision and they provide the basis for conducting similar exercises elsewhere at the substate level in India.

2

Size and Structure of Rural Markets

A 1997 World Bank Study has rekindled the debate on whether economic growth is central to poverty alleviation in India. Invoking the main findings of a research project based on household surveys over a 40-year period, the study, India: Achievements and Challenges in Reducing Poverty, claims that "overall growth accounted for the lion's share of poverty reduction: 80 per cent of the decline in the number of households below the poverty line between 1951 and 1970, and almost 100 per cent since 1970."

Further, the findings "clearly refute any presumption of immiserizing growth—that is growth that tends to marginalize or impoverish significant sections of the population—in India over this 40-year period." The message therefore is that "it is through rapid growth that India will be able to reduce poverty and generate the resources to invest in the health and education of its people—who will in turn sustain this growth." Although the overall antipoverty strategy is similar to that advocated in the 1990 World Development Report—in as much as the main components are labour-intensive growth, human capital development and social safety nets—the former is distinguishable in its greater emphasis on growth. In the present chapter, we contest this claim.

While growth matters, its contribution to poverty alleviation is much less than the World Bank claims. The related claim that growth did not immiserize or impoverishes certain sections is inconsistent with panel evidence. In fact, there is a large core of poverty that persists despite rapid growth. The issue then is whether there are specific factors that tend to exclude the poor from participating in growth. In this chapter we will attempt to identify some key factors through an analysis of a panel survey. As noted, the primacy of growth in the World Bank strategy rests not just on its direct poverty-reducing effect, but on the generation of additional resources for poverty alleviation (interpreted broadly to include human capital development). The latter claim is examined with state data on two major anti-poverty programmes, the Jawahar Rozgar Yojana (JRY) and the Integrated Rural Development Programme (IRDP).

Finally, based on the analysis of factors that impeded participation of sections of poor households in growth, we elaborate some major components of an anti-poverty strategy. Although there is some overlap with the World Bank strategy (specifically regarding human capital formation), the emphases differ. The present study focuses more on the design and implementation of this growth focused strategy. In this context, community initiatives have a potentially significant role. But such initiatives seldom work, as the impediments are not easy to overcome. A review of some recent field evidence on the functioning of the Panchayats (an elected body), following the implementation of the 73rd Constitutional Amendment Act in 1993, yields useful insights. Although a strong coalition of the poor would help overcome some impediments, it is not obvious how the coalition could be strengthened.

Extent and Severity of Poverty

Despite over four decades of planned development in India, a large section of the population continues to live in abject poverty. According to a National Sample Survey for 1993 and 1994, about 36.7 per cent of the rural population and 30.5 per cent of the urban population live in poverty—implying a national average of 35 per cent. Although there has been some reduction in the proportion of the poor over time—especially between the mid-1970s and late 1980s—their aggregate number has risen. From about 164 million in 1951, it rose to 312 million in 1993 to 1994. There are also sharp regional disparities. In Bihar, for example, the proportion of poor in the rural population (64 per cent) in 1993 and 1994 was two and a half times higher than that of the combined states of Punjab and Haryana (25 per cent). Similarly, there are wide variations within states. Of the 10 poorest regions in 1987 and 1988, five were either in Bihar or Orissa. Poverty was evenly distributed across the five regions in these two states. But in Uttar Pradesh (UP)—another poor state (with about 42 per cent of the rural population classified as poor)—barely 8.4 per cent of the rural population in the Himalayan region was poor, the lowest incidence in all of India.

Classifying all of India's rural population into various groups, 68 per cent of the landless wage earners, 51 per cent of scheduled tribes/castes (STs/SCs) and 45 per cent of illiterates were poor in 1993 and 1994. Using the poverty gap index to measure depth of poverty in seven out of the 14 states for which estimates are available, the gap in rural areas ranged from a low of about 5 per cent in West Bengal to a high of well over 17 per cent in Bihar in 1993 and 1994. Given the low poverty threshold, these estimates point to the extreme poverty of large segments of the rural population in several states. As noted earlier, the 1997 World Bank Study asserts the centrality of growth in poverty alleviation. The rate of reduction in poverty was indeed faster during periods of rapid growth (i.e., between the mid-1970s and 1980s); the average annual reduction (2.4 per cent) was three times as fast as during a period of slow growth (i.e., from 1951 to 1975). These patterns hold for both rural and urban areas. At the state level, while the centrality of growth in poverty alleviation is maintained, the study notes that human capital and infrastructure have important roles as well. However, as argued below, an effective anti-poverty strategy must have broader concerns.

Impact of Policy Reforms

Of some concern is the impact of policy reform, initiated in India in mid-1991, on the poor. These reforms were a response to the macroeconomic crisis that erupted in early 1991. Following policy reforms, the head-count ratio for rural areas rose sharply—from 36.4 per cent in 1991 to 43.5 per cent in 1992—and dropped to 36.7 per cent in 1993 and 1994. While the 1997 World Bank Study reports that no more than one-third of the initial increase in rural poverty is attributable to policy reforms, how much of the increase is attributable to such reforms remains a debatable issue.

It is plausible that some impoverishment was a result of these reforms, even if an allowance is made for (random) variability of incomes from cultivation and associated variability of wages. Equally, the subsequent reduction in rural poverty in 1993 and 1994 should not be viewed as a result of policy reforms leading to a higher overall growth rate.

In general, whatever the contribution of the policy reforms in accelerating growth in recent years, we argue below that growth alone will have a limited impact, as there are large segments of rural poverty that persist due to the inability of some sections of the population to participate in the growth process.

Impoverishment

M. S. Ahluwalia's influential contribution to the debate on growth and poverty provoked a lively discussion on whether agricultural growth 'trickles down' to the poor. Several critiques drew attention to the impoverishment of some sections as a direct consequence of growth. Given the inequality in endowments of both physical and human capital, as well as a rigidly hierarchical social structure, it is not surprising that some sections benefit while others lose when economic opportunities expand.

Under certain extreme conditions, when inequality in the distribution of land manifests itself in an oligopsonistic labour market with few large landholders dominating through wage-setting, shifts in labour demand may have a small effect on agricultural wages relative to that in a competitive labour market. Consequently, poverty persists despite growth.

Indeed, if dominance of large landholders also precludes some remunerative supplementary options (i.e., working part-time on another farm), poverty could worsen through a dampening effect on the earnings of agricultural laborers. A recent analysis confirms that while agricultural growth reduces rural poverty, a measure of oligopsony exacerbates poverty. The 1997 World Bank Study relies on a decomposition of change in rural poverty into three components: growth, redistribution and the residual.

If poverty falls over time, part of the reduction may be due to a higher average income without any change in its distribution (i.e., the growth component); some reduction may be due to a change in the distribution itself without any change in the average income (i.e., the redistributional component); while the remaining reason for reduction may be due to the interdependence between growth and distributional change (i.e., the residual).

The issue is whether the favourable effect of growth is neutralized or reinforced by income distributional change. The study found that growth accounted for 80 per cent of the decline in the head-count index over the period 1951 to 1994 and almost 100 per cent since 1978. This, however, is suspect. Two problems with this decomposition procedure suffice. One is the presumption that the growth and distributional components are separable. In case they are not, the decomposition is ambiguous.

Based on 1997 World Bank estimates, illustrates vividly that changes in mean consumption and changes in the Gini coefficient in Uttar Pradesh—one of the poorest Indian states—moved together over the period 1959 to 1994 (i.e., higher values of change in consumption were associated with higher values of change in the Gini coefficient).

Another problem is that changes in consumption distribution understate income distributional changes when there is consumption smoothing. To that extent, the redistributional component would therefore be lower. A surprising claim in the 1997 World Bank Study is that the decomposition refutes any presumption of immiserising growth over the period 1951 to 1994. All that the decomposition shows is that the growth component was the largest, implying that most of the reduction in the head-count ratio was due to growth. However, as will be demonstrated below, if a subset of the poor who cross the poverty threshold is larger than a subset of the non-poor who slip into poverty, this ratio falls.

As the decomposition is confined to changes in the head-count ratio, it cannot capture changes in the composition of the poor and nonpoor over time. The latter can only be captured through a more detailed analysis of a panel survey, as shown below.

Even though income from cultivation grew rapidly during this period (about 6 per cent annually), about 27 per cent of the households became impoverished (i.e., categories 1 and 4). Among the impoverished, the poor who became poorer were the dominant group.

Although both groups suffered substantial income losses, the non-poor who became poor recorded a much larger reduction (about 57 per cent versus about 25 per cent among the poor who became poorer).

Table. Change in Poverty Status of Households in Maharashtra, 1979 to 1984

Poverty Status	Relative Frequency	Per Capita 1979	Income(*) 1984
Poor who become poorer	15.07	134.49	101.22
Poor who ceased to be poor	24.65	117.73	239.58
Poor who remained poor without becoming poorer	13.70	100.04	131.33
Non-poor who became poor	12.33	253.21	108.40
Non-poor who remained non-poor	34.25	348.01	411.19

(*) Per capita income is at constant prices. The poverty threshold is 180 rupees (Rs) per capita annually. This is based on the cost of a nutritionally adequate diet. For details of how this poverty threshold was determined and its applications. Over the period in question, the head-count ratio registered a reduction—from about 53 per cent to about 47 per cent—as the poor who ceased to be poor exceeded the non-poor who became poor. However, the intensity of poverty rose slightly, as the average income of the poor fell from 118 to 113 rupees (Rs). Of considerable interest is the subset of the poor who ceased to be poor.

Their average income was well below the poverty threshold (barely 65 per cent of the latter) and it doubled in about five years, suggesting that even among the poorest there is considerable income mobility. The factors that enabled a quarter of the poor households to overcome poverty are analysed below. This analysis has some important implications for the persistence of poverty.

Persistence of Poverty

If there is a large core of chronic poverty—among the sick, physically weak and disabled who are unable to participate in gainful employment—the effect of growth on poverty will be weak. A detailed analysis with the ICRISAT data yields a range of estimates of chronic poverty for the period 1975 to 1984.

Three alternative measures of poverty were computed. The first is a simple head-count measure over multiple periods. It identifies households whose actual incomes fall under the poverty threshold (Rs180 per capita annually) for several years, in the extreme case, for all nine years.

Such households are designated as chronically poor. The second measure is based on expected poverty (as opposed to actual income) falling below the poverty cutoff point. The third measure is similar to the second but with the refinement of control for unobserved household fixed effects, representing ability, management and other household endowments in the estimation of the above relationship.

This measure provides the most stringent measure of poverty and identifies households that are innately poor (i.e., those likely to remain poor not only in the absence of random/ transitory income shocks but also if they were to have the same physical assets as the sample averages).

Table. Actual, Expected and Innate Poverty Estimates: Rural South India, ICRISAT Sample, 1975 to 1984

Year	Poverty Estimates Actual	Expected	Innate
1975-76	70.00	74.00	69.00
1976-77	68.00	74.00	62.00
1977-78	61.00	68.00	58.00
1978-79	54.00	59.00	46.00
1979-80	56.00	59.00	44.00
1980-81	59.00	53.00	39.00
1981-82	54.00	54.00	38.00
1982-83	44.00	55.00	36.00
1983-84	51.00	58.00	36.00
All 9 years	57.00	61.00	48.00

Over the nine years, the extent of poverty based on actual income averaged 57 per cent, but with a wide range from 44 to 70 per cent. The incidence of expected poverty was somewhat higher at 61 per cent, but declined from 74 per cent in the period from 1975 to 1976 to 53 per cent in 1980 and 1981, increasing thereafter to reach a level of 58 per cent by 1983 and 1984.

Finally, as anticipated, the magnitude of innate poverty, averaging 48 per cent during the sample period, was smaller than that of actual and expected poverty But it is still surprisingly large, considering that it identifies those households that would remain poor despite short-run changes in their assets and other characteristics (such as family size). While the monotonic decline in the magnitude of innate poverty over the sample period (from a level of 69 per cent in 1975 and 1976 to 36 per cent in 1983 and 1984) is encouraging, the fact that over one-third of the sample households during the last year of the sample period were likely to remain poor despite policy interventions in the short run, is both disturbing and pessimistic.

Slightly more than 60 per cent of households were poor roughly half of the time (i.e., during five of the nine sample years). Finally, a little more than one-fifth of the households were poor during all nine years (i.e., chronically poor). Sixty per cent of households classified as poor on the basis of actual income and 52 per cent of expected poor were also innately poor. However, because of the stringent definition of chronic poverty (i.e., poor throughout the sample period), only a relatively small proportion of the actually, expected and innately poor households were also chronically poor (i.e., 38 per cent, 34 per cent and 33 per cent, respectively).

The varying estimates of poverty reflect the heterogeneity among the poor and demonstrate that the poor are not a monolithic group; they are composed, inter alia, of households that are poor owing to transitory shocks, households that are poor owing to low levels of owned physical assets and households that are poor owing to long-run inherited disadvantages. Growth alone may not accomplish much, as different sets of policies are needed to reach each of these disparate groups.

Factors

Some further insights into the persistence of poverty are obtained from an analysis of the factors that impeded (or facilitated) the movement of the poor out of poverty. This analysis is based on the ICRISAT panel survey of two villages in Maharashtra over the period 1979 to 1984, which was marked by a rapid growth of farm and non-farm activities. Income from cultivation, for example, grew by six per cent per annum. The main findings of an econometric analysis are analysed below.

That it was harder for poor households with a high dependency burden to move out of poverty over the period in question is plausible, since, in general, a larger proportion of children implies not just fewer earners but also fewer employment options for female members. Equally relevant is the unfavourable effect of an aging household head on moving out of poverty.

Given the harsh agro-climatic environment of the semi-arid tract, it is likely that earnings fall sharply with a decline in physical strength and stamina. In addition, the possibility that older age-groups tend to be risk-averse, and therefore not inclined to experiment with innovative agricultural practices or seek out new avenues for higher labour earnings, cannot be ruled out.

That some poor households ceased to be poor by acquiring cultivable land is significant, especially in the context of a highly unequal distribution of land. Since the period 1979 to 1984 witnessed expansion of both farm and non-farm activities, it is a fair presumption that poor households with higher educational achievements were better able to seize income—augmenting opportunities to get out of poverty. It might appear surprising that, independent of physical and human capital endowments and of demographic characteristics of households, the caste affiliation had a significant effect on movement out of poverty. The low caste households—the lowest in the caste hierarchy being the scheduled castes—are typically the most disadvantaged in terms of both physical and human capital.

Evidence on their exchange entitlements, however, is scanty. Why returns to physical and human capital vary with the caste rank may reflect discrimination (in various forms) against lower castes in specific markets (i.e., labour and credit markets) or their weak motivation to engage in more rewarding pursuits. To the extent that there are traces of the former, it follows that market imperfections act as an impediment.

To summarize, while agricultural growth will undoubtedly make a difference, a substantial reduction in poverty is feasible only if barriers to acquisition of physical and human capital—and to their productive and remunerative use—are eliminated.

ANTI - POVERTY PROGRAMME OUTLAYS

As noted earlier, the centrality of growth in poverty alleviation rests on the strength of its direct and indirect effects. However, not only is the direct effect much weaker than claimed in the 1997 World Bank Study, but the presumption that growth generates resources for poverty alleviation programmes, including those for human capital formation, is somewhat naive, if not mistaken.

Given the fiscal squeeze, some components of public expenditure are more vulnerable than others, depending to some extent on the nature of the political regime. A positive relationship between outlays on poverty alleviation and growth is thus unlikely, as illustrated below.

More importantly, given the outlays, what really matters is whether these are well-targeted. In case they are not, serious doubts arise about the efficacy of the indirect effects. As state governments contribute large shares of outlays to poverty alleviation programmes (varying from 20 to 50 per cent of the total) and variations in political regime are also more pronounced at that level, it is worthwhile to analyse state outlays on two programmes: the Integrated Rural Development Programme (IRDP) and the Jawahar Rozgar Yojana (JRY). Changes in net state domestic product (NSDP) and IRDP outlays (IRDP) diverge over the period 1992 to 1995.

In a few cases (e.g. Bihar), a positive [Delta]NSDP was associated with a negative [Delta]IRDP. The correlation coefficient is positive (0.15) but statistically not significant. Thus, increases in domestic product do not necessarily entail increases in outlays.

ANTI-POVERTY STRATEGY

As a comprehensive discussion of an anti-poverty strategy is not feasible here, we shall concentrate on a few major concerns. Given the key roles of land and education in overcoming poverty a major concern is how to enhance the access of the poor to these resources. In addition, during periods of economic stress rural public works (RPW) have an important role. Finally, the old and incapacitated warrant special protection. These concerns are addressed below.

Land

As noted earlier, acquisition of land enabled a subset of the poor to overcome poverty over the period 1979 to 1984. Land redistribution would thus help alleviate poverty. Besides, since it is unlikely to reduce farm output, the equity-efficiency tradeoff in land redistribution would be low, if any. In fact, an econometric analysis with the ICRISAT data further strengthens the efficiency case.

It suggests that redistributing land from large landowners to those owning even tiny quantities of land would raise farm output. How this redistribution may be accomplished is of course not straightforward. Land ceilings are seldom implemented. One possibility is a progressive land tax. This may induce intensive use of land and discourage the holding of land for speculative purposes. In addition, the dismantling of input subsidies may further reduce the attractiveness of land to the rich.

At the same time, and contrary to conventional wisdom, a cautious approach to regulations concerning land tenure contracts, including tenancy reforms and land rent, is necessary. In particular, restrictions on share tenancy in the absence of insurance and credit markets do not help the poor. However, the rights of leaseholders already established must be preserved and made transferable. It is imperative that complementary policies for the provision of credit, agricultural inputs and extension services be designed appropriately for smallholders.

Education

The 1990 World Development Report (WDR) assigns a key role to education: "There can be little doubt that educating the children of the poor greatly improves their chances of escaping poverty. Since labour is the one scarce resource on which all able-bodied poor can rely, increasing the productivity of this labour is clearly the most effective way to escape poverty."

However, in its advocacy, the 1990 WDR does not go much beyond recommending a shift in the allocation of funds from "higher level services to basic health and primary education" to enable greater access of the poor to these services, "increasing the number of female teachers" and "paying parents to send their girls to school" to limit gender inequality. Drawing upon some recent work, we will concentrate on breaking the vicious circle between low quality of primary education—especially in rural areas—and weak motivation among poor families for education. Values have an important role in both public provision of education and its utilization. Public provision of education—especially for the benefit of lower castes—is often constrained by the perception of politicians and policymakers that education is not particularly important for them.

Equally, the traditional attitude among lower castes that they can engage only in some unskilled occupations results in a neglect of schooling among their children—especially among the female children. The deprivation of the latter reflects a limited role for women. Weak motivation and lack of incentives are inextricably linked. The opportunity cost of the time spent in school imposes a huge burden on poor families, since children play an important role in household chores and farm activities. The gender division of labour (combined with patrilineal property rights) tends to reduce the perceived benefits of female education.

The norms of patrilocal residence and village exogamy (requiring a woman to settle in her husband's village), prevalent in large parts of India, further undermine the parental incentive to educate their female children. Dowry and hypergamous marriage (i.e., a woman should "marry up" in the social scale), also prevalent in large parts of India, turn female education into a liability.

The abysmal quality of school education is also a strong disincentive. Absenteeism and shirking among school teachers are rampant. Vocational content is low, if not nil. Given the permanence of posts, bureaucratic protection and the absence of a link between performance and remuneration, there is no incentive for reform from within the school system, though pressures from the outside may have desired effects.

Active public campaigns have a decisive effect on the demand for education. School meals and related incentives enhance school attendance rates by reducing the opportunity cost of attending school. Special incentives in the form of fee exemptions or scholarships for girls would have a favourable effect on their enrollment. Whether compulsory primary education is a feasible alternative is debatable, since views on the time frame, age limits, enforcement mechanisms and social security arrangements designed to obviate the need for child labour vary a great deal.

Whatever the merits, compulsory education on its own will not remedy the inefficient functioning of schools in rural areas. Much depends on whether the school system is accountable to the community and whether the latter can exercise effective control.

Rural Public Works

Rural public works (RPW) confer transfer and stabilization benefits. Transfer benefits can be direct—the gross benefit to a participant less any cost he/she incurs in participating—or indirect—including the effect on agricultural wages and higher incomes through the creation of productive assets (e.g. roads) in rural areas. To the extent that an additional source of income during agricultural slack periods helps stabilize consumption and prevent costly adjustments (through, for example, liquidation of assets), RPW confer stabilization benefits as well. The analysis summarized below focuses on the targeting of RPW, as both transfer and stabilization benefits depend crucially on it.

Less than one-third of the households participating in the survey (about 31 per cent) were classified as poor. However, the share of poor that participated in RPW was slightly higher (5.1 per cent as against 4.1 per cent of the non-poor). As poverty and landlessness are closely associated, RPW participants were cross-classified into three landholding intervals: 0 to 0.4 hectare; 0.41 to 2 hectares; and over 2.01 hectares. About 38 per cent of the total participating households were nearly landless (i.e., belonged to the first interval), and the majority had access to some land.

In fact, about 27 per cent of the participants had access to land exceeding 2 hectares. In addition, the proportion of households participating in RPW was highest in this interval (8.2 per cent versus 3.4 per cent in the first and 4.6 per cent in the second interval). Members of the scheduled castes and scheduled tribes were among the poorest. These two groups accounted for less than half of the participants (about 42 per cent). However, the proportion participating in RPW was higher among them (6.1 per cent as against 3.8 per cent in the rest). In sum, the presumption that a work requirement by itself would be an effective deterrent for the non-poor is not corroborated by this analysis.

In fact, a substantial proportion of the total participants—if not a large majority—were non-poor. Although the 1997 World Bank Study draws attention to a few familiar design and implementation problems, it does not throw much light on the exclusion of the poor. More revealing insights are obtained from an analysis of the Employment Guarantee Scheme (EGS). Concentrating mainly on the net benefits from the EGS, it is arguable that these were higher for the non-poor, resulting in the exclusion of the poor.

Although the opportunity cost of time is not likely to vary much between the poor and non-poor during slack periods, other costs do, making it more difficult for the poor to participate in EGS due to bureaucratic red tape. Such costs relate mostly to long waiting periods between registration and work opportunities and to long distances between the residence and worksite.

On the benefit side, the actual remuneration (and not so much the wage rate) and the periodization of payments matter. Given the piece-rate system, there is a premium on physical strength and dexterity. But piece-rates cause long delays in the payment of wages as an assessment of the quantity and quality of work done takes time. Although it is stipulated that wages must be paid once a week (or fortnight at the latest), it is not uncommon for wages to be delayed for up to eight weeks.

More seriously, wages paid are often less than the recorded amount. Given the wage rate, the actual remuneration is substantially lower for the poor because they are more likely to be physically less strong and more exposed to being cheated because of their illiteracy. Thus, the disincentives to the poor on the benefit side (i.e., delays in payment of wages) may be just as strong as those associated with long delays in offers of EGS work—especially if they are subject to a tight liquidity constraint. Given budgetary constraints, improvements in the design and implementation of the EGS would enable greater participation by the poor. Specifically, replacement of the piece-rate contract by a time-rate one for some routine tasks is necessary.

This would help reduce delays in the payment of wages. A wider dispersal of EGS projects may add to the attractiveness of this scheme to the poor, since the guarantee is effective only at the district level, requiring participants to travel distances longer than the stipulated eight-kilometre limit. Simplification of registration procedures and reduction of the waiting period between registration and work would further facilitate the participation of the poor. With these improvements, which are indeed feasible, both transfer and stabilization benefits of the EGS to the poor would be substantially greater.

Social Security

The concern for the aged and infirm—both highly prone to chronic poverty—has grown over the years as a result of the aging of the population and the weakening of traditional family and community support. Formal social security is limited largely to urban areas and the benefits are small. Particularly relevant in the present context are old age pension and subsidized life insurance, as they provide a modicum of social security to the poor.

A means-tested old age pension scheme operates in all Indian states. Some states also have pension schemes for destitute widows and the physically handicapped, and some provide for survivor benefits to families when a family member dies as a result of an occupational hazard. Recently, the central government introduced a group insurance scheme for agricultural laborers and IRDP beneficiaries.

The coverage of the old-age pension scheme varies considerably among the states. The low coverage (no more than 20 per cent of the old people in poverty) is due partly to lack of information among the eligible beneficiaries, but it is mainly due to restrictive qualifying conditions relating to age, destitution, residence and ad hoc financial ceilings. Corruption and procedural delays limit effective access. The pension amount is paltry, ranging from Rs30 to Rs60 per month.

The coverage of voluntary insurance is considerably lower, covering barely 8 per cent of the adult population. Further, the coverage of the rural population is substantially lower than its share in the total. The survivor benefits in the group insurance for agricultural laborers are a paltry Rs 1,000, not adequate even to meet funeral expenses.

However, extension of social security to the rural poor—particularly old age pensions and survivor benefits—on a comprehensive scale is affordable, as the overall resource requirement is no more than 1 per cent of India's GNP and no more than 4 per cent of the combined resources of the central and state governments. Part of the premia could of course be financed from contributions of the insured persons. A recent initiative to strengthen social security for the poor, while laudable, is "belated redress rather than radical reform."

Implementation

The World Bank critique is standard: overcentralized administration, multiplicity of official agencies and hesitant devolution to the Panchayats of poverty alleviation programmes. Each of these concerns is dealt with sketchily. As devolution to the Panchayats following the 73rd Constitutional Amendment Act is in some ways a landmark, these concerns deserve a more detailed and critical review.

The 73rd Constitutional Amendment provides for a uniform three-tier structure of the Panchayats—specifically at the district, block and village levels—mandatory elections after five years, proportional representation of the scheduled castes/ scheduled tribes, a quota for women, periodic auditing of accounts and specification of areas of responsibility of the Panchayats. As a definitive assessment of this structure is not feasible for lack of detailed data, the focus is restricted to a few aspects of the devolution. A major concern is the implementation of two anti-poverty programmes for which the Village Panchayats are responsible: the Jawahar Rozgar Yojana (JRY) and the Integrated Rural Development Programme (IRDP). Drawing largely upon the fieldwork carried out by researchers at the National Institute of Rural Development (NIRD), in Uttar Pradesh and Karnataka, as well as from our own survey in selected villages of Uttar Pradesh (UP), some useful insights are obtained. Briefly, far from empowering the poor, the Panchayats have not even smoothed their formal participation.

Participation

There were delays in holding the 1995 Panchayat elections, partly because of political uncertainty, but mostly because of social resistance to quotas. In general, chairpersons and deputy chairpersons—especially at the block and district levels—tend to be from relatively affluent sections and often manipulate elections, thereby reducing the Panchayat meetings to a mere formality.

Decisions taken by the chairpersons are formally approved by the members present. But even if the chairperson belongs to the SCs/STs and other reserved categories, the dominance of the affluent sections means that the outcomes are often similar. Quotas for the poor have mixed effects. The possibility that they divide or weaken the poor cannot be ruled out. Also, as noted above, to the extent that the local power structure is deeply rooted, those elected typically serve the interests of locally powerful groups. On the other hand, quotas may legitimize power sharing over a period of time. On balance, therefore, the impact on the poor may be favourable but limited.

Devolution

Both the UP and Karnataka case studies point to serious aberrations regarding local governance. These aberrations took different forms: arbitrary reassignment of areas of responsibility, shortfalls in financial allocations and lack of administrative and other forms of support. These are considered in turn. Out of all areas assigned to the Panchayats in the UP Act, only rural sanitation was in fact devolved to them. All other areas remained under the overall control and supervision of district/ state agencies. That the bureaucracy or official agencies could overextend their domain in violation of the provisions in the State Acts had a lot to do with an unstable coalition (between the Samajvadi Janta Party and the Bharatiya Janta Party) and unsettled conditions in the hill areas.

The Karnataka case points to other sources of aberrations: relative bargaining strength and skills of the Panchayats at different levels. Given a relatively stable political environment and a properly carved-out role for the bureaucracy, the battlefield shifted to the Panchayats. Most of the major schemes were monopolized either by the Zilla/District Panchayats or the Taluk/ Block Panchayats, with a minimal role for the Gram Panchayats.

The Karnataka case study also underscores the ambiguity in the roles of some key functionaries (e.g., executive officers of Taluk Panchayats) and absence of support staff. As a result, the Panchayats have not functioned well. Our own survey in UP revealed that the long absence of the village development officer—a key link between official agencies and Village Panchayats—delayed and/or disrupted implementation of some important programmes.

Some field evidence from the Rae Bareli district in UP points to larger underutilization of JRY and IRDP outlays following the installation of the new Panchayat system. It is difficult, however, to ascertain whether it was the need for greater transparency or general unfamiliarity with the new procedures that resulted in delays in utilization of funds.

Anti-Poverty Programmes

Jawahar Rozgar Yojana

Some glaring shortcomings in the implementation of the JRY came to light in our survey of villages in UP. The amounts received by a Gram Panchayat ranged between Rs16,000 and

Rs 18,000 in 1996 and 1997, and these were utilized mostly for making brick roads. The chairpersons claimed that 200 to 250 persons participated in this activity for 7 to 10 days. Some of the participants denied receiving wages, but admitted contributing free labour to prevent water-logging in residential areas. The number of participants reported seems grossly inflated also because the wage rate implied was well below the official JRY wage.

That the whole operation was masterminded by the chairpersons, Panchayat secretaries and village development officers for their personal benefit is further corroborated by the fact that none of the Panchayat members knew anything about the scheme—the financial outlays, the nature of activities or the number of participants. In fact, in one case, it was discovered that the bricklaying activity was completed well before the JRY grant was received. Whether the poor benefited at all from this scheme seems doubtful.

Integrated Rural Development Programme

IRDP was a dismal failure as well. Instead of the Gram Sabha identifying the beneficiaries, the chairpersons of the Gram Panchayats selected them. In one case, it was widely known that the chairman exacted hefty fees.

Following complaints, he absconded. Even under the new chairperson, little seems to have changed. Lack of awareness of the scheme and weak accountability mechanisms in the village community tend to perpetuate the status quo.

Other Related Programmes

The role of the Gram Panchayat in other rural development schemes, including village hygiene and sanitation, literacy, consolidation of holdings (chakbandi) and land transfers, reflected gross negligence or the unmistakable influence of a few dominant groups.

Few Panchayat members (including the chairpersons) seemed concerned about lack of access to drinking water, primary health care facilities, nonfunctioning schools, unhygienic conditions, etc. When their attention was drawn to some of these concerns, they blamed the district agencies for the meagerness of the outlays. Several instances of chakbandi favouring a few influential/wealthy individuals came to light. For example, the chairpersons, in connivance with a few village officials, assigned them large plots near the main road for a "fee." Equally, land transfers—specifically the leasing out of Panchayat land—invariably benefited a few influential individuals, when the beneficiaries were supposed to be exclusively SC/ST families.

Reforms

Since the Panchayats are expected to play a key role in implementing poverty alleviation programmes, some recommendations for reform are sketched below. Given that the Panchayats are ill-equipped to carry out the responsibilities assigned to them, there is a strong case for selectivity. A small cluster of responsibilities could be identified through a systematic application of some economic considerations.

Economies of scale and inter-jurisdictional externalities favour responsibilities assigned to the higher levels, while need for local information and accountability favour assignment to the Gram Panchayats. Areas of responsibility that complement one another may also favour joint provision. Simultaneous involvement of more than one level of the Panchayat in an area may be necessary when each level has specific comparative advantages. Consider, for instance, primary education: the buildings could be constructed by the district or Block Panchayat while the responsibility for running the schools could be vested in a Gram Panchayat.

Incentive incompatibility between the Panchayats and official agencies raises a serious concern. This results in delays in the disbursal and utilization of funds—especially at the Gram Panchayat level. A similar incompatibility exists between the Panchayats and support staff drawn mainly from state government departments, often delaying implementation of the schemes. Although there is considerable emphasis in the State Acts on accountability of the Panchayats to higher authorities, it is not matched by a concern for accountability of the Gram Panchayat to the Gram Sabha. There are, in fact, some glaring lacunae in the existing provisions. Although the Gram Panchayat is required to place the statement of accounts, budgets and other proposals before the Gram Sabha, its approval is not binding.

Nor does the Gram Sabha have the power to dissolve the Gram Panchayat in case there is deliberate default (e.g. embezzlement of funds). There is thus a case for broadening the functions and powers of the Gram Sabha and for making its approval mandatory with a view to preventing the "capture" of the Gram Panchayat by locally influential groups. But these reforms by themselves may not guarantee that the interests of the poor will be better protected or promoted. A strong coalition of the poor could make a difference.

Greater awareness among them of their collective strength, combined with more "voice" given to them in the Panchayats, may help develop a collective identity. As pointed out by Bardhan, "changing the local political structure in the village gives more 'voice' to the poor and induces them to get involved in local self-governing institutions and management of local public goods." Over time, this would facilitate a more active and decisive role of the poor vis-a-vis locally powerful groups. From this perspective, the forging of closer links among the Panchayats, cooperatives and labour unions is thus imperative.

As emphasized in the 1997 World Bank Study; the primacy of growth in poverty alleviation efforts rests on its strong direct and indirect effects. But as shown in this chapter, both the direct effect of growth on poverty alleviation and the indirect effect through the generation of resources for poverty alleviation programmes are weaker than claimed.

Poverty tends to persist among those who are old, lack physical and human capital and/or belong to lower castes. Growth alone will not make a significant difference unless combined with specific interventions. These include land reforms through a market-mediated mechanism, the provision of school education of higher quality—especially at the primary level—and social safety nets (rural public works and social security). Community involvement has considerable potential for making such interventions effective, but as our analysis of the restructuring of the Panchayats following the 73rd Constitutional Amendment Act emphasizes, there are serious functional aberrations. In a politically unstable environment, official agencies maintained their domination, while in another there was a reallocation of responsibilities among different levels of the Panchayats.

In either case, contrary to the state's objectives, the Gram Panchayats were left with a minimal role. More seriously, other evidence points to the "capture" of the Gram Panchayats by a few influential persons, resulting in large-scale diversion of JRY and IRDP funds. Delineating a few proposals for reforms—selectivity in assigning responsibilities at different levels of the Panchayats; incentive compatibility between the Panchayats and official agencies; and greater accountability of the Gram Panchayats to the Gram Sabhas—we emphasized that these must be accompanied by efforts to strengthen coalitions among the poor.

Greater awareness among them of their collective strength together with their increased "voice" in the Panchayats may make a difference. In conclusion, it is not so much lack of growth as the exclusion of some sections of the poor from growth that perpetuates their poverty.

Growth alone will not accomplish much unless it is combined with measures designed to promote the participation of the poor. Community initiatives in the implementation of such measures, backed with a strong coalition of the poor, could make a significant difference.

3

Factors Influencing Rural Marketing

Gone are the days when a rural consumer went to a nearby city to buy any "branded products and services". In the present era, rural markets are critical for every marketer - be it for a branded shampoo or an automobile. Time was when marketers thought van campaigns, cinema commercials and a few wall paintings would suffice to entice rural folks under their folds. But the days have changed now. Thanks to television!!! Today a customer in a rural area is quite literate about myriad products that are on offer in the market place.

The rural markets have acquired significance, as the overall growth of the economy has resulted into substantial increase in the purchasing power of the rural communities. The price-sensitivity of a consumer in a village is something the marketers should be aware of. Rural income levels are largely determined by the vagaries of monsoon and, hence, the demand there is not an easy horse to ride on. Britannia Industries launched Tiger Biscuits especially for the rural market. It clearly paid dividend. Its share of the glucose biscuit market has increased from 7 per cent to 15 per cent within a very short period.

An important tool to reach out to the rural audience is through effective communication strategies. "A rural consumer is brand loyal and understands symbols better. This also makes it easy to sell look – alike". The rural audience has matured enough to understand the communication developed for the urban markets, especially with reference to FMCG products. Television has been a major effective communication system for rural mass and, as a result, companies should identify themselves with their advertisements. Advertisements touching the emotions of the rural folks could drive a quantum jump in sales and it has already shown results previously. The brands have to be made relevant by understanding local needs and customise according to that. Even offering the same product in different regions with different brand names could be adopted as a strategy.

The main four factors influencing demand in rural India are - access, attitude, awareness and affluence. HUL has successfully used this to influence the rural market for its shampoos in sachets. The company had developed a direct access to markets through wholesale channel and created awareness through media, demonstration and on ground contact. Since marketing is to target the growing segments, the village then becomes a location or a suburb of a district. In addition, the district becomes the basic geographical entity. Since the urban-like populations in the villages are considered as a part of the district, they will represent the dominant part of the market in most of the districts.

A districts perspective removes the complexities, heterogeneity, access and targetability that have hindered rural marketing initiatives. The rural marketing requires every element of marketing including product, pricing, packaging, advertising, and media planning to have the rural customer as the target. This becomes possible when we have districts marketing as a separate entity. Marketers need to understand the psyche of the rural consumers and then act accordingly. Rural marketing involves more intensive personal selling efforts compared to urban marketing.

To effectively tap the rural market, a brand must associate it with the same things the rural folks do. This can be done by utilizing the various rural folk media to reach them in their own language and in large numbers so that the brand can be associated with the myriad rituals, celebrations, festivals, "melas", and other activities where they assemble. One of the ways could be using company delivery van, which can serve two purposes - it can take the products to the customers in every nook and corner of the market, and it also enables the firm to establish direct contact with them, and thereby facilitate sales promotion.

However, only the bigwigs having hefty investments plans can adopt this channel. The companies with relatively fewer resources can go in for syndicated distribution where a tie-up between non-competitive marketers can be established to facilitate distribution. Periodical "melas" organized are quite popular and provide a very good platform for distribution because people visit them to make several purchases.

"Haats" are another potential low cost distribution channel available to the marketers. Also, every region consisting of several villages is generally served by one satellite town (termed as "Mandis" or Agri-markets) where people prefer to go to buy their durable commodities. If marketing managers use these feeder towns, they will easily be able to cover a large section of the ruralpopulation. Firms must be very careful in choosing the vehicle to be used for communication.

Only 16% of the rural population has access to a vernacular newspaper. Therefore, the audio visuals must be planned to convey a right message to the rural folk. The rich, traditional media forms like folk dances, puppet shows, etc., with which the rural consumers are familiar and comfortable, can be used for high impact product campaigns.

One very fine example can be quoted of escorts where they focused on deeper penetration. They did not rely on TV or press advertisements, but rather concentrated on focused approach depending on geographical and market parameters like fares, melas, etc.

Looking at the 'kuchha' roads of village, they positioned their bike as tough vehicle. Their advertisements showed Dharmendra riding Escort with the punch line 'Jandar Sawari, Shandar Sawari'. Thus, they achieved whopping sales of 95000 vehicles annually. ITC is setting up e-Choupals, which offers the farmers all the information, products and services they need to enhance farm productivity, improve farm-gate price realization and cut transaction costs. Farmers can access latest local and global information on weather, scientific farming practices as well as market prices at the village itself through this web portal - all in Hindi. It also facilitates supply of high quality farm inputs as well as purchase of commodities at their doorstep. Thus, looking at the challenges and the opportunities, which rural markets offer to the marketers, it can be understood that the future is very promising for those who can understand the dynamics of rural markets and exploit them to their best advantage.

A radical change in attitudes of marketers towards the vibrant and burgeoning rural markets is called for, so they can successfully impress on the 230 million rural consumers spread over approximately six hundred thousand villages in rural India. When Victor Hugo first dreamt of the United State of Europe, it might have been nothing more than a utopian dream. Today, it seems to be a logical conclusion.

How far apart are the concept of this utopia and realpolitik, how relevant is it to talk of achieving this goal, these are the issues European Union needs to address in order to move out of the Sisyphean challenge it has landed into. EU is 'caught in the middle', neither can it dissolve without causing significant distress to its member states, nor is it progressing along the path envisaged.

The need for European Union emerged out of the need for lasting peace in the wake of two world wars. The war is still on, but on the economic and political front. And if Europe wants to reclaim the competitive edge it once had, it might be a good idea to fight this war as one entity. European Union has evolved on the 'principle of subsidiarity', i.e. the EU and its institutions act only if the action is more effective at the EU level than at national level.

Today, it would be an exercise in futility for the European states to try and compete with the US and the emerging Asian economies on their own. Individual action is a luxury that few European nations can afford; the writing on the wall seems to point towards an integrated European Union. In what follows we will try to establish a case for complete political and economic union of the European Union. We would like to find a satisfactory explanation as to why European integration is significant, how it can be realistically attained, how it can change the world panorama and where is it headed.

We will try and compare the Indian union with the EU and see if we can draw some future direction from the world's largest democracy. The British left a legacy of more than 650 independent states at the time of Indian independence, half of them not even the size of the smallest European states. All these states were different in terms of language, religion and culture, yet the one theme binding these states was the desire of its people to achieve the objective of democracy, freedom and social justice.

The Indian union comprises of an amalgamation of these princely states, promoting unity while preserving diversity. Why am I not surprised to find EU espousing the same ideals as its building blocks? To maintain this diversity of opinion and culture within the framework of its guiding principles, the Indian nation adopted a federal form of government. The powers conferred upon the central and the state governments are decided by three schedules, each of which consists of a list of areas under the purview of the Centre, the State and under both (the Common List).

Parliament has the exclusive right to legislate in respect of items appearing in the Union list which includes area such as defence, foreign affairs, income tax, railways, posts and telegraphs, etc. State Legislatures have the exclusive power to make laws in relation to items appearing in the State List that includes items like police, public health, communications, agriculture etc. Both Parliament and the State Legislatures have the power to legislate in items appearing in the Concurrent List that includes items like electricity, newspapers, trade unions etc.

Likewise, all European nations can identify areas of common interest, for example anti terrorism, transport, education, scientific research etc. where they can work together synergistically to achieve stellar results. All those topics that would create minimal conflict among nations can be pooled together in a "EU List" which can be placed under the jurisdiction of the European Council. For example, education in Germany is free for all, so if the EU allows education across borders, more and more British people would flock to Germany for higher education.

In return for this, Germany might be compensated by being allowed it to use the higher education facilities of British universities. Sensitive issues like police, nuclear power, taxes can be under the purview of individual states with no interference from the EU. Contentious areas like foreign policy, common currency, common military umbrella etc. in which the member states might have differing opinions can be put in the 'Concurrent List'. Both the EU and individual states will have a right to legislate, with the member nation interests taking precedence over that of the EU. In essence, the idea is to design a political system where all actions are based on the doctrine of "Maximum benefit to all member states, or in case of a loss, the member states suffer losses lesser in magnitude to what they might have suffered had they acted alone". Either everybody gains, or nobody loses at least.

ACCOMMODATING DIFFERENCES IN POLITICAL OPINION

The European Union requires its member states to have a uniform political system guaranteeing democracy, which makes it a long drawn process for the East European countries still under the effect of communism to join the EU. In contrast, the Indian union is a democratic state with a tilt towards free market economy, yet the Communist party of India has ruled two member state governments for the past 26 years.

The West Bengal and the Kerala governments have worked amicably under the central rule of successive non communist governments. Kerala boasts of the best demographic statistics including the highest literacy rate and the most favourable sex ratio across India. Not only that, with the opening of foreign direct investment in India, these communist states are pursuing privatization and economic reforms to attract more foreign capital. The moral of the story is, uniformity in political systems is not a guarantee to a stable union and even communist governments are no deterrent, as long as the member country follows the rule of law, respects human rights and shows respect for and protect the rights of minorities. If we go by this argument, the process of granting membership to the 10 waiting countries can be expedited, accelerating the political union of EU.

Ensuring a Level Playing Field

One apprehension that has hampered EU integration is the fear in the minds of the smaller member states of being marginalized by the bigger members like Germany and France. On the other side, the large member states fear that the economically poor member states would have a parasitic effect on their economic system.

Comparing it again to the Indian state, the economic condition of member states varies considerably, from the very rich to the not so well off states. The states have their own sources of fund generation, also the centre provides for grant according to need and performance. This ensures that all states have a level playing field.

The European Union has its own sources of funds derived from member states based on their capacity to pay. These funds can be used to grant soft loans to the economically deprived states and provide them an opportunity to equal the other member states. What in case of a difference of opinion? Who decides who is right? In the Indian context, we can take a look at the Cauveri water dispute, involving four states.

The Cauveri River supplies water to four states in south India based on a fixed quota system. The dispute arose when one state kept more than its share, citing bad monsoons. Even after 10 years of across the table talks, when the matter could not be resolved, the central government established a water tribunal comprising of impartial ombudsmen acceptable to all parties. After renewed talks, the states finally came to an agreement that has held since.

A similar system is in place in Europe, what needs to be done is the appointment of an independent body with representation from all member states that looks into matters that might snowball into a major controversy later in the day. The basis of the Indian constitution is the fundamental rights given to all citizens, rights that nobody can violate and rights that are enforceable in court. The European union needs to set up independent institutions in member states to check for rights violations.

These fundamental rights, if implemented would give equal rights to all EU citizens, regardless of boundaries, thereby enhancing the faith of people in this institution. "If I want to talk to Europe, who do I phone?" - Henry Kissinger What happens if European Union achieves its ultimate goal of political and economic integration?

Will it emerge as another trade bloc viewed with suspicion by non EU countries, will it emerge as the other power centre in the US dominated unipolar world, or will it be the precursor to the ultimate goal, a world economy. On the economic frontier, the European Union countries have been dwarfed in terms of the size of economy as compared to the United States or the emerging economies of the Asia - Pacific region.

While countries like China and India are experiencing double digit growth, most European economies are growing at a sluggish pace of 2-3%. None of the European countries can match the economies of scale these countries can generate. All countries big or small are forming trade blocs or strategic partnerships. Given this scenario, the European countries must pool resources together if they want to be able to compete on a global scale. Also, the domestic market is not big enough for any of these countries; a common European market would allow corporations to operate on a larger scale.

Seen individually, none of the European states can flourish alone in the long run, but as one entity, they can emerge as a formidable force to reckon with. Take for example the recent EU ruling against Microsoft. The European Commission found Microsoft guilt of antitrust and the company was fined 497 million euros. Had it been a single country, the results could have been markedly different. Politically, the EU might emerge as another power centre apart from the United States. The European Union has traditionally had good relations with

Asian countries and in the past few years, trade has multiplied. For example, ten years ago, Chinese exports to Europe amounted to roughly a fifth of those of United States. Today it is more than 75%. Also, a politically united EU can play a crucial role in the consolidation of trade blocs in the Asia-Pacific region.

The European Union is at a stage where it can emerge not only as a Superstate, but also as a huge economic force on the world panorama. As we can see from the analogy with the Indian Union, the EU can have everything going for it if its member states leave behind their petty differences and come together with a motive to establish an Integrated Europe, dedicated to the ideals of democracy, freedom and social justice.

EU integration is a win-win situation for all parties involved: the member countries, non EU states, trade blocs and most importantly, the common man. The wheels have been set in motion; EU is slated to emerge as the next superpower, a tool to facilitate global integration. The contents of the fictitious newspaper article are going to be published sooner than later.

4

Rural Market Index: Thompson Index

The risk inherent in business location, expansion, or site closing decisions cannot be eliminated, but it can be minimized through sound market analysis. For example, the strength of the retail sector of a community can be examined in relation to communities with similar economic characteristics. A strong retail sector usually indicates that a phenomenon known as "in-shopping" is occurring in which consumers come from outside the local market area to shop.

Inshopping indicates that opportunities may exist for small businesses to capitalize on the flow of shoppers into the community. Dr. Brockway is associate professor of marketing at Murray State University in Kentucky. His research interest lies in developing practical solutions to small business problems.

Dr. Mangold is associate professor of marketing at Eastern Kentucky University. He is particularly interested in the marketing problems of service businesses. If the retail sector of an area is weak, however, the local population may be going outside the community to shop. This "outshopping" means that strategies are needed that will encourage consumers to shop at home.

This chapter presents a method that allows small business managers to assess the strength of a market area based on its ability to convert income into retail sales. The method develops an estimate of the net inshopping or outshopping that takes place in the market area. The data required are readily available to small business managers, and the analysis can be conducted without large investments of time or money.

MEASURING ECONOMIC HEALTH

Various techniques have been used to measure the economic health of the retail segment of a given market area. First, a number of studies have been published that deal with inshopping and outshopping. These studies are generally time consuming and subject to respondents' recall of their purchasing patterns. Also, they usually employ sophisticated research techniques and are costly.

Various indexes have been developed to assist small business managers in analyzing the health of a given community's retail sector. Sales and Marketing Management magazine calculates a sales activity index for publication in its annual "Survey of Buying Power." The sales activity index is the ratio of a market area's percentage of national sales to its percentage of national population.

"Because the numerator... includes all sales made in the market, and the denominator...includes only residents of the market, a high index may indicate a strong influx of non-resident shoppers. The buying power index and the quality index are other measures developed by Sales and Marketing Management to assist in analyzing the economic health of a retail trade area. The buying power index is a weighted measure which combines effective buying income, retail sales, and population into an indication of a trade area's ability to buy. This measure is expressed as a percentage of the total U.S. potential.

The quality index is computed by dividing a market's percentage of the national population into the buying power index. A fourth indicator of retail market strength is the net trade flow index. This index expresses the retail sales as a percentage of the effective buying income available for retail purchases in a given market area. In illustrating the trade flow index, LaForge, Reese, and Stanton assumed that the income available for retail purchases is about 50 per cent of effective buying income. Based on their analysis, then, a conversion rate of 50 per cent or more indicates that a strong retail sector exists in the market. Nationally, about 49 per cent of buying income is converted into retail sales, but regions differ significantly in this respect. For example, in 1986, New York and Illinois converted 40.7 and 43.0 per cent, respectively, of buying income to retail sales.

Oregon and Tennessee, on the other hand, converted 52.7 and 58.1 per cent, respectively. Overall, the state of Arkansas converted 51.2 per cent of buying income to retail sales, but metropolitan areas in Arkansas converted 55.4 per cent and non-metropolitan areas converted only 47.8 per cent. Existing indices do not adequately account for these regional differences.

DIFFERENCES AMONG MARKET AREAS

The sales activity index, the buying power index, the quality index, and the net trade flow index share a common limitation. They do not enable small business managers to readily compare their subject market with market areas that have similar economic characteristics, such as household incomes and non-retail expenditures. These variations among market areas are especially important to small businesses, since they are usually limited to one or a few geographic areas.

Two factors limit the ability of these indexes to provide a common basis of comparison among market areas. First, the indexes do not take into account variations in household incomes within market areas. These variations affect the amount of income available for retail expenditures. The indexes also fail to account for regional differences in non-retail expenditures such as housing costs, home mortgage interest, and utilities.

For example, the median price for an existing one-family home in the San Francisco area was $129,900 in 1984 compared to a median price of $48,900 in Louisville, Kentucky. These costs, too, affect the retail expenditures and the economic health of the retail sector. Because of the weaknesses inherent in existing indexes, the sales conversion index was developed to enable small business managers to analyse a market area in relation to a benchmark area with similar income and non-retail expenditure characteristics. The method provides an estimate of net inshopping or outshopping behaviour relative to that benchmark.

The sales conversion index also permits examination of retail activity in specific categories such as food, eating and drinking places furniture and appliances, drugs, automotive, and general merchandise. Because the method uses simple calculations and readily available secondary data, even those small businesses with very limited resources can employ it.

DEVELOPMENT OF THE SALES

The existence of a population with the ability to purchase goods and services does not guarantee the economic health of a retail trade area. The population's income must be converted into retail sales if trade is to flourish. The purpose of the sales conversion index is to provide a measure of a trade area's ability to make this conversion. This ability is measured in relation to a benchmark market area which is comparable to the subject area in the areas of income, housing costs, and other non-retail expenditures.

The data needed to calculate the sales conversion index can be found in Sales and Marketing Management's annual "Survey of Buying Power."

The following data are required:

- Total retail sales for the retail trade area(s) being examined. Sales and Marketing Management provides this information for metropolitan areas and for each city and county in the metropolitan area. For rural areas, the information is provided by county.
- Retail sales for an appropriate "benchmark" unit. Appropriate criteria for selecting a benchmark are discussed below.
- Retail sales for the subject and benchmark areas in each of the product categories delineated in Sales and Marketing Management's "Survey of Buying Power." These product categories are food, eating and

drinking places, general merchandise, furniture/ furnishings/appliances, automotive, and drug.

- Effective buying income (EBI) for the subject and benchmark areas being examined. Effective buying income is defined as "personal income less personal tax and nontax payments."

The sales conversion index is calculated in five steps:

1. *Step one*: determine the retail trade area to be examined. The subject area may be a metropolitan area, a city in a metropolitan area, or a county.
2. *Step two*: establish an appropriate benchmark trade area. The German statistician, Ernest Engel, observed that as income increases, the percentage spent on food declines while the percentage spent on housing and household operations remains constant. Also, as income increases, the percentage put into savings and spent on other categories such as clothing, transportation, recreation, health, and education increases.

The benchmark selected, then, should be similar to the subject area in terms of median effective buying income, income distribution, and percentage of effective buying income spent in such service establishments, sales taxes, carrying charges for credit, interest, utilities, and savings. This information is provided in Sales and Marketing Management's "Survey of Buying Power," except for income spent in non-retail categories. This amount can be calculated by subtracting total retail sales from effective buying income. Additional insights regarding income spent in non-retail categories can be gathered by examining such non-retail economic factors as housing prices, interest rate ceilings, and utility costs. For example, if the subject market is located in a non-metropolitan area, the non-metropolitan areas will usually provide a reasonable basis for comparison.

If the subject market is a metropolitan area, the metropolitan areas within the state or the state as a whole may be appropriate benchmarks. These benchmarks are convenient to use because Sales and Marketing Management's "Survey of Buying Power" provides aggregate data for each group. In some cases, a different benchmark may be needed. For example, a small business manager may be thinking of opening an operation in market X. Market X is very similar to market Y, which already has an established, profitable business very similar to the one proposed for market X. In this case, market Y may serve as a more appropriate benchmark.

3. *Step Three:* Retail sales must be divided by effective buying income for both the trade area examined and the benchmark area. The resulting percentages are referred to as conversion factors and indicate the relative amount of effective buying income that is being converted into retail sales.
4. *Step Four*: The subject area's conversion factor is divided by the benchmark area's conversion factor. The resulting figure is the sales conversion index (SCI). In effect, the sales conversion index is a relative measure of a trade area's ability to convert buying income into retail sales as compared to a benchmark area. The formula for the sales conversion index can be expressed as follows: A market area's retail sales expressed as a per cent of its total EBI SCI The benchmark area's retail sales expressed as a per cent of its total EBI
5. *Step Five*: Calculate sales conversion indexes for each of the retail categories delineated in the "Survey of Buying Power." (The retail categories are food, eating and drinking places, general merchandise, furniture/furnishings/appliances, automotive, and drug.) A high sales conversion index for a given retail category indicates a high degree of economic health relative to the benchmark. A low sales conversion index indicates a relatively low degree of economic health.

ESTIMATING INSHOPPING AND OUTSHOPPING BEHAVIOUR

The sales conversion index can be used to provide an indication of the amount of inshopping and outshopping occurring in a given market. Inshopping and outshopping are reflected in the trade area's ratio of retail sales to buying income and can strongly affect the economic health of a retail trade area. As explained earlier, net inshopping takes place when more retail purchases are made by consumers coming into an area to shop than by consumers who leave to shop elsewhere.

Net outshopping takes place when more retail dollars are spent by consumers who leave the trade area than by those who come in from outside. Inshopping and outshopping have been shown to be related to consumers' perceptions of such factors as the variety of merchandise available, quality of merchandise available, and price of merchandise. Other factors can influence inshopping and outshopp-ing. For example, areas offering entertainment and/or recreation facilities can be expected to attract consumers who will inshop for restaurant services, clothing, gasoline, and other products and services. Therefore, assuming the benchmark is comparable to the subject area, the sales conversion index provides an estimation of the net inshopping or outshopping behaviour that a trade area is experiencing.

A sales conversion index of more than 100 indicates that the subject area is benefitting from net inshopping relative to the benchmark. A sales conversion index of less than 100 indicates that the subject area suffers from net out-shopping. The following examples illustrate the use of the sales conversion index as a tool for analyzing specific market areas. In the first example, two non-metropolitan areas in the state of Oregon are examined. Two metropolitan areas in the state of Tennessee are analysed in the second example.

A Rural Oregon Example

The subject areas are two adjacent counties in rural northeast Oregon, Umatilla County and Morrow County (pop.58,861 and 7,519, respectively). Umatilla County's larger population is concentrated in some of the more heavily populated towns in that part of the state, including Pendleton (population 14,521), Milton-Freewater (population 5,086), and

Hermistown (population 9,408). Morrow County, with a population of only 7,519, has several very small towns, but no large ones. The benchmark area selected for comparison purposes consists of the non-metropolitan counties in the state of Oregon.

Morrow County, with a sales conversion index of 47, is converting a smaller portion of effective buying income to retail sales than the benchmark. This low sales conversion index indicates that Morrow County's retail sector is suffering from a largeBureau of the Census, 1980 Census of Population: General Population Characteristics amount of net outshopping. This makes sense, because there are no towns in Morrow County large enough to support major shopping areas. The individual retail categories provide additional evidence that Morrow County is suffering from substantial amounts of net outshopping.

The lowest sales conversion indexes are found in the general merchandise, furniture/furnishings/ appliances, and drug categories. The sales conversion index is higher for eating and drinking places, food and automotive, but all are substantially below 100. Conversely, Umatilla County's sales conversion index of 113 indicates that, in relation to the benchmark, it is converting a large portion of effective buying income into retail sales.

This, too, makes sense in light of the fact that Umatilla County contains some of the largest towns in northeast Oregon and can be expected to draw shoppers from Morrow County as well as other surrounding counties. Therefore, it appears that Umatilla County is experiencing net inshopping at the expense of the surrounding counties that do not have towns large enough to support substantial retail trade.

When the various product categories are analysed, Umatilla County's sales conversion indexes are particularly strong in the automotive, food, and drug categories. The sales conversion indexes for the eating and drinking places, furniture/furnishings/appliances, and general marchandise categories are low in relation to the benchmark, but considerably stronger than Morrow County's

A Metropolitan Tennessee Example

The subject areas are metropolitan areas in Tennessee: the Knoxville metropolitan area and the metropolitan area which comprises the "tri-cities" of Johnson City, Kingsport, and Bristol. The Knoxville metropolitan area has a population of 599,000. It is also the home of the University of Tennessee with an enrollment of approximately 30,000 students.

The Johnson City, Kingsport, Bristol metropolitan area has a population of 450,000. The benchmark chosen for similar characteristics consists of the metropolitan areas in the state of Tennessee. The Knoxville metropolitan area's sales conversion index of 115 indicates that it is converting a larger percentage of effective buying income into retail sales than the benchmark. The inshopping behaviour of the University of Tennessee's 30,000 students probably accounts for the high sales conversion indexes in the food store, eating and drinking places, and drug store groups.

The sales conversion index of 115 for the furniture/furnishings/appliances group indicates that people may also be coming to Knoxville to shop these stores. The Johnson City, Kingsport, Bristol metropolitan area, on the other hand, has a sales conversion index of 89, suggesting that this area converts a smaller percentage of effective buying income into retail sales than the benchmark and appears to be losing retail trade to other shopping areas. Johnson City, Kingsport, and Bristol are three relatively small cities making up a single metropolitan area. Because they are smaller, they do not contain shopping facilities as extensive as those found in larger cities such as nearby Knoxville and Asheville, North Carolina, to which they may be losing shoppers. An examination of the store groups indicates that the loss of trade is occurring in eating and drinking places, general merchandise, and furniture/furnishings/appliances.

IMPLICATIONS FOR SMALL BUSINESS

Assessing the economic health of a market area is the first step in identifying retail market opportunities for small business. A sales conversion index that is significantly above

100 indicates that, relative to the benchmark area, the subject area is converting a high percentage of buying income into retail sales. A high conversion index provides an indication of economic health in the retail sector and suggests that a significant amount of inshopping is occurring.

Large amounts of inshopping may indicate opportunities for small businesses to capitalize on the inflow of trade. Existing businesses may choose to serve the inshoppers more effectively by expanding into other lines of merchandise and into additional services. Businesses that are not getting their share of inshoppers may want to increase sales by locating near shopping malls and businesses that are likely to attract shoppers from other areas. Promotions and advertising can be directed to high-potential communities through local media such as newspaper and radio stations.

In some cases, an area may be attracting inshoppers only for the purchase of certain categories of products. If so, an opportunity may exist to develop sales in the other categories. For example, Umatilla County's sales conversion index in the general merchandise category is low relative to the benchmark, while the sales conversion indexes in the food, automotive, and drug categories are relatively high. This situation suggests that the small business that is able to offer a general merchandise product mix could attract inshoppers who are coming into the area to make other purchases.

A sales conversion index that is significantly below 100 indicates that, relative to the benchmark, the subject area is converting a low percentage of buying income into retail sales. Again, this situation suggests that the subject area is suffering from substantial amounts of outshopping behaviour. In these cases small business managers should realise that their real competition is with nearby communities rather than with each other.

When the amount of outshopping is large, these managers need to cooperate in an effort to collectively compete with nearby trade areas. Collective promotional efforts, development of complementary merchandise assortments, elimination of parking meters and other barriers to shopping, and beautification of downtown shopping areas may increase retail trade. vFurther, the existence of large amounts of out-shopping may indicate that opportunities exist for retail businesses that are less vulnerable to out-shopping behaviour. Retail stores that offer merchandise that is purchased on the basis of convenience are least likely to be affected by out-shopping. Grocery stores, hardware stores, convenience marts, and fast food restaurants, for example, are less likely than clothing stores to be affected negatively by out-shopping.

Significant amounts of out-shopping may also indicate that opportunities exist for businesses which, by their presence, can keep trade in their market area. The existence of a retail store with a large depth and breadth of assortment, for example, may keep shoppers at home. Finally, small businesses in areas that are experiencing large amounts of out-shopping may try to develop product-service mixes that are difficult for businesses in other trade areas to duplicate.

For example, an appliance dealer in such an area may want to place strong emphasis on quality service and rapid response to service problems. Clothing stores may want to emphasize quality alterations, convenient pick-up of altered clothes, convenient merchandise returns, and personalized service.

STRENGTHS AND LIMITATIONS OF THE SALES CONVERSION INDEX

The sales conversion index enables managers to focus on specific local markets in relation to markets that are similar in terms of income and non-retail expenditures. Therefore, the sales conversion index is particularly useful for small businesses in the retailing and service sectors. Larger firms, such as manufacturers whose markets span regions, will find the sales conversion index to be less useful.

The greatest strengths of the sales conversion index as a market analysis tool are low cost and ease of application. The approach uses readily available data and calculations can be made with simple arithmetic. Nor does calculation of the index require a great deal of a busy manager's time. Delaying marketing decisions until in-depth research can be completed may result in lost opportunities. The sales conversion index is a market analysis tool that can be applied quickly. Other advantages of the sales conversion index are: (1) its accuracy does not depend on respondents' ability to recall the dollar amount or percentage of budget spent on outshopping; and (2) unlike the sales activity index and quality index, it enables the small business manager to select a benchmark area that is comparable to the subject area. (Note, however, that although a market area may be healthy in comparison to its benchmark, it may be significantly less healthy than market areas not included in the benchmark.)

The sales conversion index is subject to several limitations. Another limitation of the sales conversion index is that only the net effect of inshopping and outshopping is estimated, so that managers cannot focus on inshopping and outshopping separately. In addition, Sales and Marketing Management provides data by state, metropolitan area, city within a metropolitan area, and by county. In non-metropolitan areas, data for towns and villages within a county are not available. Therefore, the sales conversion index cannot be calculated on a less-than-county basis in non-metropolitan areas.

Finally, in analyzing the sales conversion indexes by retail category, the manager can only focus on the six groups delineated in Sales and Marketing Management's "Survey of Buying Power." Retail sales that occur outside these six retail categories are accounted for in the total sales figure only. The amount of retail sales that are unaccounted for can be determined by taking the sum of the retail sales for the six categories and subtracting this amount from the total retail sales for the area.

For small business managers, assessment of a given market area's economic health is often crucial to effective decision making. While the financial risk inherent in such decisions cannot be eliminated, it can be minimized through sound market analysis. The sales conversion index is a tool for measuring the strength or weakness of a retail market and assessing small business market opportunities that exist there. The index provides an estimate of the amount of net inshopping or outshopping that occurs in a market area and has significant implications for small business managers. While it can be used as a "stand-alone" measure, many small business managers will want to use it in conjunction with other indicators of economic health.

The sales conversion index uses readily available data, is easy to calculate, and requires little investment in time or money. Because the sales conversion index can be calculated quickly, it is a valuable tool for managers who must make immediate decisions rather than wait weeks or months for the results of survey research. Unlike other indexes based on national data, the sales conversion index enables managers to analyse a subject area in relation to a comparable benchmark. This feature may be particularly valuable for small businesses that operate in one or more sites in a limited geographic area.

5

Rural Market Strategies

Financial product marketers need to manage their product portfolio in response to the changing environment and consumer needs, in addition to managing customer relationships effectively for achieving long-term profitability. The concept of a product can be understood in terms of the following four terms - actual product, expected product, augmented product, and potential product.

For a financial product, the product strategy is greatly influenced by customers, competitors, technology, and government & legislation. Depending on these factors, the product mix strategy could be product mix expansion, product mix contraction, and product modification. Branding in financial services is done more at the corporate level than at the product level.

Branding should start with a clear strategy for targeting and positioning. The brand image should be consistent with the marketing strategy. Advertising can be successful in building the brand only if the financial product caters to the requirements of the consumer and the entire service experience is consistent with the brand image that is communicated. In the financial product sector, brands can occur in three tiers – master brand, core brands, and sub-core brands.

When there are multiple tiers, the brands in all the tiers should convey the same organizational values. These values can be communicated through brand logos and taglines. CRM is a strategic tool for marketers to acquire customers, retain them, and maintain long-term profitable relationships with them. It uses information technology to achieve these objectives. Competitive pressures have led marketers to realise the necessity of customer retention to survive in a deregulated economy. CRM has enabled the shift in approach from being product-centric to being customer-centric. In addition to maximizing customer value, CRM helps marketers to cross-sell products, achieve long-term profitability, and build the brand. Relationship marketing is concerned with relationships that exist between any two stakeholders of a business. It involves relationship building with both external customers and internal customers.

In an organization, relationship marketing can be at one of the following five levels — basic, reactive, accountability, proactive, and partnership levels. One-to-one marketing essentially involves knowing about each and every possible need of the targeted customers and developing tailor-made solutions for them.

To implement one-to-one marketing, the marketer needs to identify the target customers, differentiate them into groups, interact with each customer group, and provide customised products and solutions in a cost-effective manner. This can be done using the technique of mass customization. Customer knowledge, customer loyalty, and customer switching are three important concepts in CRM.

The components of customer knowledge can be classified into three broad categories: knowledge about the customer, knowledge to support the customer, and knowledge from the customer. Customer loyalty can be either affirmative loyalty or reluctant loyalty. The level of affirmative loyalty is influenced not only by traditional factors, such as customers, product offerings, employees, and measurement systems, but also on emerging practices such as electronic customer care.

Eight different reasons have been identified for customer switching. They include (a) core service failures, (b) service encounter failures, (c) price failures, (d) inconvenience, (e) employee response to service failures, (f) attraction by competitors, (g) ethical problems, and (h) involuntary switching. The first five reasons in this list can be addressed through the use of CRM techniques. Implementation of CRM includes customer knowledge management, technology adoption and implementation, and performance measurement. The customer knowledge management process (journey) is a cycle with four inter-related steps - developing a customer-focused strategy; developing the customer buying process; implementing actions, tactics, campaigns; and customer learning.

Technology implementation has become the key to CRM implementation in an organization as huge volumes of customer data can be stored, managed, and retrieved using the latest technologies. CRM software tools can be categorized into operational CRM tools and analytical CRM tools. When the performance measurement of the CRM activities is done using a carefully defined basket of metrics, it helps in managing and controlling the CRM initiatives in the organization.

In the future, large enterprises in India are expected to opt for CRM applications which have pre-built interfaces with standard ERP applications, while the small and medium business enterprises may still continue to use stand-alone CRM applications. The usage of CRM in India is expected to evolve from ensuring operational efficiency (in customer handling) to yielding strategic benefits — through real-time customer segmentation, and co-creation of products with customers. he marketing of bank products to corporate customers is discussed in the chapter.

On the basis of sales volume and/or capital employed, banks may classify corporate customers into three segments – large corporations, mid-size companies, and small and medium business enterprises (SMEs). Corporate customers may also be segmented into industry verticals, such as automobiles, aviation, tourism, etc.

As part of their marketing efforts, banks develop long-term relationships with their corporate customers. Strong relationships help the banks improve profitability and retain customers in a competitive market. The interactions and relationships between the banks and their corporate customers are influenced by three groups of factors – the external environment, the atmosphere of the interactions, and the interaction process. The 'Partnership Relationship Lifecycle Model' describes the evolution of the bank-corporate customer relationship, beginning at an early stage where a 'customer' shows interest in the bank's offerings, and maturing to become a mutually beneficial 'partnership relationship' between the 'client' and the bank.

Banking products are broadly classified into fund-based products and fee-based services. Fund-based products are further sub-divided into asset products and liability products. Liability products include salary accounts, current accounts, fixed deposits, and payment cards. Asset products include various kinds of credit products like trade finance, corporate finance, project finance, and term loans.

New product development and innovation are considered vital for a bank's long term sustainability. Banks need to address the changing requirements of their clients through new product development. However, financial products can be easily copied.

To maintain differentiation, banks also need to come up with innovations on how they deliver the new product. The pricing of banking products directly impacts customer retention and customer acquisition, in addition to profitability and long-term viability.

For the marketer, price is a mechanism to cover the costs of operations which include production costs, distribution costs, promotion costs, and other operational expenses. The pricing decision is influenced by cost, competition, customers, and other constraints. With the advent of deregulation and the consequent increase in competition, many of the banks have adopted a competitive pricing strategy.

RBI has deregulated the pricing mechanism for both asset and liability products. Every bank has to set its own Benchmark Prime Lending Rate (BPLR) to price its asset products. A bank may price its asset products (for a given customer either above or below the BPLR, depending on situational factors such as creditworthiness of the customer, stage of relationship, etc. Personal selling is the most important component of the promotional mix for corporate banking. As personal selling is a two-way interaction, it also plays an important role in the service delivery. To reduce the overall cost of personal selling, banks may use direct-response advertising or telemarketing to identify high potential customers, who are then approached through the personal selling option.

Advertising is used to reach out to a vast audience in a cost-effective manner, as at the time of introducing a new product or service. Public Relations (PR) is used to provide publicity to the bank, to improve its public image, and to overcome a negative image (if any). PR tools include press releases, annual reports, seminars and speeches, cause-related marketing, in-house magazines & newsletters, corporate social responsibility (CSR) initiatives, and event sponsorships.

As part of sales promotion, banks give employees incentives to achieve business targets such as volume of new business, extent of cross-selling, etc. Customer promotions (such as gifts) are less important as banks can decide the price (interest rate) for customers on a case-to-case basis.

Corporate banking products are distributed mainly through bank branches and a direct sales force, supplemented by phone and Internet banking.

Relationship officers are based at different branches; they make frequent client visits to nurture relationships and to develop new business opportunities. Banks attempt to develop an optimal distribution mix using personal/non-personal modes of delivery, in order to achieve multiple objectives such as superior customer service, operational efficiency, and profitability.

Integrated banking software applications – usually referred to as Core Banking Solutions (CBS) — are vital to the real-time synchronization of the transactions that happen through the different modes of distribution. The small and medium business enterprises (SME) sector is considered as the growth engine of the Indian economy; it generates employment for nearly 30 million people and contributes around 30 per cent to the nation's GDP.

However, corporate bankers neglected this segment for a long time due to the high incidence of Non-Performing Assets (NPA) and the lack of proper methods to assess the credit rating of the SMEs. This trend is changing and the SME segment is now one of the focus areas of growth for many banks.

This shift has been influenced by the policy initiatives introduced by the Government and the RBI in favour of SMEs. With large enterprises getting access to cheaper funds from other channels, their bargaining power has increased with respect to the banks. This situation has also induced corporate bankers to look at SMEs as an avenue for profitable growth.

6

Marketing of Services

Post the economic slowdown, policymakers and companies are busy designing strategies to sell products and services to larger markets. While boosting profits quickly is no longer the essential parameter, Atmanand, MDI Dean of Executive Post Graduate Programmes, believes that revisiting age-old management theories and sticking to basics is the most cost-effective marketing tactic.

THE RURAL FOCUS

"The strategy taken by Hindustan Unilever Ltd. (HUL) to enter the rural sector, which has remained insulated so far, is a good one," says Atmanand. "In states like Maharashtra, Gujarat, Andhra Pradesh, Delhi and Haryana, the company is expanding steadily by expanding their network of dealers and making themselves household names." Of course, replicating the HUL model may be difficult for a startup, but it does serve as a valuable lesson in marketing: Don't put all your eggs in one basket. The entire gamut of white and brown goods has found a place in the rural market, driving several industries to actively explore it. "In the current scenario, companies should change their strategies for marketing. For market sustainability, we have to look at the rural markets. This would include products that have been especially designed for these markets at prices that will suit the sector," says Atmanand.

Tailor-made Products for Rural India

The company should provide rural folk with products and services that would meet their requirements. Take Cavin Care, for instance, which launched its shampoo in sachets. Also consider Britannia, which packaged its Tiger brand biscuits at a low price tag. Such companies obtained an understanding of the rural customer's needs and provided them with the desired products. Atmanand's emphasis is clearly on parameters that change the dynamics of marketing a product. Rural markets offer a great potential to help India Inc (which has reached the plateau of its business curve in urban India) bank on volume-driven growth. With a larger market to play with, virtually any marketing initiative can be cost effective.

Aspects that are seldom ignored are also key drivers in marketing. Some do not cost a penny, and the benefits are huge. "Consumer satisfaction is very important. Gone are the days when products were sold solely on their brand name. Today, people want value for their money; they want the product to meet their expectations and utility. The company should focus more on quality and the consumer satisfaction index," says Atmanand. A consumer with a high level of satisfaction and a good image of your pro-duct is likely to be your best brand ambassador and proponent of your product.

Changing the Profile of Managers

Philip Kotler's theory of a short lifecycle of a product does not really hold good, as most products in India have a lifecycle of two to three years. "Take, for example, a Maruti 800; one drives it for about three years before switching to a new car. A consumer wants a product that has resale value," Atmanand says. Understanding the preferences of the rural masses is crucial, and your company manager could be the answer.

Companies should hire managers who are familiar with rural India and are in sync with the demands and preferences of people in these regions. While management graduates are conversant with strategies applicable for the western countries, their mindset and training may not allow them to understand the requirements of rural consumers.

Marketing with the Help of Traditional Media

Traditional media would serve as a great driver to generate

awareness among rural consumers. Skits, magic shows and educational drives by NGOs are among the preferred traditional media that marketers can use to good effect. These engage the interest of rural consumers and go a long way in establishing your brand in their minds.

Things are certainly changing. Consumer financing schemes, insurance schemes and promotion associated with delivering products to consumers will be preferred. Says Atmanand, "Understanding the needs and desires of the Indian consumer, price competitiveness, innovation and R&D form the key to unlocking the potential of this vast market."

The tiny, family-owned and managed household enterprise is the overwhelmingly dominant form of private, non-farm, economic organization in the developing world. Harnessing the latent potential of these own account enterprises (OAEs) is now widely acknowledged as a legitimate policy objective to generate productive employment and to promote sustainable long-term growth.

The design of appropriate institutions, and the reform of existing ones, is recognized as occupying a key part of this process now that the "market-versus-state" dichotomy has been replaced by the more pragmatic "market-and-state" approach. Such a programme assumes particular urgency in rural areas. In the countryside, entrepreneurs face daunting hurdles relating to both the startup and consolidation of business. Two of the most significant are raising finance at affordable terms and acquiring necessary skills. The purpose of our paper is to highlight, through a village study, these constraints in the populous Indian economy.

We argue that problems of administrative complexity, limited information, discrimination and gender bias, and stymied access to formal institutions have helped to create and perpetuate a culture of corruption. The result is that entrepreneurs are forced to fall back on a weak local resource base and to rely heavily on informal avenues of finance and know-how. This condemns the majority of OABs to operate on the margins of viability and the households to remain in poverty. The Indian state of Punjab is a region where we might reasonably expect appropriate rural institutional support to be already in place. This is primarily due to the spectacular success of the Green Revolution. In order to support the spread of the high-yielding varieties of seeds, the banking and training infrastructure expanded enormously during the mid-1960s.

Located in the northwest of the subcontinent, Punjab, although a small state in terms of population and area, has a disproportionately large and modern agricultural sector compared to the rest of India. According to the 1991 population census, Punjab represented only 1.7 per cent of India's total land area and constituted 2.4 per cent of its population. Punjab's share of India's cultivated area is disproportionately high, and it has a fully modern irrigation system.

It is primarily on the strength of its agricultural performance that Punjab, along with neighboring Haryana, has the lowest poverty ranking in India. As a consequence, the state has enjoyed the highest per capita annual income in the Union for a generation, i.e., Rs.6,274 ($369 at the prevailing exchange rate) in 1988-89—two-thirds higher than the all-India average of Rs.3,875. However, many small farmers scarcely benefitted from the new technology and have been keen to diversify into off-farm activities.

Nevertheless, central and state government policies, driven by the powerful farmers' lobby, continue to favour agriculture, but increasing mechanization has reduced its labour-absorbing capacity. Furthermore, growing urbanization has meant that many rural inhabitants could not secure jobs in the towns and cities partly because of the influx of large numbers of migrants from elsewhere in the Union.

Although these circumstances are hardly unique to Punjab, institutional failure in an agriculturally advanced area is novel, has inhibited the transitional failure from farm to firm, and has been a factor in the decade-long civil unrest and terrorist activity. Against this background, the off-farm sector occupies a pivotal position in the rural economy. However, it faces severe institutional constraints marked by the existence of widespread administrative complexity and pervasive corruption that hinders job creation and arrests the general economic development of the region. To investigate problems at the grassroots level, we collected data in a fieldwork study of 100 households from three villages in a development block (the smallest planning unit in India), Rurka Kalan, of which 89 operated OAEs. The villages are situated in Jalandhar district and lie close to the geographical heart of Punjab.

Detailed interviews were conducted with the proprietors of the OAEs to identify the major constraints they faced. These activities included both manufacturing and services and ranged from "traditional" pursuits to "modern" enterprises. In addition, we interviewed bank managers located within the district and examined branch accounts. We also toured the regional training centres.

The Financing of Own Account Enterprises

A large and sophisticated literature on the subject of informal sector credit has emerged since the early 1980s. Topics have ranged from the general role of banks and financial intermediaries on the supply side to the specific difficulties that small local enterprises face in meeting collateral requirements on the demand side.

The most recent initiative concerns the provision of "micro-finance" by revolving credit unions such as the highly acclaimed Grameen Bank. Although this is a promising development, which even the large international financial organizations are starting to take seriously, coverage remains extremely patchy and confined to certain well-publicized countries and sectors.

Certainly we found little evidence of such innovating institutions in Punjab despite the existence of the dense banking and credit infrastructure that had financed the Green Revolution. Unfortunately, provision has not been forthcoming for the needs of non-agriculturalists.

In seeking to identify the problems QAE operators encountered for both start-up and growth, we probed the source of their capital. The most common was family and friends, with more than half of OAEs dependent upon this avenue. Indeed, 82 per cent of OAEs relied on informal sources.

Institutional loans were far less important, and only a fifth of respondents obtained capital from banks or other formal agencies. Given the considerable expansion of rural banks in Punjab, this finding is disappointing. In 1965-66, when the high-yield varieties were introduced, there were 1,584 banks; this had risen fourfold by 1989, giving the state an exceptionally high banking density. This absolute increase was matched by a reduction in the number of persons served per branch. In 1970, one bank served less than 8,000 persons; 20 years later, this had fallen to 3,000.

Despite this expansion, rural entrepreneurs continued to rely upon informal avenues for capital. Part of the reason undoubtedly is the bias that exists on the part of bank managers to cater to the credit needs of the farming community. The data suggest that over the decade for which information was available, only 196 loans were sanctioned. Although the bank was unable to provide details on the number of applications, and the rule governing confidentiality precluded the release of information on the number of depositors, this absolute figure was extraordinarily low.

We estimate that Bank A held approximately 2,200 agricultural accounts, and it is reasonable to assume that a large number of these were in receipt of annual loans. This, in turn, suggests that loans to OAEs averaged less than 1 per cent of the total loan portfolio. Moreover, the amount sanctioned per loan was very modest.

Respondents argued that the size of loans granted by a second commercial bank, Bank B, serving the villages was pitifully small. Indeed, data collected from this bank offer strong support for this contention (a view that was widespread). It reveals that one-quarter of all loans were less than Rs.5,000.

The single largest category (40 per cent) ranged from Rs.5,000 to Rs.9,999. The vast majority of applicants—a little under 84 per cent—obtained less than Rs. 15,000, and only 16 per cent of applicants were awarded more. In a few instances, the funds exceeded Rs.20,000. Despite the rapid expansion in banking, the number of OAE operators who were able to obtain finance from this source was very limited. There is no question that cultivators had first call and that a strong bias in favour of agricultural interests is now an in-built characteristic of rural banking practice in Punjab.

Several non-banking agencies were instructed to provide loans to help develop the off-farm sector. These included the Integrated Rural Development Programme (IRDP); the Punjab State Land Development Corporation; the Backward Classes Financial Corporation; the District Industries Centres (DICs); and the Ex-Servicemen Association.

However, our research revealed that the amounts they offered were far too small to be worth the convoluted processes of borrowing. Several institutional constraints relating to the banks and these other lending agencies were identified.

Access, Administrative Practice, and Information

The agricultural-led expansion of banking in Jalandhar district has now resulted in at least one co-operative or commercial bank branch serving an average of eight villages. Few members of the rural population are physically far from a branch: none of the 61 villages in Rurka Kalan development block are further than 10 kms away. Despite the wide coverage, individuals often experience difficulty in reaching a branch.

Although all villages are connected by roads that are officially designated as paved, our research revealed that not all were usable. Road engineering is still rudimentary in the countryside, and the surface is frequently washed away following heavy monsoon rains or melts and breaks up during the hot summers.

Few people own an independent means of transport. Many villages are not served by public transport, and for others, the bus service is irregular. In these circumstances, villagers rely upon private tempo (an indigenously manufactured three-wheeled vehicle) operators to undertake the journey. However, their reliability is notoriously poor; the owners never operate by printed timetables and only start off when they have a full complement of passengers. Even relatively short distances mean that trips to banks can be exceedingly time consuming.

In addition to travelling to the local branches, much longer journeys are required to Jalandhar city since the paperwork necessary for loans can only be completed at the law courts in the district headquarters.

Such administrative practice can usually take days and involve frequent visits to the court. Legal and banking procedures are extremely cumbersome because of the volume and complexity of the documentation that accompanies the most modest application.

Long delays in processing of paperwork are due to the drawing up of legally binding repayment schedules, and further time is expended on producing estimates for intended OAE purchases. Even when borrowers are cognizant of the conventions, the process is protracted. At the national level, the Indian bureaucracy has a well-deserved reputation for functioning at a snail's pace: the country is close to the top on the "Index of Red Tape" drawn up by Business International. Our findings are consistent with this tarnished image.

Lawyers required our respondents to return time and again to the court, and only when "speed money was paid could paperwork be completed reasonably expeditiously. Respondents applying for loans through government-sponsored schemes find themselves further disadvantaged because they are required to make further trips to the city where the offices of these agencies are located. In the case of the major development sponsor, the IRDP, beneficiaries first have to be identified by the sarpanch (the village headman), which lengthens the procedure and increases vulnerability to corrupt practice.

Applicants must also carefully consider additional costs. Although difficult to quantify, these costs were significant in the case of households with an income below the existing poverty datum line (PDL)-Rs.3,600 pa in 1993. For this group, the bus fare alone was a considerable expense, especially since numerous trips were necessary. Further, the opportunity cost of forgone earnings could mount up alarmingly depending on the number of trips necessary. Of course, some applicants minimize losses by making visits on slack days or to coincide with other business in the city. But, more often than not, the trip needed to be dedicated entirely to the loan process because arrangements associated with applications invariably took whole days, and appointment times are unpredictable.

The problem of providing adequate collateral to secure loans was severe. In this respect, the Punjab OAEs are far from being special. However, this proved to be a very real deterrent because the amount demanded was wholly unrealistic. Indeed, an examination of the records of Bank B revealed that in every traceable case the sum required was greater than the loan. From the bank manager's point of view, the need for security was crucial, and the most common form of collateral demanded was land and property—depending on whether the applicant's title was absolute. Where not, it was occasionally possible to use an intermediary to act as guarantor.

However, the difficulties in persuading family or friends to act in this capacity were obvious, and so this course of action was rare. A further barrier to access was the requirement that applicants possess sufficient know-how (jaan-cary) prior to any disbursement. In the absence of formal qualifications, it was difficult to demonstrate such business competence. As we will argue, this is a classic "Catch-22" situation since there are significant barriers to acquiring such qualifications.

Another formidable hurdle was the requirement that applicants had to have established a bank account two years prior to lodging a request. This problem was most acute for the poorest households (those qualifying for IRDP assistance), as their incomes fell below the official PDL, and they did not possess sufficient savings to establish an account.

This requirement by the bankers actually contravened government policy since neither security nor a banking history was obligatory. In fact, the reality was quite different: a track record was mandatory in all circumstances that we investigated. This conflict of interest between standard commercial bank procedures and development policy is long-standing and applies to many regions and countries around the world. Such an impasse helps to explain the recent publicity accorded to the micro-credit initiatives of Muhammed Yunus and the activities of the Grameen Bank of Bangladesh. In Punjab, however, during the period of our fieldwork, no similar banking innovations were in evidence partly due to the continued stranglehold of the existing institutions. We found that only two OAEs were involved with revolving credit arrangements, and upon detailed investigation, these instances bore little resemblance to the Grameen Bank system.

Respondents' dealings with the financial institutions were seriously impeded by poor information. Applicants received information regarding financial terms by word of mouth. Even when institutions were approached directly, the necessary information was seldom presented in a simple, straightforward manner. For example, posters, leaflets, application forms, and special promotions, which should ordinarily have been on display and in the public domain, were kept from view; they usually gathered dust in filing cabinets.

Since borrowers were usually unaware of formal procedures, actual banking practice differed markedly from state policy. By limiting information, officials circumvented conventions to their own benefit. Promotional loan deadlines frequently passed without the knowledge of the intended beneficiaries. The tight hold and tardy release of information were important means of ensuring that corrupt practices enriched the few at the expense of the many.

Corruption

Although there is a general perception that the Indian economy and society as a whole are mired in a culture of corruption, this is obviously difficult to substantiate. At the village level, however, we encountered firsthand evidence of the incidence of corruption and its baneful effects. A web of corruption, bribery, and fraud was found to be pervasive in virtually all aspects of OAE's attempts to raise finance from the formal sector.

The key mechanisms of malfeasance were the overt (budhi) and the covert "greasing-the-palm" (chai-pani) bribes. OAE operators were caught between village accountants (patwari) and headmen (sarpanch) on the one hand and bank staff and government officers on the other. All loan applications from the OAEs that we tracked involved the payment of budhi to one or more of this quartet. In order to ease the negotiating process, chai-pani accompanied all interface transacting. This took the form of material gifts and offers to help pay for school fees. Both u sually began with the demands of the patwari who hold the property deeds required for surety and with the sarpanch, whose signature is needed by all IRDP applicants.

Those villagers legally entitled to receive loans from the banks and non-bank sponsoring agencies responsible for administering the rural uplift programmes were forced to forfeit a significant part of their entitlements. For example, our respondents who received IRDP loans lost the 20 per cent subsidy. This was not released by bank staff, but had instead been retained illegally.

Moreover, adding insult to injury, recipients complained that they were required to pay interest on this subsidy. Naturally, this led to feelings of great resentment and helped to explain why so few respondents persisted in seeking institutional finance. Those who did, and were prepared to pay, reasoned that the eventual returns from the sum borrowed would exceed the bribe and the loss of subsidy.

All the bank managers whom we interviewed denied that these practices occurred in their own branch. The credibility of this denial is undermined, however, given the mode of recruitment of bank staff. Upon investigation, we found that obtaining a position and eventual promotion seldom occurred without either nepotism or money changing hands. This helps to explain the voracious demands by officials at all levels of the bank hierarchy for ex-gratia payments from OAE applicants.

A good example came to our attention during the fieldwork. A young man applied to join a bank as a junior officer but confided that he could only fill the vacancy after a "donation" of Rs. 100,000 had been paid to the manager. Since this was beyond the means of many potential recruits, the only option available was to borrow the money from friends and relatives. Since the debt could never be repaid legitimately out of the monthly salary of Rs. 4,000, the amount could only be cleared if he collected bribes. Furthermore, higher-ranking bank officials expected to share the bribe.

This vicious circle casts doubt on the view that corruption may not be harmful to economic performance in that it may, for example, accelerate decision making and enable agents to overcome bureaucratic inertia. Our evidence is unambiguous and supports the interpretation that it is harmful and damaging to nascent OAE entrepreneurs.

Bias and Discrimination

A specific complaint emanating from the Scheduled Castes (who include "Untouchables" and other low-status groups) and the Hindu minority was the fact that most rural banking officials belong to the dominant Sikh community. They claimed that as a result there was institutional bias, and that managers were more inclined to award loans to kinsmen, especially Jat (agriculturalist) Sikh farmers.

Although in the view of the respondents this propensity was obvious, it could be defended in terms of the wider policy prescribed by the credit allocation regime that favoured the agricultural sector. However, the most vehement charge of bias expressed by the Scheduled Castes—that discrimination was the norm—could not be shrugged off so conveniently because there was plenty of evidence of its ubiquity throughout the country. Certainly, we found support for the accusation.

Scheduled Castes occupy the lowest rung on the caste ladder. They find it especially difficult to secure finance, which manifests itself in a complex of ways. Perhaps the clearest barrier concerns collateral. We can say that it is virtually impossible in the villages where the fieldwork was conducted for this group to obtain a bank loan. They therefore have to rely on the IRDP.

Under the standard procedure, they are not required to provide surety for loans up to Rs. 5,000. Nonetheless, we found that the issuing authority insisted on surety. When questioned, officers openly admitted operating contrary to regulations, and this is supported by the IRDP's own Evaluation Report. It found that of the 30 banks examined, 13 insisted that applicants provide security. Furthermore, it proved extraordinarily difficult for the Scheduled Caste applicants to obtain formal recognition of their own status—identification necessary to tap some lines of credit.

They were compelled to bribe the sarpanch and District Rural Development Agency personnel to obtain a pela care (yellow card). This important document formally identifies individuals as legitimate IRDP beneficiaries. The going price for a signature was Rs. 100. Of course, the Scheduled Castes were least able to meet the other legal and administrative "charges" that accompany loan applications.

Once an IRDP loan was approved, the agony did not disappear—eventual disbursement has to go through a local bank. Our respondents claimed that the bank managers refused to actually hand over the sins due because they stated that it would not be used for the intended purpose, but for general consumption purposes or to finance marriage.

In addition, the managers argued that the Scheduled Castes were likely to default. This negative attitude towards the poorest and most socially disadvantaged was exemplified by a barber (Nai) operating out of a rented wooden hut (cooka). His implements were modest, comprising a wooden bench, a mirror, a few pairs of scissors, and combs. Working from temporary premises placed his business at a disadvantage.

He claimed that customers were more hesitant to visit him than other barbers in permanent (pukka) premises. Clients who could afford to pay a higher price preferred to visit those barbers equipped with "modern technology." In hopes of increasing his customer base, the respondent approached the local bank for a loan of Rs.5,000.

The application dragged on for more than a year, during which time officials made no effort to visit or assist with the application, even though the bank was located 50 meters away. Eventually, using savings and money borrowed from friends, the respondent was able to rent pukka premises (situated directly opposite the bank). He also purchased two chairs, larger mirrors, and a hair dryer. Following this investment, the number of customers swelled, and he hired an apprentice. Despite discrimination and against the odds, the example of this barber suggests that the micro-credit movement and the model of the Grameen Bank have great potential in the Punjab since it targets groups subject to discrimination. Irrespective of caste issues, clear cases of gender bias were identified. This was hardly surprising in view of the burgeoning empirical evidence of prejudice against female business enterprise throughout the developing world in general and the Indian subcontinent in particular.

Our female respondents claimed that they were also the victims of institutional discrimination. Of the 149 credits issued by Bank B to OAEs, only 16 were for women. This represented a little more than 10 per cent of all advances, although we could not ascertain the total number of female applications. As the prevailing social milieu only allows women to enter clearly defined pursuits, the loans were used to establish dry goods stores (karyana), to purchase knitting machines, to enter the ready-made garment trade, and to open roadside tea shops.

The prospect of female entrepreneurs using bank credit to branch out from socially accepted employment was remote. This was due to the nominal nature of most loans; more than a third were less than Rs.5,OOO. Bank managers were hesitant because, first, they argued that the bulk of applications were of a surrogate kind ("pipelining") in that the female in the household was applying for the loan on behalf of her husband or another male relative.

During inspection visits, however, male members of recipient households insisted that the assets did belong to the women. As in the case of Scheduled Castes, managers argued that the loans were used for consumption or marriage, rather than for the stated purpose. Second, managers maintained that loans made to unmarried women were very risky, since they were hard to trace after marriage because they invariably leave their home village to join their husbands. Where there were no tangible assets, little could be seized to recover any outstanding debt. Even if the assets were intact, the procedure for recovery was lengthy, and the legal costs were often greater than the amount defaulted. In these circumstances, debts would have to be written off. As a result, loans to unmarried women were avoided. Despite the obvious unwillingness, banks were compelled to do so by sponsoring agencies—but they would try to keep these to the minimum. This general attitude seems very shortsighted in light of the success of the Grameen Bank and other micro-credit programmes.

Accusations of a poor repayment record were also levelled at females, but not exclusively. However, our data did not lend support to this charge. Actually, loans to females, Scheduled Castes, and other QAB operators—from whatever background—were not especially risky. Of 196 loans issued by Bank A during 1981-90, 31 per cent had been repaid in full, and only 4 per cent were written off.

Two-thirds of the loans were still active, and of the oldest, 13 of the 21 (62 per cent) granted in 1981 had been repaid. For the next three years, the repayment rate was 68 per cent, 61 per cent, and 75 per cent, respectively. Only in 1985 had none of the loans been repaid, but this was for an exceptional reason.

There was a change of local administration earlier that year, and, as is common practice, there was a statewide cancellation of debts to government institutions. In the following year, normality was restored with a little less than 40 per cent of loans being fully repaid. Overall, the data do not support the widely held view of bank managers that loans to OAEs are highly risky.

Marginalization

As a consequence of the difficulties encountered in accessing institutional finance, the majorities of OAE operators were compelled to turn to informal sources and were therefore placed in a marginalized position. The most sizable segment (57 per cent) relied on family and friends. There were good reasons for this. Since the persons to whom they appealed were well known, the question of collateral rarely arose. Creditors were invariably familiar with the borrowers and therefore better informed about repayment viability. This offered an attractive degree of discretion and flexibility; and in those instances where interest was required, it was usually pitched below the prevailing market rate charged by commercial banks or private money lenders (Banias). There were also several genuine cases of altruism where family and friends waived interest altogether. Lengthy procedures associated with institutional borrowing could be avoided.

Owners of OAEs were able to obtain funding speedily and without the "customary" bribe. There were, however, drawbacks with this source. The principal limitation was the small sums available. A variety of other informal channels were used. Savings from wage employment, both overseas and domestic, was one: 7 per cent of the sample fell into this category.

A compelling motive for seeking work abroad, especially those travelling to the Arabian Gulf states, was to accumulate sufficient capital to establish an enterprise. Examples of individuals who obtained funds in this way included an investor in a "tent house" business, i.e., providing marquees for use at marriages and other religious ceremonies; while another person established a truck and private taxi service. Seven per cent had accumulated savings from previous domestic employment.

Another channel was surpluses generated in cultivation (6 per cent). These individuals obtained funds by diverting income from farm work; making use of rental receipts where assets had been retained; and occasionally, and most reluctantly, from the sale of land. Inheritance accounted for only 5 per cent of the funding. The remittances of family and relatives who resided abroad were responsible for a further 3 per cent. The large numbers of out-migrants who returned to Punjab for holidays or business provided finance for friends and relatives. This source has dried up recently, and the importance of remittances has fallen off sharply. The remainder generated funds from the sale of previous businesses (2 per cent).

The severe constraints that OAE operators face in trying to raise finance from formal financial institutions means they take recourse through informal avenues. Although this accords with the wider picture that has emerged from research elsewhere in India and the developing world, it is a source of particular disappointment for observers who might have expected a different outcome given the successful financing of Punjab's agricultural sector. Quite clearly, the off-farm sector has a much lower significance and priority for those who control the agenda of banks than the farm lobby. The result is marginalization. One way of overcoming these hurdles is to enhance the skills of existing and potential OAE operators.

Skill Acquisition

Investment in humans is now widely recognized as an important ingredient underpinning the establishment and successful operation of viable household enterprises. Appropriate training can empower rural entrepreneurs and enable them to impart skills to family and employees. It may also assist entry into mainstream OAEs. This will certainly require greater access to formal sources of education and training than is currently available. Of course, such access cannot guarantee business success, and some observers have argued that once basic financial requirements have been met, even the very poor will find ways of establishing and developing village enterprises.

However, in Jalandhar the constraint upon acquiring appropriate skills proved to be a serious impediment to entrepreneurs, particularly those interested in modem OAEs. Furthermore, the lack of formal skills acts as a handicap in loan applications to banks (jaan-cary). On the basis of our fieldwork, we show that poor access to formal training, inappropriate courses, corruption, limited information, and the discrimination and bias against sections of the rural community mean that the needs of OAE operators cannot be met. This perpetuates the cycle of marginalization so that the poor miss out on both finance and skills.

Access, Appropriateness, and Information

The general educational qualifications of our current generation of OAE operators were higher than their parents.

Intergenerational illiteracy fell from 16.8 to 3.4 per cent. The greatest improvement was in the fifth grade (five years of schooling). Around a third of the parents had achieved this level, but among their children the percentage had risen to just under half.

However, the percentage reaching metric level (10 years of schooling) remained the same. Not surprisingly, degree holders still represented a small proportion of the total, and there was scarcely any rise discernable across the generations. Despite this overall gain, there was little evidence to suggest that the skill profile had improved. This was demonstrated by a detailed investigation of the sample.

General education widens and deepens human capital but does not assure acquisition of specific business skills. For this, specific courses are normally required. The two main local sources of further education, Khallsa College (Jalandhar) and the Government Training Institute (Phagwara), admit only young people between the ages of 18 and 25.

This limits access, and no lifelong learning programmes are currently in place in Punjab. The courses offered did little to enhance entrepreneurial capacity, as most are not vocational. Recently, computing has been introduced into the curriculum, but the hardware and software are obsolete; moreover, they focus on dated programming languages and do nothing to provide an appropriate range of information technology skills. Unlike the ultra-modem training facilities offered in Bangalore (the "Silicon Valley" of India) and the imaginative Cyber Kiosk development programme planned for Bangladesh in the early years of the new millennium (financed by the Grameen Bank and supported b y Hewlett-Packard), the situation in rural Punjab is backward. Far from a purposeful scheme of introducing computers and the Internet, the course profile in Jalandhar did not even cover the fundamental subjects relating to business competence.

Lacking the ability to acquire business skills through further education, those interested in receiving training had to consider the next best alternative. This involved enrolling in courses offered by the more specialist national and state agencies. There was no apparent shortage of such agencies, and there were no less than 21 bodies registered in the Jalandhar area. Upon close investigation, however, most of their activities were not relevant to delivering appropriate training services and issuing information. The key point was that not a single OAE operator in our sample had had any dealings whatsoever with any, and few respondents had knowledge of their existence.

The reason for this was quite straightforward: the agencies targeted large-scale urban businesses, rather than those located in the countryside. Further, since their offices were all situated in the cities, they were too remote for rural dwellers to attend. A partial exception was the Rural Industries Development Centres (RIDCs), whose charge was to provide training to rural youth. Although there were two in Jalandhar district, one (Rurka Kalan) had closed down, and the other (Adampur) was too far away. No state or central government body was functionally active.

With regard to private training providers, we found that there was little interest or uptake among our respondents. Information on courses was not disseminated widely, and rural dwellers had to rely on word of mouth. None of our sample was even aware of fees and timetables, and it was therefore not surprising that there were few enrollments from our cluster of villages.

That tiny minority of respondents who had attended courses in the urban areas reported several serious problems in provision. To begin with, where there was a quota of places available, demand exceeded supply for entry, and providers required a "donation." Patronage and personal contacts featured in the allocation of places.

Parents were often compelled to pay bribes (chai-pani) to administrative staff. Another example of corrupt practice concerned the exemption of course fees when total household income fell below the PDL. In order to qualify, money had to change hands. All respondents complained about the haphazard attendance of the trainers. Students stated that classes were often cancelled without notice. They claimed that trainers took time off to attend to personal matters though paid to provide instruction. Indeed, this was a charge levelled at many in government whose jobs centre on servicing rural areas. The range of courses was narrow.

The limited number that did provide employment-based training w as invariably confined to pursuits that our respondents considered to be outdated. Respondents claimed that, as these trades were overstocked already, they had little to offer. For example, those who had received training in well construction were unable to find work.

Finally, there was confusion over the standardization and acceptability of the qualifications; the inflation of certification (the "diploma disease") made it much more difficult and complex for rural dwellers to assess the relative quality of the training programmes.

Discrimination and Gender Bias

There was a widespread perception by our respondents of discrimination and gender bias in access to formal training institutions. The Scheduled Castes, for example, claimed that their applications for admission to colleges and courses were not treated in an equitable manner.

Further, villagers suggested that a distinct urban biased admissions policy operated, as administrators were far more likely to be personally connected to urban applicants and tended to show them favour. Furthermore, although not exclusively male preserves, there were very few females registered in the Khalsa College and the Government Training Institute. Since the social milieu discourages females from undertaking routine travel to the towns and cities in order to attend courses, gender bias was manifest.

In the rural areas, we found few training institutes that could provide females with appropriate skills. This helps to explain the exceptionally low participation rate of females in OAEs. In our development block, the sole provider of training for females was the government high school at Sang Dhesian. This enabled pupils aged 16-18 to study "suitable" courses such as shorthand, typing, literature, art, and music. The probable purpose of these courses was to improve the chance of finding eligible spouses, particularly from abroad. Such a stereotypical approach does little to provide the necessary skills needed for business. In this respect, Punjab mirrors the situation elsewhere in the developing world.

Marginalization

As a consequence of stymied access and serious training blockages, OAE operators requiring additional skills had little alternative but to rely on informal channels. The fieldwork confirmed that any planning, communication, organizational, managerial, or marketing skills gleaned by our respondents had been acquired from a parent or friend or through apprenticeships, previous employment, or learning by doing. This meant that they were locked into informal arrangements that reinforced their marginal position.

As with finance, the largest category of respondents relied upon family members and relatives (45 per cent). Skills were acquired over a long period. The rudiments were gained by observing the family at work and by providing practical assistance. For example, in the case of an electrical motor repair workshop, younger family members begin by learning the most basic tasks such as coil winding. These operations were straightforward, and juniors could easily operate homemade winding tools and were usually only required to turn a handle and count.

The contribution of young members was often part-time. Assistance was usually confined to seasonal peaks that coincided with the heavy irrigation phases of the agricultural cycle. The number of burnt motors rose dramatically during these periods since cultivators ran irrigation pumps extensively. The more skilled, dangerous aspects of the business and contact with customers were left to older brothers.

Generally, this method of skill acquisition was appropriate for traditional occupations that had undergone little technical change, such as carpentry and masonry, and also pursuits that did not require specific training. For traditional occupations that had experienced technical improvement but where the trade had not been wholly transformed, as in iron mongering, skills needed to be updated. The new processes were usually picked up informally through trial and error, and only in very exceptional cases was formal retraining necessary.

In those activities where demand had declined or stagnated, for example, pottery and basket making, or had disappeared all together, such as water carrying, effecting a transition to modern occupations required the villagers to obtain fresh skills. Apprenticeships were the chosen means, and nearly 40 per cent of the sample took recourse in them. Their duration extended from one to three years, the exact period depending on the type of activity undertaken. For tire repair, for example, only a year was necessary as the key elements could be picked up relatively quickly; but other activities, such as scooter and tractor repair, required substantially longer.

For most apprenticeships, wages were not paid, and so trainees needed parental support. Where a wage was given, it was only after the apprentice had gained sufficient competence to make an effective revenue-earning contribution. Another means of skill acquisition was previous employment (9 per cent). Here, individuals drew upon experience accumulated as employees either in OAEs operated by others or as wage workers.

Good examples included service providers such as private tutors and house painters. In one case, an individual who engaged in tutoring deployed skills from his previous work as a government stenographer. After retirement, he returned to his home village and established a small school for typing and shorthand. The painters, having left their last employment, chose to set up their own enterprises.

They relied upon their skills and network of business contacts to obtain decorating contracts in surrounding villages and nearby towns. For 8 per cent of our sample, informal consultation and business information were further routes into QAE formation. New entrants sought advice from people who were well-versed in the business, and skill specifications were acquired on the job. This method was most appropriate for activities such as cycle repair, photography, and video-taping social functions (video barona). These fields did not require protracted training. After obtaining initial advice, new entrants acquired the necessary acumen either on the job or through learning by doing. This did not always provide a sound platform for new ventures.

For example, one disgruntled former university graduate had decided to start up a karyana store. Since a parent was in wage work, he was unable to refer to him, but instead turned to fellow villages for advice. The venture proved to be unsuccessful, and the store closed within a year in considerable debt.

The key problem was that his product range was too limited and insufficiently differentiated from his competitors. The cause of the failure was attributed to poor information, incomplete advice, and inadequate business skills. Informality therefore characterizes the way in which rural entrepreneurs obtain skills. Such expediency condemns OAEs to the margins. Institutional lacunae in training provision means having to "make do" (kurna penda) and is part of the daily reality of business life.

The lack of formal alternatives was particularly acute for those diversifying out of cultivation and establishing OAEs for the first time—the majority grouping. It is they who experience the most difficulty in gaining skills. Since their backgrounds only permitted peripheral exposure to business, they were most dependent upon formal training avenues.

As a result, they usually ended up in wage employment. Only a minority took up occupations such as driving (taxis, private buses, and trucking), installing electric motors in wells, and tractor repair. They were only able to exercise this option because there was the possibility of drawing upon skills learnt in agriculture.

But of course, this was subject to having surmounted the obstacle of obtaining finance. The absence of an appropriate training infrastructure has undoubtedly inhibited skill formation and confined many rural dwellers to "traditional" pursuits. This suggests the need for more formal training if they are to make the transition to "modern" OAEs. In addition, the lack of training facilities constrained the capacity of OAEs to absorb labour.

Nonetheless, our sample OAE operators demonstrated resourcefulness and initiative, as entrepreneurs have done in the rest of the Union and elsewhere in the developing world. Despite the advantages of a developed rural infrastructure, including banking and training facilities, we have shown that the off-farm sector has experienced great difficulties in gaining access to key capital and human development resources.

This has had serious implications for the diversification away from agriculture and towards manufacturing and services—the hallmark of structural change and economic development. In the cluster of villages that we studied, OAE operators faced difficulties at every turn. They have had to deal with a whole series of institutions that have palpably failed to address their needs.

With regard to obtaining adequate finance, institutional failure has resulted in lengthy and cumbersome loan application procedures, which have deterred borrowing. There has been the added burden of corruption and bribery. We found that the difficulty is neither necessarily one of banking provision nor is it one of inadequate savings, given Punjab's relative prosperity.

Rather, the problems we have identified appear to centre upon poorly functioning institutions that have hostile lending policies towards off-farm enterprises. The banking system continues to tilt heavily towards cultivators. The practice of demanding excessive collateral is strictly enforced even among the very poorest, which is illegal for IRDP recipients.

We also discovered a bias against those belonging to Scheduled Castes and females. Given these formidable obstacles, entrepreneurs have had little choice except to fall back on informal sources that are necessarily limited. Designing public policy to address stymied access, obstructive administrative practice, incomplete information, rampant corruption, and bias and discrimination is a huge challenge.

These are national problems that cannot be tackled easily at the state and lower levels of government. Perhaps the most that could be expected is a reduction in administrative complexity and more transparency.

The success of micro-credit programmes similar to the Grameen Bank provides one practical plan for future progress. But confronting and reducing the culture of corruption is easier said than done. However, it is certain that unless measures are taken to reform institutions and change the ideas of the key agents who run them, little of lasting value can be expected to materialize.

As far as the acquisition of training and appropriate business skills is concerned, we have identified many kinds of difficulties faced by OAEs when encountering formal institutions. These include limited spatial coverage, small intake, the exclusion of more "mature" persons, and largely irrelevant curricula. Few of our respondents had access to the training agencies, and most had only the vaguest notion of what little they had to offer. In these circumstances, there was no practical alternative to the traditional informal channels. While these provide some elements of basic training, they cannot possibly be regarded as a suitable option.

Addressing these weaknesses will not necessarily require any substantial new commitment of scarce public funds, but rather a more efficient and targeted use of current resources. The structure and content of courses need to be re-orientated towards meeting the skill gap, and wider publicity will better inform rural dwellers of what is offered.

In truth, a high price is paid f or institutional failure, especially by the poor, whose recourse to informality is scarcely an effective substitute. Of course, radical policy reform and investing in people are surely the firmest foundations for building sustainable development. But they need to be moved up the agenda so that the financial and training requirements of OAB operators in rural Jalandhar are met. Only then can there be any hope of meeting the competitive challenges that lie ahead.

7

Rural Marketing Channels

The effective coordination and maintenance of interorganizational exchange relationships in channels is extremely important to business practitioners. The environment in which businesses operate has become intensely competitive. As a means of competing, organizations are becoming strategically focused. Long-term strategic relationships are replacing the short-term transactional type relationships of the past.

The current research investigated the adoption of Electronic Data Interchange (EDI) because it is often the glue that ties long-term relationships together. EDI is a communications technology that offers a variety of benefits to channels. EDI has been defined in the literature in numerous ways. Laughlin defines it as "a method of computer-to-computer data transmission intended to improve the speed and accuracy of transactions among trading partners."

According to Reich, EDI is "a way for a computer in one company to communicate directly with a computer in another company to perform business transactions and to access data." Akerman similarly defined EDI as "the direct computer-to-computer exchange of standard business forms." Oskroba defined it as "the computer-to-computer transmission of business data in a standard format."

Stenger defined EDI as electronic transmissions in certain prescribed formats either requested from or given to another company. According to Sokol, "EDI is the intercompany computer to computer communication of standard business transactions in a standard format that permits the receiver to perform the intended transaction." For the purpose of this research EDI will be defined as "...the interorganizational exchange of business documentation in a structured, machine-processable form." This definition was chosen because it describes the interorganizational nature of EDI and the structured nature of the transmitted data.

The definition also limits the type of data transmitted to business data. By enabling fast and effective communications, EDI provides the means for efficient channel coordination. It allows managers to transmit information from one channel member's computer system directly to another channel member's computer system.

By its very definition EDI is interorganizational. Thus, studying its adoption required an interorganizational or channel perspective. Two types of channels identified by Bowersox, Closs, and Helfrich were investigated in the present study. The transaction, or marketing channel, that focuses on negotiating long-term relationships between buyers and sellers, was represented by sampling customers and suppliers in the channel. The logistical channel, that coordinates and manages the actual flow of products, was represented by sampling shippers and carriers in the channel. EDI adoption within both channel types is investigated because our understanding of EDI adoption within each channel and the differences between the channels is rather limited.

The purpose of this research is to contribute to our understanding of adoption behaviour between and within channel types by testing theoretically founded and practitioner-supported variables. The theoretical variables found in the literature were selected because of their ability to determine technology adoption within organizations. Since the objective of this study is to expand our knowledge of adoption in logistical and marketing channels, these same theoretical variables were tested to determine their predictive power in channel adoption.

Prior research from organizational behaviour, economics, marketing, and logistics is integrated to develop a framework of interorganizational EDI adoption. Organizational behaviour theory has suggested that such organizational factors as the size and structure of the organization positively influence the adoption of technological innovations. Economic theory and marketing researchers have indicated that adoption is not only influenced by internal factors but by the organization's external environment as well.

The extension of adoption from a single organization to the channel requires the inclusion of channel power. Significant contributions about power have been made by both marketing and logistics disciplines. The use of power in the channel is expected to affect EDI adoption significantly. Thus, the model is not only an integration of theories and research but an extension of the adopting unit from the single organization to the distribution channel. The next section provides theoretical support for the model and development of testable hypotheses.

FRAMEWORK OF INTERORGANIZATIONAL EDI ADOPTION

Internal/Organizational Dimension

Researchers have argued that the structural characteristics of an organization significantly influence its adoption behaviour. The contention is that certain features of organizations facilitate or encourage adoption of an innovation. This research investigated two variables, organizational size and structure, in relation to interorganizational EDI adoption.

Organizational Size

Numerous empirical findings document a positive relationship between size and adoption behaviour. Researchers have found that organizations do not adopt technologies because of their pure size, but because size leads to economies of scale, capital accumulation, and/or volume of transmissions. Larger organizations process a sufficient volume of transactions and have substantial capital to justify the adoption of a new technology, such as EDI. Smaller organizations, however, with fewer transactions and less capital availability might not reasonably expect to benefit from adopting similar innovations. The null form of the organizational size hypothesis for both channel types is presented below.

- *Hypothesis A1*: The relative size of channel members in the marketing channel will not significantly explain the variance of EDI adoption within the marketing channel.
- *Hypothesis A2*: The relative size of channel members in the logistical channel will not significantly explain the variance of EDI adoption within the logistical channel.

Organizational Structure

Nearly all researchers hold that organizational structure is important to innovation adoption. The relationship between centralization and adoption of innovation has been found to be positive in some cases and negative in others. Rarely, if ever, has it been found to have no impact.

The position taken in this research resembled that taken by Gatignon and Robertson. The researchers propose that centralization facilitates acceptance of innovation for technologies requiring organizational standardization, e.g., telephone systems and EDI. Since EDI implementation requires an organization to standardize its business transactions in an electronic format to be transmitted to a channel member, top management's support and approval is often required.

Thus, a centralized decision-making structure is expected to facilitate the interorganizational adoption of EDI faster and more efficiently than a decentralized decision-making structure because senior managers can adopt EDI despite the resistance of lower managers. A decentralized structure is expected to slow the interorganizational adoption of EDI as the adoption decision ascends through the levels of management, because lower managers do not have the same power and influence over upper managers. The null organizational structure hypotheses are listed below for both channel types.

- *Hypothesis A3*: The organizational structure of channel members within marketing channels will not significantly explain the variance of EDI adoption within marketing channels.

- *Hypothesis A4*: The organizational structure of channel members within logistical channels will not significantly explain the variance of EDI adoption within logistical channels.

External/Industry Dimension

While a significant body of research has contributed to our understanding of the impact environmental conditions have on the distribution channel,(19) our understanding of how they influence the adoption of technology has been under explored. This research investigates the influence that environmental variables, industry competitiveness, and demand uncertainty have on EDI adoption.

Industry Competitiveness

The structural characteristics of the industry are important to the adoption of a technological innovation. However, economists have disagreed about the environmental condition most conducive to technology adoption. A conflict often arises between the true monopoly and pure competition. Both theoretical and empirical studies have suggested the existence of a degree of concentration that lies between pure monopoly and atomistic (perfect) competition that is best for organizational adoption performance.

The acceptance of a technological innovation is posited to be maximized in more concentrated industries. The logic is that industry participants operating under oligopoly conditions pay close attention to each others' competitive moves and that the benefits of adopting an innovation increase as the number of competitors decreases. The participants also are more likely to have the discretionary financial resources necessary to innovate than those in industries characterized by numerous firms with small market share.

Industry competitiveness, e.g., concentration of competition in the industry, was expected to have a significant impact on the adoption of interorganizational EDI within distribution channels. Under high competitive intensity, greater resource allocations and more aggressive pricing policies are likely to materialize, thus encouraging more rapid diffusion. Gatignon and Robertson hypothesize that high levels of competitive intensity lead to more rapid diffusion and the achievement of higher levels of market penetration for the innovation. Presented below are the null hypotheses for industry competitiveness.

- *Hypothesis B1*: Industry competitiveness will not significantly explain the variance in EDI adoption within marketing channels.
- *Hypothesis B2*: Industry competitiveness will not significantly explain the variance in EDI adoption within logistical channels.

Demand Uncertainty

A turbulent market environment created by fragmented markets with less brand loyal customers, coupled with intense global competition and rapid product innovations, highlight the need for incorporating the element of demand uncertainty in the framework. It has long been viewed that occurrences in the channel's external environment affect the degree of uncertainty experienced by channel members. Uncertainty is a pivotal notion in organization behaviour theory. Thompson views it as the "cutting edge" of organizational analysis and sees coping with uncertainty as the "essence of the administrative process."

Pierce and Delbecq hypothesize that "environment uncertainty will be positively related with organizational innovation (i.e., initiation, adoption, and implementation)." Based on data from five in-depth case studies of the adoption of innovations in five shoe firms, Duchesneau *et al.* found that to reduce uncertainty firms are "more likely to adopt new innovations." The research hypotheses are:

- *Hypothesis B3*: Demand uncertainty will not significantly explain the adoption of EDI within marketing channels.
- *Hypothesis B4*: Demand uncertainty will not

significantly explain the adoption of EDI within logistical channels.

INTERORGANIZATIONAL DIMENSION

Channel Power

Among the phenomena that occur in distribution channels, probably none has gained the attention of researchers as much as interorganizational power. The degree of scholarly interest in this topic may come from power's significance and utility in the real world of distribution, as well as its potential as an explanatory construct in the realm of scientific understanding. Power is defined as the influence one channel member has over another channel member.

According to Emerson, power is a relational concept inherent in the channel. In other words, there will always be some power existing within distribution channels due to mutual dependencies that exist among channel members, even though that power may be very low. However, power can also be fully concentrated in a single organization, which then appears as the undisputed channel administrator.

Channels with an undisputed channel administrator are described as having a unilateral power system. Because of the numerous flows that tie the channel together, the more common case is where different firms exercise control over different flows, functions, or activities. The latter can be referred to as a mixed power system.

The power construct was thought to be more influential when there is a unilateral power structure. Literature suggests that channels with unilateral power structures will adopt EDI because the more powerful member will "push" EDI on the less powerful member.

Therefore, the research hypotheses stated in the null are presented below:

- *Hypothesis C1*: Channel power will not significantly explain the variance of EDI adoption within marketing channels.
- *Hypothesis C2*: Channel power will not significantly

explain the variance of EDI adoption within logistical channels.

The research was conducted in two phases. The first phase of the research utilized interviews from firms that represented organizations from both channel types. In addition, consultants and EDI third-party providers were included to provide an impartial and unbiased perception of EDI adoption within both channels. Phase one was conducted to determine if there was practitioner confirmation of the study's theoretical variables and to investigate whether there were other variables practitioners thought influenced adoption.

The second phase collected data through a national mail questionnaire. Questionnaires were mailed to customers and suppliers in the marketing channel and shippers and carriers in the logistical channel. A combined total of 540 questionnaires were mailed and 156 usable questionnaires (28.9% response rate) were returned. Selected sections of the customer and supplier questionnaires were designed so that supplier responses could be directly compared with customer responses. Likewise, sections of the shipper and carrier questionnaires were constructed so that shipper and carrier responses could be directly compared.

Questionnaire Design

The questionnaire consisted of a series of interval scales. Seven-point semantic differential style scales with bipolar descriptors and 7-point Likert scales anchored with "strongly disagree" and "strongly agree" were used to gather data. Each construct of interest—organizational size, organizational structure, industry competitiveness, demand uncertainty, and channel power—had multiple operational-izations. Each variable suggested by practitioners in phase one was assessed through single measures.

The customer, shipper, and supplier sample from phase II represented a convenience and judgment sample taken from the membership list of the Council of Logistics Management (CLM). The carrier sample was obtained from both the CLM membership roster and the 1992 Second Annual Mason

Symposium attendee list. After duplication of firms was eliminated by subjectively selecting the most appropriate title for the respondent, and after firms not classified as shippers, carriers, suppliers, or customers were deleted, the questionnaires were mailed to the remaining members.

Several data analysis techniques were performed on the data, Since nonresponse bias is inherent in all survey research that does not have 100% compliance, a test for nonresponse bias was performed.

The data was then analysed using Cronbach's alpha to assess internal consistency and reliability. Items with reasonable Cronbach alphas were an indication that the items were consistent and reliable in measuring the research variables.

Third, the reliable measures were further analysed using principal component factor analysis to determine the number of factors present in the data. To interpret the factors, test for validity, and calculate composite factor scores, factor analysis with varimax rotation was performed. Variables that demonstrated reasonable reliability and validity were used to develop regression models. The regression models were used to test the research hypotheses.

Nonresponse Bias

The test for nonresponse bias required contacting nonrespondents. The test then compared responses from the nonrespondents to those from questionnaire respondents on eight key questions.

There were no statistically significant differences at the .05 level. Therefore, it was inferred that the results could be generalized to the target population.

Cronbach Alpha

The Cronbach alpha was used to test internal consistency of questionnaire responses, and to provide information about similarity in measurement across items. It was an appropriate test for inter-item consistency because the item measures were scored on a scale ranging from one to seven.

Factor Analysis

Scree plots and the eigenvalue greater than one criterion were used to determine the number of factors in each data set. Nine factors were retained for the supplier and shipper data sets and eight for the customer and carrier data sets. The factors were rotated using varimax rotation to investigate whether a simple interpretable structure existed.

Regression Model Development

The forward stepwise regression technique was used to develop regression models. The forward stepwise regression technique inserts variables into a regression model until a satisfactory regression equation is reached. The order of insertion is determined based upon the partial coefficient. The partial coefficient determines the importance of variables not yet in the equation. The results of the forward stepwise regression technique are discussed below.

Marketing Channel Regression Models

Performing stepwise regression on all measures, both theoretically founded and interview supported, resulted in the following regression models. The supplier and customer multiple regression models were significant at the .05 level.

Marketing Channel

Suppliers within the marketing channel are characterized as having large organizational size and high levels of demand uncertainty. The sign on the beta suggests that large suppliers perceive themselves as operating within highly uncertain markets. According to prior research, demand uncertainty in the environment may drive them to adopt EDI, but the firm's size, i.e., profitability, actually makes adoption possible.

Another characteristic of the marketing channel is customers' perception of high levels of demand uncertainty. The findings suggest that customers may adopt EDI because of its ability to reduce demand uncertainty in the environment. EDI enables both suppliers and customers to reduce demand uncertainty because the channel becomes electronically tied.

Each member is able to look into its partner's production schedule, inventory levels, and freight tracking systems. This immediate access reduces time and uncertainty while conceptually bringing the channel closer together.

Logistical Channel

Based on the responses by both shippers and carriers, there appears to be a different set of factors that characterize the logistics channel. It appears that shippers not only have unilateral power but exercise it by giving carriers mandates to adopt EDI. Those choosing not to adhere to the request will either pay surcharges on every paper document or suffer complete loss of the shipper's business. The findings also suggest that sometimes carriers adopt EDI for more proactive reasons. As discussed above, carriers reacting to shippers requests are often "forced" to adopt EDI. However, some carriers as a means of competing in a highly competitive environment will proactively adopt EDI. EDI enables them to differentiate their service offerings from the competition.

Between Channel Differences

The research findings suggest that marketing channels are typically characterized by suppliers and customers that view EDI as a means of reducing environmental uncertainties. Logistical channels that adopt EDI are characterized as having significantly powerful shippers that forcefully persuade carriers to become EDI-ready. A significant portion of the sample came from the membership roster of the Council of Logistics Management (CLM).

Firms belonging to CLM and participating in the Mason Symposium may be more proactive in recognizing the importance of logistics and organizational interrelate-dness. Thus, these firms may be more receptive to EDI and more proactive in EDI adoption. Future research should include a cross section of respondents from other sources other than CLM. The research centered on the adoption of EDI between only two organizations in each channel type. Since channels can be comprised of multiple members, the study is limited because it did not explicitly consider the adoption of EDI linkages between three or more channel members. Future research should recognize the large numbers of intermediaries that may represent both channel types.

Contribution to Theory

The study contributes to theory by investigating the impact channel type has on interorganizational EDI adoption. Researchers have defined the distribution channel in terms of two separate channels. The present research contributes to understanding channel behaviour by determining how channel type affects adoption behaviour. The study also contributes to theory by extending the study of innovation adoption beyond single organizations. By using the distribution channel as the focal unit of analysis, the study extends prior research by testing the ability of theoretical variables to explain channel adoption.

Contribution to Practice

The information from the research enables managers to perform self analysis. Managers provided with characteristics of EDI adopting channels can determine if their channel has the characteristics that make them likely adopters of the technology. In addition, the same information can allow managers to evaluate channel members with whom they should adopt EDI. The findings from this research also provide managers with market intelligence information. By knowing the characteristics of adopting channel members, managers will be able to determine the likelihood that the competing channel will adopt EDI. Armed with this information, managers can proactively implement EDI in an attempt to gain or protect the firm's competitive position.

There are also implications for EDI providers. By determining the predictive power of variables in the model, EDI vendors may be able to assess which organizations are likely to adopt EDI. With this information, their managers will be able to improve sales force efficiency by allocating the sales force to those organizations worthy of the time and investment.

8

Marketing of Consumables and Durables

The typical approach followed by national brands to attack the lower end of the market is to introduce an offering, which is priced just above the unorganised market's offering. The idea is to upgrade the consumer from that to the branded one. A-1 in tea, Britannia's Tiger brand of biscuits (introduced by Britannia) and the Nirma brand of detergent are some examples of success with regard to the approach.

But companies which target huge volumes through this strategy may face two risks: the volumes may not be adequate given the cost of building the brand and the brand so developed may make a dent in the other brands (offerings) of the company, adversely affecting product-line profitability. Aim was a toothpaste introduced by Hindustan Lever in the lower end of the market and the brand is not found in most retail outlets.

The same company introduced a tea brand, Tiger (the formula was a unique one in which tea was blended with tapioca for the first time in the world to reduce costs). This brand is also not found with most retailers who handle other HLL brands. The Tiger brand of biscuit introduced by Britannia has been a major success at the lower end of the market with the company launching several variants of the brand within a short span of five years. India is a market of diversity - diverse with regard to incomes, price points of products, culture and preferences and marketers would have to get used to these diverse characteristics of the market.

THE UNORGANISED SECTOR

Apart from national brands and unorganised offerings, there are also regional brands in certain product categories at the lower end of the market. The regional brands may be present in a geographical area which covers several markets of the unbranded offerings (normally present within a State which may typically comprise 8-10 town markets).

Apparel, edible oil, dish-washing powders, ice-creams, detergents, tea and fans are some categories in which regional brands are present. These brands advertise in cost-effective local media (regional newspapers, cable TV options, radios and wall-painting). Cable TV options consist of several local cable TV operators who may be running local channels which are viewed in a specific town/locality.

This kind of media is very effective for regional brands. Sabena and Shineit dish-washing powders (regional brands) have forced Vim (a national HLL brand) to revamp its marketing mix in the recent times. The marketing strategy for the lower end of the market could be a combination of low price, an offering with adequate efficacy, high brand-building efforts across the country, developing a distribution network which would go beyond cities and using 'locality-specific' media.

Hindustan Lever uses video vans in certain rural areas to create awareness about its brands. The video van screens movies which may be of interest to the consumers of the locality and in between, the commercial breaks advertise the company's brands to create awareness.

Durable Products in Diverse Markets

There are around five million colour television sets sold in India and there is a great demand for used colour television sets. It is also interesting to note that 50 per cent of the colour television sets belong to the replacement market. Akai entered India and institutionalised the second-hand market. It introduced a promotional exchange scheme by which a consumer could exchange his/her old colour television for a new 29 inch-colour TV set by paying almost half the cost of a new colour TV set. This strategy, besides opening up the 29-inch TV market which was almost non-existent, also ensured retailers in rural areas made margins by transporting used sets from urban areas.

The rural consumers also benefited by getting a colour television set (though a used one) at an unimaginable price. A number of brands have introduced exchange schemes in several categories (though not as attractive as Akai's) after the success of Akai's scheme. LG, another TV brand, has been able to effectively tap a niche TV market in rural areas (though the brand markets TVs above mid-price range) by introducing TV models with a programming menu in regional languages.

These models are of the sub-brand, Sampoorna. BPL, another well-known brand, markets several models (mostly over the mid-price range) in urban and rural markets with a retail distribution chain of around 4,000 outlets.

The colour TV market is shared between major brands BPL, Onida and Videocon Fifty per cent of the total market for CTVs is accounted for by the semi-urban/rural markets. The brands of yesteryear, such as Beltek, Salora and Crown, are concentrating on such regional markets with models at lower price points and they account for about 20 per cent of the total market.

Consumables and Diversity of Markets

Managing diversity in consumables is accomplished by brands using price points and packaging. Around 60 per cent of the shampoo consumption in the country is attributed to sachets (8-10 ml packs). Almost all well-known brands have 50 gm soap packs distributed almost by all well-known brands both in urban and rural areas.

Tea packs are also sold in sachets more in the rural areas. Toothpastes and beauty creams are also sold in sachets. Both Nestle and Cadbury recently introduced a form of liquid chocolate bars priced at Rs 2 (the lowest price point for chocolate bars). Incidentally, in a topical country like India, liquid chocolates do not require refrigeration. Cadbury has a number of price points for its variants in the product line. This has resulted in millions of consumers trying out these low-priced variants. About 95 per cent of retail outlets are small shops (*kirana* shops) and most retailers would readily stock product units of a low price. Economy packs across almost every category are also being marketed by leading brands through supermarkets and larger retail outlets in urban markets.

Small unit packs also enable the retailer to rotate his capital faster, especially given the fact that most of these retailers cannot afford to invest in huge stocks. Packaging at a low unit cost is extremely advantageous for a brand in any product category. Edible oil, cigarettes, biscuits and chocolates are distributed in small quantities by retailers who buy large packs.

This practice is followed both in urban and rural areas. This is because given the frequency of income (apart from the income being low), there are several consumers who are paid on a weekly or even daily basis. Hence there is very strong generic competition among several consumable brands across categories. The "small" purchasing power with the masses could provide several options to them in terms of what they would like to buy at a given point of time.

Traditional snacks could compete with ice-creams or a cola drink (both Pepsi and Coke have introduced 200 ml bottles in several markets in India). Besides, there may be special occasions during which a toothpaste may be used (the penetration of toothpaste is quite low and a number of consumers at the lower end of the market either use toothpowder or traditional herbs and neem sticks).

Low unit packs enable consumers in the lower segment to choose and buy different product categories. ven in higher-end detergents like compact detergents (Surf Excel and Ariel), a significant portion of sales is from sachets (small packs which could be used twice only).

In cassettes, the T-Series brand was extremely successful with its low pricing and value (providing more songs per pre-recorded cassette). There are around two hundred brands of mineral water in the country, most of them in the unorganised sector. National brands including Aquafina from Pepsi and Kinley from Coca-Cola target urban consumers with their retail network.

Diversity and Marketing Communication

Most brands (durable and consumables) which have an urban orientation carry Western appeals in their advertisements which are formulated in English. There are around 100 regional language TV channels and these brands also have advertisements in regional languages. There may also be cosmetic variations of these advertisements when they are launched across the country. Regional celebrities who appeal to consumers may also be used in advertisements intended for various regions.

Coca-Cola is currently following this approach. Soaps, personal care products and household appliances are some of the categories where this approach may be observed. Regional dailies and magazines (in various languages) are also important media vehicles for both regional and national brands.

National brands in consumables categories normally advertise on TV networks in important channels but they made use of regional dailies when they hold region-specific or market-specific sales promotion. Hoardings are used by regional brands.

Wall paintings, as stated earlier, are popular as a medium in semi-urban and rural areas for local offerings in the unorganised sector (a few of them advertise in local markets as 'brands' in certain categories). Regional dailies and magazines across languages and geographical areas along with the retail store names in almost all markets are very popular for durables categories.

While national brands in consumables categories and durable categories make use of TV channels to advertise, they are selective about the channels depending on the target segments. Zee, Sony and ESPN are channels used for consumable brands which address national markets. (Zee and Sony are Hindi channels. Hindi is the national language and these channels have a huge following across different social economic strata.) Star Plus and Star News channels are most suitable for consumables and durable product categories which are urban-centric - like cars, toys and TVs, washing machines and refrigerators. National brands may use both national and regional channels for consumable categories depending upon the target segment and the demand for the product in specific regional areas.

9

Marketing of Agricultural Products

Agricultural marketing involves in its simplest form the buying and selling of agricultural produce. In olden days when the village economy was more or less self-sufficient the marketing of agricultural produce presented no difficulty as the farmer sold his produce to the consumer on a cash or barter basis. Marketing functions.

In modern marketing the agricultural produce has to undergo a series of transfers or exchanges from one hand to another before it finally reaches the consumer. This is achieved through three marketing functions (a)assembling, (b)preparation for consumption, and (c) distribution. Concentration pertains to the operations concerned with the assembly and transport from the field to a common assembly field or market. The produce may be taken direct to the market or it may be stored on the farm or in the village for varying periods before its transport.

It may be sold as obtained from the field or may be cleaned, graded, processed and packed either by the farmer or village merchant before it is taken to the market. Some of the processing is done not because consumers desire it, but because it is necessary for the conservation of quality. At the market the produce may be sold by the farmer direct to the consumer or more usually through a commission agent or a broker. It may also be purchased by traders, wholesalers or retailers. The transactions may be carried out by direct negotiation or through middlemen, by barter or cash, by open or under cover auction, on the spot or in future markets. The transactions take place at one or more levels in the primary, secondary or terminal markets or all three. Distribution (dispersion) involves the operations of wholesaling and retailing at various points. By a series of indispensable adjustments and equalising functions, it is the task of the distribution system to match the available supplies with the existing demand.

MARKETING FUNCTIONARIE (AGENCIES)

The transfer of produce or goods takes place through a chain of middlemen or agencies. In the primary market the main functionaries are the producer, the village or itinerary merchant, pre-harvest contractors, commission agents, transport agents etc. In the secondary market the processing and manufacturing agents are the additional functionaries. Financing agents such as shroffs, banks and co-operatives may also take part. In the terminal or export market the commercial analyst and shipping agent also gets involved in the transfer of goods.

The functionaries have their own set up. They may be individuals, partners or co-operatives who may buy and sell on ready and future basis at a price determined by forces of supply and demand. Each functionary renders some service in the process of marketing and also earns a varying margin of profit for himself. This procedure makes marketing rather complicated and inflates the price of the produce. The nature of some of the agricultural products for eg. their bulk form and perishability and their seasonal availability further add to the complexity of agricultural marketing.

MARKETING IMPROVEMENTS

India being a primary producing country, agriculture plays a vital role, both as an essential infrastructure and a development component in generating and sustaining a higher national income. Out of a natonal income of about Rs 38,921 crores in 1972-73 as much as Rs 17,500 crores or about 44.9% is contributed by agriculture and allied sectors. It is estimated that about 50% of the agricultural produce is available as marketable surplus. The marketing system in India provides sustenance for abour 3 million persons who are engaged in performing various marketing function . In the field of exports too, the agricultural sector accounts for about 50% of the total value.

The process involved in the disposal of such a substantial produce of great economic importance are significant not only for the farmer but also for the country as a whole. The unreasonably low return that the farmer gets for his produce and the excessive margin of profit retained by the intermediaries attracted the Govt's attention and it was felt that the economic condition of the agriculturists could not be improved unless determined steps were taken to establish an orderly system of marketing in the country.

GOVERNMENT REGULATORY PROGRAMMES

With this object in view, a number of marketing surveys were conducted by the Directorate of Marketing and Inspection which revealed the shortcomings in the country's marketing system. A rectification of these deficiencies was sought to be achieved by rationalizing various activities and standardizing various practices in the markets through legislation or otherwise.

The primary objective of improving the system of agricultural marketing was not only to remove the handicaps from which the producer-seller was suffering but also to increase his income by ensuring him a fair price.

Regulation of Markets

Prevailing market practices and market charges made a deep cut in the share of the producer in the price paid by the consumer. Some of the market charges were authorized whereas others were more than what the service rendered warranted. It was felt that a remunerative price to the producer could only be ensured if the market practices and market charges were regulated and rationalised. And thus the regulation of the markets has been given a high priority in the various Five Year Plans. The markets are sought to be regulated through an Act of each legislature. The Act is generally known as the Agricultural Produce Markets Act and it is provided for the removal of various malpractices widely prevalent in the markets for the settlement of disputes between sellers and buyers and for the promoting of orderly marketing of farm produce in general. Various state govts have made considerable progress in this field by bringing in the necessary legislation.

The Acts enabling the respective states to regulate the markets generally provide for the notification of market areas and the commodities to be covered in the act in different areas. A 'Marketing Committee' consisting of the representatives of growers, traders, merchants, local bodies and govt nominees administers the working of each market. The functions of the market committee are to frame bye-laws, define local market prices, fix market prices payable to various functionaries, licence the functionaries, settle disputes, supervise weightment and promote the development of orderly marketing in general. The committee is generally empowered to raise funds for its working by levying a small fee on the produce bought and sold in the market in addition to the licence fees received from the functionaries.

Market Surveys

A survey conducted in 496 markets in 1961-62 has shown that after the regulation the market charges have been reduced by 48%. Another survey of selected commodities revealed that for some commodities market charges have been reduced by as much as 98%. Although the first market to be regulated was Karanja in 1886 the regulation of markets did not make headway till the first Five Year plan. It got a fillup in the second and third five year plan.

The states and union territories which have regulated the markets are: Andhra Pradesh (335), Bihar (62), Chandigarh (1), Delhi (3), Gujarat (212), Mysore (102), Madhya Pradesh (233), Haryana (80), Kerela (6), Maharashtra (212), Orissa (34), Punjab (95), Rajasthan (90), Tamil Nadu (136), Tripura(1), Uttar

Pradesh (264), Goa, Daman and Diu (1), West Bengal (15), and Himachal Pradesh(5). The states and union territories which are yet to regulate markets are Assam, Andaman and Nicobar islands, Arunachal Pradesh, Dadra and Nagar Haveli, Jammu and Kashmir, Laccadive and Minicoy islands, Meghalaya, Mizoram, Nagaland, and Pondicherry. Necessary measures to regulate markets in these states and union territories are at various stages of progress. It is expected that these states and union territories will regulate the markets by the end of the Fifth plan.

All the states where necessary legislation has since been passed, have formulated phased programmes for the regulation of markets. By the end of the fifth plan it is expected that all the wholesale assembling markets would be brought within the regulatory orbit. As a result of this scheme, excessive commissions and other market charges have been substantially rationalized. Unauthorized and arbitrary deductions have been prohibited and malpractices stopped. The issue of sale slips by licensed commission agents to the sellers, indicating the details of sale proceeds, deductions effected etc has been made obligatory. Weightment is also done by licensed weightmen of the market committee.

The dissemination of marketing information and news is one of the functions of the market committees. This is done through the displaying of the prices prevailing in the market and also in the neighbouring markets on the notice boards and announcements through loud speakers at regular intervals. This information is also supplied to the Central Govt and the State Govt and also to other market committees. Arrangements have been made for the maintainence of reliable statistics arrivals, sales, stocks, prices etc which are maintained by the market committees.

It is also obligatory on the part of the market committee to provide the market yards with the necessary amenities. In some of the markets that have been regulated amenities like rest houses, cattle sheds and water troughs have been provided by the market committees for the convenience of the producer sellers. Facilities for grading before sale and storage have also been provided. A survey of 500 regulated markets was undertaken by the Directorate of Marketing and Inspection in the Ministry of Agriculture in 1970-71 and 1971-72, with a view to assessing the adequacy and efficiency of the existing regulated markets and highlighting their drawbacks and deficiencies and suggesting measures to develop them.

One of the most important drawbacks has been the inadequate financial resources of some of the market committees. During the fourth plan, a central sector scheme was drawn up by the Ministry of Agriculture to provide a grant at 20% of the cost of development of market, subject to a maximum of Rs 2 lakhs. The balance will have to be provided by the commercial banks.

An important development in the field of regulated markets is the keen interest taken by the International Development Agency (IDA) in the development of the infrastructure in regulated markets. The IDA is financing the development of infrastructure in 50 markets of Bihar. The World Bank has approved a loan assistance of 6.5 crores to Karnataka also for the development of markets.

Under the existing trade practices, the sale of produce in a primary market takes place on the basis of the visual inspection of the goods, and in the secondary and terminal markets on the inspection of the samples. Thereafter the buyer and the seller decide upon the terms either orally or through written contracts. The contract terms specify the quality and quantity of the produce, the time and place of delivery, the price and terms of payment, handling and incidental charges, the procedure for settlement of disputes and penalties.

The terms of contract were not standardized and thus varied for every individual transaction, and were more favourable to the buyer. With a view to improving trade practices, All-India standard contract terms have been drawn up for a number of commodities.

In standard contract terms the definition of quality and allowances in respect of refraction, damaged goods has been specifically standardized though the adoption of these standard contract terms by traders is voluntary they have to a large extent strengthened the position of the producer-seller and have improved the quality of the product marketed.

STANDARDISATION AND GRADING

In order to gain the confidence and establish a rational relationship between the quality of a produce and its price, it is necessary to devote some attention to the proper preparation sifting and sorting of a material according to certain attributes before it is taken to the market. This is sought to be achieved by grading the produce in conformity with certain accepted quality standards viz. shape, size, form, weight, and other physical and technical characteristics.

The produce brought to the market is very often contaminated with dust, stones and other foreign matter added either deliberately or by accident. Sometimes the produce is immature or not properly dried or contains shrivelled grains or damaged and rotten material. Such a produce brings a lower price to the farmers. Care should be exercised while assembling the produce of different farmers so that the good material is not mixed with the inferior material brought in by some farmers.

The Govt. of India had recognized the need to introduce the standardization of agricultural produce which would enable the farmers to derive the benefits of grading in terms of fair practices according to the prescribed standards and enacted the Agricultural Produce Grading and Marking Act in 1937. The Act empowers the central govt. to prescribe grade standards indicating the quality of articles included in the schedule and specify grade designation marks to represent particular grades or qualities.

The Act provides for the grading and marketing of agricultural produce. The grade standards prescribed under this act are based on both physical and chemical characteristics and are formulated after analysing representative samples of each commodity collected from different regions and different seasons. Besides the international standards and special requirements of overseas consumers are also taken into account while formulating these standards for the commodities which are exported. The grade standards are reviewed and amended from time to time in the light of the shift of the pattern of production and trade and changes in the consumer's preferences. The grades are designated as the 'Agmark' grades.

A central Agmark Laboratory at Nagpur with sixteen regional laboratories at Guntur, Madras, Bombay, Kanpur, Cochin, Rajkot, Calcutta, Sahidabad, Jamnagar, Bangalore, Patna, Tuticorin, Virudhunagar, Mangalore, Alleppey and Kozhikode are assisting to provide adequate laboratory facilities for fixing grade standards for new commodities, for revising old grade standards and for routine qualtiy control work.

GRADE FOR EXPORT

Grading of agricultural produce under the A.P. (G and M) Act is voluntary. Exports of certain agricultural commodities have however been prohibited unless duly graded and marked in accordance with the grade standards laid down under the A.P. Act 1937. The power to so prohibit exports was derived under the provisions of the sea-customs act. The Directorate of Marketing and Inspection under the Ministry of Agriculture exercises a three tier control on the quality of agricultural commodities that are graded under 'Agmark' before they are exported. This is done through inspection.

GRADING FOR INTERNAL TRADE

Commodities such as cotton, ghee, butter, rice, wheat, atta, gur, eggs, arecanut, potatoes , fruits, bura, pulses, vegetable oils and ground spices are being presently graded under ; Agmark' on voluntary basis.

GRADING AT FARMERS LEVEL

The grading of agricultural commodities under 'Agmark' has been consumer oriented. Generally the grading was done at the level of the traders. At this stage the producer was not a direct beneficiary of the grading scheme. It was felt the need to introduce grading at the producers' level. Thus the

Directorate of marketing and inspection introduced a scheme for setting up commercial grading units.

GRADING OF FRUITS AND VEGETABLE PRODUCTS

With a view to exercising quality control over fruits and vegetables the govt promulgated the Fruits Product Order under the essential Commodities Act. The preservatives and colors to be used are also clearly laid down. The order also stipulates the hygeinic and sanitary methods which must be adopted by the manufacturers. The licence for all this is issued by the executive Director, food and Nutrition board.

The total number of licensed factories was 1194. The total average production of fruits and vegetable products in the country during 1970 has been estimated as 156 thousand tonnes valued at Rs 32.66 crores. Some of the products are very popular in foreign markets and are a good source of foreign exchange. In 1970 alone fruit products worth Rs 2.92 crores were exported from India.

REGULATION OF COLD STORES

Most of the problems relating to the marketing of fruits and vegetables can be traced to their perishability. Perishability is responsible for high marketing costs, market gluts, price fluctuations and other similar problems. At low temperature, perishability is considerably reduced and the shelf life is increased and thus the importance of cold storage or refrigeration. The first cold store in India was reported to have been established in Calcutta in 1892.

However significant progress in the expansion of the cold storage industry in the country has been made only after independence. An ad-hoc survey of the cold stores carried out by the directorate of marketing and inspection in 1955 showed that the total available cold storage in the country was only 77 thousand tonnes. The survey also highlighted the need to regulate the cold storage industry in a planned manner. With a view to ensuring the observance of proper conditions in the cold stores and to providing for development of the industry in a scientific manner, the govt of India and the ministry of agriculture promulgated an order known as "cold storage order, 1964" under Section 3 of the Essential Commodities Act,1955. The order is applicable in respect of every cold store with a capacity more than 8.4 cu m.

The jurisdiction of this Order extends to the whole of India except West Bengal. Under this order, it is obligatory on every operator of the cold store to obtain a licence from the Licensing Officer before using the installation for storing any food stuffs eg. fruit, vegetables, meat, fish, dairy products. The Agricultural Marketing Advisor to the govt of India is the Licensing Officer.

The directorate of marketing and inspection is enforcing the cold storage order. The field staff posted in the regional and sub offices located in different states regularly inspects the cold stores and offers necessary guidance for better and scientific preservation of foodstuffs. Besides the directorate of marketing and inspection gives general guidance on all technical matters concerning the setting up of cold stores to the intending entrepreneurs.

The govt of India constituted a Central Cold Storage Advisory Committee consisting of official and non official members, representing the growers, owners, machinery manufacturers, research organizations etc. The Committee advises the govt on all matters pertaining to the enforcement of Cold Storage Order and the future development of the industry. At the end of 1973-74 there were 1503 cold stores in the country with a capacity of 18.70 lakh tonnes. Uttar Pradesh had the maximum number of cold stores of 9.37 lakh tonnes followed by Bihar with 169 cold stores with 2.10 lakh tonnes capacity and West Bengal with 133 cold stores with 3.15 lakh tonnes capacity.

Out of 1217 cold stores licensed during 1970, 1021 representing 84% of the total were owned by the private sector, whereas 121 and 75 were owned by the public and co-operative sector respectively. The respective capacities are 13.88 lakh tonnes, 0.25 lakh tonnes and 0.73 lakh tonnes. Though numerically the cold stores in the co-operative sector were less than those in the public sector the capacity was more. The National Co-operative Development Corporation (NCDC) has formulated a scheme for financial assistance for setting up new cold stores in the co-operative sector.

Potato is the most important commodity which is presently placed in the cold stores accounting for as much as 92 % of the total capacity in the country. The remaining 8% is being utilized for other perishables viz. fruits, vegetables, meat, sea-foods, dairy and poultry products. With the attainment of self-sufficiency in the production of food grains, greater attention is being paid to the increased production of protective foods such as fruits, vegetables, fish, poultry and dairy products. These products being highly perishable are required to be kept in cold stores.

Owing to the inadequate cold storage facilities at present considerable losses occur in the case of these commodities. There is enough scope for expanding the cold-storage industry with a view to providing facilities for preserving and prolonging the shelf life of these protective foods which are essential for human health.

CONSUMER PROTECTION

In the marketing process the producers and consumers are the two weak ends of the chain. It is incumbent on the part of the govt. to protect the interests of both of them. Producers are sought to be protected through the regulation of the markets, grading at the producers level and other similar measures.

Consumer's interests on the other hand are safeguarded by grading under 'Agmark' at the level of traders. The progress towards making the consumer quality conscious is slow. With the growing popularity of semi-processed foods the danger of sub-standard food articles being marketed has become manifold.

With this in view steps have been taken in many directions. Acts relating to grading and standardisation of agricultural commodities, certification marks in respect of manufactured goods, pure food laws, laws relating to weights and measures, and laws relating to the manufacture of fruits and vegetable products have been passed and enforced. Commodities such as ghee, vegetable oils, butter, honey and powdered spices are being graded and marked under 'Agmark' under the provisions of the Agricultural Produce (Grading and Marking) Act 1937.

The Agmark attempts to provide a third party guarantee for the consumer. It not only certifies the purity of the product but also gives an indication of their quality by the grade-desiganting mark. The economic incentive to the producer-manufacturer is reflected in the premium the Agmarked product fetches in the market over the ungraded products. Running parallel to the enforcement of laws, certain measures to complement the effort of achieving the overall objective of consumer protection are also being adopted.

Monopoly procurement of foodgrains being operated by the Food Corporation of India and other state departments achieves the two objectives of ensuring a remunerative price to the farmers and a uniform and reasonable price commensurate with the quality of the produce to the consumers. The task of consumer education and protection is formidable and the govt. machinery alone will be inadequate to accomplish this task.

There is a need of active consumers' movement as in other countries. The Consumers' Guidance Society has been established with the objective of educating the consumers about their rights and responsibilities and advising them on the quality of products available in the market. Similarly it has advised the producers and manufacturers to abide by such standards as are necessary for the health and safety of the users.

CO-OPERATIVE MARKETING

The existing institutional structure of co-operative marketing is such that the co-operatives are functioning at the primary level, at the secondary level (taluka or district) and at the state level. In pursuance of a recommendation of the Dantwala Committee, efforts have been made to persuade the state govts. to divert the middle tier viz. the district marketing federations, of the functions legitimately falling within the purview of the state or primary marketing societies, so that a two-tier system can be brought into operation.

The co-operatives in different states have been federated into a central level federation viz. the National Agricultural Co-operative Marketing Federation (NAFED). At the end of 1960-70 as many as 3335 primary cooperative marketing societies were operating. Of these more than 500 were specialized commodity marketing societies for special crops, cotton, fruits and vegetables. In certain states intermediate organizations at district and state levels have also been established. At the end of 1960-70, 232 such societies were functioning.

They included some commodity federations also. At the state level 28 apex co-operative marketing federations are functioning. They are normally handling all the commodities. There are a few apex cooperative societies which are handling exclusively a particular commodity eg. two apex societies in Gujarat are handling cotton, one is handling fruits and vegetables and one in Uttar Pradesh is handling sugarcane only. In order to strengthen and develop co-operative marketing to an extent where it may have an impact on the marketing of agricultural produce, several measures have been initiated.

Steps are also being taken to see that there is an effective co-ordination between the state cooperative departments and their counterparts dealing with agricultural marketing. Consequently there has been a significant expansion in the operations of marketing co-operatives. This is exclusive of the value of agricultural requisites and consumer articles handled by the marketing cooperatives.

The main commodities marketed by the cooperatives were sugarcane, cotton, oilseeds, fruits, vegetables and plantation crops. In pursuance of the decision of the govt., a scheme of outright purchases of agricultural produce by the co-operative marketing societies was launched in 1964-65 in 200 selected marketing societies. The basic theme of this scheme has been to bring the small producers within the fold of co-operative marketing together for such farmers. To provide the necessary financial backing the scheme envisaged the creation of a price-fluctuation fund. The fund envisages to meet losses if suffered by the co-operative marketing societies at different levels as a result of outright purchases of agricultural produce.

The scheme has been operative in several states. During 1969-70 the value of the agricultural produce purchased under the outright purchase scheme was about 34 crores. As a result of this scheme there has been a greater involvement of cooperative societies in the marketing of agricultural produce. Besides this scheme has given impetus to inter-state trade by the cooperatives. They transacted about Rs 66.55 crores worth of agricultural produce during 1969-70.

Inter State Trade

The co-operative marketing societies are devoting increasing attention to inter state trade in agricultural produce. The main commodities are wheat, pulses, plantation crops, copra, spices, fruits and vegetables. The bulk of the transactions were made by the Punjab Apex Federation. During 1970-71 the NAFED acted as the agency of the co-operatives of Jammu and Kashmir for marketing their apples outside the state.

Co-operative Export of Agricultural Produce

The export of agricultural produce by the co-operative sector continues to be a growing activity. The bulk of the exports are made by National Agricultural Cooperative Marketing Federation Ltd., which accounted for exports worth Rs 5.64 crores. Besides , the Gujurat State Cooperative Marketing Federation Ltd., the Khanna Cooperative Marketing Federation Ltd., the Kerela state Cooperative Marketing Federation Ltd., the Jalgaon district fruit sales societies and the coconut oil millers society also cooperated to exports to countries like Kuwait, Malaysia, Ceylon, Singapore, Bahrain, Doha, Dubai, Iran ,Muscat. The Khanna Solvent Extraction Plant in the Punjab State exported de-oiled cake worth Rs 35 lakhs during 1969-70. The main commodities exported by the cooperatives were pulses, chillies, onions, pepper, de-oiled cake, potatoes and kardi extraction meal. The exports were mainly made to Ceylon and other important markets were Mauritius, Kuwait, Doha, Bahrain, Hong Kong, the USSR, the UK, Iran, Czechoslovakia and France.

Some of the traditional items of export have been marketed in non traditional areas. Pulses were exported to Cuba and onions to Malaysia and Singapore. The cooperatives also assisted various agencies to export agricultural commodities. In this connection exports of coffee and raw sugar were made. During 1970-71, NAFED exported agricultural produce worth Rs 5.26 crores. The Jalgaon District Fruit Sale Societies Cooperative Marketing Federation Ltd., directly exported bananas worth Rs. 34 lakhs to Kuwait and Bahrain Islands.

Co-operative Cold Stores

Co-operatives are also to facilitate the storage and marketing of perishable commodities especially seed potatoes. By the end of the Third plan the cooperatives had established 87 cold stores and the target for the fourth plan was set at 45 more. At the end of December 1971 there were as many as 96 cooperative cold stores with a capacity of 1.42 lakhs tonnes.

TRAINING OF MARKETING PERSONNEL

Several training courses, viz. (a)11 months Diploma Course in Agricultural Marketing in Nagpur, (b) 4 months Market Secretaries Course at Chandigarh, Lucknow and Hyderabad, (c) 6 months Diploma in Livestock Marketing at Nagpur, (d) 3 months training for grading supervisors at Nagpur (e) 3 months Graders Course at Hubli, Lucknow, and Chandigarh, (f) 4 months Training Course in Cotton Classing Centre at Surat, (g) 6 months Training Course in Tobacco Grading at Guntur, and (h)3 weeks course at Demonstration cum training centre in animal casing at Bombay and New Delhi are being run by the directorate of marketing and inspection. In addition short term condensed training courses of one week duration organized for the state govt. personnel in Kapas grading. As many as 407 candidates in the 11 months Diploma course, 1596 in 4 mths course; 212 in 3 mths course; and 76 in 3 mths grading course were trained by the end of 1972-73.

Market Extension

The directorate of marketing and inspection has set up a separate extension wing for the dissemination of information valuable to producers as well as to consumers. The primary aim of the scheme is to enlighten the producer seller on consumer preference and to advise him on the proper methods of preparation for marketing, grading, storing, packaging, handling and transporting and to improve the quality of the produce and to secure a better return to the growers. Since 1969, the Directorate of marketing and inspection has in collaboration with the directorate of extension launched a series of 'Agmark' exhibitions known as 'vital link between farm and home'. These have been held in New Delhi, Lucknow, Chandigarh, Trivandrum, Bombay, Calcutta, Bangalore, Nagpur, Ahmedabad, Madras and Hyderabad. These have designed to educate the general public in the field of agricultural marketing to promote quality consciousness among producers.

Marketing Intelligence

With a view to disseminating the marketing intelligence to the interested parties the directorate of marketing and inspection publishes the following journals:

- *Agricultural Marketing*: A quarterly journal.
- *Marketing Newsletter*: A monthly letter.
- *Agmark Statistics*: Yearly.
- Commodity Intelligence Bulletins for tobacco, wool, bristles, potatoes etc.

MARKETING RESEARCH AND INVESTIGATION

The role of market research in the establishment of an efficient system of marketing cannot be overemphasized. In order to be able to introduce reforms one should know the defects and shortcomings of the prevailing system. This calls for and justifies the necessity of intensive research and investigation. Under the third five-year plan an elaborate scheme for conducting survey, and research in the various facets of agricultural marketing has been undertaken by the Directorate of marketing and inspection.

Particular attention is being paid to the collection of market information, with regard to price spreads, shifts in marketing practices, consumption pattern, consumer preferences, directional movements, packaging, assembling, transportation, distribution, etc. Authentic statistics and data are being collected so that up-to date information may be maintained in respect of all important agricultural commodities.

Besides the market surveys cover studies on the organisational aspect of the mktg. system, problem oriented studies etc. Under the fourth five year plan a specialized study to estimate the post harvest losses and marketable surpluses of agricultural produce have been taken up on an all-India level. The Research Wing of the Directorate of marketing and inspection has been further strengthened by creating the Market Research and Planning Cell. The cell has a big component of exports in the field of agricultural marketing research and is expected to increase the tempo of development in this field .

Marketing is a multistage process. For the improvement and development of marketing structure, a co-ordinate approach aiming at removing all the weak links of the marketing chain is essential. A package of improved marketing services in the form of regulated markets, grading, weighing, storing, transporting, handling services and marketing finance need to be made available to ensure the producer a fair return from his production efforts and a better share in the price paid by the consumer.

At the same time, market research programmes should be oriented to the developing of an orderly and efficient marketing system. A piecemeal approach at this stage can be disastrous and can nullify the advantages gained by the farmer on the production front. The agricultural marketing system in India operates primarily according to the forces of supply and demand in the private sector. Indian Government intervention is limited to protecting the interests of producers and consumers and promoting organized marketing of agricultural commodities.

In 1991 there were 6,640 regulated markets to which the central government provided assistance in the establishment of infrastructure and in setting up rural warehouses. Various central government organizations are involved in agricultural marketing, including the Commission for Agricultural Costs and Prices, the Food Corporation of India, the Cotton Corporation of India, and the Jute Corporation of India. There also are specialized marketing boards for rubber, coffee, tea, tobacco, spices, coconut, oilseeds, vegetable oil, and horticulture.

A network of cooperatives at the local, state, and national levels assist in agricultural marketing in India. The major commodities handled are food grains, jute, cotton, sugar, milk, and areca nuts. Established in 1958 as the apex of the state marketing federations, the National Agricultural Cooperative Marketing Federation of India handles much of the domestic and most of the export marketing for its member organizations.

Large enterprises, such as cooperative Indian sugar factories, spinning mills, and solvent-extraction plants mostly handle their own marketing operations independently. Medium- and small-sized enterprises, such as rice mills, oil mills, cotton ginning and pressing units, and jute baling units, mostly are affiliated with cooperative marketing societies. In the late 1980s, there were some 2,400 agro processing units in India in the cooperative sector. Of all the cooperative agro-processing industries, cooperative sugar factories achieved the most notable success.

The number of licensed or registered units remained at 232, of which 211 had been installed by March 1988. During the October 1987-September 1988 sugar season, 196 cooperative sugar factories were in production. They produced nearly 5.3 million tons of sugar, accounting for about 57.5 per cent of the country's total production of 9.2 million tons. The National

Federation of Cooperative Sugar Factories (India) rendered advice to member cooperatives on technical improvement, financial management, raw materials development, and inventory control.

In the early 1990s, the cooperative marketing structure comprised 6,777 primary marketing societies: 2,759 general-purpose societies at the MANDI (wholesale markets in India) level and 4,018 special commodities societies for oilseeds and other such commodities. There were also 161 district or central societies covering nearly all important MANDIS in the country and twenty-nine general-purpose state cooperative marketing federations. The total value of agricultural produce marketed by cooperatives amounted to about Rs54.2 billion in FY 1988, compared with Rs18 billion in FY 1979. The total value of food grains handled by marketing cooperatives increased from Rs5 billion in FY 1979 to about Rs11.3 billion in FY 1986.

The Indian Ministry of Agriculture's Directorate of Marketing and Inspection is responsible for administering federal statutes concerned with the marketing of agricultural produce. Another function is market research. The directorate also works closely with states to provide agricultural marketing services that constitutionally come under state purview.

Under the Agricultural Produce (Grading and Marketing) Act of 1937, more than forty primary commodities are compulsorily graded for export and voluntarily graded for internal consumption. Although the regulation of commodity markets is a function of state government, the Directorate of Marketing and Inspection provides marketing and inspection services and financial aid down to the village level to help set up commodity grading centres in selected markets.

By the 1980s, warehouses for storing agricultural produce and farm supplies played an increasing role in government price support and price control programmes and in distributing farm commodities and farm supplies. Because the public warehouses issue a receipt to the owners of stored goods on which loans can be raised, warehouses are also becoming important in agricultural finance. The Central Warehousing

Corporation, an entity of the central government, operates warehouses at major points within its jurisdictions, and cooperatives operate warehouses in towns and villages. The growth of the warehousing system in India has resulted in a decline in weather damage to produce and in loss to rodents and other pests.

Most agricultural produce in India is sold by farmers in the private sector to moneylenders (to whom the farmer may be indebted) or to village traders. Produce is sold in various ways. It might be sold at a weekly village market in the farmer's own village or in a neighboring village. If these outlets are not available, then produce might be sold at irregularly held markets in a nearby village or town, or in the MANDI. Farmers also can sell to traders who come to the work site. The Indian government has adopted various measures to improve agricultural marketing.

These steps include establishing regulated markets, constructing warehouses, grading and standardizing produce, standardizing weights and measures, and providing information on agricultural prices over All India Radio (Akashvani), the national radio network. The government's objective of providing reasonable prices for basic food commodities is achieved through the Public Distribution System, a network of 350,000 fair-price shops that are monitored by state governments.

Channeling basic food commodities through the Public Distribution System serves as a conduit for reaching the truly needy and as a system for keeping general consumer prices in check. More than 80 per cent of the supplies of grain to the Public Distribution System is provided by Punjab, Haryana, and western Uttar Pradesh.

The Food Corporation of India was established in 1965 as the public-sector marketing agency responsible for implementing government price policy through procurement and public distribution operations. It was intended to secure for the government a commanding position in the food-grain trade. By 1979 the corporation was operating in all states as the sole agent of the central government in food-grain procurement. The corporation uses the services of state government agencies and cooperatives in its operations. The Food Corporation of India is the sole repository of food grains reserved for the Public Distribution System. Food grains, primarily wheat and rice, account for between 60 and 75 per cent of the corporation's total annual purchases.

Food-grain procurement was 8.9 million tons in FY 1971, 13.0 million tons in FY 1981, and 17.8 million tons in FY 1991. Food grains supplied through the Public Distribution System amounted to 7.8 million tons in FY 1971, 13.0 million tons in FY 1981, and 17.0 million tons in FY 1991. The corporation has functioned effectively in providing price supports to farmers through its procurement scheme and in keeping a check on large price increases by providing food grains through the Public Distribution System.

10

Rural Industry in India

Rural Markets are defined as those segments of overall market of any economy, which are distinct from the other types of markets like stock market, commodity markets or Labour economics. Rural Markets constitute an important segment of overall economy, for example, in the USA, out of about 3000 countries, around 2000 counties are rural, that is, non-urbanized, with population of 55 million. Typically, a rural market will represent a community in a rural area with a population of 2500 to 30000.

In recent years, rural markets have acquired significance in countries like China and India, as the overall growth of the economy has resulted into substantial increase in the purchasing power of the rural communities. On account of the green revolution in India, the rural areas are consuming a large quantity of industrial and urban manufactured products. In this context, a special marketing strategy, namely, *rural marketing* has taken shape.

Sometimes, *rural marketing* is confused with *agricultural marketing* – the later denotes marketing of produce of the rural areas to the urban consumers or industrial consumers, whereas rural marketing involves delivering manufactured or processed inputs or services to rural producers or consumers. Also, when we consider the scenario of India and China, there is a picture that comes out, huge market for the developed products as well as the labour support. This has led to the change in the mindset of the marketers to move to these parts of the world. Also rural market is getting an importance because of the saturation of the urban market. As due to the competition in the urban market, the market is more or so saturated as most of the capacity of the purchasers have been targeted by the marketers. So the marketers are looking for extending their product categories to an unexplored market i.e. the rural market. This has also led to the CSR activities being done by the corporate to help the poor people attain some wealth to spend on their product categories.

Here we can think of HLL (now, HUL) initiatives in the rural India. One of such project is the Project Shakti, which is not only helping their company attain some revenue but also helping the poor women of the village to attain some money which is surely going to increase their purchasing power. Also this will increase their brand loyalty as well as recognition in that area.

Similarly we can think of the ITC E-Chaupal, which is helping the poor farmers get all the information about the weather as well as the market price of the food grains they are producing. In other view these activities are also helping the companies increase their brand value. So as it is given above the significance of the rural market has increased due to the saturation of the urban market as well as in such conditions the company which will lead the way will be benefited as shown by the success of HUL and ITC initiatives.

STRATEGIES

Dynamics of rural markets differ from other market types, and similarly rural marketing strategies are also significantly different from the marketing strategies aimed at an urban or industrial consumer. This, along with several other related issues, have been subject matter of intense discussions and debate in countries like India and China and focus of even international symposia organized in these countries.

Rural markets and rural marketing involve a number of strategies, which include:

- Client and location specific promotion
- Joint or cooperative promotion..
- Bundling of inputs
- Management of demand

- Developmental marketing
- Unique selling proposition (USP)
- Extension services
- Business ethics
- Partnership for sustainability

Client and Location specific promotion involves a strategy designed to be suitable to the location and the client. Joint or co-operative promotion strategy involves participation between the marketing agencies and the client. 'Bundling of inputs' denote a marketing strategy, in which several related items are sold to the target client, including arrangements of credit, after-sale service, and so on.

Management of demand involve continuous market research of buyer's needs and problems at various levels so that continuous improvements and innovations can be undertaken for a sustainable market performance. Developmental marketing refer to taking up marketing programmes keeping the development objective in mind and using various managerial and other inputs of marketing to achieve these objectives. Media, both traditional as well as the modern media, is used as a marketing strategy. Unique Selling Propositions (USP) involve presenting a theme with the product to attract the client to buy that particular product. For examples, some of famous Indian Farm equipment manufactures have coined catchy themes, which they display along with the products, to attract the target client, that is the farmers.

English version of some of such themes would read like:

- The heartbeats of rural India
- With new technique for a life time of company
- For the sake of progress and prosperity

Extension Services denote, in short, a system of attending to the missing links and providing the required know-how. Ethics in Business form, as usual, an important plank for rural markets and rural marketing. Partnership for sustainability involve laying and building a foundation for continuous and long lasting relationship. "Building sustainable market linkages for rural products: Industry's role, scope, opportunities and challenges." Rural products of India are unique, innovative and have good utility and values. Large number of these rural products (like handicraft items, food products, embroidery, clothes & other products) sustains a significant segment of the population in the rural areas.

Several attributes of rural products can be identified, for which, it has a demand in the market. Out of the lots, 'ethnic origin' and 'indigenous design & appearance' are two traits of rural products, attracting a premium in the market. But, contrary to this, the non-uniformity of rural products (from one another) and lack of its quality control measures has been creating a negative demand.

Besides, the small sized and dispersed production units of these rural products hinder realization of the economies of scale in marketing and result in high transaction costs per unit of output. Niche-based products have no local market. Products in local use are also not marketed horizontally; they often first travel down to market through a long chain of intermediaries and then up to more difficult locations in the rural areas. In the process, the people in rural areas suffer from both low prices as producers and high prices as consumers. In this conflict, rural products loss its equilibrium and the supply side becomes exponentially high. Because of this hazard, rural entrepreneurs face acute economic loss and rural markets become stagnant. Therefore, there is an emergent need for Building sustainable market linkages for rural products, so that, it can be connected to larger markets and farmers can get a sustainable livelihood.

Market Linkages for Rural Products

There are, broadly speaking, three ways in which they can be connected to the markets. They can do it on their own — through cooperatives. Or, the state can do it for them — through its procurement engines. Stages one and two, in a manner of speaking. Today, developmental thinking on market linkages has reached stage three — linkages through companies or industries. Rural markets are regarded as organizations for marketing of non-farm products in a traditional setting. Developing rural markets is one of the major concerns of government and Non-governmental organization in India. This subject has attracted large number of research studies over past. Among which noted contributions are made by Rajagopal, PhD, FRSA; faculty members of Institute of Rural Management Anand, IIMA and others.

Across India, previous attempts to create such linkages have floundered. Take Assam and other eastern states itself. Around the Eighties, the state government here decided that cooperatives were a great way to consolidate its political base. Loans went to the undeserving. Debts were written off. The institutions slowly got corrupted.

As for the linkages provided by the state, these offer uncertain sustainability. Given this context, one can conclude that profit-oriented industry linkages are a more sustainable, more scalable alternative. In this scenario, companies can use the social infrastructure (the self help group *et al.*) as an alternative procurement and distribution chain and vise versa.

Industry's Role in Building Market Linkages

To make an effective market linkage, industries have to play as an engine of market, which can generate a brand image of the rural products. This initiative of industries will also strengthen the backward and forward linkages of the rural market, besides, accelerating the innovations of the rural products. Definitely, this strategy will also give a remarkable dividend to the industries & profit making companies. In micro level, it is observed that to create a sustainable market linkage for rural products, industries can develop an ecosystem of Self Help Groups (SHGs) by involving the local communities through village level empowerment. It is nothing less than the next phase in the democratization of commerce.

Under this paradigm, industries can create a network with viable marketing channels covering all the linkages from villages to the global level. This architecture provides the right value of procurement through the village procurement centres and rural entrepreneurs can sell their products faster with better price realization. This model is also capable of generating a consumer business and an output business in a win-win scenario, where rural producers can get a wide marketing horizon and the industries shall get a new, lower cost 'salesforce'.

Another role of industries in building market linkages for agro-based rural products can be the 'dynamic contract farming'. If a conventional industry can kick off a contract farming business, and export niche horticulture crops like cucumbers, the small and marginal farmers who could grow these small cucumbers would make Rs 30,000 in profits in a year. KRBL, one of India's largest basmati exporters, has contract farming agreements with 24,000 farmers; Global Green buys from about 12,000 farmers.

Moreover, in the current era of information technology, industry and private companies can also creatively use ICT for building sustainable marketing linkages. This approach creatively leverages information technology (IT) to set up a meta-market in favour of small and poor producers/rural entrepreneurs, who would otherwise continue to operate and transact in 'unevolved' markets where the rent-seeking vested interests exploit their disadvantaged position.

ITC e Choupal is the best example in this context. Through creative use of Information Technology, ITC eChoupal has been creating sustainable stakeholder value by reorganizing the agri-commodity supply chains simultaneously improving the competitiveness of small farmer agriculture and enhancing rural prosperity. eChoupal also sidesteps the value-sapping problems caused by fragmentation, dispersion, heterogeneity and weak infrastructure. ITC takes on the role of a Network Orchestrator in this meta-market by stitching together an end-to-end solution.

It eliminated the traditional 'mandi' system which involved lot of middlemen as a result of which farmers failed to get the right value for their produce. The solution simultaneously addresses the viability concerns of the participating companies by virtually aggregating the demand from thousands of small farmers, and the value-for-money concerns of the farmers by creating competition among the companies in each leg of the value chain.

Scope & Opportunities

The basic scope of this novel initiative will be the mutual benefits of the rural entrepreneurs and industries. The entrepreneurs – primary beneficiaries, SHGs – bridge with the community, participating companies/industries and rural consumers have befitted through a robust commercial relationship. These models of marketing linkages demonstrate a large corporation which can play a major role in reorganizing markets and increasing the efficiency of a rural product generation system.

While doing so it will benefit farmers and rural communities as well as shareholders. Moreover, the key role of information technology—provided and maintained by the industry/company for building linkages, and used by local farmers—brings about transparency, increased access to information, and rural transformation. Besides, this strategy of market linkage, addresses the challenges faced by rural entrepreneurs due to institution voids, numerous intermediaries and infrastructure bottlenecks.

Moreover, the prime scope of this model is the creation of opportunities for the rural entrepreneurs for product differentiation and innovation by offering them choices. Because of this sustainable market linkages, rural producers can participate in the benefits of globalization and will also develop their capacity to maintain global quality standard. Nonetheless, it creates new stakeholders for the industry sector.

And subsequently, they become part of the firms' core businesses. The involvement of the private /industry sector at the rural product and market development can also provide opportunities for the development of new services and values to the customers, which will find application in the developed markets. It will be worth mentioning that building a sustainable market linkage through industry's intervention will also empower the rural mass (producers, farmers &

entrepreneurs) to cope with socio-economic problems in the rural society and will ensure economic self –reliance.

Challenges

There are significant challenges to the entire process the most important being the capacity building of the rural entrepreneurs. For decades, the entrepreneurs associated with very conventional/traditional knowledge of business, humiliation with government, so they are likely to look at these initiatives with skepticism. Only consistent performance can convince the skeptics.

Therefore, the industries must play a catalytic role to cope with this challenge and should also train the entrepreneurs to develop their managerial and IT skills. On the other hand, the products of the existing and popular brand also stand as threat to the rural products. These global giants (brand) may try to suppress the rural products in the markets with its communication hype.

Therefore, developing alternative and additional market linkages for these products is an absolute necessity. Moreover, the low volumes of rural products, high operating cots, high attrition, and absence of local know how and relationships may also create problem in the process. Henceforth, it is essential to make a way out to cope with these odds.

These issues gain added complexity under globalization, where markets are characterized by extreme competition and volatility. While rural products has been perceived traditionally as catering to the local market, or at best, to a wider national market through limited formal channels, the reality of globalization since the 1990s introduced a new dimension to the market for such products.

The issue of rural product generation through industrialization, therefore, needs to be viewed from a new angle and on far more scientific lines. The core of a scientific approach is to understand the market opportunities for rural products along with the country's development priorities and to chalk out a strategy where rural industries have an important role to play. While rural products are forced to increasingly become part of global supply chains, these products need to adapt themselves, not only according to the changing tastes of the national market, but also according to changes in tastes in the international market. Therefore, a process is essential to explore the market linkages and capacity building for SHGs through a bottom up approach and continuous dialogue with stakeholders of rural enterprise.

This process should ensure the participation of rural people as consumers and producers in the globalization mechanism, with better livelihoods and global access to markets. The real challenge of building a sustainable market linkage starts here.

Present Position

Rural markets, as part of any economy, have untapped potential. There are several difficulties confronting the effort to fully explore rural markets. The concept of rural markets in India, as also in several other countries, like China, is still in evolving shape, and the sector poses a variety of challenges, including understanding the dynamics of the rural markets and strategies to supply and satisfy the rural consumers.

As a constructed category of human difference, 'ethnicity' has given way to 'culture' in its shared genealogy in the new millennium. Public knowledge about such phenomena as 'ethnic cleansing', debates on immigration, and the use of ethnicity as both a dependent and independent variable in research and policy are central realities in the domestic and foreign policies of many nations. The social psychology of group affiliation, nationalism, and the use of ethnicity (as well as gender) in workplace diversity, or the deployment of ethnicity in electoral politics continues to perplex and complicate human social interaction.

One of the anomalies of culture as a way of life among 'subcultures' is the degree to which ethnic differences constrain or expand human freedom and the right of access to the benefits and resources of the planet. Globalization and transnationalism, in particular, has affected the way culture-as-difference is deployed in identity politics and the manipulation of culture in the reconstruction of societies.

Race or ethnicity is often a marker of advantage or disadvantage. Structured inequalities, over consumption, and the competition for scarce resources. Social conflict and political unrest only further exacerbate the possibilities of economic freedom for the poor and deepen the economic divide creating dimension's of stratification based on power, privilege, and prestige.

Conventional social science has examined these challenges historically, but the new globalization of capitalization and increasing political tensions among governments have caused many social advocates, non-governmental organizations, and financial institutions to take their case to the micro-level in a bid to alleviate poverty through small business development -microenterprise from rural settlements to the urban centres. This has led to a confrontation with indigenous knowledge and indigenous people.

The question is when and where ethnicity or culture is compatible or oppositional to commerce. Who are these ethnic entrepreneurs and do they control the course of their ethnic traditions in the new market economy? Philosophical ideas concerning race were formulated by academic disciplines in nineteenth century followed by new knowledge about the seemingly infinite range of ethnic groups identified at the height of imperialism. Social science and anthropology have claimed two streams of thinking on how ethnicity is defined. One stream of thought characterizes ethnicity and its derivations to common descent and cultural continuity. Another focuses on other distinct markers such as phenotype (physical appearance), name, language, history, and religion, factors formerly associate with race.

Globalization has expanded how individuals define themselves as well as how state institutions define them. In any case, the indigenous is experienced as ethnic and, therefore, both are part of the long-standing colonial relationship. The heritage debates located in the tourism industry involve not only the rights of ethnic peoples (human and intellectual), but create a striking convergence with issues of environmentalism, fair trade, and sustainability. What further complicates these social and economic relations is the correlation between ethnic groups and poverty and the new income-earning potential of ethnicity in the handicrafts industry. Some critics refer to links between tourism as an extension of neocolonialism in the developing world. Therefore, the question of ethnicity and artisans may be reframed as an indigenous/colonial relationship, one which exposes the possibilities of the western/elite consumer once again pursuing those objects of pleasure and desire once promoted as "the exotic other."

Within international development, however, there exist genuine commitments to the alleviation of poverty and numerous social and financial organizations have made their mark, some well before the inauguration of the UN Millennium Development Goals. In this chapter ethnicity is being presented as an aspect of economic mobilization in the developing world and In emerging economies specifically focused on material culture as a product of ethnicity in the handicrafts industry.

Historically, material culture, particularly crafts have played a diminishing role In the GNP of many countries because they have been situated in the informal sector, undervalued as 'folkways', or associated with 'women's domestic work', thus unaccounted for in the formal economic picture.

Further, the emergence of credit options for the poor, prominently associated with the Grameen Bank In Bangladesh, suggested new banking models from the World Bank to national financial systems of microfinance. Besides ethnicity then, the poor have become a target market for micro-finance institutions, where a century ago it was assumed that the poor were bad financial risks having no collateral besides their labour.

How we define and value different types of human labour appears to occur in renewable cycles. An insinuating industrialization and the demand for mechanized goods marginalized the cottage industries as labour-intensive industries that focused on the hand manufacture of products associated with rural life and cultural heritage. A time consuming process, the production of handicrafts as rare objects of personal consumption eventually lost their niche markets and patrons with few exceptions. As a result many of these industries died out from the silk-weaving tradition of Laos to the pottery-making traditions of the Amazon region, or the sculptors of Tengenengue in Zimbabwe. However, to focus on not merely the artisan industries but the artisans themselves reveals shifts in how we think about ethnicity in the new millennium.

As such, identity issues, the sense of ethnic self, and the preservation of that sense of ethnic traditional ways though that priceless social product-the craft- represents the central preoccupation of current theory, practice, and policy among these small business artisans and the legion of international social entrepreneurs who are providing capacity-building skills to these artisans.

Whether, this occupational Interest in artisans and their traditional crafts is seen as ethnic exploitation by formal organizations, capitalistic institutions, or by the altruistic values of a new generation of social entrepreneurs, the private ownership of production, the revitalization of ethnic values, and the spiritual focus on the essential nobility of men and women, especially the poor, is creating new forms of social cohesion, economic empowerment, and a resurgence of interest in the professional artisan in the social hierarchies of many local communities in developing nations. Artisans are achieving a new spiritual status all over the world, one that elevates not only their social and economic conditions, but also their role as players in cultural continuity

ETHNIC ARTISANS

Ethnic artisans are defined as native-born producers of indigenous handicrafts and other culturally specific products in developing nations who self-identify as 'native' or 'indigenous'. In the ancient world, east and west, an individual who possessed artisan skills were part of a merchant class who were servants to kings, emperors, rulers, chiefs, sheiks and pharaohs alike. The production of art and artifacts is a much older project that dates to pre-literate societies engaged in traditional ideas concerning "faber", the making of objects both utilitarian and aesthetically unique.

By the middle ages, artisans became associated with the guild system, an intricate network of master artisans who were "licensed" by local and national authorities. The guild system existed from Europe, to Japan's Edo period, to the court artisans of life and Benin in medieval Mali and Songhay. This system was partly a self-regulating association that administered quality control, managed all components of production and distribution, and provided protection from competitive markets.

One passed through stages of professional growth from apprentice to journeyman, from journeyman to master artisan, the latter accredited through the production of a "masterpiece". Individual artisans, guilds, or artisan families gained reputation and status by creating objects that met the standards of the guild or court, but extended the bar to produce unique objects that defined personal style becoming the signature of the artisan, both male and female, or of a family. Cultural transmission of knowledge and technique become key factors in how ethnic artisans learned and passed on the making of their craft.

As master craftsman and craftswoman, artisans provided the aesthetic labour necessary for the construction of both objects and ceremonies that preserved national and group identity through state sponsored and religious patronage. The master-apprentice model, guild systems, and indigenous knowledge that characterized old world development among artisans have given way to new forms of development. However, in many regions from Puerto Rico to Southeast Asia, artisan skills are passed down through families, extended family members, or young people in local communities.

The Santeros of Puerto Rico, its lace bobbin weavers, and the Mascaras of Loiza, east of San Juan have become family traditions. Such practices of cultural transmission retain the creative wealth within communities in home-based enterprises in which mentoring and training workshops validate heritage and the production of handicraft objects. From a commercial standpoint, one of the primary interventions in the promotion of handicrafts has been a tourism sector.

However, their focus has been on the promotion and sale of marketable objects selling ethnicity- and less on the capacity building of the artisan. Other organizations have increasingly stepped up to provide more comprehensive social and business development skills to assist artisans in meeting the demands of small businesses in the global market.

Browse through the über-stylish pages of home furnishings, travel, and food industry journals for direct marketing advertisements by artisan industry brokers or the travel and tourism sections of popular newspapers who lure travelers to "exotic" destinations such as Istanbul and its 550 year old Grand Bazaar, the oldest and the largest covered market place in the world.

MICROENTERPRISE AS DEVELOPMENT

In the paradigm shift from traditional ways of life to modern ways of life, the imposition of western ideas on ethnic groups has been sweeping both in the way the west has defined wealth purely in economic terms and the press of globalization on a shrinking planet driven by overconsumption and underdevelopment. While the era of historical imperialism may have ended with the Age of exploration, the economic, political, and cultural engine of colonialism was driven by a need to exploit and subjugate both ethnicity and ethnic groups. The destructiveness of policies of imperialism and colonialism has been followed by what the western world now refers to as 'development'.

The scope and scale of penetration into the financial world of poverty has been the work of micro-finance institutions (MFIs), commercial banks, and NGO's. Latin America has taken a lead In advancing small business loan opportunities for individuals and households who have "an established minimum capacity to repay a loan". However, the economic realities of urban and rural poverty are regionally dependent.

In Africa and Asia, most of the poor reside in rural areas, while in Latin America "The majority of the poor live in urban areas while at the same time the poorest people live in rural areas. By 2002 the distribution of extreme poverty in Latin America including the Caribbean was 13+% in urban areas and 37+% in rural areas. "Indigence" in both rural and urban settlements is, therefore, conditional on region.

However, microcredit clients in the artisan sector have emerged as sustainable phenomena in Latin America, Asia, Africa, and increasingly In the Middle East as ethnicity and cultural heritage become policy magnets. Data collected on specific artisan industries points to the dynamism of integrated approaches to social and economic empowerment of low-income families and the poor. However, the role that women have been playing in the economic activity of their local and national artisan industries including the informal sector is gaining significant momentum. Historically, women's work as often been relegated to the informal sector.

Not until 1993 were international statistical definitions of informal sector employment adopted and fewer than 100 countries provide national statistics since 1995. The difficulties in quantifying the contributions of women to the artisan industries of developing nations that lack statistics are an inherent drawback in measuring their labour as artisans. The larger goals of collecting data by sex in order to monitor comparative wage earnings between men and women, while increasing, do not pull out the occupational output of artisans. This data frequently shows up conflated with tourism statistics or in individuated NGO reports.

However, the numbers of handicraft workers across countries and regions as exemplars of the growing interest in stimulating entrepreneurialism among the poor, especially women continue to grow. Here are some reasons why women dominate and thrive in artisan industries.

WOMEN-SURVIVING AND THRIVING

By the late 1990's the World Bank and other international and national aid agencies recognized that women, especially poor and low-income women, were dependable financial risks. A now growing revolution in universal banking models that historically preferred assets or capital as collateral for loan-making, poor and lowincome women are now playing a competitive role as full participants in small business owners in the developing world.

The loan repayment rate of microcredit loans reported by MFI's has surpassed more than 98% as generally reported by the Grameen Bank, Acción, and Finca, leaders in the microfinance movement. However, beyond the economic factors that have made artisan industries sustainable, the role of women as central agents in the lives of families and communities is increasingly evident.

Homebased entrepreneurs (HBE's) are a critical sector of developing nation economies as prospective clients in artisan industries. As artisans, many have been the recipients of handicrafts traditions transmitted from master craftswomen or are newly trained in the revival of traditional crafts once central features of their ethnic groups. Globally, gender, the role of women's empowerment schemes, and the political nature of gender inclusion from a human rights and governance point of view are increasing foci.

Barriteau (2001) looks at the Caribbean political economy and gender and Otero (1998) follows gender-related policymaking and Mf. To further document the history of artisans and ME. Nearly 85% of the world's poor live in developing nations. The 'feminization of poverty' describes the disproportionate effects of poverty on women and children.

Due to transportation challenges between rural and urban markets and the prominence of street vendors (male and female), house-bound constraints of (e.g., Moslem) women and the resulting home-based (formerly cottage industries), lack of access to equal education and training, the home-based sector, street vendors, the informal economy, and the cooperative have been viable labour sites in which women artisans can participate in local economies. Tourner and Fouracre address the challenges of differential transport access for women particularly in developing nations and the need for gender awareness in developing policies of urban planning that overcome the lack of access to safe, affordable, and efficient transport. Further, advances in e-commerce can, in some cases, reduce the reliance on conventional transportation for all entrepreneurs.)

CRITIQUES OF ETHNIC-BASED MICRO-ENTERPRISE

Critics of microenterprise and microfinance suggest that 1) small-scale businesses will not necessarily move the national economies of developing nations and 2) that, perhaps, direct giving (philanthropy) may be a better route to reversing the entrenched, transgenerational, and historical poverty present in many countries.

It is possible that a whole scale reversal of poverty and its long-term effects can no more be reversed than global warming. The primary concern here is ethnicity. Entrenched poverty is primarily characterized by race-based, ethnically rooted deprivation and inequality and the systematic underdevelopment of ethnic communities globally.

From this vantage point, the current fever of (over) development appears as a continuation of the exploitation (of ethnic artisans in this case) to satisfy the insatiable demands of the global market.

While the study of race and culture may seems an embedded or implicit correlative with poverty in many nations, the way that race or culture-based poverty operates, particularly among artisans has yet to be directly addressed.

This is for several reasons:

- Increasingly, studies bypass race in favour of cultural identity as a variable of policy interest;
- Income generated by artisan industries is not often incorporated in the databases of developing nations, unless it is conflated with tourism or the new formula called "creative industries;
- "Creative industries" policies are initially associated with fine arts and entertainment (music, theatre, and

film) and have distinct differences as economic industries

- A shift in focus to gender-focused policy initiatives has weighed in on gender, but not always gender and race as "double jeopardy" in poverty studies;
- Marketing ethnicity as "cultural heritage" content for the tourism industry and as global policy development sheds light on the priorities of philanthropists and entrepreneurs, economists, and activists in the developed world.

A critical perspective of artisans themselves is missing From the global vista, UNESCO's Global Alliance for Cultural Diversity (ACP countries-African, Caribbean, Pacific) with ILO (International Labour Organization) and UNCTAD has been investigating key elements of how nations preserve culture. The international policy framework of "Intangible Heritage" and "Living Human Treasure" are preservation measures that seek to associate human rights and diversity with the endangerment of ethnic heritage in a time of globalization.

And given the enormous challenges of reducing and eliminating global poverty in a market economy matrix, many social scientists, human rights and legal advocates, and development economists have addressed the related Issues of social inequality and injustice which are at the heart of the structural inequalities that plague both developing and developed nations.

Luttrell and Dickson discuss corporate and government social responsibility models, fair trade practices, and their impact on artisans industries. In a treatise on trade and social justice and Bhala has considered how the international development community participates in and confronts national, global, and local policies that purport to enhance access to justice for the 'have-nots'.

There is no dearth of writing and research on how to reduce poverty and eliminate it. However, I would argue that poverty reduction must move in tandem with wealth reduction. Microenterprise among ethnic artisans is, beyond its critics, producing profound opportunities for artisans to remain in rural areas, preserve their traditional knowledge, and offers new insights into the essential nobility through innovative human economic occupational development.

COTTAGE INDUSTRY

The putting-out system was a means of subcontracting work. It was also known as the workshop system. In putting-out, work was contracted by a central agent to subcontractors who completed the work in their own facility, usually their own home.

It was used in the English textile industry, in small farms, and lock making trades as late as the 19th century. Historian David A. Hounshell writes, In 1854, the British obtained their military small arms through a system of contracting with private manufacturers located principally in the Birmingham and London areas ... Although significant variation occurred, almost all of the contractors manufactured parts or fitted them through a highly decentralized, putting-out process using small workshops and highly skilled labour. In small arms making as in lock production, the "workshop system" rather than the "factory system" was the rule.

It was replaced by inside contracting and the factory system. All of the processes were carried out under different cottage roofs. The *domestic system* was a popular system of cloth production in Europe. It was also used in various other industries, including the manufacture of wrought iron ironware such as pins, pots, and pans for ironmongers.

It existed as early as the 1400s but was most prominent in the seventeenth and eighteenth centuries. It served as a way for entrepreneurs to bypass the guild system, which was thought to be cumbersome and inflexible. Workers would work from home, manufacturing individual articles from raw materials, then bring them to a central place of business, such as a marketplace or a larger town, to be assembled and sold.

The raw materials were often provided by the merchant, who received the finished product, hence the synonymous term putting-out system. The advantages of this system were that workers involved could work at their own speed while at home or their home and children working in the system were better treated than they would have been in the factory system, although the homes were polluted by the toxins from the raw materials.

As the woman of a family usually worked at home, someone was often there to look after any children. The domestic system is often cited as one of the causes of the rise of the nuclear family in Europe as the large amount of profits gained by common people made them less dependent on their extended family. These considerable sums of money also led to a much wealthier peasantry with more furniture, higher quality food, and better clothing than they had had before. It was mostly centralized in Western Europe and did not take a strong hold in Eastern Europe.

The development of this trend is often considered to be a form of proto-industrialization and remained prominent until the Industrial Revolution of the nineteenth century. A cottage industry is an industry—primarily manufacturing—which includes many producers, working from their homes, typically part time. The term originally referred to home workers who were engaged in a task such as sewing, lace-making or household manufacturing. Some industries which are usually operated from large centralized factories were cottage industries before the Industrial Revolution.

Business operators would travel around, buying raw materials, delivering them to people who would work on them, and then collecting the finished goods to sell, or typically to ship to another market. One of the factors which allowed the Industrial Revolution to take place in Western Europe was the presence of these business people who had the ability to expand the scale of their operations.

Cottage industries were very common in the time when a large proportion of the population was engaged in agriculture, because the farmers (and their families) often had both the time and the desire to earn additional income during the part of the year (winter) when there was little farming work to do. The use of the term has expanded, and is used to refer to any event which allows a large number of people to work part time.

For example, eBay is said to have spawned a cottage industry of people who buy surplus merchandise, and sell it on their auction system. Cottage industries were the precursor to the factories that would characterize the Industrial Revolution. Their formation was prompted largely by the enclosing of the common lands.

Common lands were lands set aside for the common people on which to garden or graze their livestock. Over time the rich aristocrats enclosed the common lands, largely without censure or punishment of any kind, leaving the poor people in a major predicament. Bear in mind that if one was not a land owner, highly skilled, or highly educated there were few opportunities to make a good living. Cottage industries were the solution to this problem and saved many of the common people. Most of the work was carried out in the home and was often combined with farming. There were three main stages to making cloth: carding, spinning and weaving. Most cloth was made from either wool or cotton, but other materials such as silk and flax were also used. The woven cloth was sold to merchants called clothiers who visited the village with their trains of pack-horses. Some of the cloth was made into clothes for people living in the same area. However, a large amount of cloth was exported.

The process of the cottage industry involved the entire family as most work performed in the 18th century did. In fact the entire process moved from child to the mother then to the father. First was the process called carding. Carding was usually done by children. This involved using a hand-card that removed and untangled the short fibres from the mass. Hand cards were essentially wooden blocks fitted with handles and covered with short metal spikes.

The spikes were angled and set in leather. The fibres were worked between the spikes and, by reversing the cards, scrapped off in rolls (cardings) about 12 inches long and just under an inch thick. The second process was known as spinning and this was performed by the mothers. The spinning of wool, cotton or flax was originally done by the spindle and distaff. The distaff, a stick about 3 ft long, was held under the left arm, and the fibres of wool drawn from it were twisted spirally by the forefinger and thumb of the right hand. As the thread was spun, it was wound on the spindle.

The spinning wheel was invented in Nuremberg in the 1530s. It consisted of a revolving wheel operated by treadle and a driving spindle. This slow process of spinning was a tedious process that remained unaltered until the invention of James Hargreaves who invented what is known as the Spinning Jenny. It is claimed that one day his daughter Jenny, accidentally knocked over the family spinning wheel.

The spindle continued to revolve and it gave Hargreaves the idea that a whole line of spindles could be worked off one wheel. The machine used eight spindles onto which the thread was spun from a corresponding set of rovings. By turning a single wheel, the operator could now spin eight threads at once. The last process was performed by the fathers or the men of the household, this process was called the weaving. The weaving was done on a machine known as the handloom weaver so weaving was also referred to as handlooming. The handloom was devised about 2,000 years ago and was brought to Britain by the Romans. The process consisted of interlacing one set of threads of yarn (the warp) with another (the weft). The warp threads are stretched lengthwise in the weaving loom. The wefts, the cross-threads, are woven into the warp to make the cloth. Like the process of spinning, weaving remained unchanged for a great period of time. Then the twelfth child of a Yeoman farmer, John Kay invented the flying shuttle, which enabled a weaver to knock the shuttle across the loom and back again using one hand only.

The speed of weaving was doubled; and a single weaver could make cloths of any width, whereas previously two men had sat together at a loom to make broad cloth. Unfortunately John Kay had to fight for the royalties of his invention his whole life and died a poor man. Recently cottage industries have been encouraged by environmental groups to preserve areas of the rainforest by aiding the local tribes in a sustainable way. The Maisin tribe and others in Papua New Guinea is a notable example to sustain the rainforest for future generations.

11

Problems in Rural Marketing

Rural people consume most products such as shampoo, biscuits, tooth powder, etc in micro units. This is majorly linked to the fact that they earn in daily or weekly wages. The following discussion is to reason out why do they prefer daily/ weekly wages in turn to explain the popularity of shampoo sachets (and not a shampoo bottle).

If you visit any rural household or a surrounding retail stores please observe what kind of things they have. Tooth powder in sachet, Coconut oil in sachet, Fail & Lovely in sachet, only one soap bar (though they might be using multiple soaps in a month), small biscuit packet (Do you know the very popular Britannia Tiger?? it just contains 3 pieces instead of regular 10 pieces), the telephone usage with a 1 Re coin box, mobile phone usage in small top-ups (10/- or so), chota pepsi, etc. Basically consumption world is a miniature here.

Basic reason for this micro-units of consumption is to use them for a day or for at most a week. Their consumption budget is just about a week or less. That is because their earnings fall under in similar periods. Typically in rural locations, the work contract period is about a week or less. In fact, it is day-contracts which rules here.

Before proceeding further discussion on these consumption patterns, let me talk about an interesting topic and it is about you. Assume, after a shopping exercise, you came out of a shop to return your home. As you are with some luggage, you wanted to return home with a auto-rickshaw. You found 3 autos standing on the road and you know it takes about 45/- to reach your home. When you asked each auto driver, you were told 3 prices, first guy – 100/-, second guy – 50/- third guy – 10/-. Then which one will you take to reach home? and why? Think for a while before reading further. Coming back to our original discussion, rural people plan weekly budgets unlike the Indian government which does 5-year budgets. As we have seen before that is because rural people earn in similar periods. And surprisingly, it is their choice to earn in daily but not monthly. Yes, you read it right, it is their preference.

Why is that so? It is because, their logical capability to think is very limited. Just like birds, they can do additions up to 10, beyond which it is difficult for them to count. To understand things for a year period, you need to foresee a lot of things, and plan accordingly. This requires arithmetic skill-set. So it is skill-set deficiency that makes an issue with them. Again, what exactly is the issue??

By the way, did you find out which auto you would prefer? I am damn sure that it is not the one which charges 100/-. Moreover, it is not the auto that charges 10/- either. Second guy who charges 50/-, which is a little more than the usual charge of 45/-, is the one you prefer. Why is that so? Why do you wish to pay higher, when there is a guy who would take you as cheap as 10/- (and in fact, you are willing to pay more than the usual charge)?

The reason is simple. You know that it is not economically feasible for him to run at 10/-. Because you know if the usual charge is 45/-, then any auto must be making 10-15/- (or 25%-40% margin). This means actual cost is about 30/-. Then you would start doubting the guy who just charges 10/- instead of some price more than the actual cost of transportation, that is 30/-. You would believe that he would make money in another fashion perhaps by robbing you or so and not by direct charge. That's what is known as fear of uncertainty.

Rural Indians can't take decisions beyond a week or more is due to their incapability of logical thinking or arithmetic calculations. Beyond anyone's capability falls under uncertainty. Rural people don't wish take those unknown risks. This is the reason for their earnings in short periods, and so, they spend on micro-units of consumable goods. As rural economies restructure, will creative economy strategies that nurture the arts and heritage resources be appropriate for the transition? Creative economy strategies often build on existing assets and are relatively economically and environmentally sustainable when compared with large-scale industry.

Arts-based projects also recognize the value of art in our society and can be an important source of pride in rural communities. However, the benefits and challenges of initiating a creative economy in a rural setting, and its links to the concept of sustainability, are not well understood. In this chapter I seek to determine the unique characteristics of creative economy strategies in Chatham County, North Carolina and, in a context of rural gentrification, examine links between the creative economy and sustainability.

I address quantitative trends and describe creative projects in the county, then turn to qualitative research on the challenges and benefits of creative economy in a rural setting and a critical examination of sustainability, exclusion, and discourse. Although creative strategies appear to contribute more effectively to economic goals than to environmental and social justice goals, as is often the case in urban locales, conditions specific to a rural setting affect the outcome.

These conditions include ideas about landscape and community change, few formal resources for artists, the nature of rural gentrification, social isolation, and debates over art and development. Economic development strategies based on the arts are part of a larger shift in economic theory that prioritizes knowledge, ideas, and creativity.

Arts advocates, academics, and governments treat cultural or creative industries as a fundamental part of modern, particularly urban, economies. Richard Florida argued that arts activity will help encourage a socially tolerant atmosphere and a revitalized downtown, which in turn will attract knowledge-based workers, or the creative class. Arts projects are often put forth as examples of sustainable development because they improve community collaboration, learning outcomes for children, and civic participation, bridge ethnic and class divides, and contribute to environmental sustainability through connections with nature and "clean" industry. Much of the literature on creative economies has focused on urban settings, yet many artists choose to live in rural locations near metropolitan areas because of affordable living costs, access to markets, and the attractiveness of a rural landscape. Based on evidence from case studies in rural Minnesota, Ann Markusen finds that artists centres, artist live/work spaces, and performing arts facilities are attracting extralocal spending and new residents.

And David McGranahan and Timothy Wojan apply quantitative analyses based on Florida's model to find that natural amenities in U.S. rural areas are the strongest lure for creative class workers. Rural examples of successful arts-based strategies—such as the Massachusetts Museum of Contemporary Art in North Adams, Massachusetts; Asheville, North Carolina and its surrounding counties; and the Rockingham Arts and Museum Project in Bellows Falls, Vermont—share key characteristics, such as long-term backing by energetic leaders and multiple organizations, locations with established tourism ties, access to larger populations, and a historic downtown building stock.

It is also important to consider sustainability in a rural community as different from that in an urban setting. A rural landscape is a place of imagination and idealized lifestyles, resulting in complex layers of urban-to-rural migration, class conflict, and land-use change. Rural gentrification can stimulate rural economies and environmental preservation in a simultaneous, if contested, process; and rural environmental justice movements, particularly in the U.S. South, have linked social justice and environmental aims under a concept of "just sustainability".

Examining creative projects in terms of sustainable development offers insight into the complexities of rural and creative economies. Sustainable development is most often defined as "development that meets the needs of the present generation without compromising the ability of future generations to meet their own needs," from the 1984 U.N.

World Commission on Environment and Development meetings, further refined by the 1995 U.N. World Summit on Social Development's "Copenhagen Declaration" to include "economic development, social development and environmental protection".

Many authors have explored contradictions in the combination of "sustainable" and "development"; others argue that sustainability discourse is used in a superficial manner to make development projects appear more palatable. The search for alternative development strategies is taking place in the context of neoliberal restructuring, in which cities and regions have had to become increasingly entrepreneurial.

Place-marketing competition, which includes creative city development, can lead to increased surveillance and elite-controlled spaces, and creative strategies often neither address social inequality nor benefit local residents. Malcolm Miles and Jamie Peck both contend that, although in theory creative economy rhetoric promotes social tolerance and environmental preservation, its implementation facilitates status quo urban development and elite-centered policies.

The relationship between creativity and the economy is complex and problematic, for the value of the creative process cannot be explained in economic terms and cannot be directly induced by policy. The concept of "cultural economy" has been the subject of lively debate in recent geographical literature that, according to Chris Gibson and Lily Kong, has focused both on the economic geography of creative activities and on a more poststructural understanding of culture and the economy as mutually constitutive ideas. David Throsby suggested that we add "cultural capital" to traditional economic categories of physical, human, and natural capital, as a way of measuring items and activities that have cultural value in that they contribute to "shared elements of human experience," such as a historic building, a novel or a poem, a work of art or a piece of music.

Cultural capital, which Throsby also suggests using to evaluate "culturally sustainable development", is a particularly useful concept for rural settings, for it not only relates to economic value and tangible products but also encompasses subjective qualities such as place, well-being, and aesthetic values.

LINKING ARTISTS, ECONOMIC DEVELOPMENT, AND SUSTAINABILITY

This study derives from interviews and participant observation conducted in the winter and spring of 2005 in Chatham County, North Carolina. While studying economic and community development at the University of North Carolina at Chapel Hill, I worked with a local nonprofit organization assessing the economic impact of the arts in the state. Because many arts-based policy ideas come from macrolevel economic data, I sought to discover and address the practical obstacles in implementing arts-development projects on the ground.

I chose Chatham County, south of Chapel Hill, as a research site because it has a well-established artist community and arts activities with economic development implications, yet official economic policies do not centre on the arts. In addition, the county is experiencing intense development pressure, has a growing Latino community, a historic African American population, and marked income inequality, making it well suited to an exploration of questions about arts-based economic development, rural transition, inclusion, and equity.

My approach builds on the extended case study method, combining qualitative research with quantitative contextual data, and on the ethnographic "snowball" method, which asks an initial set of contacts to name additional contacts. I collected social, political, and economic statistics about Chatham County and identified organizations and actors likely to be involved in economic development and arts-related activities.

I identified artists through the directory of local artists and word of mouth, attempting to gather a diverse group in terms of financial success, affiliations with local arts groups, ethnic background, and artistic medium. For arts organizations, I began with the Chatham County Arts Council and extended my research to other organizations and arts-related businesses, such as galleries, cafes, and music and art stores. I identified economic development actors by focusing on local planning, administrative, educational, and community development entities. Approximately 80 per cent of my interviews were formal, lasting from twenty to ninety minutes, most often at the interviewee's home though occasionally at a public cafe, and the remainder on the telephone, all recorded in handwritten notes.

I focused my questions on whether my interviewees saw a role for the arts in economic development and on whether they perceived obstacles or useful strategies in potential and existing arts-related projects. I also attended several arts events—including a play, gallery openings, music concerts, an annual studio tour, and street fairs—participated in three Arts Council board meetings and one planning board meeting, and made several site visits to arts projects.

ECONOMIC AND DEMOGRAPHIC TRENDS IN CHATHAM COUNTY

Chatham County is in central North Carolina, adjacent to two major metropolitan areas with more than 1 million inhabitants each: the Research Triangle area, encompassing Raleigh, Durham, and Chapel Hill, three major research universities, and Research Triangle Park; and the Piedmont Triad area, including Greensboro, Winston-Salem, and High Point. Chatham County, by contrast is rural, with a population density of seventy-two people per square mile in 2000, compared with the state average of 165 people per square mile. It had a population of more than 55,000 in 2004 and is growing fast, with a population increase of nearly 12 per cent between 2000 and 2004, 5.5 per cent higher than the state as a whole for this period.

The county's municipalities comprise Pittsboro, 2007 population 2,490, on the county's eastern side, Siler City, population 8,372, on the western side, Goldston, population 352, on the southern end of the county, and part of Cary, population 88, a Raleigh suburb that barely stretches into Chatham County. Residential development is generally dispersed, most often single-family homes surrounded by acres of open space but with several upscale planned communities between Pittsboro and Chapel Hill. Between 1990 and 2000 the white population in Chatham County increased by 21 per cent; the African American population decreased by 5 per cent, and the Latino population increased by a remarkable 741 per cent. In 2000, Chatham's population of about 50,000 was 72 per cent white, 17 per cent African American, and 10 per cent Hispanic or Latino. Significantly, the white population of Pittsboro grew 36 per cent but decreased in Siler City by 18 per cent, the African American population of Pittsboro grew 48 per cent yet decreased by 5 per cent in the county as a whole, and the Hispanic populations in both towns grew by more than 1,000 per cent.

In 2007, only one-fifth of the county's population lived in its municipalities. Between 2000 and 2007, Pittsboro grew nearly 12 per cent, Siler City grew 20 per cent, and the part of Cary that lies in Chatham County grew 363 per cent, indicating suburban growth. Chatham County's economy historically relied on agriculture, livestock, and textile production, but these have declined because the residential tax base now far outpaces commercial revenue.

The homeownership rate was about 77 per cent in 2000, and the median value of an owner-occupied house was $127,000, both above state medians. The median household income was nearly $43,000 in 2000, the sixth highest in the state; median incomes in Pittsboro and Siler City were nearly 20 per cent lower. In 2000, more than 55 per cent of Chatham residents commuted outside the county for work.

In 2007, the private sector accounted for 94 per cent of all county employment; manufacturing, for 31 per cent; and arts, for less than 2 per cent. Finally, Chatham had the lowest retail sales in the region in 2005, having lost an estimated 55 per cent of its potential retail sales to surrounding counties. Demographic and economic trends in Chatham County indicate challenges in providing employment, retail establishments, and infrastructure for its growing population. In coming years the county will likely struggle to update its roadways, sewer and water pipelines, reservoirs, and school system, given the 15,000 new homes whose construction had been approved for construction over the next ten years and given a populace reluctant to vote for increased property taxes. Residential development is a source of fierce controversy, as a local newspaper report noted: "Chatham, which has long offered an affordable retreat for young professionals, retirees, artists and nature-lovers, is headed for widespread clear-cutting in the Triangle's most unregulated county".

The controversy has effectively split the county: The eastern portion, tied to Chapel Hill and Raleigh, has organized several antigrowth citizen advocacy groups; the western portion, more closely tied to the Piedmont Triad area, is generally pro-growth because it will benefit from greater tax revenue without landscape change or infrastructure problems.

Although the situation in 2005 was characterized by growth, the current downturn in the housing market and overall economy is affecting the outlook for housing construction and population increase in Chatham County, at least in the short term. For example, residential building permit requests have dropped sharply, and some developments have been put on hold or are seeing slow home sales because of general problems in the housing market.

ARTS ACTIVITIES IN CHATHAM COUNTY

Chatham has historically been home to potters, craft artists, bluegrass and blues musicians, and writers. Since the 1970s artists have been drawn to the county by the rural landscape, affordable housing, proximity to an academic community and metropolitan areas, and, over time, by the presence of established artist networks. More than 240 artists live in the county, working in visual, literary, and performing arts, and several arts-based projects related to development are in the area. Many projects and activities in Chatham help artists participate in the community and local economy. A long-running annual studio tour features nearly sixty juried artists, clustered mainly in and north of Pittsboro, who sell their work to visitors from their home studios. An arts-based small business incubator, funded in part by state and local government and recently opened in downtown Siler City, provides business assistance, inexpensive studio space, and a gallery for twenty artists. Siler City also has a public art programme, including murals on downtown buildings. The Chatham County Arts Council coordinates an online Artists' Directory, a gallery in Pittsboro, business-skills workshops for artists, an artist-in-residence programme for local schools, a summer arts festival, and charity fund-raisers using donated art. Pittsboro also has a contemporary art gallery, a cafe that presents live music and sells work by more than fifty local artists, and a renovated textile mill containing small businesses, an organic food cooperative, and art and performance space.

Tourists visit the county for writing workshops run by local authors, cooking schools at high-end restaurants, and agro-tourism at one of the more than forty organic farms, some of which also offer work by local artists. Several public music events are held, such as a summer music series at a historic general store near Pittsboro and a large-scale, three-day music festival at a nearby farm. Artists have made innovative connections with environmental and social justice causes. Several artists who first worked together making life-size chess sets from scrap metal recently founded a biodiesel plant, which makes alternative vehicle fuel. They use their metalworking skills in their new enterprise and draw visitors to the grounds through large outdoor sculptures, informal dance performances, and amateur film shoots.

Artists are also part of a green building boom in Chatham, collaborating with builders on homes that feature green design and custom interior painting and detailing. The local community college is a site of informal networks, drawing artists and environmentalists through thriving programmes in ceramics, sustainable farming, and green building. In addition, artists volunteer their time in local schools and social service organizations, help run a foundation that supports local blues musicians, and regularly donate work to charity fund-raisers. Minority populations in Chatham have a wealth of talented artists and artistic entrepreneurs who are not well represented in formal art organizations. African American artists in Chatham include painters, quilters, writers, and a large group of musicians who draw on traditions in blues and bluegrass-style string music. One African American musician and entrepreneur owns a successful music staging business, allowing it to employ local youth, support gospel music in church, and run a small recording studio at reduced rates.

An artist from the substantial Latino community in Siler City creates complex airbrush paintings for automobiles and restaurants, and another makes decorations from dolls, glassware, and craft trimmings for weddings, baptisms, birthdays, quincineras, and other events. Latino artisans are employed in the construction industry, and musicians play in mariachi bands for hire.

However, at the time of this research, the Chatham County Arts Council board had only one Latino member and no African American member, very few minority artists are listed in the Arts Council's Artists' Directory, and none is either on the studio tour or represented at the arts incubator.

CREATIVE ECONOMY IN A RURAL SETTING

Its rural setting offers a particular set of resources to artists in Chatham, who expressed a great appreciation for the beauty of the rural landscape, in addition to county's affordability, access to a large market, and nearby university communities. One successful artist explained that he had moved to a rural part of Chatham from elsewhere in the state for several reasons, including "the beauty of the county, its artistic reputation, a diverse and tolerant community, and the ability to afford a nice house."

Another artist described the intangible value of the setting, saying, "I live in an old farmhouse on many acres that feed my growth and development but that wouldn't show up on economists' radars!" All groups expressed some ambivalence about the role of the arts as an economic engine and provider of a social good. Most of the economic development actors considered the arts important for society but did not think they should be publicly subsidized, in part because of their subjective, unquantifiable value and because other demands, such as maintaining the county's infrastructure, were more pressing. Arts supporters countered that arts should be publicly subsidized because of their role in the community, variously stating that the arts "enrich people's lives through enjoyment and participation," "contribute to learning, especially for children," "create a unique identity for Chatham and Pittsboro" and foster an inclusive community by "creating meeting places for different people."

Although some artists referred to their role in the local economy, they emphasized how art contributes to personal growth, helping people express their identity and putting emotions into tangible form. Artists were split about whether they should receive subsidies, some insisting they should succeed or fail like other entrepreneurs, others explaining that the market does not account for the full value of their work. One artist expressed both a desire for support and fierce economic independence: "I'd love to be able to work less and be paid more! But so does everybody else in the world. My biggest need is for the economy to remain healthy, for people to have good incomes to spend on art.

I also need more time to develop my ideas. I'd like more freedom from economic constraints,... but I'm not expecting it to be given to me." Despite this tension, artists suggested many avenues for government assistance, such as helping them find health insurance, marketing the arts, giving grants to individual artists and art in the schools programmes, and sponsoring festivals and performance venues.

Art differs from other industries because of its solitary nature, which is amplified in a rural setting. All of the artists said they tend to work alone, and a writer added, "Writing doesn't have any visual or immediate result.... It's very contained, solitary, reserved work." One person suggested that artists in general are individualistic and hard to organize, so, without a representative organization or an official spokesperson, their concerns are difficult to represent to politicians. Most artists also pointed out that the arts are difficult to promote in an organized way because they are so diverse and unique, explaining that word of mouth and self-promotion were more effective than formal marketing campaigns. They did, however, appreciate limited collaboration in the Artists' Directory, participation in the studio tour, and sharing Web site and mailing costs. Other artists said they do not need local promotion because their market is international and Internet based.

The individual isolation of artists and paucity of resources for arts projects contribute to a fractious environment for arts-support groups. The Arts Council negotiates a tension between its aim to assist artists and its need for artists' donations and volunteer time. After collaborating for more than ten years, the studio tour formally split from the Arts Council, at least in part because artists on the tour felt that the council was more involved in bringing art to the public, often by asking artists to donate work or volunteer for charity events and festivals, than in assisting artists as businesspeople.

Other artists chose not to participate in the tour because it is juried, which they viewed as overly exclusive. Most artists were skeptical about the incubator project, one because it only allows incubator artists, not artists from the studio tour, to display their work in the gallery; and another described "geographical cliques" of artists in particular areas of the county.

I found little interaction between artists and economic development actors, due in large part to the divergent nature of their daily activities, and almost no common places where artists and government representatives cross paths or have occasions to work together. For example, both groups considered the cafe in Pittsboro that sells art a gathering place for artists but not government representatives, even though it is adjacent to municipal buildings.

None of my interviewees was a member of both an arts organization and the county's economic development commission, and few artists or arts supporters had participated in local government beyond antigrowth advocacy. Furthermore, planning and creating art are fundamentally different activities. One planner insightfully characterized the difference: "Art is transformative, while business is a transaction, and can the two ever meet?" The planner went on to note that planning has a regulatory nature and takes a long time to produce something, whereas art is not regulated, does not need much infrastructure in order to create, and visible results occur relatively quickly. Artists speculated that they differed from economic development actors because they did not prioritize economic success.

For example, some artists said they did not want to expand their business, despite high demand, because they were satisfied with their current level of work and income, and other artists said they would not sell their work to developers or other projects with which they did not agree. Each group's perceptions of the other groups of interviewees were generally misinformed and at times overtly judgmental. Several in the economic development group speculated that artists would be difficult to work with because they imagined artists to be poorly organized and not serious businesspeople.

One suggested that, for artists to be taken seriously, "They have to dress the part—they have hands covered in paint and clay, or they're in tie-dye dresses—they must come in with a business plan." Some countered that they saw artists as intelligent and hard working; others stressed their respect for artists who held a second job, as many of them did. However, several interviewees wanted to see economic data on the contribution of the arts to the local economy and expressed concern about artists who avoid paying sales tax on their work by selling it "under the table."

When informed of these speculations, the artists emphasized that they did pay sales taxes; one exclaimed, "I'd be afraid not to!" When asked whether they worked with "economic development officials" on any projects, many artists thought I meant developers. Planners, however, did not see themselves as aligned with developers, but rather as intermediaries; as one said, "We're more involved in just dealing with all the new development requests and trying to manage them in a controlled way." A businessperson remarked, "The common ground is money: Everyone wants money, but it will take work. Each group needs to come to the table and let down the barriers," suggesting that a partnership between artists and planners must come from mutual interests. Social fragmentation also affected the involvement of minority groups in the arts.

As noted, few minorities were involved in the studio tour, Arts Council, or the arts incubator despite some efforts to reach out. For example, when the Arts Council noticed that few minorities were at a summer music festival in 2003, they invited local African American gospel choirs and a school step group to the 2004 event. These performances attracted a large African American audience, but, as an observer noted, "the council got people there, but they still stood separately." A spokesperson told me that the arts incubator was trying to establish ties with Siler City's Latino population by working with a nearby Hispanic store owner and by looking for a translator, remarking, "We've been trying desperately to get Hispanics here ... and we've been doing some things for low-income people as well, such as offering free space and help with business plans."

However, another incubator affiliate thought that the Latino community was "more interested in soccer and their own social events" and added that the language barrier was a major problem. An African American arts supporter suggested that the low level of minority participation in formal arts activities had to do with a lack of initial contact and cultural differences: "There's talent out there, but who's tapping it? No one is bringing them forward.

African American artists do want to become known, but they don't know who to ask about how to do it and aren't comfortable asking people of another culture about it. They need to have a place [in which] people feel welcome, comfortable." African American musicians were also negatively affected by the lack of performance venues and the critical mass of people and other musicians who typically support live music in urban settings. Given the level of social disconnects in Chatham's creative economy, how do people connect through art projects? Art engages people in dialogue because it is often intentionally challenging or disturbing; as an arts supporter noted, "People are afraid of art. If it's cows it's fine, but a naked woman! Not fine." Several projects rely on people who have experience in many social groups and work as intermediaries, translating literally and culturally. For example, the art incubator's founding director convinced public officials to offer financial support because he could, as one explained, speak to them "in numbers."

RURAL DEVELOPMENT, SUSTAINABILITY, AND EXCLUSION

Groups in Chatham County saw the role of development differently, each in a distinctly rural context and with different implications for sustainability. For the most part, economic development actors saw the definition and purpose of development in terms of growth, specifically attracting commercial and industrial development, creating jobs, and increasing the tax base.

Many felt that economic development should also contribute to the quality of life in an area, and one mentioned "sustainable growth" as important. A major concern for economic development actors was the lack of infrastructure in the county, in terms of old or insufficient water and sewer systems, roads, and public schools, whose maintenance directly affects low-income populations.

Many were concerned that residential taxes would rise due to development, resulting in a lack of affordable housing, and many felt an urgency to attract industry and commercial development to relieve some of this tax burden. One lamented Chatham's uneven wealth distribution, noting that the county does not qualify for many state rural development grants due to its wealthy northeastern section.

Artists saw development in a similar way, in that they believed it should provide jobs and help county residents make money. However, all respondents emphasized that maintaining a high quality of life is a crucial goal of economic development, and several talked about equitable distribution of benefits from growth, environmental stewardship, growing in a "controlled way," and improving educational opportunities for residents.

Arts supporters also thought development should improve the local economy and quality of life for everyone. Significantly, most also thought the purpose of economic development was not to develop the county too much or too fast, stressing the need for sustainable small businesses, maintaining the character of the area, reducing out-commuting, and encouraging tourism. One planner remarked, "There is no good communication; everyone says they're not in the loop with development." Overall, most of my interviewees seemed confused about the evolving characteristics of impending development.

The nature of rural gentrification seems to pit different groups in Chatham County against one other. Many artists and arts supporters saw this division as one side of the county against the other, or as liberal newcomers against conservative old-timers, and as a choice between "good" development, with arts-based businesses and restaurants in small towns surrounded by preserved countryside, or "bad" development, in the form of homogeneous subdivisions and big-box stores. Although some artists and arts supporters realized that they could not begrudge new residents—because some are recent arrivals themselves—they wanted the county to retain a sense of rural beauty and uniqueness.

An arts supporter argued that the county needed to attract people with innovative ideas, "well-paid people with time on their hands to support the arts," through promoting the arts, a healthy environment, and other amenities, such as "dark night skies, a rural landscape, a healthy riparian zone, recreational opportunities, and high-tech connectivity"; an artist suggested that arts-based businesses would "bring quality people out."

This awareness of the benefits of attracting the "creative class" acknowledges that this type of growth has a better chance of supporting the arts and protecting the environment than do other types—and also that it is a form of gentrification.

When discussing the issues of impending development, gentrification, social divisions, or what government could do to support the arts, artists and arts supporters expressed a desire for "arts space" or "community space" often envisioned as a way to "bring people together," twenty-six times in twenty-nine interviews. Representative examples of arts space discourse are:

A performing arts centre ... with gallery space, and exhibits ... would bring community together, artists together. A performing arts centre would foster community spirit. Art space could bring a sense of cohesiveness.... You'd work with people you're not politically aligned with, you could help at-risk teenagers, there would be less litter, less crime. It would be a good image for the town. We need venues for artists to sell work and for performing[,]... we need a space for crossing over of social and economic groups.

Public music brings different populations together in Chatham. The problem is there is [a lack of] community space in Chatham; there is no regular space in Chatham where I see black people and will run into them. How can we have economic development and arts without having space to have a burger with a black person? The dilemma is [that] most people in Chatham ... like diversity and are open-minded, but it's also [highly] segregated. We need a community space, but it's not on the agenda because the energies are directed now for or against the new development.

People from different backgrounds and social groups do communicate through creating and consuming art, and public art programmes have turned out to be impressive community development strategies. However, in Chatham what art spaces would offer minorities or low-income residents, or how they would bring people together, are not clear. Just because people are in the same room does not necessarily mean that they will make a genuine connection or that institutionalized racism or poverty will be affected.

The sentiment reveals good intentions about a figurative space to connect with different people, and perhaps anxiety about the trade-offs of gentrification, in that the arts community clearly values a diverse community and wants to help marginalized people. The artists' antigrowth efforts may slow gentrification, which may keep the cost of living affordable, but neither result is guaranteed.

If sustainability includes meaningful action to improve the quality of life for low-income residents, then the economic development actors, who must address infrastructure and affordable housing due to the nature of their jobs, are thinking more concretely about equity. Members of the arts community involved in social justice charity and volunteer work are also working towards social equity.

Instead of talking openly about race, class, and gentrification, however, envisioning a future with a physical space for the arts becomes a way to avoid these uncomfortable topics while expressing a desire for social and economic equity. Arts development discourse is not used in a pernicious way to justify capitalist development, but it can nonetheless work subtly to steer the debate away from equity and towards obscuring the injustice of gentrification.

TOWARDS MEANINGFUL SUSTAINABILITY IN RURAL CREATIVE ECONOMIES

Study of Chatham County identified several challenges to sustainability efforts in rural creative economies, with implications for geographical theory, further research, and practical application in terms of resource availability, social fragmentation, and the role of arts discourse in gentrification. First, rural settings have resources, such as natural beauty, rural landscapes, and small-town social communities, that are not necessarily available elsewhere.

However, rural governments and organizations do not often have the resources to support artists formally, because of a lack of funds, but also because the artists are relatively few in number and because supporting entities do not have common goals. Building trust through projects that benefit both policymakers and artists, along with understanding creative workers as a diverse group, are important features of successful creative economy projects. Second, although arts organizations run by artists themselves seem to be most useful in negotiating for artists' needs, in rural settings artists are often socially and geographically isolated, making organizing or planning projects more challenging. In addition, though by no means limited to rural settings, lack of social overlap between artists and planners contributes to competing discourses.

Social fragmentation can be exacerbated by the particularities of rural development, which in this case is relatively secretive and divisive. A clear, open dialogue between developers and community members would help guide development to fit the landscape and community goals. Third, gentrification and exclusion are complex processes whose ties to race and class are referenced in particular discourse.

In his study of urban change in London, Peter Jackson found that race is talked about not directly but through discourse about "modernity," "neighborhood change," and "Englishness". Loretta Lees found that governments in the United States and the United Kingdom use the terms "livability," "environmental sustainability," and "sense of community" to promote urban redevelopment and obscure the inherent inequality in gentrification processes.

Although the presence of artists often presages gentrification, David Ley reminded us that this is not the artists' fault but the result of factors largely beyond their control, with artists often themselves the victims of rising prices. In North Carolina, as elsewhere, Community Land Trusts have been effective in creating affordable housing for artists as well as other low-income residents and merit consideration for more widespread application.

Further study of rural gentrification through the lens of creative economy, using qualitative and quantitative methods, would contribute to understanding the role and meaning of art in our communities. Music is a promising topic for research on social interaction, particularly for understanding minority participation in the creative economy. In addition, it would be useful to more specifically characterize social relationships, such as applying a networks concept to trace economic interactions and social processes, and to better define the role of intermediaries. Finally if the goal of sustainability is to benefit everyone in a community, under what conditions can arts-based activities effectively accomplishes it? Further defining the meaning of sustainability for creative projects will shed light on this and other issues in the culture/economy debate.

In the preface to his treatise on arts and the economy Bruno Frey stated, "Without a sound economic base, art cannot exist, and without creativity the economy cannot flourish". In practice, creativity and economics are intertwined: Artists must become businesspeople to have a career; a strong economy leads to greater support for the arts; and innovation and creativity contribute to ideas and a vibrant society.

Still, involving art in a planned project is complicated, in part because art expresses intangible values and ideas that are intensely personal, intuitive, and resistant to being induced. As the situation in Chatham County indicates, we should strive to better understand the complexity of these projects. Involving artists in sustainable planning holds great potential, but such efforts, if implemented with the boilerplate superficiality present in so many civic arts plans and without talking directly about uncomfortable issues like race and inequality, will lack the vitality and meaningful treatment of sustainability that inspire personal commitment and true innovation.

Our country is endowed with a good degree of ethnic and regional diversity. About three-fourth of the total population resides in the rural areas and majority of them are dependent upon agriculture for their subsistence. Agriculture contributes about 24.7% to the Gross Domestic Product (GDP) of the country. It also contributes about 13.1% to the total Indian exports. This sector provides employment to 58.4% of the country's workforce and livelihood to more than 650 million people. Despite this fact, the condition of these people has not shown any significant improvement. The development of the nation largely depends upon the development of the rural population. Mahatma Gandhi had once said: "India's way is not Europe's. India is not Calcutta and Bombay. India lives in her several hundreds of villages".

Rural Market Potential

India is an agro-based economy and the growth of most of the other sectors of economy is driven by rural demand. Urban market is reaching towards the saturation point, thus bringing in and urgent need to focus on rural development. Moreover, more than 70% of India's population lives in villages and constitutions a big market for industry because of increasing disposal incomes and awareness level.

In comparison to just 5,161 towns in India there are 6,38,365 villages in India. This in itself is an indicator where the real India resides. Companies are realizing slowly but surely that the key to gain true market leadership lies in tapping the rural potential. However, the rural sector in India suffers from different kinds of problems. Some areas are having enough money but their level of awareness and hence consumerism is very low. But there are many areas where economic empowerment, education, health etc., are major problems.

What is Rural Marketing

While there is a large growth in the urban market, the rural or latent market is yet to be tapped, and has an enormous potential for growth. A rural market can be defined as any market that exists in a area where the population is less than 10, 000. The rural market in India is scattered and spread over a wide geographical area. Indian market is divided into urban and rural markets.

- Urban market is flooded with low demand.
- Rural market witnesses a high demand

It's the rural segment of market that contributes more profit than its urban counterpart. Rural marketing broadly involves reaching customers, understanding their wants, supply of goods and services, and ultimately satisfying consumers, leading to more sales. The general impression is that only agricultural inputs like seeds, fertilizers, pesticides, cattle feed and agricultural machinery have a potential for growth in the rural market. However, there is a growing market for consumer goods now. It has been estimated the rural market is growing at the rate of five times its urban counterpart.

Challenges in Rural Marketing

Though rural markets are a huge attraction to marketers, it is not easy to enter the market and take a sizeable share of the market, in the short time due to the following reasons.

Low Literacy

There are not enough opportunities for education in rural areas. The literacy level is as low (36%) when compared to all-India average of 52%.

Seasonal Demand

Demand for goods in rural markets depends upon agricultural situation, as agriculture is the main source of income. Agriculture to a large extent depends upon monsoon and, therefore, the demand or buying capacity is not stable or regular.

Transportation

Many rural areas are not connected by rail transport. Kacha roads become unserviceable during the monsoon and interior villages get isolated.

Distribution

An effective distribution system requires village-level shopkeeper, Mandal/ Taluka- level wholesaler or preferred dealer, distributor or stockiest at district level and company-owned depot or consignment distribution at state level. The presence of too many tiers in the distribution system increases the cost of distribution.

Communication Problems

Facilities such as telephone, fax and telegram are rather poor in rural areas.

Traditional Life

Life in rural areas is still governed by customs and traditions and people do not easily adapt new practices. For example, even rich and educated class of farmers does not wear jeans or branded shoes.

Buying Decisions

Rural consumers are cautious in buying and decisions are slow and delayed. They like to give a trial and only after being personally satisfied, do they buy the product.

Media for Promotions

Television has made a great impact and large audience has been exposed to this medium. Radio reaches large population in rural areas at a relatively low cost. However, reach of formal media is low in rural households; therefore, the market has to undertake specific sales promotion activities in rural areas like participating in melas or fairs.

Career in Rural Market

While rural marketing offers a challenging career, a rural sales person should require certain qualifications and specialized talent.

Cultural Factors

Culture is a system of shared values, beliefs and perceptions that influence the behaviour of consumers. There are different groups based on religion, caste, occupation, income, age, education and politics and each group exerts influence on the behaviour of people in villages.

There is a belief among rural people that experience is more important than formal education and they respect salespersons who can offer practical solutions to their problems. Therefore, it is desirable that sales persons, especially those who have been brought up in cities are given a thorough training consisting of both theory and practical aspects of village life. The training will help these sales persons to align themselves with the market realities and settle down smoothly in their jobs. Rural market has a tremendous potential that is yet to be tapped. A small increase in rural income, results in an exponential increase in buying power.

FUTURE TRENDS

Markets which are not able to face the stiff competition posed by MNCs, can restore their profits in the rural sector. The market share of urban market when compared to the rural market is low, hence if Indian industries concentrate on rural markets their sales will increase. If rural markets are brought into the limelight of development, they pave way to prosperity. Prosperity of India lies in the prosperity of every Indian, hence no rural segment should be left untapped.

Periodic markets are centres for exchange of common goods and services, in both cities and the countryside, all over the world. Held at a regular time and place, these markets link small towns and their surroundings to create grassroots-level networking trade systems throughout the developing world. For impoverished and less-industrialized economies, periodic markets are the logical and appropriate places for peasant families to obtain goods and information.

Organized in a rational manner, a region's several periodic markets require spatial and temporal integration to work smoothly: meeting days are distributed among the seven days of the market week, with schedules taking into consideration the convenience of both traders and consumers. Diverse services are available at each market, including the buying and selling of local perishable and fragile commodities such as vegetables or earthenware pots; and employment opportunities are available for trading and other activities.

Also, farmers can easily obtain fertilizers, seeds, insecticides and pesticides; and periodic markets offer the raw materials for household-level industries, bringing development to rural areas.

The Origin of Periodic Markets

An important puzzle for geographers and planners has been to determine the genesis of periodic markets. Two main theories emerge from research to date. The first is the indigenous concept: those periodic markets developed as a result of internal demand for exchange of goods and services among local communities. The exogenous concept credits external stimuli, such as the incursion into a local area of long distance traders, for the start of periodic markets.

Our research indicates that socio-economic factors have played a vital role in the location of Gonda District's periodic markets. History reveals that the majority of markets today are held in those villages that were once the residential seats of powerful landlords.

During India's pre-independence era (the Republic of India dates from 1947), the permission of this elite, high-caste group, known as Zimindars, was needed for any socio-economic decision made by the peasants who tilled the land. Gonda District's periodic markets have emerged partly as a result of the prestige, competition, and family feuds among the Zimindars, and partly from natural needs, especially since independence.

Since 1947, this area has witnessed a breakthrough in farming and industrial development. Huge surpluses and outputs have been recorded: new markets were needed to sell this surplus. Once a road network was built, markets sprang up to meet the needs of agriculture and rural industry.

Gonda District's Periodic Markets and Trade

Gonda District's periodic markets bring together the region's agricultural products at the most local level of agricultural trading. In addition to the buying and selling of farm improvements such as pesticide and fertilizer, marketable crop surpluses are bought and sold at these markets. This provides producers with the cash they need to pay for the annual round of festivals and marriages, as well as for next season's crop seeds. Located in the southern section of Gonda District, the three periodic markets of Maddo Bazar, Sadullah Nagarm, and Kazipur account for the sale of 90 per cent of the area's surplus vegetable production. Indian handicrafts have, since antiquity, been sold at periodic markets. During the centuries of British rule, handicrafts moved into the international market from the local, village-level markets. Industrial modernization has led to a drop in the production of handicrafts and a resultant drop in the self-sufficiency of local villages, as their residents increasingly turn to cash-based jobs in modern factories.

The post-independence revolutions in farming and industry have led to a shift in the type and quality of processed goods traded in Gonda District's periodic markets. Factory-made cloth, cosmetics, farm chemicals and machinery and industrial raw ingredients dominate, in place of the handicrafts of earlier centuries.

The flow of goods from urban to rural areas and vice-versa has led to stronger linkages between city and village: the rising demand for industrially-made goods has percolated down to each and every rural resident through the periodic markets. This has led to profound socio-economic change in rural areas.

Periodic Markets and Rural Employment

Urban culture has introduced the cash-based economy to rural areas. Employment for cash income has meant more money available among farm families for investment in improved housing, farm storage, and transportation. The post-independence periodic markets have brought physical and financial incentives that supplement the numerous rural development schemes introduced by government and non-government planners.

Notable successes include the Integrated Rural Development Programme (IRDP), the Training of Youth Self-Employment (TRY-SEM), and the Jawahar Rojgar Yojana (JRY). Periodic markets have brought about rural transformation in two basic ways. One, they boost local economic growth which stimulates production, trade and employment. Two, these improvements discourage the migration of rural residents to the big cities, by providing off-farm employment for the people of rural india. The problems of rural India can be ameliorated by further strengthening the links among rural market centres, agricultural producers, small-scale manufacturers, and artisans and crafts-workers in rural areas. In addition, improved transportation can help strengthen the ties among rural markets, town markets and larger cities. In the 1992-1997 five-year plan, the planning commission for Gonda District stressed the need to augment and streamline marketing infrastructure (such as improved transportation, storage of perishable farm surplus, and auction facilities), so that local farmers can receive a fair share of the price paid for their products by consumers.

A large number of studies have shown that even today approximately 70% of Indian Population lives in Rural Areas. Today, Rural Development is essential for the development of the Indian Economy. Indian Government has realized the role of the rural development and the contribution of I.T. in the development of Rural Markets.

A large number of projects are introduced in the rural area with many upcoming projects in pipeline; which are likely to be introduced by the Government in the short span of time. Rural Literacy is ranked at the topmost position of priority. Trends indicate that rural markets are coming up in big way and growing twice as faster as urban markets. According to a study by NCAER (National Council for Applied Economic Research), the number of middle and high-income households in rural India is expected to grow from 80 Million to 111 Million by the end of year 2007 as compared to Urban India that is nearby 59 Million.

The Rural Market of India is showing an impressive growth largely due to changing lifestyle patterns, better communication network and rapidly changing demand structure of consumers of rural area. With the changing patterns of Rural Market, the role of I.T. has increased from providing only the Networks to set-up the basis of updated technological programmes in the rural area.

It is seen that the people living in the rural area have strong purchasing power and have more openness for new technology as compared to the past. Evidence of the increase in purchasing power can be drawn from the statement of Mr. D. Shivakumar (Business Head - Personal Product Division,

Hindustan Unilever Limited) who said that the money available for spending on the FMCG by Rural India is 63,500 Cr., which is much more as compared to Urban India that spends the amount of approximately 49,500 Cr.

In Rural India, Government has already provided Info-kiosks (a rural version of cyber café) which provide basic communication facilities like internet connection and telecommunication services. Modern Information and Communication Technologies (ICT's) were found to have great potential to contribute. The projects of Info- Kiosks are very popular in the region of Andra Pradesh, Delhi, Gujrat, Karnataka, Kerala, Maharashtra, Madya Pradesh, Rajasthan Tamil Nadu and Uttar Pradesh and have shown a positive response in the development of the rural area.

Government is taking serious steps for the development of the rural market, under which the activities related to the development of the rural infrastructure, subsidized food availability and rural employment schemes are at the priority. I.T. plays a major role in accurate implementing these developmental programmes in the rural area. Government has set up various centres which are spreading the I.T. web in the rural area through which people can be benefited and exploit the resources available efficiently.

I.T. AND RURAL DEVELOPMENT

I.T. has varied applications in it, through which the development of the rural area can be possible accurately. Government had introduced a number of programmes through which the people of rural India can come forward and use the I.T. enabled services and work more systematically. Some of the programmes run by the Government are.

E-Mitra

This service is launched by the RAJASTHAN GOVERNMENT for the first time for its rural citizens, so that they can deploy the I.T. enabled benefits to its fullest. E- Mitra is State Government started projects, which soon become highly popular in the region. In year 2002, two projects came into existence namely; Lok Mitra and Jan Mitra. Where JAN MITRA is an integrated electronic platform through which the citizens of Rajasthan can avail the benefit if getting the desired information regarding any Governmental Department at kiosks which is very near to there doorstep.

These Initiative programme of Rajasthan government have not only helped the Government by reducing the burden of attending every call, it has reduced the waiting time for the service and has lead to provide comfort to the citizens also, as with the inception of this service they can easily get the information required at their doorstep.

LOK MITRA is an urban electronic Governance Project which was launched in Jaipur city in year 2002, which helps the citizens of Jaipur (now other cities also) to pay their bills online (land, Water, Bus Tickets and BSNL) leading the citizen to save the waiting time. This service also ensures people that their money is going directly to the Government and provides a feeling of security related to their bills payment.

Community Information Centres

The programme is designed especially for providing the internet access and I.T. Enabled services to the citizens through which the interface between the Government and the Citizens can be setup. These centres connect seven northeast states namely; Arunachal Pradesh, Assam, Manipur, Mehalaya, Mizoram, Nagaland and Tripura. The centre helps to gain the connectivity at the time of unsuitable environmental conditions.

The centres are commonly termed as CIC which are generally situated at the school, college or any governmental office. People can come for the Internet access, and for accessing the internet, a nominal amount is charged from the people through which the daily expenses of the centres are maintained.

wi-fi Projects

One of the wi-fi project under which few villages (of UTTAR PRADESH) are connected to internet is Digital

Gangetic Plan (DGP). Through the use of DGP wireless network connectivity is created, this programme helped the people residing in villages of India to have the access of internet through which the information on various issues can be collected ad used, at the same time the people living in rural India can be updated with the new technological changes and the innovative changes taking place in the national and the international markets.For instance; BIMARI JANKARI is a portal through which the information regarding every disease and health related issues is available and DIGITAL MANDI is available as one of the portals where all the information regarding the agricultural commodities are available. This portal provides the information regarding the prices of the commodities and their relative value.

Drishtee

Drishtee is present in 5 States and is currently available in six districts. It is a private company, which was previously named as CYBER EDGE, which has the main work of developing the modules.

It is present in Bihar, Haryana, Madya Pradesh, Punjab and Rajasthan. It is generally suited in the PANCHAYAT or in the BAZAARS. They prepare the module for the poor section of the society who cannot understand the international language. The modules are designed for the rural and semi-urban areas especially.

Gyandoot

It was established in January in year 2000. It is an e-governance based module designed for the rural citizens. The project was initially initiated by the Government of MADHYA PRADESH. Gyandoot caters the need of the villagers by providing the information related to the prevailing rates of the agro-based commodities and the rate of land.

Each Gyandoot Info kiosks caters to approximately 15 panchayats and 30 villages. The module is designed with the aim to provide cost effective and sustainable delivery model to the people.

TARAhaat

It was developed by an NGO (non-government organization); with the vision to bring internet facility to the rural India. It is a franchisee based business model that attempts to generate revenues by focusing on the marketing services through the module (especial focus on the local applications). It was initiated in the region of PUNJAB with the introduction of different centres called as Kendra's which are connected to each other through the dial up internet connection facility.

These Kendra's have power backup also; in case, the electricity supply is interrupted. The info kiosks provide online and offline services information on education, prevailing opportunities in the market and other useful information for the villagers. TARAkendra's are very popular in between the local population as it provides the information in the local language and the portal is designed in such a pattern that semi literate population can also understand it without any difficulty.

Different services that TARAkendra's provide are:

- TARABazar (for product information)
- TARAdhaba (for providing connectivity)
- TARAdak (connect to relatives at distance)
- TARAgyan (educate rural youth on various issues)
- TARAguru (helps in mentoring and consultancy)
- TARAvan (delivery of orders at remote areas) and many other services are also provided.
- RURAL E-SEVA:

It was initiated by ANDRA PRADESH Government. It was initially implemented in West Godavari District to deliver e-governance facility. The centres are designed with the view to provide better governance facilities to the people of the Rural India. The popularity of e-seva can be estimated from the fact that in the year 2003, more than 400 million rupees was collected only for the electricity payment.

With the success of the e-seva in electricity bills payment, Government is looking forward for introducing it in the areas of collection of telephone bills and local Governmental Bills. E-seva is gaining popularity with passing days as it helps the citizens to avail the benefit of getting the certificates at their doorsteps; which is both relaxing and reliable.

Bhoomi

The KARNATAKA Government for maintaining the records related to the land introduced it. The Department of Revenue in Karnataka has computerized 20 million records of land ownership belonging to 6.7 million farmers of the state. With the introduction of the programme, the farmers are free from giving the bribe and are protected from the harassment. Framers can easily get the Records of Rights, Tenancy and Crops (RTC) by depositing a minimal fee of Rs. 15.

National Informatics Centres (NIC) through which the software online copies of the land records are available developed the software of Bhoomi. By giving an online request, farmers get an online enrollment number through which further processing can be done. In the software, the connectivity is through the LAN through which all the clients are connected to the hubs. With the increasing popularity of the project, Government of India has decided to introduce the project in other parts of the country also, namely: Kerala, West Bengal, Sikkim, Tripura, Punjab, Haryana, Madya Pradesh, Himachal Pradesh, Uttaranchal, Gujrat, Assam, Orrisa, Rajasthan and Pondicherry.

e-choupal

It is designed especially for the farmers of India. Through e-choupal, farmers who are living in the remote area of the country and cannot manage to have direct contact with the consumer can come forward to have a direct contact. It provides an e-procurement system through which the farmers can access the latest and updated information (local, national and international) related to different farming practices. It provides real time information and customised knowledge to the farmers through which the farmer can take better decisions and can have direct contact with the customer, reducing the amount wasted by moving through the distribution channel of intermediary. E-choupal has already become the largest initiative among all internet-based interventions in Rural India. E-choupal is present in 36,000 villages through nearly 6,000 kiosks across nine states. ITC (Indian Tobacco Company) is planning to expand the concept of e-choupal further in 15 states of India.

Aksh

It is mostly active in Northern India, it is a fibre optic cable company with its core competence in lay down and maintenance if cable. Aksh has the license to lay down the cables in the rural areas. It initially has collaborated with Drishtee for maintenance of kiosks, but with the changing times; Drishtee and Aksh have separated in different service offerings. While Urban Area has witnessed a penetration of cable T.V., rural areas have left un-served.

The fact behind the low level of cable T.V. proportion in rural as compared to urban area is due to the fact that in rural area there are a limited number of houses which can afford cable T.V. The bandwidth delivered by Aksh supports a large variety of services (including video interactions) which will lead to increase the level information exchange in between the people living in several areas of rural India.

n-Logue

N-Logue is activated in South India and due to its advantages is entering into the northern areas. The main impetus came from IIT -CHENNAI. It is a non-profit organization with the responsibility of providing rural IT based services (including hardware and software) through connectivity and application all around the rural area. It is functional with WLL Technology whose construction and maintenance is costly and the connectivity is also limited to a certain area, but has the facility of providing connectivity with a range of services as it provides the voice call facility and overcome the problem of dial up connection errors. N-Logue is further supported by IIT-Chennai, which prepares a variety of local language software for it in short time for convenience and comfort. It has also added the facility of web-cam through which the remote diagnosis of various problems can be done. Tamil Nadu Government has supported the functions of n-Logue (especially in its Madurai and Nellikuppam district). N-Logue charges for connectivity and is relatively popular in the southern region due to its easy connectivity functioning and training of handling the applications.

INCLINATION OF SECTORS TOWARDS RURAL INDIA

Income generation from Rural India has increased dramatically from past few years. Trends have witnessed twice growth rate of the rural market as compared to the urban markets. According to a McKinsey survey conducted in year 2007, Rural India, with a population of 627 million, (approximately 74.3 per cent of the total population), would become bigger than the total consumer market in countries such as South Korea or Canada in another twenty years.

Moreover, it would grow almost four times from its existing size in 2007, which was estimated at US$ 577 billion. Several sectors are showing their inclination towards the rural market area due to the increased possibility of opportunities.

FMCG

According to Federation of Indian Chambers of Commerce and Industry (FICCI), the number of rural households using fast moving consumer goods (FMCG) products has grown from 136 million in 2004 to 143 million in 2007. In a report by market research firm AC Nielsen, in April-May 2008, it was observed that rural market has shown a rapid rate of growth. The FMCG sector in rural areas is projected to grow by 40 per cent against the 25 per cent growth in urban areas.

Insurance

According to a report, 'Insurance in Next 2 Years', by The Associated Chambers of Commerce and Industry of India (ASSOCHAM), in May 2008, the insurance sector size was estimated at US$ 12.8 billion, and it is likely to see an unprecedented growth of 200 per cent, touching US$ 51.2 billion by 2009-10. Rural India may offer a business opportunity worth US$ 23 billion for the insurance companies if the segment can be wooed with innovative saving schemes at affordable premiums.

Retail

According to a study, conducted in September 2007, by Confederation of Indian Industry (CII) on the Indian rural retail sector, opportunities in Rural Retail were estimated to be over US$ 34 billion in year 2007. This figure is expected to touch US$ 43 billion in 2010 and go up to US$ 58 billion by 2015. The rural markets in 2008 have grown at 25 per cent compared to the 7-10 per cent growth rate of the urban consumer retail market.

Automobiles

The Indian Automotive Industry currently has a turnover of US$ 34 billion. However, the automobile market remains untapped in rural India that has a strong purchasing power. Nearly 50 per cent of the Indian rural market, which includes 220 million households, is potential car buyers. Two-wheeler penetration in rural belts is still very low with less than 10 per cent households owning a two-wheeler.

Pharmaceuticals

The Indian Pharmaceuticals Market is regarded as one of the fastest growing in the world. In 2006-07, this market was valued at over US$ 7 billion with the rural segment having a remarkable share of this market. Industry estimates observed that while small towns contribute 20 per cent to the country's pharmaceuticals market, rural areas account for 21 per cent. In 2006-07, the rural Indian market was estimated at around US$ 1.4 billion, having grown at about 40 per cent in 2006-07 against 21 per cent in the previous year.

Consumer Durables

A survey carried out by the Federation of Indian Chambers of Commerce and Industry (FICCI), indicated that the consumer durable goods sector is all set to witness 12 per cent growth in 2008. The rural market is growing faster than the urban markets, although the penetration level in rural area is much lower. The rural Indian market, which accounts for nearly 70 per cent of the total number of households, witnessed a 25 per cent annual growth while the urban consumer durables market reflected an annual rate of 7 to 10 per cent.

The face of Indian rural market can be transformed only with the deployment of I.T. The paper has provided the brief description of the various services offered in the rural areas of different states of India and simultaneously the advantages these services have. All the services have difference in degree of connectivity, level of service offered and basic organizational structure. It is clearly seen that the range of I.T. enabled service proportion is increasing at a rapid rate in the rural areas of India.

The fact behind it is the increasing interest of the organizations (profitable and non-profitable) to capture the rural markets and the increasing level of the education and market interface of the rural people. I.T. enabled services are growing at a fast rate and are providing several services to rural people with the common motive of having increase in the connectivity and thus creation of bigger market in the rural areas. The increase in the services provided to the rural people (in terms of various services offered) will result in the overall betterment of the society on one side by enriching the people with updated market information and providing latest technological developmental news and organizations on other side by creating more market opportunities for them and adjustment of the market prices.

For development of the rural areas proper development of the IT Communication and Infrastructural services are essential along with the utilization of the fibre optic networks. I.T. services need to be developed in reference to the present rural infrastructure. Internet based services blended with customer support services should be provided in the rural areas, which can increase the acceptance rate of the services by the rural people.

12

Approaches for Rural Marketing

INTRODUCTION

For quite some time now, the lure of rural India has been the subject of animateddiscussion in corporate suites. And there is a good reason too. With urban markets getting saturated for several categories of consumer goods and with rising rural incomes, marketing executives are fanning out and discovering the strengths of the large rural markets as they try to enlarge their markets. Today, the idea has grown out of its infancy and dominates discussions in any corporate boardroom strategy session.

Adi Godrej, chairman of the Godrej group that is in a range of businesses from real estate and personal care to agri-foods, has no hesitation proclaiming, It is a myth that rural consumers are not brand and quality conscious. A survey by the National Council for Applied Economic Research(NCAER), India's premier economic research entity, recently con_rmed that rise in rural incomes is keeping pace with urban incomes. From 55 to 58 per cent of the average urban income in 1994-95, the average rural income has gone up to 63 to 64 per cent by 2001-02 and touched almost 66 per cent in 2004-05.

The rural middle class is growing at 12 per cent against the 13 per cent growth of its urban counterpart. Even better, the upper income class those with household incomes of over Rs one million [$22,700] per annum is projected to go up to 21 million by 2009-10 from four million in 2001-02. It will have a 22 to 23 per cent rural component. Higher rural incomes have meant larger markets. Already, the rural tilt is beginning to show. A study by the Chennai-based Francis Kanoi Marketing Planning Services says that the rural market for FMCG is worth $14.4 billion, far ahead of the market for tractors and agri-inputs which is estimated at $10 billion.

Rural India also accounts for sales of $1.7 billion for cars, scooters and bikes and over one billion dollars of durables. In total, that represents a market worth a whopping $27 billion. It is no wonder that even MNCs have cottoned on to the idea of a resurgent rural India waiting to happen. Four years ago, Coke ventured into the hinterland.

Now Coke's rural growth of 37 per cent far outstrips its urban growth of 24 per cent. Coke is not the _rst MNC to have cottoned on to the rural lure. Its global rival Pepsico took a wider approach to the business when it was given permission to set up shop in India in the late 1980s and investment in food processing and farming was a pre-condition for entry. The company imported a state-of-the art tomato processing plant from Italy to Punjab. In _ve years, productivity improved from 16 tonnes to 52 tonnes per hectare and there was a tomato glut in the state. Farmers weren't complaining because even though prices fell, their incomes increased because of the huge jump in productivity. Pepsi is now heralding a citrus plantation drive in the state and other parts of the country for its brand of Tropicana fruit juices, to replace imported fruit. Hindustan Lever Ltd, the $2.3 billion Indian subsidiary of Unilever, the country's largest FMCG company, has also got on the bandwagon.

It's Project Shakti uses self-help groups across the country to push Lever products deeper into the hinterland. Its four-pronged programme creates income-generating capabilities for underprivileged rural women; improves rural quality of life by spreading awareness of best practices in health and hygiene; empowers the rural community by creating access to relevant information through community portals and it also works with NGOs to spread literacy. There are currently over 15,000 Shakti entrepreneurs, most of them women, in 61,400 villages across 12 states. By the end of 2010, Shakti aims to have 100,000 Shakti entrepreneurs covering 500,000 of India s 640,000 villages, touching the lives of over 600 million people. With such an emphasis on rural marketing, consumption patterns are changing and it signals a change in the regulatory environment. Vertical integration of the food market from farm to form to fork becomes the best way to achieve efficiency and serve the interest of every stakeholder in the chain the farmer, the processor, the retailer and the consumer.

As Ashok Gulati of the US-based International Food Policy Research Institute put its, The future of Indian agriculture in general and the farmer in particular depends on the how soon they can become globally competitive. Indian economic policy realises this. Between the 8th (1992-97) and the 10th (2002-07) Five Year Plans, successive governments have tripled the spending on rural development from $6.82 billion to $20.2 billion. All this potential has got India's big business houses rushing to enter and expand rural businesses. Telecom giant Sunil Mittal, chairman of the $2billion mobile telephony major Bharti Tele- Ventures, is another unabashedag-bearer of the 'go rural' strategy.

He is confident that the next 'explosive' phase of demand for cellular connections is going to come from the villages. In an interesting business diversification, he has tied up with the legendary Rothschilds of Europe for a $51 million food processing venture and export of fruits and vegetables. We can replicate our pre-eminence in IT agriculture and transform the country into a global food basket, he points out. Mittal's initial investments include an agriculture research centre and model farm in Punjab.

If the hinterland has caught the attention of Mittal, among the country's most recent entrants to the ranks of big business, it has also not escaped the radar of the oldest business house, the $17 billion Tata group, which has consolidated its rural operations. The group's two companies,Tata Chemicals and Rallis India, ran separate rural initiatives till 2003. Tata Chemicals ran a chain called Tata Kisan Kendra, which ofered farmers a host of products and services ranging from agriinputs to financing to advisory services. Rallis, on the other hand, was partnering ICICI Bank and Hindustan Lever in ofering deals to farmers that covered operations from the pre-harvest to post-harvest stage. In 2004, the two operations were merged and Tata Kisan Sansar, a network of onestop shops providing everything from inputs to know-how to loans, was launched. Today, the Tata Kisan Sansar has 421 franchisee-run centres in three states and reaches out to over 3.6 million farmers. Like the Tatas, the $2.6 billion Mahindra group has successfully established a synergy between its current businesses and the planned rural forays.

Its agship, Mahindra & Mahindra Ltd is India's largest farm equipment company. Its subsidiary, Mahindra Shubhlabh Services, has operations in 11 states, and leverages the strong Mahindra brand, the 700,000-strong Mahindra tractor customer base and the 400-plus dealer network, to provide a complete range of products and services to improve farm productivity and establish market linkages to the commodity market chain. Its retailing arm, Mahindra Krishi Vihar, has been instrumental in increasing the groundnut yield in Rajasthan through a new seed sourced from the state of Maharashtra, and it has also introduced a new variety of grapes in Maharashtra. Says Vikram Puri, head of Mahindra Shubhlabh Services, Almost 80 per cent of the farmers registered with us have less than five acres land.

We are making farming an attractive proposition through three basic guiding steps growing what the market requires, improving the crop yield and decreasing the cost of crop production. The activities of Mahindra Shubhlabh Services have attracted the attention of the International Finance Corporation, the financial arm of the World Bank, which recently picked up a 27 per cent stake in the company. Rural India accounts for a market worth $27 billion. No wonder even MNCs have cottoned on to the idea of a resurgent rural India.

BY COMMUNICATING AND CHANGING QUALITY PERCEPTION

Companies are coming up with new technology and they are properly communicating it to the customer. There is a trade-of between Quality a customer perceives and a company wants to communicate. Thus, this positioning of technology is very crucial. The perception of the Indian about the desired product is changing. Now they know the difference between the products and the utilities derived out of it. As a rural Indian customer always wanted value for money with the changed perception, one can notice difference in current market scenario.

By Proper Communication in Indian Language

The companies have realized the importance of proper communication in local language for promoting their products. They have started selling the concept of quality with proper communication. Their main focus is to change the Indian customer outlook about quality. With their promotion, rural customer started asking for value for money.

By Target Changing Perception

If one go to villages they will see that villagers using Toothpaste, even when they can use Neem or Babool sticks or Gudakhu, villagers are using soaps like Nima rose, Breeze, Cinthol etc. even when they can use locally manufactured very low priced soaps. Villagers are constantly looking forward for new branded products. What can one infer from these incidents, is the paradigm changing and customer no longer price sensitive? Indian customer was never price sensitive, but they want value for money. They are ready to pay premium for the product if the product is offering some extra utility for the premium.

By Understanding Cultural and Social Values

Companies have recognized that social and cultural values have a very strong hold on the people. Cultural values play major role in deciding what to buy. Moreover, rural people are emotional and sensitive. Thus, to promote their brands, they are exploiting social and cultural values.

By Providing What Customer Want

The customers want value for money. They do not see any value in frills associated with the products. They aim for the basic functionality. However, if the seller provide frills free of cost they are happy with that. They are happy with such a high technology that can fulfill their need.

As "Motorola" has launched, seven models of Cellular Phones of high technology but none took of. On the other hand, "Nokia" has launched a simple product, which has captured the market.

By Promoting Products with Indian Models and Actors

Companies are picking up Indian models, actors for advertisements as this helps them to show themselves as an Indian company. Diana Hyden and Shahrukh Khan are chosen as a brand ambassador for MNC quartz clock maker "OMEGA" even though when they have models like Cindy Crawford.

By Associating Themselves with India

MNCs are associating themselves with India by talking about India, by explicitly saying that they are Indian. M-TV during Independence Day and Republic daytime make their logo with Indian tri-color. Nokia has designed a new cellular phone 5110, with the India tri-colour and a ringing tone of "Sare Jahan se achcha".

By Promoting Indian Sports Team

Companies are promoting Indian sports teams so that they can associate themselves with India. With this, they inuence Indian mindset. LG has launched a campaign "LG ki Dua, all the best".

ITC is promoting Indian cricket team for years, during world cup they have launched a campaign "Jeeta hai jitega apna HindustanIndia India India". Similarly, Whirlpool has also launched a campaign during world cup.

By Talking About a Normal Indian

Companies are now talking about normal India. It is a normal tendency of an Indian to try to associate himself/herself with the product. If he/she can visualize himself/herself with the product, he /she becomes loyal to it. That is why companies like Daewoo based their advertisements on a normal Indian family.

By Developing Rural-Specific Products

Many companies are developing rural-specific products. Keeping into consideration the requirements, a firm develops these products. Electrolux is working on a made-for India fridge designed to serve basic purposes: chill drinking water, keep cooked food fresh, and to withstand long power cuts.

By Giving Indian Words for Brands

Companies use Indian words for brands. Like LG has used India brand name "Sampoorna" for its newly launched TV. The word is a part of the Bengali, Hindi, Marathi and Tamil tongue. In the past one year, LG has sold one lakh 20-inch Sampoorna TVs, all in towns with a population of around 10,000. By the end of 1999, roughly 12Thats Rs 114 crore worth of TV sets sold in the villages in a year.

By Acquirng Indian Brands

As Indian brands are operating in India for a long time and they enjoy a good reputation in India. MNCs have found that it is much easier for them to operate in India if they acquire an Established Indian Brand. Electrolux has acquired two Indian brands Kelvinator and Allwyn this has gave them the well-established distribution channel. As well as trust of people, as people believe these brands. Similarly Coke has acquired Thumps up, Gold Spot, Citra and Limca so that they can kill these brands, but later on they realized that to survive in the market and to compete with their competitor they have to rejuvenate these brands.

By Effective Media Communication

Media Rural marketing is being used by companies. They can either go for the traditional media or the modern media. The traditional media include melas, puppetry, folk theatre etc. while the modern media includes TV, radio, e-chaupal.

LIC uses puppets to educate rural masses about its insurance policies. Govt of India uses puppetry in its campaigns to press ahead social issues. Brook Bond Lipton India ltd used magicians efectively for launch of Kadak Chap Tea in Etawah district.

In between such a show, the lights are switched of and a torch is ashed in the dark(EVEREADYs tact). ITC's e-chaupal (chaupal is the common place where villagers gather) has been the most elaborate and extensive venture in this field so far. Conceived by ITC's international business division and launched in 2000, the e-chaupal project has since grown to around 2,700 chaupals covering a population of around 1.2 million in five states {Madhya Pradesh, Karnataka, Andhra Pradesh, Uttar Pradesh and Maharashtra}.

Rural marketing requires the understanding of the complexities and this article reviews some of the key issues. Indian agricultural industry has been growing at a tremendous pace in the last few decades. The rural areas are consuming a large number of industrial and urban manufactured products. The rural agricultural production and consumption process plays a predominant role in developing the Indian economy. This has designed a new way for understanding a new process called Rural Marketing.

The concept of rural marketing has to be distinguished from Agricultural marketing. Marketing is the process of identifying and satisfying customers needs and providing them with adequate after sales service. Rural marketing is different from agricultural marketing, which signi_es marketing of rural products to the urban consumer or institutional markets.

Rural marketing basically deals with delivering manufactured or processed inputs or services to rural producers, the demand for which is basically a derived outcome. Rural marketing scientists also term it as developmental marketing, as the process of rural marketing involves an urban to rural activity, which in turn is characterised by various peculiarities in terms of nature of market, products and processes. Rural marketing di_ers from agricultural or consumer products marketing in terms of the nature of transactions, which includes participants, products, modalities, norms and outcomes. The participants in case of Rural Marketing would also be di_erent they include input manufacturers, dealers, farmers, opinion makers, government agencies and traders.

The existing approach to the rural markets has viewed the markets as a homogeneous one, but in practice, there are significant buyer and user differences across regions as well as within that requires a differential treatment of the marketing problems. These differences could be in terms of the type of farmers, type of crops and other agro-climatic conditions. One has to understand the market norms in agricultural input so as to devise good marketing strategies and to avoid unethical practices, which distort the marketing environment.

Many of the inputs used for production process have implications for food, health and environmental sectors. Rural marketing needs to combine concerns for profit with a concern for the society, besides being titled towards profit. Rural market for agricultural inputs is a case of market pull and not market push. Most of the jobs of marketing and selling is left to the local dealers and retailers. The market for input gets interlocked with other markets like output, consumer goods, money and labour.

The importance of rural marketing can be understood from the fact that today modern inputs, i.e., diesel, electricity, fertilisers, pesticides, seeds account for as much as 70Green Revolution areas. Further the percentages were higher at 81of land. Strategic aspects Rural marketing in India is not much developed there are many hindrances in the area of market, product design and positioning, pricing, distribution and promotion.

Companies need to understand rural marketing in a broader manner not only to survive and grow in their business, but also a means to the development of the rural economy. One has to have a strategic view of the rural markets so as to know and understand the markets well. In the context of rural marketing one has to understand the manipulation of marketing mix has to be properly understood in terms of product usage. Product usage is central to price, distribution, promotion, branding, company image and more important farmer economics, thus any strategy in rural marketing should be given due attention and importance by understanding the product usage, all elements of marketing mix can be better organised and managed.

By Adopting Localised Way of Distributing

Proper distribution channels are recognized by companies. The distribution channel could be a Big scale Super markets, they thought that a similar system can be grown in India. However, they were wrong, soon they realized that to succeed in India they have to reach the nook and the corner of the country. They have to reach the "local Paan wala, Local Baniya" only they can succeed. MNC shoe giants, Adidas, Reebok, Nike started with exclusive stores but soon they realized that they do not enjoy much Brand Equity in India, and to capture the market share in India they have to go the local market shoe sellers. They have to reach to local cities with low priced products.

By Associating themselves with Indian Celebrities

MNCs have realized that in India celebrities enjoyed a great popularity so they now associate themselves with Indian celebrities. Recently Luxor Writing Instruments Ltd. a JV of Gillette and Luxor has launched 500 "Gajgamini" range of Parker Sonnet Hussain special edition fountain pens, priced at Rs. 5000. This pen is signed by Mr. Makbul Fida Hussain a renowned painter who has created "Gajgamini" range of paintings. Companies are promoting players like Bhaichung Bhutia, who is promoted by Reebok, so that they can associate their name with players like him and get popularity.

Melas

Melas are places where villagers gather once in a while for shopping. Companies take advantage of such events to market their products. Dabur uses these events to sell products like JANAM GHUTI(Gripe water). NCAER estimates that around half of items sold in these melas are FMCG products and consumer durables. Escorts also displays its products like tractors and motorcycles in such melas.

Paintings

A picture is worth thousand words. The message is simple and clean. Rural people like the sight of bright colours. COKE, PEPSI and TATA traders advertise their products through paintings. Case Studies-1: AKASHGANGA This case study is about a product and service named Akashganga sold by a small, entrepreneurial business named Shree Kamadhenu Electronics Private Ltd. (SKEPL). Akashganga is for diary farmers and it is intended to enable to them to increase their efficiency and productivity.

The Indian diary industry is plagued by several problems, the major ones being low productivity of Indian cows, the delays in processing milk, low quality caused by manual handling, corruption and mismanagement, and, of course, endemic dilution of milk with water. Akashganga attempts to alleviate some of these issues. Akashganga is a computerized system.

When a farmer gets milk into the collection point, it's weighed and the amount of fat measured and immediately an entry is made on the farmer's swipe card. The money can be collected immediately. This is marked contrast to the previous system where the financial calculation was done later to avoid holding up the queue of farmers ready for milking; the calculation was done by hand and was somewhat complicated.

With the new system, calculation is done automatically which makes it possible to pay the farmer on the spot rather than having him wait for a couple of days. Also the potential for cheating is reduced. An entry is made electronically on the farmer's swipe card. When SKEPL wanted to market this service, it ran up against the skepticism of the Indian rural people against unproven technology. This is the classic catch-22 situation as the farmer does not trust the tool till he tries it, and is reluctant to try it till he trusts it. SKEPL got around this problem by opening free trials and delayed payment schemes stretching up to several months. The company also provided responsive and ancient after-sales service.

It established a service network covering the rural areas, and typically would attend to a compliant within a few hours of receiving it. It's important to note that the company's local presence whether for marketing, sales or service helped tremendously, since the villagers would not be disposed to make a journey to a town or city to learn about their products. The company also used a name Akashganga that Indian villagers can relate to.

This helped earn the trust of the villagers. Also, Shree Kamadhenu Electronics used local people for marketing, sales, service, etc. This was a very important factor that helped the farmers relate to and trust the company. Of course, the company had a solution that was superior in terms of time, transparency, fairness, etc, and that played a big role in their success. As a result of these factors, SKEPL gained a threshold in this large market and earned respect among farmers. Case-Study 2: ITC e-Choupal About ITC-IBD ITC is one of India's foremost private sector companies with a market capitalisation of over US $14 billion and a turnover of US $3 billion. ITC has a diversified presence in Cigarettes, Hotels, Paperboards & Specialty Papers, Packaging, Agri-Business, Packaged Foods & Confectionery, Branded Apparel, Greeting Cards and other FMCG products. Its International Business Division (ITC IBD) was created in 1990 as an agricultural trading company; it now generates US $150 million in revenues annually. Initially, the agricultural commodity trading business was small compared to international players.

By 1996, the opening up of the Indian market had brought in international competition. Large international companies had better margin-to-risk ratios because of wider options for risk management and arbitrage. For an Indian company to replicate the operating model of such multinational corporations would have required a massive horizontal and vertical expansion. In 1998, after competition forced ITC to explore the options of sale, merger, and closure of IBD, ITC ultimately decided to retain the business. The ITC-IBD taken the challenges to use information technology to change the rules of the game and create a competitive business that did not need a large asset base. Today, IBD is a US $150 million company that trades in commodities such as feed ingredients, food-grains, coffee, black pepper, edible nuts, marine products, and processed fruits.

ITC e-Choupal and the Strategy

ITC followed a different media/communication strategy which is more elaborate and extensive in rural marketing so far, which benefits both the farmers and the organization. The strategy is use the Information Technology and bridge the information and service gap in rural INDIA which gives an edge to market its products like seeds, fertilizers and pesticides and other products like consumer goods.

With this strategy it can also enhance its competetiveness in global market for agri exports. A pure trading model does not require much capital investment. The e-choupal model, in contrast, has required that ITC make significant investments to create and maintain its own IT network in rural India and to identify and train a local farmer to manage each e-choupal. The company has initiated an e-choupal effort that places computers with Internet access in rural farming villages; the e-Choupals serve as both a social gathering place for exchange of information (choupal means gathering place in Hindi) and an e-commerce hub.

The computer, typically housed in the farmers house, is linked to the Internet via phone lines or, increasingly, by a VSAT connection, and serves an average of 600 farmers in 10 surrounding villages within about a five kilometre radius. Each e-Choupal costs between US $3,000 and US $6,000 to set up and about US $100 per year to maintain. Using the system costs farmers nothing, but the host farmer, called a sanchalak, incurs some operating costs and is obligated by a public oath to serve the entire community; the sanchalak benefits from increased prestige and a commission paid him for all e-choupal transactions. The farmers can use the computer to access daily closing prices on local mandis(governmentmandated markets), as well as to track global price trends or find information about new farming techniqueseither directly or, because many farmers are illiterate, via the sanchalak (the village farmer who runs the e-Choupal and acts as ITCs representative in the village). In addition they can also know about weather forecast(local) and best practices in the world from e-Choupal website. They also use the e-Choupal to order seed, fertilizer, and other products such as consumer good from ITC or its partners, at prices lower than those available from village traders; the sanchalak typically aggregates the village demand for these products and transmits the order to an ITC representative.

At harvest time, ITC o_ers to buy the crop directly from any farmer at the previous days closing price; the farmer then transports his crop to an ITC processing centre, where the crop is weighed electronically and assessed for quality. The farmer is then paid for the crop and a transport fee. Launched in June 2000, 'e-Choupal', has already become the largest initiative among all Internet-based interventions in rural India. 'e-Choupal' services today reach out to more than 3.5 million farmers growing a range of crops - soyabean, coffee, wheat, rice, pulses, shrimp - in over 31,000 villages through 5200 kiosks across six states (Madhya Pradesh, Karnataka, Andhra Pradesh,Uttar Pradesh, Maharashtra and Rajasthan).

Vision and Planning Behind the e-Choupals

Implementing and managing e-Choupals is a signi_cant departure from commodities trading. Through its tobacco business, ITC has worked in Indian agriculture for decades, from research to procurement to distribution. ITCs translation of the tactical and strategic challenges it faced and its social commitment into a business model demonstrates a deep understanding of both agrarian systems and modern management. The principles followed in implementing the e-Choupals are Re-engineer, Not Reconstruct Present Mandi system have some success factors in it. ITC decided to build e-Choupal on existing system. Already ITC has trading agents in local mandis for its tobacco business. It retained the efficient providers and created roles for inefficient people. It recruites and engages members of landscape thereby making their expertise available to ITC.

With this principle ITC can avoid the reinventing the system in areas where it can add no value with its presence i.e., in areas where efficient agents are there. Address the Whole, Not Just One Part The farmers various activities range from procuring inputs to selling produce. Currently, the village trader services the spectrum of farmers needs. He is a centralized provider of cash, seed, fertilizer, pesticides, and also the only marketing channel. As a result, the trader enjoys two competitive benefits. First, his intimate knowledge of the farmer and village dynamics allow him to accurately assess and manage risk.

Second, he reduces overall transaction costs by aggregating services. The linked transactions reduce the farmers overall cost in the short term, but create a cycle of exploitative dependency in the long-term. Rural development efforts thus far have focused only on individual pieces rather than what the entire community needs. Cooperatives have tried to provide agricultural inputs, rural banks have tried to provide credit, and mandis have tried to create a better marketing channel. These efforts cannot compete against the traders bundled offer. Functioning as a viable procurement alternative, therefore, must eventually address a range of needs, not just the marketing channel.

ITC e-Chopal provide services as a bundle what the entire agricultural community needs. Conclusion ITC e-Choupal, an innovative strategy which is elaborative and extensive in rural markets sofar. Critical factors in the apparent success of the venture are ITCs extensive knowledge of agriculture, the effort ITC has made to retain many aspects of the existing production system, including retaining the integral importance of local partners, the companys commitment to transparency, and the respect and fairness with which both farmers and local partners are treated.

13

Rural India Consumers

It was thought that passage of the Consumer Protection Act in India in 1986 would encourage consumers to stand up for their rights and lead to an overwhelming number of disputes in consumer courts. Although a consumer movement has yet to get going in India, existence of the act has stimulated the creation of many consumer organizations across the country. The number has such organizations has more the doubled in the last few years so that there are now 600-800 organizations in the voluntary sector.

The movement has not blossomed because not all of the organizations are active enough to make an impact, there has hardly been any unified action which would demonstrate their strength, and there has been no active consumer participation in the movements. Consumers claim that the lack of consumer education makes them passive and apathetic, and blame consumer organizations. The majority of consumers in the country are even unaware of the existence of consumer courts to which they make take their grievances.

Consumer rights organizations, however, counter that they lack sufficient funds and blame the government for their inaction. The author acknowledges criticism that the Indian consumer movement is elitist and considers the need to focus upon rural consumers, the significant contributions that organizations have made in laying the foundations for change, the need for consumer education, the need for specialists, the particular need for consumer protection with regard to health-related products, and support by voluntary health groups. Since 1967 when the High Yielding Varieties (seeds)

Programme (hereafter HYVP) was introduced in Indian agriculture, a lot has been written for and against the green revolution. It would, however, be erroneous to equate the green revolution with HYVP alone. The green revolution has to be understood as a broader ideology of rural transformation, whereas programmes such as HYVP, the Integrated Rural Development Programme (hereafter IRDP), and the like are specific institutionalized measures for translating the green revolution ideology into practice.

Even at the risk of appearing to be stating the obvious rather simplistically, it is necessary to emphasize that the green revolution as a package (ideology and programme) is to be defined as the large-scale application of modern science and technology to agriculture. Green revolution technology involves extensive use of farm machinery (as labour-saving, efficient devices), high-yielding hybrid seeds, energized well irrigation and lift irrigation, use of large quantities of fertilizers and pesticides, and the like.

In short, "extensive and intensive use of improved production technology and high yielding varieties of seeds" has been the essence of the green revolution. To varying degrees, all areas of rural India have been humming with developmental activity. Initial measures for rural development in the form of the Community Development Programme, land reforms, and cooperative institutions, introduced in the first two decades after Independence (1947-67), had not been particularly effective either in increasing farm productivity substantially or in removing the specter of rural poverty, unemployment, and ever-growing socioeconomic inequalities. The green revolution — the U.S.-sponsored technological package for agricultural development — was accepted in India somewhat overenthusiastically and uncritically.

It was hoped that improved farm production would not only be a lasting solution to the perpetual problems of rural poverty and hunger, but would also generate a new resource base — a launching pad for rural industrialization that would create new employment opportunities and would improve the quality of life at the grass roots to an appreciable measure.

In both theory and practice, the green revolution has been the dominant, much discussed orientation for rural development programmes in India for the past two decades. Meanwhile two midterm reviews of the net outcome of the green revolution and its impact on the Indian countryside were attempted by two separate voluntary institutions in the early 1970s, within just five years of the introduction of the HYVP and other similar programmes.

One of these was a symposium or ganized in 1973 by the Centre for the Study of Social Change that brought out both the positive and negative aspects of the green revolution. On the positive side it was claimed that the impact of the green revolution was apparent in food-grain production, which had increased in India in the post-HYVP period (1963-73), by 19.1 per cent over the pre-HYVP period 1961-65).

This increase was 87.2 per cent in Punjab, and 64.9 per cent in Haryana where the gains in production performance were impressive. Hence some scholars believed then that to improve the backward regions in general and agriculture in particular there was no alternative to the green revolution. However, this rosy picture of the green revolution was not endorsed even by its staunch protagonists.

For example, it was asserted at the CSSC symposium that the green revolution was not really taking place, that the new agricultural technology was accessible only to the large-scale farmers, and the prosperity unleashed by the green revolution was distributed differentially to the various categories of farmers, putting the small-scale and marginal farmers at a relative disadvantage. The reasons for differential distribution were obvious.

The high-cost, high-yield cereal technology of the green revolution called for substantial capital investments generally beyond the means of the majority of small-scale and marginal farmers. The second review was attempted in 1973 by the Londonbased, Halslemere Declaration Group (HDG). Its report assailed the green revolution as a propagandistic and highly misleading way of describing an annual growth rate of 5 per cent in wheat achieved in Punjab and Haryana from

1967 to 1973 with the introduction of HYVP, whereas the annual compound growth rate of food grain in India during the same period, using locally improved varieties of seeds, was about 3 per cent.

The Halslemere Group further criticized the Indian government for making institutionalized subsidies and cheap credit as well as other similar facilities relatively more accessible to big landowners and rich farmers than to small-scale and marginal farmers. The HDG report did admit that in Punjab and Haryana the trickle-down effect of the green revolution was partially visible in the improved daily wages for agricultural labour, which increased by 89 per cent from 1961 to 1968.

However, this seeming gain was totally offset by a rise in prices of about 93 per cent over the same period in spite of the substantial increase in agricultural production. In our view both the reviews discussed above were somewhat premature assessments of the green revolution in India. Until 1973 the green revolution measures had been introduced only in a few selected areas whose propensity to adopt new farm technologies was an established fact.

Moreover, the trial period of the five years from 1967 to 1973 was too short for any assessment to be fair. Thereafter several studies have reported their findings, revealing the complexity of the precise impact of green revolution measures on farm output per acre, on wages, on total household incomes of different categories of farmers, on consumption patterns, and on rural poverty alleviation in general. The research literature has grown into a massive body.

This proletariani-zation process is most striking in the green revolution areas. In view of this process, the improvement that the green revolution was expected to bring to the conditions of wage laborers appears to be no more than a distant mirage. At least the position of the rural poor — particularly agricultural labour — as a class is not likely to be altered substantially vis-à-vis the rich farmers who virtually monopolize economic resources and control credit institutions in the countryside. This chapter attempts to sift through some of this material to examine the nature of the impact of the green revolution on different sections of rural society. It is aimed at finding out whether or not this developmental strategy has succeeded in lifting a sizable section of the rural poor above the poverty line and in reducing socioeconomic inequalities in rural India. The exercise is based on the use of secondary source material.

Of course different researchers have used different measures to quantify growth or impact. Since such quantitative measures evoke disagreements among economists more often than they evoke unanimity of opinions, some sets of data are and can be used to support and sustain different standpoints or interpretations. It would be difficult to defend a claim that such an exercise is or even can be totally value-free.

Nonetheless we have attempted this assessment of the green revolution in the hope that it would provide us with at least qualitative answers to our questions and would suggest future lines for rural developmental strategies in India. Initially the green revolution measures were considered to be "scale-neutral." It was therefore expected that, whether it is HYV seeds, pesticides, insecticides, and fertilizers, or whether it is lift irrigation, mechanization of farm operations, and other farm subsidies, small landholders would benefit as much if not more than large landowners would.

The agricultural development bureaucracy working at the grass roots, however, has had different perceptions. Their understanding rarely conformed to the notion of scale-neutrality, and their actions almost always reflected a tacit pro-rich policy of rural development. Joan Mencher, for example, has reported that most of the agricultural officers she had interviewed in the Chinglepet district of Tamil Nadu appeared to be far from neutral.

"What they thought was needed to further the Green Revolution was to forget about small farmers (i.e. holders of less than 5 acres of irrigated land — defined as uneconomic holding), because they could not really contribute to increased production. To these officials, progressive farmers are those who have viable farms and who are fairly well-off." However, the reality was to the contrary. Mencher found that some of the small-scale landholders in Chinglepet were as interested in trying new inputs and were as innovative as the rich landowners were. But the farmer often lacked facilities to try new methods, and seldom received encouragement from the development bureaucracy.

The National Seed Project, started in India with World Bank assistance in 1976 as a part of green revolution measures, is yet another example of how rural development strategy is founded on similar pro-rich assumptions. Production and marketing of HYV seeds to augment production in agriculture has been the professed aim of this project. The actual implementation of this schemes — an integral part of the green revolution — has been critically investigated by Satya Deva using the specific case of the Haryana Seeds Development Corporation.

The policy underlying this project was to support the expansion of the private sector to maintain a reasonable balance between the public and private sectors in agriculture. The farmers in the project area of nine blocks of about 100 villages each were to buy two shares of Rs 100 each per acre of seed-producing land; share money was paid over five crops. Within four years of the establishment of the Seeds Corporation in Haryana, there were 285 shareholder seed growers.

About one-third of these were growing seeds in plots of five acres each, another one-third in plots of five to ten acres, and the remaining third used larger plots ranging between ten and 100 acres. Since seed was generally being grown in only parts of their larger land holdings, obviously mainly rich farmers with substantial holdings were benefiting from the project. After all, the very agreement terms requiring a farmer to buy two shares (of Rs 100 each) per acre favoured the rich farmers.

And at any rate, even the smallest seed grower with a five-acre plot under seed cultivation required an initial investment of Rs 1000 in share capital if he wanted to benefit from this scheme. As to utilization of seeds, a survey of sixty users and seventy-three nonusers of certified wheat seeds also brought out some interesting facts regarding the growing disparities in green revolution areas. "It was found that users came *only* from among landowners and high caste farmers and not even one came from among tenants or low (scheduled) caste ones." Satya Deva's conclusion suggests unmistakably that "agricultural development through the application of new scientific knowledge" was just a euphemism for using the public sector to promote the private seed industry.

In this process of development, the benefit of new scientific knowledge was allocated almost invariably to the upper-caste, rural, rich farmers; it seldom reached poor tenants and low-caste farmers who needed it most. The introduction of High Yielding Variety seeds as inputs in green revolution areas was thus yet another measure that created new kinds of inequalities, and at times exacerbated the old ones.

The pro-rich peasant bias of Indian rural development planning draws its justification from a fallacy that green revolution technology, being capital-intensive, suits rich farmers much better than small-scale and marginal farmers. The rich farmer alone has adequate resources to afford that technology of production, and expensive inputs are within the reach of only the more affluent farmers – therefore the latter are better placed to derive benefits.

This assumption is then developed into an argument, somewhat hypothetical, that overall yield rates as well as productivity per acre would be positively correlated to farm size. The built-in fallacy in this assertion has been clearly revealed by the findings of a pioneering survey conducted in Punjab by Bhalla and Chadha.

Conducted in three separate regions of Punjab, this survey, following the methodology of the thirtieth round of the National Sample Survey, selected some 180 villages and collected valuable data from 1,663 cultivating households. The methodology of classifying households into six categories demarcated exclusively by the size of the operational holdings suffers from certain inadequacies since it may not adequately describe or approximate rural social stratification.

Nonetheless, the findings of this survey are quite revealing. Analysis of the material costs, such as expenditure on seeds, manure, fertilizers, diesel, electricity, care of bullocks, and repair and maintenance of equipment has shown that in all three regions expenditure on material inputs per acre of cropped area was inversely related to farm size. This is likely to create an impression that green-revolution measures and inputs have truly benefited the small-scale and marginal farmers more than the rich. But such an assumption would be quite misleading.

In other words, there is enough evidence to suggest that the smallest farmers are at least as productive as, if not more productive than, the biggest farmers. Hence the argument of productive potentialities and efficiency of large farms is not sustained empirically; certainly it cannot offer any convincing justification for such an inequalitarian distribution of a scarce resource like agricultural land, as well as inputs through green revolution measures, as one finds in India in general and in Punjab in particular.

As Bhalla and Chadha tell us, "On marginal and small farms, a lion's share of material costs is on account of expenditure on draft cattle — some 48.63 per cent of total material cost incurred by the marginal farmers for the state as a whole." When it comes to per-acre expenditure on diesel, electricity, and repair and maintenance of machinery, costs continue to increase with farm size.

What is interesting and important to note is that despite their greater dependence on traditional capital inputs such as draft cattle, small farms were found to be supplementing their own stock of productive assets by renting machine services. Hence, per-acre expenditure on machine rental charges is much higher on marginal and small farms compared to large farms.

The Punjab survey makes it abundantly clear that the small-scale and marginal farmers, for whom competing with the rich farmers is an uphill task, do not hesitate to take risks. In fact, they are enterprising enough to make every possible effort to improve their farm inputs. But the entrepreneurial initiatives of small-scale and marginal farmers do not seem to have helped them substantially nor have they been able to reduce the growing inequalities in rural Punjab. The distribution of the 1,663 households in the Punjab survey demonstrates some of these inequalities. Bhalla and Chadha found that in their total sample there were 140 (8.4 per cent of the total) households having marginal farms of the average size of 1.6 acres; at the other end of the spectrum were seventy-four (4.4 per cent of the total) large farms of an average size of 32.8 acres.

Thus, the large farms were average about twenty times larger than the smallest farms. Such inequalities are then perpetuated and further reinforced by developmental bureaucracy's known preference for favouring owners of large farms on the grounds of the assumed high productivity of large farms.

This assumption is not, however, validated by the Punjab survey data which show that the agricultural farm business annual income per acre was Rs 754.50 in the case of the smallest farms and Rs 740.40 for the largest ones. In other words, there is enough evidence to suggest that the smallest farmers are at least as productive as, if not more productive than, the biggest farmers.

Hence the argument of productive potentialities and efficiency of large farms is not sustained empirically; certainly it cannot offer any convincing justification for such an inequalitarian distribution of a scarce resource like agricultural land, as well as inputs through green revolution measures, as one finds in India in general and in Punjab in particular. In India the farm policies pursued by the government from the 1960s onwards have tended to increase the degree of inequality between perennially irrigated regions and regions mainly dependent on rainfall for cultivation.

It is a known fact that farms in the wet areas are better served and reached by the state bureaucracy that implements development programmes than are farms in the dry areas. This is true because the green revolution package of programmes was devised with a primary focus on the perennially irrigated farms. Production of high yielding varieties of grain with heavy doses of fertilizers has mainly affected irrigated areas that are already favoured. Therefore, seen in terms of average household income, inequalities in rural areas are even more glaring in the relatively more irrigated and hence more prosperous areas.

Several researchers have undertaken studies comparing the relative economic opportunities in wet areas and in dry areas. For example, V. Athreya and his co-researchers have studied six villages sampled from two Panchayat Unions in the Tiruchi District of Tamil Nadu. Their inquiry was aimed at identifying the class status of individual households.

As a part of a wider inquiry into production relations, this study compared the mean incomes of rural proletarian households — both poor peasants and agricultural laborers — in the wet and dry areas. For poor peasants in the wet areas the annual cash income from agriculture was Rs 1,458 in contrast to Rs 346 in the dry areas.

The income disparity in the wet and dry areas here is in the ratio of 4.2 to 1.0, suggesting that in the wet areas a poor peasant household's agricultural income is more than four times the average income of a'corresponding household from the dry areas. However, poor peasants from the dry areas apparently make up the difference to some degree by supplementing their income substantially through nonagricultural sources.

Initially the green revolution measures were considered to be "scale-neutral." It was therefore expected that, whether it is HYV seeds, pesticides, insecticides, and fertilizers, or whether it is lift irrigation, mechanization of farm operations, and other farm subsidies, small landholders would benefit as much if not more than large landowners would. The agricultural development bureaucracy working at the grass roots, however, has had different perceptions.

Even more revealing are the disparities between the economic conditions — measured by mean incomes — of the poor peasants and agricultural laborers' households. The study by Athreya and others has further discovered that the cash wages from agriculture earned by a laborer household in the wet areas totaled Rs 1,030 compared to Rs 530 in the dry areas. Thus the wages in the wet area are almost twice the wages in the dry zone.

If one takes into account total cash income from all sources for agricultural labour households, then the disparity between the dry and wet areas is somewhat reduced, to the ratio of 1 to 1.5. Even so, the overall economic condition of wage labour in the wet areas remains one-and-a-half times better than that of laborers in the dry areas.

The most fascinating development in rural India is that even while the gap between economic conditions in the dry and wet areas is steadily widening, the economic returns of agricultural labour households are fast outstripping the incomes of the poorest peasant families. This process is occurring equally in both the wet areas and the dry areas. In the Tamil Nadu study conducted by Athreya and his associates, again it was found that in the wet areas the total annual average cash income (from all sources) of an agricultural labour household was Rs 1,686, while it was Rs 1,333 for a poor peasant household.

These incomes ranged between Rs 1,217 and Rs 1,103 for the laborer and poor peasant households respectively in the dry areas. Thus the gap is a more serious problem in the wet areas than in the dry areas. Despite its somewhat mixed findings, the Tamil Nadu study by Athreya and his associates highlights an unmistakable trend in the emerging class structure and the social inequalities or disparities attendant on it. Apparently the size of the rural proletariat is much the same in the wet-area and dry-area villages.

However, the greater polarization in the wet areas is reflected in the composition of the proletariat there. More than 60 per cent of the rural proletariat in the wet areas do not cultivate any land. They are thus truly "landless" laborers, without any tenurial, sharecropping, or proprietary holdings. In the wet areas, therefore, polarization has led to greater proletarianization, while the class of poor peasants (implying those with some land) is a minority. In the dry areas the reverse is the case. There only 36 per cent of the agricultural laborers do not cultivate any land (which means they are totally landless), but conversely it also means that 64 per cent of laborers do operate some piece of land and thereby swell the ranks of poor peasants. Thus in dry areas poor peasants constitute a majority.

Qualitative differences further reinforce the disparities between the agricultural laborers in the dry and wet areas. The rural proletariat in the wet areas is a more specialized work force with less nonagricultural income and higher forms of work-organization (gang-system etc.), which are practically nonexistent in the dry-zone villages. The most striking difference between the dry and wet areas covered by the Tamil Nadu study is seen in the size of the middle peasantry. In the wet areas a mere 21 per cent belonged to this category in contrast to nearly half (46 per cent) of the agrarian population which belonged to the middle peasant category in the dry region.

This polarized nature of class structure in the wet areas is also reflected in the fact that an impressive 14 per cent of the rural population in the wet areas are "surplus appropriators" — either rich peasants, capitalist farmers, cultivating landlords, or pure landlords. The proportion of surplus appropriators in the wet areas was three to four times higher than that in the dry areas.

The polarization process that accentuates rural class differences has been further intensified by the green revolution. Both the number of landless laborers and their proportion to the rural population as a whole have grown in most regions. Many tenants, including sharecroppers, have lost their lands since landlords were able to evict them.

A microlevel longitudinal study of two villages in the Mandya district of Karnataka conducted at two different points in time — 1955 and 1970 — has also revealed certain growing disparities. Here Scarlett Epstein found that as irrigation facilities were extended to the two villages, the acreage of holdings owned by upper-caste Lingayat and traditional peasant castes increased, whereas the percentage of land belonging to Adikarnataka (untouchable or Scheduled Caste) households actually decreased. Wet lands had also attracted outsiders – nonagriculturalists from nearby towns – to invest capital in buying farms. In the two Karnataka villages, Epstein also noticed that rural cooperative societies, particularly credit societies, were serving the wealthy farmers better than they did poorer farmers.

Rich farmers controlled cooperative institutions not for symbolic gains of 'status,' but to serve their vested interests. The richest could easily get loans from cooperative societies at an official rate of 6 per cent interest, which were just half the rate private moneylenders charged. The rich peasants were also reported to be in a much better position to buy large quantities of fertilizer on credit and thereby ensure agood harvest than were poorer farmers.

The inequitable income distribution among rural households from Punjab studied by Bhalla and Chadha reveals a similar, perhaps even more striking disparity. Their survey found that the total yearly farm business income of the smallest farmer's household – i.e. marginal farmers having less than 2.5 acres of land – was Rs 1,231, while that – of the biggest one – with operational holdings above 25 acres – was Rs 24,283. The disparity between the two incomes was found to be in the ratio of 1 to 20.

In other words, the small farmer who is no less productive than the biggest one, and whose entire family has to work on the farm, was much poorer than the one who hardly ever performed any manual work himself. It is particularly noteworthy in the findings of the Punjab study that the marginal farmers were working much harder to supplement their income through nonfarm sources (through means other than crop farming, such as dairying, poultry farming, etc.). Thus, the average annual nonfarm income of the smallest farmer (per capita) was Rs 392.53, but that of the biggest farmer was only Rs 352.84.

As a percentage of the total household income, 64.84 per cent of the marginal farmer's household income was from nonfarm activities, compared with only 12.84 per cent in the case of the biggest farmer. Equally interesting is the fact that although the farm business income of the smallest farmer was just one-twentieth that of the biggest one, the farmer's gross investment in farm assets per acre operated was about Rs 60 as compared with Rs 85 for the biggest farmer. Thus, the most marginal farmer in Punjab invested as much as about 5 per cent of his total household income for improvement of his farm assets; in the case of the biggest farmer, however, it was even less than one-half of one per cent.

The risk-taking propensity of the small-scale and marginal farmer is too evident here to need any more elaborate comment. The Punjab data have thus demonstrated that marginal and small-scale farmers are no less enterprising than rich farmers. The former are apparently more willing to take risks in their farm operations than the latter when the bulk of their household income is actually derived from nonfarm sources and activities.

This suggests, as Satya Deva has put it, "that a more equitable distribution of land would [in fact] lead to a much larger investment in the farm sector and hence would lead to a stupendous rise in productivity. The possibility of a truly revolutionary rise in [agricultural] productivity flowing from greater equality in land ownership has been all but missed [in Punjab]." Obviously this rise in productivity would be even greater than that which has been achieved so far in the so-called green-revolution areas where both policies and practice have favoured the rich farmer.

Rural inequalities begin to unfold their hitherto unnoticed dimensions if we look into some statistics on electricity connections on farms. Such statistics clearly indicate that only the needs of the rich farmers are catered to by electricity boards on a priority basis. For example, the Punjab Electricity Board had a system of providing priority connections on payment of Rs 10,000, which was subsequently reduced to Rs 7,000 a few years ago.

Apparently the system has now been discontinued; nonetheless, as of 30 March 1984 the Board still charged Rs 2,000 per service connection. It is interesting to note that the

Expert Committee which investigated the electricity tariff for agricultural consumers in Punjab was conscious of the fact that some 67 per cent of the 1.027 million farm operators in Punjab have landholdings of less than 4 hectares, with an average holding size of only 1.74 hectares.

Estimates of the Department of Economics and Sociology of the Punjab Agricultural University for the year 1981-82 showed that this holding size Was capable of generating an average disposable income of Rs 7,000 per annum – an amount which is about the bare maintenance level of income for an average family of six. But this was also the amount the Electricity Board in Punjab charged for providing connection on a priority basis.

At any rate, the Expert Committee mentioned above found that by 1983-84 there were just 350,000 consumers with agricultural connections, which constituted only a little over 14 per cent of the total consumers in the whole of Punjab. It can therefore be surmised that only about 35 per cent of the total farm-holders had sought service connection from the electricity board and that these must have been mostly rich farmers who alone could afford the high cost of service connection and installation.

The small-scale and marginal farmers are disadvantaged because very few of them can afford electricity and diesel. It is pertinent to note in this context that the Punjab survey by Bhalla and Chadha found electricity expenditure to be positively correlated to farm size.

Mechanization of farm operations in green revolution areas has undoubtedly strengthened the economic position of the rich farmers in India. However, for the landless agricultural laborers, some of the incidental effects of modernization of farm technology have been far too damaging, and in some instances they are simply disastrous. The degree of farm mechanization has exceeded all expectations in Punjab, so much that in 12,000 villages of the state there were as many as 200,000 farm machines of different types, mainly wheat threshers and combine harvesters. But the detrimental effects of such speedy mechanization are apparent when one considers that there were a total of 5,000 deaths in India resulting from farm machine accidents by 1978; of these 500 occurred in Punjab alone. A recent report has further revealed that every year more than 300 farm workers are incapacitated during the wheat harvesting season in Punjab. A majority of these accidents occur to workers while they are working on wheat threshers.

It is further estimated that in 1985 alone, nearly 1,000 farm workers in Punjab, Haryana, and Western Uttar Pradesh lost their limbs in thresher accidents. Most of the victims were migratory laborers, and it has been estimated that by the end of 1985 more than 10,000 farm laborers from Bihar, Uttar Pradesh, and Orissa had been maimed while working on such machines.

According to the official information given in the Punjab assembly on 7 September 1978, 841 cases of loss of limb or life occurred in the period from 1975 to 1978; of these eight agricultural laborers were killed and twenty-four lost two or more limbs. The government's attitude towards the problems of treatment and rehabilitation of the victims of accidents on farm machines is, however, that of total ambivalence. In Punjab, for example, the Workers' Compensation Act of 1923 has not been implemented properly.

This act requires farmers to insure their workers' against accidents. Insured farm laborers are supposed to get Rs 15,000 for the loss of a limb. Instead the government provides compensation which is usually just one-third of this amount. The government doesn't take effective steps to prevent farmers from using substandard threshers, nor does it prevail upon them to give rightful and adequate compensation to victims or to protect potential victims from such hazards.

The government clearly adopts a mothering attitude towards rich farmers, whom it protects by promptly reducing costs of consumer electricity connections as discussed earlier; but it does not consider it necessary to implement rigorously and urgently the provisions of the compensation act for farm laborers injured or incapacitated in machine accidents. The health hazards for rural agricultural laborers in the green revolution areas are not confined to incapacitation resulting from machine accidents. The agricultural work in these areas has become dangerous because of the increasing largescale use of poisonous chemical sprays for plant protection. The high-yielding varieties of seeds – used as an indispensable part of the green revolution strategy – are apparently highly susceptible to diseases, and in Third World countries poisonous pesticides are used both extensively and intensively for plant protection with little realization of hazards that result for agricultural laborers.

A recent report of the International Development Research Centre in Ottawa has revealed that there were 750,000 cases of acute poisoning with different varieties of pesticides. Half of these were reported from Third World countries, out of which one-third were reported from India alone. Victims of such poisoning are almost always agricultural laborers, and only rarely rich farmers themselves. For example, a study of seventy patients of acute poisoning reported from the civil hospitals of Vadodara and Surat (in Gujarat) in the three years from 1976 to 1978 were all agricultural laborers, including two women.

Surprisingly no legal protection is available to the victims of poisoning accidents on farms as the Workers' Compensation Act applies only to industrial workers in this respect. Comparing the income distribution and consumption units of both the rural rich peasants (magnates) and agricultural labour households in 1955 and in 1970, Epstein has concluded that the rich have grown richer and the poor have become poorer. Agricultural real wages had declined mainly because of increase in the number of labour households, and steady inflationary pressures.

Some other scholars who have examined the impact of the green revolution on the weaker sections of the population have argued, somewhat optimistically, that conditions of the rural poor – particularly agricultural laborers – are not necessarily deteriorating. On the contrary, these scholars see a general prosperity ushered in by modernization of agriculture in the green revolution areas, which percolates to the grass roots in rural society. When this percolation process is arrested by the rich through machinations, the agricultural laborers tend to get better organized and more militant, with the result that they struggle and thereby stand to benefit from higher wages and improved working conditions. Group bargaining thus strengthens the position of agricultural labour in rural power equations.

However, this optimism is founded on the assumptions of perfect competition and an ideal labour market. In fact, with imperfect labour market conditions like those in India, the bargaining power of rural labour is more apparent than real. There is also another assumption: that the green revolution necessarily raises the rate of agricultural growth in the affected areas.

But some scholars even question this assumption. Some economists tell us that in India agricultural production grew at best at a constant rate on an average over the period from 1950-51 to 1973-74; at best the green revolution might have just managed to arrest a tendency towards decline in the agricultural production growth rate observed in the late 1950s. In this context it is significant that owing to the growing capitalist penetration of the countryside there area fewer and fewer peasants, with large numbers of small and marginal farmers or poor peasants pushed into the ranks of landless laborers.

This proletarianization process is most striking in the green revolution areas. In view of this process of proletarianization, the improvement that the green revolution was expected to bring to the conditions of wage laborers appears to be no more than a distant mirage. At least the position of the rural poor — particularly agricultural labour — as a class is not likely to be altered substantially vis-à-vis the rich farmers who virtually monopolize economic resources and control credit institutions in the countryside. In general, findings of different studies show that the green revolution has had a contradictory impact on rural employment and agricultural wages. The pessimism of the Halslemere Group or Reddy's skepticism about the potentialities of the green revolution in raising the agricultural growth rate could be temporarily ignored. One may generously admit that by raising the productivity of land and by making it possible for farmers to grow two or even three crops on a piece of land, the green revolution has made it possible for rural workers to obtain more employment for the year as a whole.

But then Billings and Singh have discovered that in Punjab the demand for agricultural labour went up from fifty-one man-days to 60.1 man-days with the introduction of the Persian wheel as a means of irrigation and with the use of chemical fertilizers and pesticides. However, when pump sets, wheat threshers, corn shellers, and tractors are introduced, the average demand for labour drops down to 25.6 man-days.

In certain prosperous parts of India such as Haryana, the green revolution has led to formal contracts replacing paternalistic relations between capitalist farmer-employers and workers, but in most other parts of the country attached laborers are simply being thrown out of work or are being converted into casual day laborers.

Where mechanization of farm operations appears to brighten the employment opportunities and wages in green revolution areas, migration of workers from less favoured areas – such as Bihar, eastern Uttar Pradesh, Orissa, or Rajasthan – have tended to depress the bargaining position as well as wages. The pattern of consumption in the green revolution areas is equally inequitable, and there are a staggeringly high number of people below the poverty line. The case of Punjab – the most prosperous state in India – once again calls our attention to what is wrong.

The Bhalla-Chadha study has revealed that about one-third of the marginal farmers (cultivating up to 2.5 acres), one-fourth of the small farmers (cultivating between 2.5 and 5 acres), and one-fifth of the medium-scale farmers (cultivating holdings of 5 to 7.5 acres) were living below the poverty line, i.e. were living on a starvation diet: In the total sample of 1,663, 16.48 per cent of the farming households were living below the poverty line, and their proportion was positively correlated to the farm size in all the three regions of Punjab. If we add the 16 per cent of households of landless laborers, then the proportion of rural households living below the poverty line comes to over 32 per cent, which is distressing considering that Punjab is the most developed state in India. This finally raised doubts about the efficacy of green revolution technology, which was originally visualized as a poverty-alleviating measure.

Since the green revolution was projected as the new official ideology for rural reconstruction in order to effectively fight poverty, it is pertinent to examine here whether its implementation and consequences have actually alleviated poverty, or whether it has served only to widen the gap between the rich and poor farmers who represent the two extreme ends of the agricultural development spectrum in India.

In fact, all available statistics indicate greater and greater immiseration and pauperization as the green revolution technology package has spread in different parts of India. Studies of Indian poverty, measured by per capita expenditure and consumption of calories, further expose the hollowness of claims often made by planners of the green revolution. "The process of rural development during the 1960-69 decade has benefited the upper middle and the richest sections more than the middle, lower middle and the poorest sections."

Consequently socioeconomic inequalities in rural India have been steadily growing. While Dandekar and Rath found some 45 per cent of the total population to be below the poverty line at the 1960-61 prices, Bardhan came out with an even grimmer picture. He compared the proportion of rural population below the minimum level of living (defined as Rs 15 per month at 1960-61 prices) in 1960-61 with that in 1967-68. Without exception all the Indian states had experienced a massive increase in the percentage of rural people below the poverty line.

It ranged from 80 to over 84 per cent in states like Bihar, Orissa, Uttar Pradesh, and West Bengal in 1967-68. Even in Gujarat, the, most prosperous state, it had increased from 25.01 to 63.97 per cent; while it had increased from 40.14 to 67.61

per cent in Maharashtra, and from 13.56 to 49.98 per cent in Punjab. So, in the throbbing heartland of the green revolution, Punjab-Haryana, this percentage had nearly quadrupled from 1960-61 to 1967-68. This trend was confirmed a decade after Bardhan's study by a study conducted in 1979 by the International Labour Organisation.

Drawing its sample from the four states of Punjab, Tamil Nadu, Bihar, and Uttar Pradesh, this survey was aimed at determining trends in absolute and relative incomes of the rural poor. It revealed the steadily worsening distribution of income and the declining real income of the rural poor. In the rich farmlands of Punjab, the real per capita income was reported to have risen by 26 per cent during the 1960s, or at a rate two-and-a-half times as fast as in India as a whole. Despite this, the proportion of rural population living below the poverty line increased in Punjab from 18 per cent in 1960 to 23 per cent in 1970.

In Tamil Nadu the ILO study found that the percentage of population earning less than the costs required to buy enough food to survive had gone up from 36.04 per cent in 1961-62 to 48.63 per cent in 1969-70. Taking the "basic-needs line" into account these percentages had gone up from 66.49 to 73.98 for the corresponding years. About the social origins of the rural poor, the ILO survey has revealed that in all the states it was the agricultural laborers — the landless and near-landless families — who constituted the core of rural poverty. For example in Tamil Nadu, in 1971, 56 per cent of all cultivators, 85 per cent of "other workers" (mainly artisans) and 87 per cent of agricultural laborers were living below the poverty line.

However, some economists have provided us with a more optimistic picture. Using the data from the 32nd round (197778 revised) and the 38th round (1983-84) of the National Sample Surveys, C. H. Hanumantha Rao has pointed out that the decline in the number of people below the poverty line for the total population is estimated at around 12.5 per cent in rural areas as against 7.8 per cent in urban areas. However, he accepts that between 1977-78 and 1983-84 this decline is less notable for Scheduled Castes and Tribes (7.6 and 7.1 per cent respectively) than it is for the rest of the population for whom the rate (15.1 per cent) of decline in poverty ratio is more than double the rate for Scheduled Castes and Tribes.

Even assuming that Hanumanth Rao's inferences are close to reality, they imply an admission that poverty alleviation programmes, whether the Integrated Rural Development Programme (IRDP) or the National Rural Employment Programme (NREP), have failed to bring about a sizable reduction in the rural poverty ratio in a highly developed state like Punjab where between 1977-78 and 1983-84 the poverty ratio declined by only 17.1 per cent.

The poor performance of Punjab in poverty alleviation programmes becomes even more striking in the light of the following facts: (a) the average per capita consumption expenditure was the highest in Punjab (Rs 81.69 compared to the All India average of Rs 70.94), and (b) the expenditure on the anti-poverty (Poverty Alleviation) programmes like IRDP, NREP, etc. for the years 1980-84 was the highest in that state – Rs 31.22 for Punjab compared to the national average of Rs 8.33.

Two points come out clearly in Hanumantha Rao's analysis: first, that although the poverty alleviation programmes have succeeded in bringing about an appreciable decline in the proportion of the rural population below the poverty line, their performance is far less impressive for the Scheduled Castes and Tribes, traditionally the weaker sections of Indian society.

Secondly, the regional variations in the decline of the rural poverty ratio clearly suggest that more developed states, particularly Punjab, are not performing as satisfactorily as some of the less developed states, such as Madhya Pradesh, Orissa, and West Bengal. The implications of these points are too obvious to need any elaboration.

Agricultural growth may be a necessary but not a sufficient condition for reducing social and income inequalities. A more genuine political will and commitment to the philosophy of distributive justice must match the rising level of agricultural growth – a dictum almost dicounted in the Indian planning for rural development. There are other economists who do not share Hanumantha Rao's optimism about poverty alleviation measures, nor do they accept the official versions of the so-called achievements of IRDP or NREP.

For example, N. Rath has attempted to demonstrate the multifaceted failures of IRDP/NREP and has even commented that it should not come as a surprise if another National Sample Survey on consumption expenditure in the mid-1980s shows no visible impact of the IRDP on the dimensions of rural poverty in India.

A similar view was expressed earlier by Raj Krishna. To him the IRDP and NREP schemes have brought only small, often negligible, benefits to the rural poor; at least these are not substantial enough to ensure that the households that are often claimed by official sources to have been lifted above the poverty line would remain permanently above the poverty line. Raj Krishna's apprehension is fully justified in the light of the fact that the Draft Plan (1976-83) had estimated the size of the rural poor as 290 million in 1978, whereas a World Bank estimate had suggested that there are as many as 327 million rural poor.

In fact, Raj Krishna feared that despite the official claims about the decline in rural poverty ratio, the Sixth Five Year Plan figure of the poor population (339 million below the poverty line) for 1980 might grow to 472 million by the end of the century, which would be more than India's population at the time of Independence.

For nearly two decades now green revolution practical measures have been experimented with by the state in different parts of India. In the name of spreading green revolution technology, even the transnationals have been permitted to operate in rural areas under the official cover of the state. However, in most areas the green revolution has failed to raise the incomes of the rural poor appreciably, or to contribute substantially to their effective purchasing power. On the contrary, in many parts of India the real earnings of agricultural laborers and poor peasants were lower at the beginning of the 1970s than they were during 1960 and '61. Several studies of Punjab, Uttar Pradesh, Bihar, and Tamil Nadu have produced convincing data on this point. The main thrust of the green revolution has been towards productivity and growth.

The policy makers were concerned primarily with augmenting per acre yield. The assumption underlying the planners' priorities was that growth in itself suffices as it would have percolation effects and would in turn help in resolving problems of unemployment and poverty in rural India. This perspective now stands virtually discredited.

An alternative perspective is being advocated which does not treat growth and poverty alleviation as two distinct goals, but stresses that the latter has to be built into the growth processes. This approach advocates socialization of productive assets and more egalitarian distribution of these infrastructural facilities through the promotion of cooperative activity. Streaks of socialistic thinking are evident in the new perspectives on rural development in India.

However, ideas for reorientation and reorganization of IRDP, etc., seldom go beyond suggestions for decentralization of decision making, entrusting Penchayat bodies (Zilla Parishad) with responsibilities for planning and overall monitoring of antipoverty programmes, or for altering plan allocation priorities "for shifting from individual to group approaches," whatever that may mean.

Rarely do we examine the adequacy and suitability of the constitutional framework that treats the institution of private property as sacrosanct, and considers property, and not work, as a fundamental right. The pertinent question is whether and to what extent the given institutional framework is conducive to systemic changes — changes that is often offered as palliatives in the populist discussions on rural development and poverty.

The growing domination of the new class of rich farmers is a fact to reckon with and not to be wished away. It is naive even to believe that the green revolution and the IRDP measures (for poverty alleviation) constitute a point where growth and social justice converge or dovetail, and that both goals could be targeted simultaneously without any fundamental restructuring in the institution of property. Without some rethinking on development strategies for basic changes in the system, rural inequalities will never be reduced, let alone eliminated. India has been observing 15 March since 1989 as the National Consumers' Day. This day has a historic importance as it was on this day in 1962, when the Bill for Consumer Rights was moved in the US Congress. During his speech President John F. Kennedy had remarked:

"If a consumer is offered inferior products, if prices are exorbitant, if drugs are unsafe or worthless, if the consumer is unable to choose on an informed basis, then his dollar is wasted, his health and safety may be threatened, and national interest suffers." John F. Kennedy had equated the rights of the ordinary American consumer with national interest.

He gave the American consumer four basic rights:

1. *The Right to Safety*: To be protected against the marketing of goods which are hazardous to health or life.
2. *The Right to Choose*: To be assured, wherever possible, access to a variety of products and services at competitive prices: and in those industries where competition is not workable and Government regulation is substituted, an assurance of satisfactory quality and service at fair prices.
3. *The Right to Information:* To be protected against fraudulent, deceitful or grossly misleading information, advertising, labeling, or other practices, and to be given the facts s/he needs to make an informed choice.
4. *The Right to be Heard:* To be assured that consumer interests will receive full and sympathetic consideration in the formulation of Government policy, and fair and expeditious treatment in its administrative tribunals.

Kennedy recognised that consumers are the largest economic group in the country's economy, affecting and affected by almost every public and private economic decision. But they were also the only important group who were not effectively organised, whose views were not heard. Therefore, the Federal Government, by nature the highest spokesman for all people, had a special obligation to the consumer's needs.

Thirteen years later President Gerald Ford felt that the four rights constituted in Kennedy's Bill of Rights were inadequate for a situation where most consumers are not educated enough to make the right choices.

So he added the Right to Consumer Education, as an informed consumer cannot be exploited easily. While these rights served the interest of the American consumer well enough, they did not cover the whole gamut, because a global consumer did need, apart from them, other well-defined rights like basic needs, a healthy environment and redress. The Consumers International (CI), former International Organisation of Consumer Unions (IOCU), the umbrella body, for 240 organisations in over 100 countries, expanded the charter of consumers rights contained in the US Bill to eight, which in a logical order reads:

1. Basic Needs
2. Safety
3. Information
4. Choice
5. Representation
6. Redress
7. Consumer Education and
8. Healthy Environment.

This charter had a universal significance as they symbolised the aspirations of the poor and disadvantaged. On this basis, the United Nations, in April 1985, adopted its Guidelines for Consumer Protection.

BIRTH OF CONSUMERS' DAY

Considering the importance of Kennedy's speech to the US Congress on this day, and the resultant law, the CI took a decision in 1982 to observe 15 March as the World Consumer Rights Day from 1983. Peculiar though it may sound, 15 March is not observed as a special day in the world's largest and most pulsating consumer society - the US. But at home in India the Government, adopted 15 March as the National Consumer's Day. India is a country, which never fell behind in introducing progressive legislation - we were among the first in the world to introduce universal adult franchise for women. *Gandhi had rightly said*: "A customer is the most important visitor on our premises.

He is not dependent on us. We are dependent on him. He is not an interruption in our work - he is the purpose of it. We are not doing him a favour by serving him. He is doing us a favour by giving us the opportunity to serve him."

BIRTH OF 'COPRA'

The right to redress lead to the passing of the Consumer Protection Act (COPRA) in 1986 in India which has been defined as the Magna Carta of consumers but, it recognises only six of these eight rights:

1. Safety;
2. Information;
3. Choice;
4. Representation;
5. Redress and
6. Consumer Education.

Besides this statutory recognition, COPRA has succeeded in bringing about revolutionary judicial reforms by providing juristic quasi-judicial courts solely for redressal of consumer grievances (where a price has been paid), for adjudication within a limited time frame of 90 to 150 days. The rights of basic needs and healthy environment could not be provided in COPRA as these symbolised the aspiration of the poor and the disadvantaged, and were not the subject matter of priced commodities and services available in the market place. However, these are the backbone of peoples' movements in both the developing and the developed worlds.

Yet, inspite of pulsating movements, the rights of consumers could and were trampled on and often. There existed a vacuum in the definition of rights. It was often seen that boycotts would be spontaneous or organised in an adversarial situation, examples of, which are numerous. On an occasion in Calcutta a boycott of fish was successfully organized and the marketing cartel had to bow down, by cutting the inflated prices, rather than store rotting fish.

RIGHT TO BOYCOTT

Taking a leaf out of India's freedom movement, when Mahatma Gandhi had successfully organised various boycotts of foreign cloth, salt etc. we at CUTS, declared and adopted the 9th Consumer Right on India's Independence Day - 15 August 1990: "The right to resist and boycott any person, goods or services in the event of conflict with consumer's interest". This right was the ultimate one, to be used when all methods fail. And many a times they do: the seller does not heed, the administration does not listen, and the judiciary fails. This right inherently signifies consumer unity as an individual consumer can be helpless or even apathetic, and it is a collective action that succeeds.

While the right to boycott epitomises the enability of consumer rights, the right to basic needs remained abstract. It only defined a consumer's necessities required to survive and live a dignified life but it did not demand the means to obtain them - the right to work. However, the right to work is also vague, as this colloquially meant easy jobs, and did not feature in the existing charter of Consumer's Rights. In the interlude, a new Union Government in India raised a debate to recognise the right to work, as a fundamental right on the one hand, and advocating self employment schemes for everyone, including the poor, on the other.

Observing the societal disarray created by government job and dole schemes, whether permanent or temporary, and how they maim the spirit of enterprise which prevails in the mass humanity of India, 'CUTS' was inspired to declare and adopt the 10th (enabling) Consumer Right on 26 January 1991: "The right to opportunities to acquire basic needs which will enable one to work and to earn a living, without exploitation." This inherently demands execution of the state's singular responsibility to provide productive infrastructure, work ethos, job opportunities, social justice and economic equity. Both these rights were adopted at the Third National Convention of Consumer Activists at Calcutta during 1-3 November 1991, calling and urging the now (CI) IOCU to recognise and take suitable steps in expansion of the Consumer Rights internationally.

INDIA'S GLOBAL REPUTATION

Laws, rules, regulations and orders (for which India has unparalleled distinction in the Guinness book of records) alone do not protect consumers, but it is the rights' movement of people which produce results in a democracy. One of the greatest achievements of the Indian consumer movement is the enactment of the dynamic consumer law: COPRA. Coming 39 years after Independence, it has acknowledged the rampant consumer abuses, including those of the government owned public utilities like telephones, transport, power etc. These utilities, in the first place, were created as state monopolies ostensibly to protect consumers!

Critics of COPRA rightly conclude that it can't do anything about rising prices, but it has succeeded in bringing about fair-play in the supply of goods and services available in the market place, giving substance to the adage: Customer is King. Also, COPRA has encouraged active consumer bodies to demand, and perhaps see in the near future, independent Public Utility Regulatory Commissions to debate costing, pricing and promote competition.

This confidence emanates from the empowerment of voluntary organisations in COPRA and other consumer laws. While right to information is enshrined in COPRA, addition of the enlarged Right to Know in the fundamental rights chapter of the Indian Constitution would only result in meaningful empowerment - no more tight rope walking, but total glasnost.

In fact the Central Consumer Protection Council has recommended to the Government to enact a Freedom of Information Act on the pattern of a similar law in the US.

Another major achievement of the Indian consumer movement in the context of the world scenario, was to get the government in 1989, to adopt 15 March, the World Consumer Rights Day, as the National Consumers' Day. Unlike the Labour Day on 1 May, which has roots in the US, the Consumer Rights Day, which also has roots in the US, is not even observed there?

Today India is the only country in the world, which has exclusive courts for consumer redressal. At the IOCU's 13th World Congress held in Hong Kong during 7-13 July 1991 it came in for praise and developed countries were called upon to emulate. In the same year, these developments inspired Jim Sugarman, a noted US consumer activist and a close associate of Ralph Nader, to candidly observe: "India is getting a global reputation for the rapid development of its consumer movement."

BUREAUCRAT'S REVENGE

COPRA, which was amended by an ordinance in June 1993, is a mixture of sad and happy tidings. And tragic because of one surprise which our bureaucrats sprung onto the bill, a matter which was not even discussed in the high power working group of the Central Consumer Protection Council. The law then proposed a limitation of one year to file complaints, where none existed. An utter nonsense, which goes beyond the principles of our well established Limitations Act of 1963, wherein courts cannot be approached after the expiry of three years of the last cause of action.

Since there was no limitation period prescribed under COPRA, in one matter, the apex consumer court, the National Commission had pronounced that the principles of the Limitations Act do not apply but can be relied upon, though not religiously. This proposal would not only have put consumers at a terrible disadvantage but also annoy them badly. Most warranties and guarantees on goods expire in one year, and manufacturers often drag on many consumers during this period by attending to complaints, instead of setting it right or replacing or refunding the price of the defective goods. They will thus be deprived of the easy redressal avenue by this one-year 'deadline'. Consumers will be angry because the rule on the time limit of 90/150 days provided in COPRA for disposal of cases is practiced more in the breach, and cases drag on for years.

Under this situation, expecting consumers to meet a deadline will be very irritating. Granted that delayed complaints can be entertained, but that would mean a set of lengthy arguments on just the admissibility of the case. Fourthly, the law also enables consumers to file class action complaints, which incidentally always existed, but there can be no basis to determine the deadline in such matters. For instance, if the Motor Vehicles Act, 1988 provides for certain mandatory safety features which have been ignored by manufacturers; after research, we decide to file a complaint what would be the limitation period? Due to these arguments and lobbing the time limit was revised to two years, when the ordinance was put on the table of the parliament.

BELYING EXPECTATIONS

The law belied the consumer affairs Minister note in one statement of objects and reasons, wherein he says the working of the redressal agencies has helped to arouse the expectations of the people on several other grounds as well. Housing by way of plots or flats or houses has been covered under the definition of 'services' under COPRA.

Rather than adopt the words: 'real estate', as defined under the MRTP Act, 1969 from which the whole definition clause of services was borrowed in the first instance, a new jargon: 'housing construction' is added. This would mean that the consumer courts will only entertain complaints relating to: flats, land, houses purchased or to be purchased. In a beacon case involving a plot: Garima Shukla vs. UP Avas evam Vikas Nigam, the National Commission had held that the dispute is covered as a deficiency in the service of housing.

The Supreme Court upheld the orders of the National Commission. Among several other recommendations of the Central Council, another major one has also been diluted. In view of several protests by consumers, the council had agreed to recommend incorporation of an open, democratic and a transparent process of selection of the non-official members of consumer courts. The recommendation was that a selection committee headed by the minister and consisting of the secretary in charge of the department, a nominee of the chief justice of the state high court and two consumer activists (one a woman) would be the right form.

The bill now proposes a committee headed by the President of the state commission and the consumer affairs secretary and the state law secretary. It is thus heavily loaded against transparency. I have seen many a president of the State Commission sitting in the chamber of the secretary, especially when s/he is a retired high court judge.

By and large the secretary has to follow the minister's orders, therefore the transparency sought in the selection process will be doubtful. Presence of two activists would have perhaps changed the odds. However the president of the State Commission can only be appointed after consultation with the Chief Justice of the concerned high court, but those who know, consultation does not mean consent or concurrence. On several occasions, in spite of opposition, people have been appointed, after the so-called consultation.

THE BROOM STICK

The Council had made several other vital recommendations after long deliberations and critical debates, but they have been given the broomstick.

These were:

- Consumer rights were to be put in a separate chapter so that violations of the same could be an additional ground, if not the basis of a complaint. These will now continue as decorations in COPRA, for the central council to 'talk, about - only once in a year, as against twice as recommended'.
- Services rendered by public health care system and civic bodies were to be covered, as they are not charities but are run from the taxpayer money. So that consumer could get value for money and these

white elephants are brought to heel. The union health ministry prevailed.

- Lawyers were to be debarred except when the complainant had engaged one, or with his consent or if the consumer court directed the parties to engage lawyers, when questions of law were involved. This was recommended because lawyers often delay the settlement of cases by court craft etc. Apparently the belligerent lawyers lobby proved stronger.
- Writ jurisdiction of high courts has to be excluded by bringing COPRA under Article 323B of the constitution as their interference, particularly the Calcutta High Court, delays the proceedings especially when a hierarchy of appeals is provided under COPRA where the Supreme Court is the ultimate arbiter.
- Empowering Consumer Courts by giving them the authority to order cease and desist, or interim injunction or take suo motu action (of its own accord and on its own information) like the MRTP Commission, so as to meet the ends of justice have not been incorporated. For, bureaucrats felt that it would give unbridled power to over 450 district fora and 30 state commissions and that would have created havoc.

Some readers might remember the case of ITC LTD's Wills brand being injuncted by a Gangtok district judge, which cost ITC a large sum of money to get it vacated from the Supreme Court under its extraordinary jurisdiction. This type of case is a freak but without such power our consumer courts will be hamstrung in protecting the consumers interest, as it were.

Section 1(4) of COPRA says this Act will apply to all goods and services, therefore under the definition of services, where illustrations are given, it was understood that it was an all inclusive definition and exclusions had to be specified. To correct the anomaly, especially in view of the hectic lobbying by the medical fraternity and other professional groups, it was proposed to put a semi-colon, and add, "not limited to" before the illustrations. But this has also not been inserted in the amendment bill.

RECALLING UNSAFE GOODS

So much so for the bureaucratic revenge and/or sabotage. However there are many welcome steps, though confused as well, which will take the consumer movement considerably forward.

These are:

- Enhancement in the scope of relief under COPRA to stop the sale of and/or order withdrawing the marketing of hazardous goods. This will entitle consumers and consumer groups to challenge harmful goods, provided a law says so, like the BVO case when this toxic chemical was banned but continued to be used in soft drinks like Limca, Gold Spot etc.But the clause does not empower consumers to challenge hazards in services. For instance the Electricity Act provides for certain safety measures to be adopted by the suppliers, but consumers may not be able to challenge it. This is more so surprising when in all the consumer rights in COPRA 'services' have been added along with 'goods', and under the relief section power has also been given to consumer courts to remove defects and deficiencies in services.
- A major beneficial change has been added to cover agreements for purchase, as against the earlier provision for only goods or services actually purchased. This would cover disputes relating to booking of flats, cars, scooters and similar contracts, where delivery has not been made.
- Restrictive trade practices have been added, also enabling the courts to stop these, as well as unfair trade practices. This means that there would be a mini-MRTP Commission in every district.
- Monetary jurisdiction of a district forum has been raised to Rs 5 lakh, while that of a state commission

to Rs 20 lakh. Beyond this, the National Commission. Age limit of the members of the state commissions has been fixed at 67, while that of the national commission at 70. No mention of the age limits of members of the district forums.

- Complaints against goods purchased for commercial purpose will ordinarily not be adjudicable under COPRA save and except where such goods in dispute have been purchased by a self-employed businessperson like a taxi owner-driver.
- Costs would be awardable to consumers or their organisations that win cases. Simultaneously consumers who file frivolous or vexatious complaints could be penalised with a fine of upto Rs 10,000. And if they don't pay up, they could face a worse fate of paying a further fine of upto Rs 10,000 and/or undergo imprisonment of upto three years like other offenders.
- Following the Supreme Court order, in the Common Cause Vs Union of India case, administrative control of district fora will now be under the state commissions, who will in turn report to the National Commission. A proper reporting system and procedures will also be incorporated. Lastly, a quiet change has been incorporated to redefine the department of civil supplies as consumer affairs, which is what we in the consumer movement have been shouting for a long time.

14

Role of Government and NGOs in Rural Marketing

The important role of technology to promote sustainable agriculture and rural development cannot be underestimated in view of the needs within the agriculture sector often dominated by the highly differentiated small holder farming systems. There is need for generation of sustainable labour intensive agricultural production and large scale off-farm employment for a large number of landless and other rural poor.

In view of the limits reached in the expansion of agricultural land, any productivity increase has to come from intensification and or diversification of agricultural production to meet the need for both increased yields in food products per unit of land and also the requirement for increased rural employment opportunities.

Agricultural research and development budgets are very low in most developing countries within the region except in China and India (with R & D expenditures of US $ 330 million in 1997 and US $ 500 million in 1994 respectively). Yet there is high return on public investment in agricultural research which contributed to an estimated 20% of China's agricultural output growth from 1993 to 1996.

According to a recent international study published in 1999 the marginal internal rate of return of public agricultural research is estimated at over 50%. Agricultural research enhances the capacities of the small farmer to increase their production and productivity. Yet the full benefits in terms of employment and income from agricultural research for small scale agricultural producers depend equally upon complementary capacity building for improved post harvest and marketing skills. The rural poor which depend upon off farm employment will benefit from increased income opportunities from growing demand for non-farm products, tools and consumer goods in rural areas and the community in general through lower food prices.

Yet, the reality is in most developing countries that, small holder agriculture is largely bypassed in the development and dissemination of new technologies. While agricultural productivity enhancement starts at local farm level most small farmers still lack adequate access to credit, extension, improved high-yielding and drought resistant varieties, chemical fertilizers, appropriate farm tools and equipment. This is especially so in the case of women, who represent the majority of the agricultural producers in the region.

The daunting tasks of the developing countries in the field of research and extension in agriculture cannot be fulfilled by the public sector alone. Certainly not by the traditional departments concerned with agriculture, fisheries and forestry and their education and research institutions. Yet the private sector by itself is not keen on agricultural research related to low level technologies in response to local farming practices and constraints faced by the small farmers, small scale fishermen, local water users and women etc.

At the high end of agricultural research such as in biotechnology and plant genetic engineering (GMOs), the new technology development by the private sector is dominated by the international companies often acting as monopolies world-wide and unconcerned with small farmer related food and export crops produced in the region. Natural resources management technologies are rapidly increasing for promotion of sustainable agriculture, forest, water and fisheries development. Following the trend towards liberalisation of trade in agricultural products within the framework of Uruguay Round/WTO, there is increasing need in the region to promote agricultural exports which are consumer friendly in European, Japanese and US markets. Thus, new technology development will need to meet export requirements of food safety and quality of agricultural products. On a broader scale not only the products but the entire physical environment needs to be consumer friendly in terms of the standards set for environmental conservation, biodiversity and bio-safety, involving all stages including handling of agricultural products from farm to agro- industries and to the market.

Government institutions need a major shift in attitude in favour of use of local knowledge for improved productivity in local food crop production, water conservation, soil improvement, etc and develop demand driven new farm technologies in partnership with the local communities and small farmers. Government facilitation of small farmers' participation in decision-making on priorities and budget allocation for agricultural research and extension activities is of equal importance as collaboration with the private enterprises in high-end biotechnology research.

Of equal importance is research on sustainable and labour intensive agricultural production systems and on rural off-farm production and enterprise development. On this topic, APO organised in Iran a successful regional seminar in 1998. The outcome of this seminar was indeed recognition that government policies should give more priority to investment in public research on technologies to promote agro-industries based on local resources and to the establishment of institutional linkages between them and small farmers and rural workers, through their own self reliant, representative and self managed organisations, including the agricultural cooperatives.

An emerging area of research and technology development for enhancement of agricultural productivity, value added production, processing and marketing within the small holder agricultural sector is the development of rural telecom systems and related information technology and dissemination in rural areas. Rural universities, market information centres, schools, community centres, NGOs and farmers' groups become directly and independently interlinked in the exchange of information, education, extension and marketing activities. Such interactions enhance local opportunities for market oriented production as well as access to new technologies which better guarantee sustainable small farming systems development, natural resources management and off-farm enterprise development.

Information technology will also enhance transparency and efficiency in government decision-making on promotion of agricultural and rural development programmes and delivery of related public services. Yet while some villages or village clusters could become virtual rural service centres, in most cases the development of telecom based virtual market roads between the small farms and the urban markets cannot replace the need for real development of rural infrastructure, in particular farm to market roads and improved urban-rural people and goods transport linkages.

It will be obvious that research and technology development in these areas requires a well defined policy framework to incorporate new paradigms which respond to the ecological challenges in this sector. The paradigm should shift from "green revolution" to "evergreen revolution" and incorporate effectively the concept of pro-poor and gender sensitive small scale farmer participation and extension. The broader trade and ecological dimension of agriculture and rural development will demand a strong effort in human resources development as part of the needed institutional capacity building for management and coordination. Government needs to establish effective interactive frameworks of activities through a broad range of government institutions.

Agriculture and other relevant ministries need to be restructured to facilitate effective participation of small farmer led private sector and rural organisations in the planning, implementation, monitoring and evaluation of the programmes and activity mechanisms at decentralised levels between government agencies, private sector agro -enterprises and institutions including representative small farmers, producer and marketing organisations, agricultural cooperatives and community level NGOs. Asian countries are the major trading nations in food and agricultural products. Countries like Thailand and Vietnam are major rice exporters; Malaysia and Indonesia are rubber exporters and so on. About 26% of the total agricultural output in the East and Southeast Asia are exported mainly to USA, Europe and Japan, of which about 65% originates from Thailand and Malaysia alone.

While Asian countries are active international trade partners a whole range of policy issues are to be addressed within the framework of the Uruguay Round and WTO agreements. Asian countries are reluctant to further liberalize trade in agricultural products for two reasons. First, the concept of national food security/food self-reliance is still considered valid to protect the local small scale rice producers. Second, expected mutual efforts towards liberalisation of imports of food and agricultural products by the developed countries like in the European Union and USA have not taken place convincingly.

Yet there are major reasons for government institutions to be reformed and strengthened in order to promote agriculture and rural development through trade at regional and international levels. In most countries the customs departments and port authorities are among the most corrupt agencies, leading to the loss of income for the state and lack of adequate control on quality, disease, etc. Agreed quotas in imports and exports of agricultural products can not be monitored also with interstate borders, which totally lack control, transparency or even telecommunication equipment. Yet the greatest challenge for the Asia and Pacific countries lies in the development of highly modern technologies for food safety and quality control either upon demand from importing developed countries or following the emerging importance of imported GMOs, particularly the corn and soy products consumed by the Asian consumers.

According to the World Bank, about 50% of the annual development investment funds have to be reserved for meeting the sanitary and phyto-sanitary requirements (SPS) and conditions for protection of property rights (IPS).

Governments will need to build institutional capacities at the national and international levels (country representations, regional collaborative frameworks in collaboration with international agencies including UNCTAD, FAO, ILO and WTO) for research on various trade-offs in the new trade agreements and provisions in the existing agreements, which should provide necessary safety nets in trade, environmental protection and biodiversity conservation.

Many developed and developing Asian governments, though often do not subscribe to, remain rather passive towards a wide range of international conventions and codes of conduct, concerning sustainable management of agriculture, fisheries and forestry or related to quality of food and nutrition, environment, food security, etc. The whole body of international agreements affecting food and agriculture has to be taken into account within the framework of globalisation and trade in terms of their impact on food security and sustainable agriculture and rural development.

Governmental level meetings in this region, facilitated by FAO for its 26 South and Southeast Asian and 12 Pacific Island member countries, provide a regional platform for a dialogue and joint decision-making on these matters. Cereal trade liberalisation will have a profound impact the on small-scale rural food producers in both cereal production and processing. The World Bank recognises that there will be large scale changes in the agricultural sector affecting small scale producers which need to diversify their crop and agricultural production and specialise in local food products for urban consumer markets.

To meet WTO related requirements in the light of the prevailing low quality of both the social (education and health) and agricultural support services in rural areas, government institutions need to be restructured and decentralised to establish effective partnerships with private institutions, especially with the representative small agricultural producers' organisations and agricultural cooperatives. Agricultural cooperatives, used to mainly distribute agricultural inputs or related purposes, often are not able to respond to the needs of local entrepreneurship development either as agricultural or as off-farm producers. This policy area will become important within the context of WTO as the private sector is unable to fill the gap in the provision of services. Secondary level agricultural cooperatives in agro-processing and marketing will have to be developed and, where necessary, rehabilitated.

Producer groups need to be organised and trained as market oriented entrepreneurs, able to develop specific urban market demand driven production capacities based upon diversification of their produce. Export of food and agricultural products through effective agricultural cooperative networks in the Asian countries will be a major policy area in the promotion of agriculture and rural development.

To effectively guide this process, the Government needs to develop a policy dialogue. Government institutions need to consult and collaborate in the design and implementation, monitoring and evaluation activities at the local, regional and national levels with the agricultural cooperatives and small farmers based commodity organisations. A major effort in education, training and provision of credit for small and medium enterprise development will be needed.

Finally public investment for rural infrastructure will be needed to improve rural-urban transport and market linkages. Telecommunication networks and a consistent rural energy development policy are needed. Rural electricity production, if based upon fuel wood and biomass, by small farmers and rural poor, will stimulate income generation and rural employment and thus contribute to rural poverty alleviation.

It is evident that governments alone cannot mobilise all the necessary resources for the needed investments. Therefore practical solutions will have to be found at the local community and regional levels. Also large-scale donor support from the developed countries, World Bank and ADB will be needed. The most important factor is the change in attitude among the political leaders and senior level government officials in favour of agriculture and rural sector and the needs of the rural poor. That the road will be long and arduous may be clear from a comment by Mr. Thomas Fuller on the meeting of G8, word's most powerful economic countries in Geneva (Herald Tribune of 18 July, year missing?). "For Italy, globalisation had bad aspects during their Long March to modernity: inequality of incomes, concentration of wealth, poor working conditions and exposure to environmental degradation, political corruption and bribery, organised crime -all the social phenomena that crowd around any environment in the middle of radical change.

Then comes the final shot: I am sure many Italians wish to be as boringly normal as countries like Switzerland and Sweden. Here is the news they will get their wish WITHIN A CENTURY". In this long-term perspective the major issue in Asia and the Pacific is not to present ambitious agricultural and rural development policies and plans but to allocate adequate resources and to immediately put them in to operation with effective participation of the rural poor.

Environmental opposition groups have often formed in rural communities as a response to sweeping environmental regulations. They do not match the stereotypes of nongovernmental organizations funded by extractive resource industries, but have a solid grass-roots membership that is stalling, if not altogether thwarting, the momentum of the environmental movement.

Jay Hair, former president of the National Wildlife Federation, once commented that the members of the environmental opposition "...are people who would convert our national heritage to short-term wealth and damn the consequences". Another environmental leader, Sierra Club Executive Director Carl Pope, spoke of the opposition groups by noting, "Quite simply, we are in a total war over the future of the environment".

While the militaristic rhetoric may be overstated, environmental organizations have expressed alarm at the growing presence of opposition groups and their perceived influence on the decisionmaking process. This- chapter addresses the reasons and process by which nongovernmental environmental opposition groups influence environmental policies in rural areas. It uses Easton's definition of public policy-the mechanism through which values are allocated authoritatively for the society-as a starting point, and uses the theoretical framework of plural ism and the development of rural studies as a way of studying nongovernmental organizations (NGOs). It continues with an overview of the literature that explores perceived differences in attitudes towards environmental protection between rural and urban residents.

This is followed by a typology of rural environmental opposition groups and an analysis of the impact of these groups and their members in confronting, and in some cases, thwarting the efforts of mainstream environmental groups.

PLURALISM

For most policy theorists, the best paradigm for understanding the policymaking process is pluralism-the belief that people and groups pursue their self-interests through government. The early works of Bentley identified pluralism as the dominant framework for making policy decisions, made through a democratic process that involves bargaining and negotiation among groups and individuals with competing perspectives.

A more complex model of pluralism, advanced by Truman, Key, Cobb and Elder, and Dahl, argues that democracy resides in the people, who are regarded as political equals with the capacities, resources, and institutions they need to govern themselves and make policy decisions in a responsible manner. The contemporary model also notes that pluralist democracy demands that political power be fragmented to prevent a central government from dominating other institutions or to eliminate the possibility that any one group controls policy.

At the same time, pluralism can be contrasted with James Madison's view that "factions" or special interests are to be feared because they ignore the greater public interest. Proponents of pluralism instead consider interest groups critical to policymaking, because they force elected officials to be more responsive and accountable, and their decisionmaking becomes more public and less secretive.

Critics of pluralism, such as Schneider and Ingram, argue that policy issues can be manipulated by the creation of "grass-roots uprisings" that actually are carefully orchestrated public opinion marketing strategies that generate hundreds of letters or telephone calls to elected officials. "Mobilization that simply intensifies the pursuit of narrow special interests through increasingly deceptive and manipulative practices will exacerbate the problems of governance".

RURAL STUDIES

The debate over pluralism and the role of NGOs has been mirrored by the growth in the study of environmental attitudes of persons living in rural areas, especially in the several disciplines of public policy, including sociology. The study of rural communities in the United States began at the turn of the twentieth century, and by the mid-1930s researchers had begun their attempts to develop a connection between rural life and attitudes towards natural resource use.

Field and Burch termed this field of study as a more formal, or a classical ecological, explanation of behaviour and resources. Two groups, the Rural Sociological Society and the Natural Resources Research Group, gave legitimacy to the emerging subdisciplines of rural sociology and social ecology. The explanation for differences between rural and urban residents' support for environmental protection-and consequently, their participation in interest groups-continues tod ay.

There are a number of competing definitions of what constitutes a rural area; the Census Bureau in the Department of Commerce has a standard that differs from that used by the Farmers Home Administration, for example. One generally accepted definition takes into account an area's population (counties with no places of 2,500 or more population) and isolation (location relative to urban areas).

Other factors include the homogeneity of the culture, economic, and social character. What factors have led to the formation of environmental opposition groups in rural communities? For nearly five decades, researchers have grappled with questions about group formation and whether it is possible to identify the factors that influence perceived urban/rural differences over environmental protection. The conventional wisdom has been that rural residents have sharply different attitudes towards the environment than do urban dwellers.

As a result, rural communities have been viewed as pockets of anti-environmental sentiment and fertile ground for policy entrepreneurs seeking to gain converts to join opposition groups. Pioneering work on the nature of groups by Truman found that groups tend to form most often during periods of stress or rapid change, when people with shared interests interact more frequently.

This factor clearly was applicable in the mid-1970s and 1980s, when changes in the rural economic base and increased environmental regulation by federal authorities were the norm. But combining group theory with studies of support for environmental protection has resulted in a lack of consensus. Initial studies showed that rural people consistently had lower levels of support than city dwellers for environmental protection.

In looking at variables that explain the difference, Lowe and Pinhey concluded that factors like exposure to environmental degradation in cities, or the socialization process for people in rural communities that results in utilitarian attitudes towards natural resources, were inadequate to explain support or the lack of support for environmental protection.

Later studies attributed the difference in environmental attitudes to economic and social variables such as age, wealth, gender, and education. However, Gallup polls interpreted by Hueber showed little difference in the expression of environmental attitudes based on key demograph ic variables. Similarly, a study of differences in rural residents' views on forest issues concluded that rather than focusing on a simplistic dichotomous rural-urban distinction, researchers would be better served by looking at the inmigration of urban residents who give a "voice" to preexisting pro-environmental attitudes.

More recently, McBeth and Foster found that rural culture in the West, at least, has been manipulated as a consequence of the "Western myth"—the use of cultural symbols of independence, self-sufficiency, and local control. Environmental opposition groups, they argue, have used the Western myth and related populist arguments to turn rural residents against the environmental movement.

However, this view treats the environmental opposition leadership as elite urban outsiders preying on the fears of poor rural residents who do not have the resources to form groups on their own. Except in limited situations where an organization is clearly industry-sponsored is this true. This study found such groups to be the exception rather than the rule.

Studies of political organizations by Moe and Knoke and Wood became the foundation for the work of Russell, whose research on grass-roots political organizations found that low-income individuals, who are often the economic base of rural communities, joined groups for three reasons: self-interest, anger, and the group's organizational identity.

Of the three, selfinterest was thought to be the mainstay of membership incentives, although people who have been frustrated because of a perception that their needs have been ignored for too long also have an incentive to join environmental opposition groups.

A TYPOLOGY OF ENVIRONMENTAL OPPOSITION NGOS

The core finding of this analysis is that environmental opposition NGOs are part of a complex and complicated movement that is more diverse than many observers have recognized, with their roots firmly established in rural areas. The environmental opposition movement can be divided into three segments: wise use, property rights, and county supremacy groups.

There is, however, considerable overlap in their goals, types of leadership, and strategies. Of particular interest is whether these groups have a truly grass-roots constituency, whether they are initially grass roots and are assimilated under an umbrella of coalitions, or if, as is often claimed, they are corporately financed or directed.

RURAL GRASS-ROOTS OPPOSITION GROUPS

There are a number of opposition groups that even leaders of the mainstream environmental movement agree are community based and organized. Most indeed stem from issues particularly salient to rural residents.

Such is true here many of the organizations considered part of the wise use and property rights arms of the environmental opposition are found in the rural West, where the environmental movement is blamed for wrecking local economies besieged by the implementation of the Endangered Species Act or other federal laws.

One of the first opposition groups, now called the National Inholders Association, was founded in 1978 by Charles Cushman to protect the rights of property owners, or inholders, who own land in or near national parks and forests. Their membership is now estimated at 16,000, almost all of whom live in rural areas. Washington State, targeted as one of the nation's most important environmental battlegrounds, is where Cushman initially "put a name to the vague fears of small-town, recession-bound America".

Smaller grass-roots opposition groups that support the goals of the wise use movement, like the California Desert Coalition, Protect Industries Now Endangered (PINE), Workers of Oregon Development (WOOD), and Timber Resources Equal Economic Stability (TREES), were founded by local activists who neither seek nor receive support from urban interests; their leadership and resources are almost always from rural residents.

Similarly, the county supremacy groups identified by a number of researchers as operating almost exclusively in the rural West have returned to the themes first espoused by the leaders of the 1978-81 Sagebrush Rebellion. Feeling distanced from a federal bureaucracy they believe no longer represents the interests of rural residents, especially ranchers and small mining operators, county supremacists have challenged federal control of public lands, mostly unsuccessfully, in several judicial venues. However, individual activists and small opposition groups in states like Nevada, New Mexico, and Idaho that have vast tracts of federally owned land lack the elements of organizational structure and widespread geographical support of the Sagebrush rebels.

UMBRELLA GROUPS

The most established of the umbrella opposition organizations, the Centre for the Defence of Free Enterprise (CFDFE), has attempted to capture the concerns of smaller groups as a coalition of interests. The organization grew from the partnership of two policy entrepreneurs, Ron Arnold and Alan Gottlieb, who joined forces in the early 1980s to create what they termed the wise use movement. In 1989, they published their mission statement, made up of 25 goals for its supporters to work towards.

Among the issues CFDFE has tackled are a major overhaul of the Endangered Species Act, the opening of most public lands for mineral and energy production and off-road vehicle use, and eliminating restrictions on development. By developing such a broad agenda, wise use leaders have been able to attract a diverse constituency of interests, some of who are in agreement with the majority of the movement's goals, along with others who have limited themselves to specific issues. Most wise use supporters live in rural communities where issues involving extractive industries and property rights are of critical importance.

Cushman later included the National Inholders Association under a new umbrella property rights group, the American Land Rights Association (ALRA). Headquartered in Battle Ground, Washington, with a legislative office in Washington, DC, the ALRA has as its motto "Unlock the Bureaucracy."

Among the ALRA's targets has been an ecosystem management project for the Columbia Basin, developed under the Clinton administration, which planned to restrict grazing, mining, logging, and private property covering 144 million acres in seven western states. The ALRA was in turn a member of an ad hoc coalition of more than 23 other groups attempting to prevent the project from moving forward.

This strategy accounts for the proliferation of many umbrella organizations. By supporting each coalition's agenda, the umbrella groups are perceived by the media and the public as being larger and more powerful. But many of those credited as group "members" are not members in the traditional sense of being joiners and are perhaps better classified as "adherents" to the issues that are the focus of the umbrella organizations.

CORPORATELY-FINANCED OR DIRECTED GROUPS

It has been argued that corporate interests began their support for the creation of opposition groups in rural communities as a result of two factors. Their support began when extractive industries felt the sting of federal natural resource legislation and was followed by the increasing clout of the growing environmental movement of the 1970s and 1980s Initially hardest hit (or at least recognized as a threat to the timber industry) were two highly publicized protests against a proposed logging ban in California in 1976. A populist call to arms can be found in an advertisement placed in the magazine American Timberman and Trucker.

It read: Our timber communities are under siege. If we do not unite we will perish, the victims of the radical preservationist movement that is destroying our communities and timber industry. Mills are closing. Hard-working men and women-family people-are losing their jobs, the direct result of preservationist lawsuits and timber sale appeals that are locking up our forests. We must unite in our common defence. Some rural environmental opposition groups are what some observers call "astroturf" or phony NGOs because they are organizationally connected or funded by particular industries or businesses. While it is true that some rural grass-roots groups may have started at the urging of industry, many now operate independently, developing their own leadership and financial resources. For example, Women in Timber, whose chapters were initially underwritten by large timber companies, are no longer identified with the logging industry and operate autonomously.

Another large group often associated with corporate interests is the Blue Ribbon Coalition (BRC), founded in 1987 to bring together various interests associated with off-road recreation. Its board of directors is almost exclusively made up of representatives from the rural West, although the BRC serves as an umbrella for non-Western groups like the Association of Wisconsin Snowmobile Clubs and the Pennsylvania Trail Riders Association.

The BRC and its coalition members are strongly allied with the companies that manufacture and sell off-road vehicles and products, such as Kawasaki, American Honda, and Mikuni Racing Carburetors. Its corporate contributors also represent firms like the Grand Targhee Resort in Wyoming, extractive resource companies like the Rocky Mountain Oil and Gas Company and Boise Cascade, and the multi-interest, Idahobased J. R. Simplot Company. A study commissioned by the Wilderness Society suggested that the BRC's connection to Japanese commercial interests be exposed because they provide d "substantial support" to the BRC.

BRC officials respond that mainstream environmental groups have overstated the importance of the corporate influence and that the majority of their support is in the form of advertisements in the BRC's newsletter. This is no different, the BRC notes, than the ads placed by General Motors in the Sierra Club magazine, which does not in and of itself back claims that the organizations are fronts for or financed by large corporate interests.

Besides, BRC officials say, their small budget (less than $200,000) does not provide the group with resources to begin to match those of mainstream groups. One of the reasons why it is so difficult to track corporate control of the environmental opposition is that industry groups, rather than visibly supporting a "grass-roots" group, will instead pay a professional organizer to come into a community and "organize" local residents. The groups may have innocuous-sounding names, such as Citizens for a Responsible Environment, a grass-roots organization supporting a Vancouver-based gold mining company, made up of rural residents who simply state that they are supporters of a local employer.

Another opposition group, People for the West!, has a budget 10 times larger than the BRC, with the majority of its corporate members representing the mining industry. Still, the organization refers to itself as a "Grass-Roots Campaign Supporting Western Communities." But despite environmental groups' attempts to paint the opposition with an industry brush, even their own research shows that this is a local movement driven, primarily by local concerns, not national issues.

The movement's members are apparently genuinely grass-roots. That is, they are local individuals addressing local concerns who joined with other individuals, groups and funders as a matter of common concern...it is foolish to lay this movement solely at the doorstep of Exxon, Georgia-Pacific, or Kawasaki. Real people have perceived a real threat. The national wise use movement is attempting to give these grassroots groups coherence, it did not give them life.

THE IMPACT OF RURAL OPPOSITION NGOS

To date, rural grass-roots opposition groups' impact on the policy process has been minimal, especially if compared with the efforts of traditional business and industry organizations and their efforts to weaken environmental protection regulations.

The more enduring nature of business influence, which dates back to the mid-twentieth century, coupled with the use of a wider range of political strategies, uses such tactics as political action committees, contributions of "soft" money to political parties, and bureaucratic end runs that cannot be matched by rural groups. The opposition groups simply do not have the legal and financial resources of thousands of corporate interests, even when business is divided itself on how to reduce the impact of legislative initiatives like the 1990 Clean Air Act. By using the criteria of Rochon and Mazmanian's model for measuring policy success, rural groups have been unable to gain new advantages for their members, have not been accepted as valid representatives for newly defined social interests, and have not developed the ability to change social values.

In addition, the environmental opposition has not changed the salience of environmentalism for the American public. Studies continue to show that while environmental issues may not always be at the top of the policy agenda, there continues to be support for environmental protection even when there are difficult trade-offs involved.

Although it is difficult to identify any national-level victories for the environmental opposition, it is important to note that much of the focus has been on rural areas, especially where the economy has traditionally been based on extractive industries like logging or mining and where their message is more resonant than that of environmental groups. In 1993, a 50-state assessment of the influence of the environmental opposition determined that while the national movement was "more smoke than fire," its true strength lies at the local level, where it is fully engaged in scores of resource issues. If more contemporary research findings are accepted that indicate there is little difference between the environmental attitudes of rural/urban residents, then what accounts for the fact that environmental opposition NGOs are predominantly found in rural areas? There are four explanations that apply specifically to this context.

First, the fact that environmental opposition groups find niches in rural communities is exemplary of the policy window/policy entrepreneur model described by Kingdon. Fledgling grass-roots opposition organizations in rural areas frequently lack sufficient resources or skills to maintain a viable or visible political presence. Additionally, the lack of local leadership has provided an opportunity for policy entrepreneurs to take advantage of a policy window—a process described by Kingdon as the way in which individuals invest their time, energy, reputation, and money to promote an issue in expectation of a return or future gain. Policy windows open unpredictably and infrequently and may stay open for only a short period of time.

The window may close when participants feel their issues have been sufficiently addressed, when they fail to get a return on their investment or resources, when a focusing event passes, when there is a recurrence of the same kind of personnel changes that opened the policy window initially, or when there is no readily available alternative to meet the needs of the policy entrepreneurs and their followers.

Kingdon's model is an ideal way of explaining how rural NGOs have been "captured" by policy entrepreneurs like Chuck Cushman. One policy window opened in 1978 when Congress enacted the Omnibus National Parks Act and the National Park Service (NPS) adopted a policy of reducing private landholdings within the parks because they were incompatible with the mission of preserving scenic wilderness areas. Cushman, who had purchased a vacation cabin inside the boundaries of Yosemite National Park in 1970, organized his fellow property owners to oppose the NPS policy-an action that led to the formation of the National Parks Inholders Association—a grass-roots group representing the interests of rural residents.

The policy window opened for Cushman in the late 1970s for a number of reasons. His ability to organize inholders came at a time when the Sagebrush Rebellion was beginning to unite rural landholders and extractive resource interests in the West. The election of Ronald Reagan in 1980 provided Cushman and other grass-roots environmental opposition groups a political climate where their issues received a highly receptive response from the president.

That momentum was sustained throughout the 1980s and early 1990s as the policy window remained open for other entrepreneurs who developed their own organized opposition to federal and state national resource and property rights policies. As a policy entrepreneur, Cushman was able to use his rhetorical skills and organizational capabilities, just as Ron Arnold and Alan Gottlieb parlayed their marketing, direct mail, and fundraising experience in the formation of the CFDFE.

While providing technical assistance and personal attention to small groups in rural communities, all three men remain in positions of authority because they are rarely challenged and their organizational resources are unmatched. Second, umbrella opposition groups have used the same strategies as mainstream environmental organizations to effectively organize and communicate with the rural residents with whom their antigovernment messages resonate so strongly.

Cushman has boasted that opposition groups "read their [environmental groups] book on organizing". Because of their background, organizers like Gottlieb used computer technology to manage a mailing list with an estimated five million names of sympathetic supporters. The expansion of the World Wide Web, the availability of free electronic mail, and affordable facsimile machines have given even the most isolated rural resident a connection to hundreds of publications, organizational websites, and chat rooms to voice their concerns.

Those who live in remote areas are now able to be apprised instantaneously of legislative alerts, conferences, rallies, and virtual picket lines. Prior to the enhanced information superhighway, rural residents were unable to participate as easily as they can now, matching the resources of urban environmental group members byte by byte.

Third, environmental organizations appear to have been taken off guard, or were simply unprepared for the scale of opposition that formed relatively quickly in response to federal environmental statutes and regulations. Subsequently, they faced bitter accusations by their own members, who perceive that the movement is in a state of disarray.

By focusing attention, staff, and resources on well-funded national offices in New York and Washington, DC, and highly publicized accounts of salaries paid to attorneys and leaders, critics argued that groups like the Sierra Club and the Wilderness Society may have squeezed out grass-roots support that was the hallmark of the environmental movement during its growth years. Brick notes that an increasingly divided environmental movement came face to face with a well-organized and ideologically energized countermovement at a time when other social issues such as welfare, health care, and crime loomed larger than the environment in voters' minds.

Others have criticized the environmental groups for failing to tend to their original base of support. The mainstream groups now rely largely on an urban membership, with little effort (at least until the rural opposition surfaced) at recruitment in rural areas. As a result, the environmental movement itself tends to be perceived by rural residents as made up of elitists who lack an inclusive agenda, even to the point where some have accused the groups of being insensitive to rural residents living in or near areas the mainstream groups hope to save.

As one author notes, the large environmental groups are seen as catering to an urban, wealthy constituency that wants to preserve Western public lands as their summer playgrounds. Finally, rural residents who feel distanced or antagonistic towards the government's natural resource policies often act strictly out of self-interest. Although this attitude may be shared by other individuals, it is a distinctive element that characterizes the early rural opposition, best illustrated by Nevada rancher Wayne Rage, the plaintiff in the property rights case Hage v.

United States, initially filed in 1991. Hage and his attorney Mark Pollot, a former Reagan administration official, used the case as the foundation for the grass-roots group Stewards of the Range. Hage filed suit after he refused to take his cattle off federal lands that the government alleged were being overgrazed.

He sought compensation when he argued that the Nevada Department of Wildlife's introduction of elk reduced the grass his cattle might have eaten. The U.S. Forest Service confiscated his cattle, sold them, and kept the proceeds. Hage has become a martyr for many rural residents who have joined grass-roots groups in hopes t hat someday they, too, will have their day in court. At the recent 25th FAO Regional Conference for Asia and the Pacific in Yokohama (Japan) in September 2000, member governments adopted policy recommendations relevant to the above mentioned core issues.

One recommendation to the governments is that they, as well as donor organizations, increase funding for agricultural research and for supporting institutions relevant for small-scale farmers. The second recommendation is that they implement policy reforms that encourage private and public sector participation in economic activities in accordance with their comparative advantages.

A third recommendation is to encourage governments to focus on addressing market failures, ensuring competitiveness and quality of support services, protecting the environment and common property resources and promoting balanced regional development.

Member countries also adopted a recommendation that urges FAO to assist member countries to develop micro credit programmes, extension services, education and marketing support for small scale farmers, especially women, the less skilled and the disadvantaged. To support small scale farmers' entrepreneurship development FAO was recommended to assist countries in the region to establish clearly defined and enforceable land and property rights and broad based decentralised development of economic activities in rural areas.

Of immediate relevance is the request to FAO to provide direct support and capacity building services for carrying out needed agricultural sector reviews, assessment of policies for food security and poverty alleviation and studies on resource pricing policies in such cases as water and irrigation.

The recommendations adopted at the 25th FAO Regional Conference cover also such topics as fisheries, forestry, data collection, assistance to meet the WTO requirements. The Conference encouraged FAO to collaborate with all the relevant organizations in developing national and regional strategies for food security and rural development to ensure coherence and relevance of activities and adequate financial support for its own activities in the region. The outcome of the FAO Regional Conference has recently been put in to operation as part of the programme planning for 2002-03 for the Regional Office of FAO.

The Assistant Director General and Regional Representative Mr. R.B. Singh presented a programme of work to FAO Headquarters for consolidation of overall FAO world wide activities, which covers a long term period of planning based upon biennial work plans towards 2015 and gives top priority in the region to:

- Rice based livelihood systems and their role in lessening hunger and rural poverty.
- Bio-technology, bio-security and bio-diversity: towards an evergreen revolution.
- *Disasters*: Early Warning, prevention, preparedness and management.
- *WTO*: Capacity building, multilateral trade and an enabling environment.

A regional consultation with the Asian NGOs, farmers' organizations and representatives from the agricultural cooperatives and rural workers organizations was also held parallel and as an input to the discussions by member governments at the 25th Regional FAO Conference. In September 2001 another regional FAO consultation with the NGO's will take place in Bangkok. The focus of this meeting will be on the actual outcome of the World Food Summit held in 1996 in Rome and the follow up of the meeting within Asian and Pacific countries.

The FAO Regional Office has a long history of innovative ways of regional and national level collaboration with the Asian NGO's and private institutions. Two major networks which have a special relationship with FAO are the " Asian Coalition for Agrarian Reform and Rural Development" (ANGOC) representing over 13 Asian NGO country networks and the "Network for Promotion of Agricultural Cooperatives in the Asian and Pacific Region" which represents government agencies and cooperative movements jointly from about 13 Asian and Pacific countries. In partnership with these two networks and many other NGOs and farmers' and rural workers' organisations in the region, FAO-RAP supported a broad range of activities to promote sustainable agriculture and rural development at regional and country levels. The Rural Development Section within RAP has been for many years technically responsible for these activities. In fact all technical units of RAP are involved and participate in activities when relevant to them. Today the focal point for FAO-NGO collaboration in RAP is the Policy Unit.

One FAO promoted normative model for government collaboration with NGOs encourages sustainable agriculture, natural resources management, rural development and poverty alleviation. Initiated at the FAO Head Quarters in Rome by the Human Resources Division, this is one out of the annual activities implemented with ANGOC and dates back to 1990.

Called the Project Formulation for Peoples Participation in Rural Development Activities, it is still the most valid topic today. The process of dialogue among four government agencies and four NGO representatives led to effective (re) formulation of funding and operations of 19 projects covering community health services, urban poor, cooperatives and self-help groups, small scale fisheries, community forestry and environment and agrarian reform development.

What is most relevant is laying the foundation of such a collaboration based upon mutually agreed principles and a detailed framework and mechanism for participatory project formulation for people's participation in rural development activities, covering the ongoing and new project activities from planning and implementation to monitoring and evaluation. FAO-RAP has provided member countries' government agencies and people's movements active support to promote cooperative development policies and institutional capacity building enabling small-scale farmers to develop viable membership-based agricultural cooperatives. The NEDAC regional network is composed of membership paying members and autonomous entities in the region representing thousands of primary, secondary and tertiary level agricultural cooperatives covering both food and agricultural commodity sectors as well as provision of agricultural support services such as fertilisers, credit and marketing, at regional ministerial conferences and to the International Cooperative Alliance with a regional branch in New Delhi.

FAO Rural Development Section in RAP and NEDAC jointly organise regular study seminars and regional level country exchange programmes for cooperative leaders, managers and policy decision makers. Member countries include among others China, India, Bangladesh, Nepal, Sri Lanka, Thailand, and Mongolia, and provide a unique platform for policy dialogue and advocacy of favourable agricultural cooperative policies and institutional capacity building for small farmers as viable entrepreneurs in the rural sector.

The core issue in the promotion of effective partnership between government agencies and agricultural cooperatives is the recognition by law and effective administrative technical and financial support to promote genuine membership based and managed agricultural cooperative enterprises. Member governments from Vietnam, Thailand and Nepal have requested FAO-RAP technical support and are receiving technical assistance in this area.

The FAO Regional Rural Development Unit has organised country level Round Table meetings and Training of Trainers seminars based on a training toolkit on agricultural cooperative development in Thailand, Indonesia and Nepal and currently in Mongolia.

Decentralisation has become a key word in policy debate and formulation of strategies for improving coordination between the public and private institutions for agricultural and rural development.

There are many significant opportunities for effective participatory planning and implementation of agricultural and rural development activities, which combine resources, technology and local knowledge of government and private institutions. Yet there are also many pitfalls particularly in terms of regulatory framework for decentralized budget allocation, which generates local institutional resources and capacities and guarantees transparency for all stakeholders. Secondly, leadership and professional skills formation are major challenges in building local government capacities, able to timely and effectively respond to genuine local demands from the rural poor.

The FAO Regional Rural Development Unit has on behalf of the Rural Development Division based in Rome gave priority attention to capacity building of member governments in the field of decentralised participatory planning for sustainable agricultural and natural resources management and poverty alleviation.

Recently a training toolkit has been developed in collaboration with the Centre for Integrated Rural Development and the National Institute of Rural Development in India. The first draft of the document, being field tested and thoroughly discussed among experts, is practical and very enriching on normative background developed by FAO and on facts and modalities for participative decentralisation for poverty alleviation applied in the State of Maharashtra in India.

Upon request of the member countries, the FAO Rural Development Unit will assist in further development of such training toolkits in Asia-Pacific countries for strengthening capacities of government institutions to establish mechanisms for coordination between public and private institutions to promote sustainable agricultural and rural development. Requests for assistance from the Unit have been received from UNDP in Vietnam and Nepal and assistance has been provided in policy advice on this important topic.

The debate around the relative roles of markets versus bureaucrats took on renewed life with the end of the Cold War. The public policy debate shifted from focusing on the public sector to emphasizing markets and their ability to innovate, decentralize, use incentives and meet needs more effectively. Yet there remains in this public policy debate a stunning silence about the absence of property rights for the rural poor. This chapter focuses on the need to put property rights for the rural poor—the need for land reform—back on the international policy agenda. The first half of the chapter examines current land reform paradigms and looks at what has been learned, focusing on Brazil as a case study The second half of the chapter moves from what has been done to a discussion of where future research and operational work should go from here.

There are 1.3 billion people around the world who live on less than U.S.$1 a day.(1) Even though urbanization has been one of the major features of development and change in the past decade, the majority of these poor still live in rural areas. Furthermore, there are rural roots to the urban poverty seen in most countries, as those without assets migrate to urban or semi-urban areas searching for work.

Thus redistribution of assets is central to long-run progress on reducing poverty in both the city and the countryside. Researchers Michael Lipton and Jacques van der Gaag point out: For poverty reduction to succeed, the poor need some autochthonous source of income and safety. That is, they need to have an alternative, in the market place and in the polity, not to depend on a patron, monopolist or bureaucrat. Providing the poor with access to productive land is usually regarded as crucial.

Land reform is one of the most central steps in this process. The effectiveness of land-reform programmes in improving productivity and reducing rural poverty relies on many factors including land quality, access to technology and strong local agricultural markets.

However, access to land is the single most important prerequisite for improving economic conditions among the rural poor. Precisely because of the salience of land reform to the reduction of rural poverty, one of the major recommendations of this chapter is that international donors should recommit themselves to land reform and begin financing the analytical work and technical assistance it requires. The current general silence and limited operational programming of donors on land reform exacerbates the rural poverty problem.

CONCEPTUAL FRAMEWORK

Over two decades ago, Peter Dorner, a major authority on land reform, cautioned: Land reform is so intimately related with the whole development process that one feels the need to deal with issues of development in general as well as with those more specifically identified with land reform. That requires simplification of complex and nationally specific experiences. No single body of theory encompasses all the strategic variables.

Dorner's definition of land reform includes measures to redistribute land in favour of peasants and small farmers and "... embraces consolidation and registration in areas where customary tenure is prevalent and also land settlement on new lands." He places an additional emphasis on the need to make changes in tenancy rights. Each of these aspects goes to the core of rural politics, and nothing about them is easily simplified.

Indeed, to think of land reform as only a technocratic or economic problem is a mistake. It is a political economy problem with economic and social consequences amenable to resolution through good technical skills and political change. As such, land reform is a central part of the whole development process.

While development economists and agricultural economists have done most of the conceptual work on land reform, more recently attention has shifted to the ancillary fields of institutional theory (including organization theory), development management and law. Institutions, and their role in setting political and social norms, as well as legal frameworks, are now understood as endogenous, not exogenous, as economists had generally assumed.

Economists had not previously thought of institutions as directly and immediately central to achieving land reform. Rather, they assumed that the powerful case for economic efficiency gains would carry the argument to fruition. But in practice, legal, political and social changes proved to be just as important to getting land reform accepted as policy, and crucial to successful implementation.

As Michael Lipton has noted, "land reform, to achieve its aims, requires institutions that render those aims incentive compatible." Equalizing outcomes of factor and product markets provide access to technology and changing power structures through land reform—as property rights for the rural poor—are among these aims. Achieving these objectives requires conceptualizing the endogeneity of institutions.

Land policy, like other policies, must be understood by focusing attention on those institutions with the greatest capacity to achieve poverty-reduction goals. Gershon Feder pointed to the need for a new paradigm when he said that most economic analyses omit institutional analyses. He adds that "property rights are an important class of institutional arrangement. Institutions cannot be omitted without seriously distorting the analysis."

With this in mind, and in the Brazilian case discussed below, we will turn to an analysis of what kinds of institutions need to be in place in order to effect land reform. Historically, there have been tensions between neo-classical and structuralist approaches to land reform. Neo-classical economists argue for land reform on the grounds of efficiency and productivity: owner-managed farms use resources more efficiently and are more productive.

There is impressive evidence of the inverse relationship between farm size and productivity per hectare. There are fewer economies of scale in farming, especially in food crops, than there are in other sectors. Structuralists argue for land reform on grounds of equity and social justice. For them, land reform changes power relationships as it achieves more productive agriculture.

As a result, there are parallel debates between these schools over the role of the state, and hence over how to manage land reform. In addition to the two standard paradigms, a new development paradigm is evolving. This new perspective is detailed in a special issue of World Development edited by de Janvry, Sadoulet and Thorbecke. In a seminal collection of articles, they emphasize the role of institutions in the development model and the need to transform the state into a developmental state. Land reform, in the form of changes in land tenure systems, is centuries old. The disintegration of feudalism ushered in the advent of small holder farming. In more recent times, land reform initiatives have been effective in Japan, South Korea and Kerala in India. For some countries, such as Japan, land reform unleashed new potentials that served to enable subsequent development.

Other programmes, in Mexico and Bolivia for example, promised far more than they delivered. For much of the late 1950s and in the 1960s, land reform was a major issue for development assistance policy. Analytical work then included discussion of the problem of landlessness.

Taiwan and Honduras were targeted for major work. For several other countries, such as Bolivia, Brazil and Indonesia, the problems of landlessness persisted, but neither governments nor donors attempted to address the problem, with the exception of tenancy reforms in Sri Lanka. Some governments that were engaged in land reform, such as Nicaragua, were not given support for political reasons.

During the 1970s, the real text for donor engagement in land reform often took the form of opposition through counterinsurgency (e.g. El Salvador). In the 1980s land reform was completely removed from the international policy agenda by conservatives led by Thatcher and Reagan. The problem—the absence of property rights for the rural poor—was neglected. However, in the 1990s there are faint glimmers of a return to issues connected to land reform.

This record of reform success, failure and indifference brings us to the present. In today's world economy, there is more need than ever for land reform. For countries such as Nicaragua, El Salvador, Peru and Brazil in Latin America, and Zimbabwe and South Africa in Africa, the issue is central to much of the domestic political tension. The wars in Central America, especially in El Salvador, Guatemala and Nicaragua, as well as the violence in South Africa and Zimbabwe, were rooted in problems of access to land. However, nowhere more than in South Africa and Brazil is the need for reform more apparent. Post-apartheid South Africa has the greatest inequality in land ownership in the world, with Brazil following right behind.

LANDLESSNESS TODAY

In the late 1970s Cornell University undertook research to document the extent of landlessness and near-landlessness in Latin America and Asia. The Cornell Study defined "landless" as people living in rural areas who do not have ownership or control over land. These people are landless agricultural workers or tenant farmers who earn their living from their labour, or other laborers who reside in rural areas and earn their living from making or selling goods and services.

This category also includes pastoralists, nomads, shifting cultivators and scavengers. The near-landless are marginal farmers who may have customary tenure to holdings which are of inadequate size or quality to provide more than subsistence livelihood. The Cornell study documented staggering numbers of landless and near-landless peoples living in rural areas.

Taking the landless and near-landless as a percentage of total rural households, researchers found them to be 85 per cent of Indonesia's rural households; 78 per cent of the Philippines rural households; 77 per cent of Sri Lanka's and 53 per cent of India's rural households. In the case of Latin America, the percentages were very similar, ranging from 85 per cent in Bolivia and Guatemala to 55 per cent in Costa Rica. One may assume that economic growth in Latin American and Asian countries in the two decades since the Cornell data was assembled has diminished the scale of the problem of landlessness.

But even if one assumes that today those numbers are fully 50 per cent lower than those cited (which is probably overly optimistic), there remain large numbers of people who are denied property rights and live in dire poverty, without access to the single most important rural asset—land. While that study did not include Africa, it is widely accepted that the majority of Africa's population still resides in rural areas, and that 70 per cent of Africa's poor are rural. From household level data in 17 countries, a profile of the rural poor emerges: only about 40 per cent have completed primary education and only 30 per cent of rural households have access to sanitation. Their access to land is highly variable, depending upon customary access, tenure arrangements and inherited colonial land law. All too often they are subsistence farmers without land they can use as collateral to obtain the technical inputs they need to increase productivity.

Of course, in addition to skewed access to land, Africa's governance problems have exacerbated the problems of rural poverty. Agriculture was often taxed for largely urban oriented investment. The historic under-investment in human resource development by political interests with other agendas imposed agricultural policy distortions, skewed exchange rates and constrained the factors needed to increase production (such as access to technology). Malawi is a case in point; large tobacco estate owners used the power of the state to forbid small farmers from growing burley tobacco, a major source of export earnings. As Sahn and Arulpragasam have noted, in Malawi—a classical dual economy—the estates expanded by appropriating uncultivated customary land, thereby reducing the land available to the small-farm sector.

African customary law and tradition usually accords usufruct rights on communal land to those who till it. These rights can pass down over generations, but they are neither freehold nor leasehold rights. Prewar Rwanda is an example of the problem of usufruct rights versus land ownership in a densely populated country When social systems are devastated by war, resettlement is greatly complicated by disputes over land where such rights are difficult to define.

The commercialization of land in Africa, coupled with population increases and the gradual erosion of customary protections for use rights, means that land problems are becoming more severe. Women traditionally had only usufruct rights, not ownership rights, to land for cultivation. With commercialization and imported registration systems, women often lose their customary rights and do not gain access to the "modernized" system. Meanwhile, other factors have added to land problems in Africa. Desertification in the Sahelian countries, and periodic drought stretching from parts of Uganda through Zambia to Botswana to Natal in South Africa, have diminished soil quality and hence food production. Land rights were greatly skewed by colonialism in countries such as Zimbabwe, Malawi, South Africa, Namibia, Angola and Mozambique. In these countries, white settlers actively took land and used the force of law to enforce their land claims, creating a complex legacy of land hunger.

The two potentially richest agricultural producers in Africa—Mozambique and Angola—have large landless populations due to war and refugee movements. Much of the fertile land remains idle, still laden with landmines in the aftermath of war. Productive farming is also inhibited by a complex legal system governing land. Unlike their neighbors, both Mozambique and Angola practice civil law rather than common law, a legacy of their Portuguese colonial experience.

This further complicates the contract enforceability needed in order to sort out land claims. There is strikingly little research on land questions in this region, yet there is little doubt that their settler traditions, war-induced migration and land mines, have crippled real potential for rural development. The tragedy is that Mozambique, for example, with its seacoast, temperate climate and fertile soils could be the California of southern Africa if it were not for its unsettled population and landmine riddled fields. As discussed below, many of the same land tenure problems in Mozambique and Angola are directly relevant in another outpost of Portuguese colonialism—Brazil.

SOUTH AFRICA'S LANDLESS POOR

South Africa's land issues are a glaring example of the problem of dualism. The scale of land consolidation in the hands of large land holders is more extreme,, and its connections to political power more complex than anywhere in the world. Afrikaners land consolidation policies were institutionalized by the Native Land Act of 1913, which prohibited black landownership, except in designated communal areas known as Bantustans.

By the late 1980s, about 86 per cent of the land was owned by white South Africans. While land reform is a priority for the new democratic government, exactly how best to proceed, given the fragility of the rapidly evolving new state and the intricate role of commercial agriculture in the economy, is daunting. The government cannot undermine that sector without widespread economic consequences, but it also cannot forever postpone the structural changes needed to address the issues of land hunger and poverty.

Part of the challenge is that the forceful depression of the profitability of small-scale agriculture took place so completely over a long period of time that its regeneration would require serious investment in rebuilding extension services, skills, technical innovation and institutional change. Land reform could start with the reallocation of unoccupied arable land, but there is little unused arable land available for redistribution.

Furthermore, only a small percentage of the rural poor with farming skills could maintain the level of agricultural production that South Africa now enjoys, and the countries around South Africa rely upon, to meet food needs. Nearly one-third of sub-Saharan Africa is linked to the South African economy and relies on its agriculture for food imports.

Fortunately, there has been some work by leading South African agricultural economists on market-based approaches to land reform. There have also been consultations with the World Bank on the development of a particularly innovative approach for a willing seller-willing buyer, market-based model for land reform. Substantial sector analysis was conducted as a result of these consultations, and the South African government has begun to test this model on an experimental basis. While the model for a market-based approach—a willing buyer-willing seller framework—breaks away from earlier, more bureaucratic models, it still requires the use of a small grant programme. The poor rural cultivator most in need of land will be unable to pay the market price from income earned on that land without significant help in the near term. The eventual gains, however, of having smaller and more productive farms are substantial both in terms of sustainable agricultural development and in terms of greater rural employment generation.

Among the many arguments for smaller owner-managed farms for South Africa (as in many other countries, including the United States) are those which stress environmental sustainability. Environmental degradation in South Africa is serious due to its capital-intensive approach on large land holdings, coupled with extensive use of chemicals on fragile soils. Heavy modern machinery contributes to a loss of biodiversity and soil compaction; chemicals threaten the ecology of water, land, insect, plant and animal life and pose serious long-term public health hazards as well. Land reform encourages smaller holdings that are more environmentally benign.

Subsistence farming, however, by which tenants live with great tenure insecurity, also results in heavy environmental abuse. It is increasingly documented that smaller owner-managed farms make more productive use of their land and have greater incentives to manage land in ways that avoid depleting the soil. Moreover, modest to small owner-managed farms employ more labour, thus increasing opportunities for rural employment, another way in which land reform can help reduce rural poverty.

South Africa and Brazil are countries that play large roles in their respective regions and have the potential to become major regional growth centres. Both are poised to become big players in the international arena and demonstrate unprecedented leadership in the Third World. Both are also countries with extraordinary levels of inequality and dense rural poverty—factors that serve to hold them back from realizing their full potential. Furthermore, neither of these countries has received significant assistance from international development agencies to move forward on their land problems. Neither Brazil nor South Africa has sought financial assistance for land reform, in part because political concerns overwhelm the economic case for land reform. Administrations in both countries may acknowledge that the absence of land reform is acting as a brake on long-term economic growth. But they are reluctant to invite any of the leverage that borrowing from the international community might bring to bear on this sensitive issue. International donors, however, also must improve on approaches to land reform.

With more serious commitment to this issue—at the least revisiting the research needs that have remained unaddressed since the 1980s—international donors could refurbish their toolkit and re-engage with the problem. Research on what works—why and how success can be replicated—is necessary. There is a lot of work to do, both within international donor agencies in developing strategies that are acceptable to these countries and within the countries themselves, to move towards land reform.

RURAL POVERTY AND LANDLESSNESS IN BRAZIL

Brazil has the single largest population of rural poor in South America. Concentrated in the northeast of the country, they account for 54 per cent of Brazil's poor people. Brazil as a whole is not a poor country; the average per capita income in 1991 was about U.S.$3,000.

However, average per capita income in the Northeast was U.S.$1,500. But even that average hides the extent of serious deprivation, not only because of inequalities in income but because of extreme inequalities in asset ownership. According to United Nations Development Programme (UNDP) estimates, Brazil has the second lowest human development index and the greatest disparity in wealth distribution among the world's middle income countries.

Brazil has one of the most unequal land distribution systems in the world. Eighty-eight per cent of the land is in the hands of the wealthiest 20 per cent of the rural population;

the bottom 40 per cent of the population share only 1 per cent of the land. Brazil's highly unequal land distribution is one of the country's most serious problems, exacerbating poverty and limiting the potential for healthy agricultural growth. While inferior censustaking makes data gathering difficult, it is clear that land inequality is considerably worse in the northeast part of the country.

Nearly 60 per cent of all land-owners in this area control only 3 per cent of the land. Meanwhile, .6 per cent control 32 per cent of the land. The Movimento dos Trabalhadores Sem Terra—the national organization of landless people—estimates that as of 1991, over 20 million people (4.8 million families) were landless in Brazil.

Farmers tilling tiny holdings lack public services, extension services, help with marketing or legal protection for their rights. All of these constraints lead to working conditions which limit how much the poor can do to improve their situation. The result is that life expectancy rates, infant mortality rates and literacy levels in northeast Brazil are similar to those of Haiti, Zaire and Honduras, even though these countries have much lower per capita incomes than Brazil.

The political system linked to the land system, popularly termed latifundium-minifundium (extremely large land holdings—tiny land holdings) with its patron-client relations, is entrenched in Brazil's legal structure. The result today is that it is desperately difficult, especially in the northeast of Brazil, for a poor illiterate farmer to document, or get a court to enforce, his land claims.

Even if he once paid someone for land, that transaction is likely not to have been registered. He may think his "papers" are a title only to find out once in court that they are legally flawed and thus worthless. This lack of legal titling also means that the farmer has little chance to borrow against this land, since banks are not anxious to take his "papers" for collateral.

Although much of this will happen with great decorum and appeal to legal precedent, citations to other documents and abundant jargon, the result for the farmer is the same. He cannot really "sell" his property unless he convinces another hapless peasant to purchase his "papers," and he cannot get the credit needed for the tools and seeds essential to improving his income. Local registries in rural areas foster landlessness as well.

The local registry officer in rural Brazil is called the cartorio, a position inherited from one generation to the next. Visits to cartorios revealed that the records were kept in large bound volumes, in which the cartorio would keep handwritten records that were supposed to be transmitted at intervals to higher levels in the chain of command so that land registration would be actually recorded.

Cartorios make a living from their fees; they usually have a table indicating the fees charged, but there is no surveillance that might mitigate corruption. All of these factors have led to a registry system rampant with irregularities. The cartorio operates in a milieu where there is a labyrinth of land claims dating back to 16th century colonialism.

Unequal landownership is interdependent with unequal access to credit. Large landowners have easy access to subsidized credit, which allows them to extend their holdings and adds to higher land concentration. Foreclosure on loans is rare, and debt forgiveness is politically negotiated. Large landowners often extend their holdings into frontier areas because formal rural credit policies and production incentives encourage mechanization and large-scale agricultural production with its adverse environmental impacts.

Distortions in income tax and credit policies have been incorporated into the price of land. Land prices are currently greater than the capitalized value of farm profits or land rents. Investment in land for non-agricultural reasons has increased land prices and encouraged the expulsion of small farmers—the nearlandless—from the land.

High inflation in the early 1990s also led to greater investment in land for the purposes of portfolio diversification, pushing the near-landless off the land. Another consequence of landownership patterns in this area of Brazil is that large holders generate higher unemployment. Credit policies which encourage mechanization contribute to the displacement of the rural labour force through migration. As a result, there is severe underemployment in the rural areas of the Northeast. Since mid-level and smaller-sized farms provide the greatest employment opportunities for the rural poor, as well as higher productivity levels, an increase in the number of farms of moderate size would be not only economically efficient, but would provide jobs.

One result of landowning inequalities has been a steady increase in land invasions—squatters who move onto land which they occupy with, or without, an intention to later lay claim to it. Land invasions have become an important and pervasive informal institution. There are several different kinds of invasions.

Sometimes squatters move onto land on their own accord. Other times they are invited by large landowner-patrons who encourage squatters to invade public lands to which the large landowner intends to lay subsequent claim.

Landowners often induce squatters onto property instructing them to clear-cut timber and get the land under production—at which point the large landowner files his claim for the title and moves the settlers to yet another parcel to continue the process. The "settlers" or "mercenary squatters" never get access to land—only the large landowner gains in this vicious process.

REFORM ATTEMPTS IN BRAZIL

There have been sporadic attempts on the part of the Brazilian government to address these problems. Interestingly, even reforms proposed in the name of pursuing social justice for the landless have in practice added to the problem. For example, the 1964 Federal Land Statute was promulgated to pursue social justice for the rural laborer, aiming to gradually replace the latifundium-minifundium institution.

It led in part to the first survey which quantitatively identified the latifundium-minifundium situation and the severe underutilization of land. That in turn led to the Land Statute, which created many unintended negative externalities. This reform set ceilings on rents and crop shares and provided semi-permanent rights to tenants after several years. The result was a constraint on even temporary access to land for renters, as large landowners became wary of subsequent claims by renters. The Land Statute also has provisions that would expropriate farms with high numbers of renters, sharecroppers and squatters. Local sources say these provisions are rarely enforced, but serve to justify the refusal of large landowners to rent out modest land parcels.

In 1974, Brazil established the Programme of Development of Integrated Areas of the Northeast (Polonordeste), in hopes of increasing production, productivity, incomes and living standards for small-scale farmers. In addition, the World Bank approved 10 integrated rural development projects in eight selected "micro-regions" of the Northeast between 1976 and 83. Several of these projects included land components aimed at improving poor farmers' access to land. Later came the Northeast Region Land Improvement Project, which was more focused on strengthening land titling by using state-of-the-art technology to clarify state cartorios.

Judith Tendler, researching the Polonordeste projects, reports that one million hectares of "informal land transfers" took place over a period of five years in the Northeast. In 1985, the government of Brazil launched a National Plan for Agrarian Reform. Although efforts in land redistribution, land acquisition and land titling were pursued, the results were not very positive.

By 1988, three years after the National Plan of Agrarian Reform was launched, only an estimated 18,000 rural families had been settled, and these had been given inadequate land. Only four million hectares had been expropriated out of the 845,648,300 hectares in the entire country.

From 1988 to 1994, the Federal Government reduced the income tax treatments for the agricultural sector, and substantially reduced the volume of government-financed agricultural credit in an effort to bring interest rates in agriculture to levels similar to those in other sectors. These changes reduced the distortions capitalized into land prices. Yet tenure insecurity still undermines the people who are at risk—and it leaves incentives in place that result in higher levels of land degradation.

THE NEED FOR INSTITUTIONAL REFORM & ROLE FOR DONORS

The primary lesson learned from the Brazilian situation is that institutional reform is an integral part of the land-reform process. The rural poverty problem in Brazil has far-reaching consequences for Brazil's development. Donors have a central role to play, given the increasing knowledge within donor organizations about how to assist with institutional reform.

Donor organizations could contribute to reforming the antiquated cartorio system for land registration in order to improve access to local courts and access to credit for land purchase. At a different level, organizations could assist with judicial reform in order to create an enabling environment for contract enforceability, to strengthen land registration at the state level or, most importantly, to help emplace a market-based approach to land reform.

Impediments to land reform in South Africa also demonstrate the endogeny of institutional reform. The particular institutions needing reform in South Africa are different from those in Brazil. South Africa has less of a problem with contract enforceability and judicial bias because the South African judicial system is less politicized and more independent than that in the northeast of Brazil.

In South Africa, however, land reform efforts must address the enormous challenge of reversing decades of devastation wrought by the Bantustans—the homeland areas onto which Africans were forced for decades during the Afrikaner land grabs. In this case, legal reform is needed to reverse the land policies of apartheid. With an enabling environment, land reform could proceed using a market approach.

There are groups and interests within both Brazil and South Africa that are working to bring attention to the need for land reform. They are incrementally building up coalitions that will constitute political will for change. As a result, in the last decade an opportunity has emerged for the international community to contribute to these reform movements. Sometimes, financing can help leverage change. So the question is, where are the international donors on the issue of land reform?

Currently, potential donors are backing away from the problem rather than moving forward, even though, as Judith Tendler has documented, donors have sometimes embedded interesting and effective micro-level land reform initiatives within small localized projects.

The U.S. Agency for International Development (USAID) engaged in some work on land reform in the 1960s only to have it derailed by Cold War geopolitics. The World Bank had a major policy paper on land reform accepted by its board in 1975, and reissued in 1982—but it was promptly neglected for the rest of the 1980s. Among the reasons given are that the Articles of Agreement establishing the World Bank proscribe lending for the transfer of assets.

The recent work of small, skillful and dedicated groups within the World Bank and the Inter-American Development Bank has creatively managed to get some land reform work back into operations, but these groups are clearly swimming upstream. Larger scale efforts on the part of donors remain off the agenda.

In a time when traditional donors lack leadership, where is serious organizational support for land reform most likely to come from? It is possible that leadership will emerge from the non-governmental organizations (NGO) community, perhaps the fastest growing sector in development work. To date, the NGO sector has done little work on the national policy level of land reform, with the exception of the Association of the Landless in Brazil.

Within certain local projects, there have been some real successes by local NGOs in acquiring land for the rural poor. But for structural or systemic change, NGOs generally lack the authority needed to bring about land reform, and are often not inclined to make it one of their advocacy issues. Financing is needed, and thus the role for donors is vital, especially given that the more redistributive a land reform programme is, the more financing it requires. Even if a market-based approach to land reform is used, external financing is still necessary since few small farmers can finance their mortgages out of the profits earned by their holdings, particularly in their early years. Institutional financing is also needed to fund the development of agricultural technology, credit institutions and marketing systems.

MARKET-BASED APPROACHES TO LAND REFORM

There is a good case for using a market-based approach to land reform. In earlier periods many land reform programmes used either collectivist, state-mandated programmes with top-down command and control or state bureaucratic systems. Markets, however, have advantages over earlier, more administratively heavy approaches to land distribution.

If markets are transparent and competitive—a missing characteristic in the land "markets" of northeast Brazil—they provide greater efficiency in allocation, and lower transaction costs. Earlier approaches to land reform relied heavily on the power of the state through expropriation to take land. This entailed a lengthy process of determining compensatory payments, allocating land and selecting people for resettlement.

A market-based system would be more decentralized, less administratively intrusive and the allocation process would be facilitated by the market. Nonetheless, launching a sustainable market-based land reform programme requires a development-oriented state and state financing, even if it is nothing more than a modest NGO-run grant programme assisting the poor in financing land purchases.

Putting in place a market-based approach to land reform and moving away from a politically distorted land market requires several institutional changes.

The fundamentals are:

- An open titling and registration process;
- Transparency and open price competition;
- Credit, collateral and debt collection institutions;
- Freedom to contract and contract enforceability;

- Dispute adjudication institutions; and
- Financing and extension for low income cultivators.

OPEN TITLING AND REGISTRATION PROCESS

Most poor cultivators "buy" land through informal markets in deals that have no force of law. Often the unwitting purchaser is illiterate and does not know this is the case. Land bought through informal markets is not readily alienable so that struggles to strengthen title claims often ensue.

Furthermore, land bought and sold in the informal market often does not include legally determined boundaries or title verifications. Sales that are not registered also can mean that a seller "sells" land to different buyers and leaves them all with competing claims. In such cases, the first one through the gate to registration is the winner. This corrupts a market since it is widely known that multiple sales to multiple purchasers can take place, and frequently do in marginal areas. Registered land commands a higher price. Most rural poor are thus caught in a relentless squeeze: what they can buy cannot be registered, nor can they ever know for sure whether the title is clear.

Moreover, searching registries is difficult. In Brazil, for example, registries can only be searched with official permission—hardly likely to be given to a rural peasant. The data within them is not organized for ease of retrieval. Often the registries themselves cannot detail the formal legal standing of the titles they have within their data banks. The result is that prices for credit—interest rates—are affected. Because land parcels with clear title command higher prices, prices do not reflect competitive interaction between demand and supply, but rather the selective access to scarce information about what is being sold, by whom, and with what competing claims.

When one assumes a mortgage, it is wisely preceded by a title search or, alternatively, title insurance that ensures against the risk that the title bought is not free and clear of encumbrances: Many developing countries lack title search companies or agencies serving this purpose. If sellers cannot certify that boundaries have been demarcated and the parcel they are selling is legally owned, buyers are less willing to go forward. Informal markets may be a last resort, but the risk is borne entirely by the most vulnerable, who lack recourse. Without a formal title management mechanism, title is often enforced through violence. In countries marred by social, political and economic turbulence, the use of violence in land disputes is frequent precisely because there are few, if any, legal and respected title search or title insurance companies.

In some countries the severe problems surrounding titling and registration have been bypassed by techniques involving securitization. Under this process an agency with approval from the government can undertake demarcation of the boundaries of land occupied and give occupants a certificate recognized by the government as providing security of tenure for the occupant on that land. Further, the occupant can use that certificate as collateral for obtaining credit, or can sell it to others.

TRANSPARENCY AND PRICE COMPETITION

Price information is critical to market competition, as crony capitalism often leads to limited information about land sales and land prices. In many developing countries, land markets are purposefully opaque. Precisely because land is coveted and central to future income possibilities as well as status and political influence, much of the land market is shrouded from public view, thus inflating prices. Transparency requirements would go a long way towards making land markets more competitive. Local governments could institute disclosure requirements along with changes in the registration system. The media, too, have important roles to play in highlighting information about land markets and farm prices. In this Information Age, even donor-financed computerization of land and farm prices could enhance freer exchange of price information.

Index

H

I

J

K

M

N

P

Q

R

S

T

W